D1559297

# Seriatim

# Seriatim

## *The Supreme Court before John Marshall*

EDITED BY

*Scott Douglas Gerber*

*New York University Press*
NEW YORK AND LONDON

NEW YORK UNIVERSITY PRESS
New York and London



Library of Congress Cataloging-in-Publication Data
Seriatim : the Supreme Court before John Marshall / edited by Scott Douglas Gerber.
p. cm.
Includes index.
ISBN 0-8147-3114-7 (cloth : alk paper)
1. United States. Supreme Court—History. 2. Judges—United States—Biography. 3. Judicial review—United States—History. 4. Law and politics—History. I. Gerber, Scott Douglas, 1961–
KF8742.S47 1998
347.73'26—dc21 98-9056
CIP

New York University Press books are printed on acid-free paper, and their binding materials are chosen for strength and durability.

Manufactured in the United States of America

10 9 8 7 6 5 4 3 2 1

*For George Athan Billias,*
*who represents what the profession*
*is supposed to be about.*

# Contents

# Preface

The Founders of the American regime were truly remarkable men. George Washington, John Adams, Thomas Jefferson, James Madison, Alexander Hamilton, John Marshall—these are the familiar names of men who established a form of government that today serves as a model for much of the world. There were other great men of the Founding, men who are not as well known but who, nevertheless, made major contributions to America's form of government. This volume of essays examines ten of these men; individuals who served on the U.S. Supreme Court before John Marshall, and who have suffered undeserved obscurity as a result.

This book grew out of two of my intellectual passions: the first, in the history of the American Founding; the second, in an interdisciplinary approach to scholarship. Although much has been written about the American Founding, little has been done to examine the history of the early judiciary, particularly as it existed before John Marshall. With respect to interdisciplinary scholarship, my time spent in the academy has convinced me that, unfortunately, most scholars prefer a traditional single-discipline approach. The contributors to the present collection hold otherwise. We believe it is more fruitful to examine American history from a variety of perspectives.

In the spirit of interdisciplinary scholarship, each contributor was given free rein on how to approach her or his particular justice. Each was asked, however, to provide a brief biographical sketch of the justice and, more importantly, to analyze the contributions he made to American law and politics in general and to the Supreme Court in particular. These relatively unknown justices, as shall be seen, contributed a great deal.

It is hoped that this focus on the justices who served before John Marshall will help correct the impression that the Supreme Court appeared full-blown with Marshall like Athena from the forehead of Zeus. Certainly it should explode the myth that the concept of judicial review began with *Marbury v. Madison* (1803), which, though well known to be false, continues to be perpetuated by innumerable nodding scholars. Indeed, this volume is exploratory in nature and, it is hoped, will provoke scholars to research the early Court more carefully than they have in the past.

All but two of the essays were written specifically for this collection. Sandra VanBurkleo's essay about John Jay and Dan Degnan's essay about William Paterson first appeared in somewhat different form in the *Journal of the Early Republic* and the *Seton Hall Law Review,* respectively. Permission to reprint them is gratefully acknowledged.

Mark Hall, a friend and classmate from graduate school, was the only contributor I knew before this project began. Mark had written his dissertation—since published as a book—on James Wilson's legal and political philosophy, so Mark was an obvious choice to write the Wilson chapter. I then identified, with Mark's help, the leading authorities on the other justices to be considered and I wrote to these authorities to ask if they would be willing to write an essay about their particular justice. All agreed.* None of the prospective authors knew who I was when I requested this substantial commitment from them. Consequently, I credit my 100 percent success rate to a shared enthusiasm for the subject of this volume. The essays reflect this enthusiasm. I thank each of the contributors for his or her fine work, and for the kindness and patience they all have shown me on this, and other, matters. Grateful acknowledgment is made to the Earhart Foundation, to Florida Coastal School of Law, and to the University of Toledo Federalist Society and the Stranahan National Issues Forum for their support of this project. I also want to thank the administration and staff of the Social Philosophy and Policy Center (especially Mary Doilsaver) for their assistance in helping this volume see the light of day, and my editor and friend Niko Pfund, the direc-

*No one now living had written anything of substance on two of the justices I wanted to include, William Cushing and Bushrod Washington. I asked political theorist Jim Stoner, author of a fine book on the influence of the common law on the Founding, if he would be willing to write on one of the two. Jim picked Washington. I was "left with" Cushing. (Why I place quotation marks around "left with" is made clear in my Cushing essay.)

tor of New York University Press, for being so supportive of it. Finally, I would like to thank George Athan Billias, a great early American historian and an even better human being. The academy would be a better place—the kind of place it is supposed to be—if there were more people in it like "Mr. B." I am proud to call him my mentor.

S. D. G.
Hampton, Virginia

*Chapter 1*

# Introduction
## *The Supreme Court before John Marshall*

*Scott Douglas Gerber*

### *The Pre-Marshall Court in the American Mind*

Students of judicial institutions in recent years have come to appreciate more than ever that to understand any court we must understand its origins.[1] Nowhere is this more correct than in the case of the Supreme Court because the origins of that institution are so closely identified with one justice—John Marshall. This holds true no matter what one thinks of Marshall. For those who hold Marshall in high esteem—and most scholars today do exactly that—the study of the Court prior to 1801 makes more plain the stamp Marshall placed on the institution. For those who view Marshall less heroically—as do several contributors in this volume—studying the pre-Marshall Court reveals what the institution might have been like had Marshall not accepted the nomination to be chief justice.

Jumping ahead two centuries to the present—and some three hundred fifty pages to the end of this book—an examination of the Supreme Court before John Marshall reveals much of interest to students of the institution. Marshallphiles will note, for example, the absence of the institutional voice Marshall's leadership was able to

I thank Mark Hall for his contributions to this essay; Todd Ellinwood for his research assistance; and George Billias, Bill Casto, Chuck Hobson, Wythe Holt, Steve Presser, Jim Stoner, and Sandra VanBurkleo for their suggestions for making it better. An earlier version was presented at the 1996 meeting of the Northeastern Political Science Association. I thank the participants on the "Elements of Judicial Culture" panel—John Brigham, Nancy Kassop, Jeffrey Morris, Suzanne Samuels, and Grier Stephenson—for their enthusiasm about this project.

provide—an institutional voice that has been absent for much of the twentieth century as well.[2] Those who view Marshall less heroically will find in these pages, by contrast, that, among other things, judicial review—the Court's most important power in the American system of constitutional government—was understood by the early justices, was argued for by them, and was practiced by them.

The conventional wisdom is, of course, that the Supreme Court became an important institution only after Marshall's arrival and the opinion rendered in *Marbury v. Madison* (1803). It is not exactly accurate to say that the pre-Marshall Court has been completely ignored by students of the judicial process, but most scholars on the subject stress the Court's lack of significance. Bernard Schwartz, for instance, concludes in *A History of the Supreme Court* (1993) that "the outstanding aspect of the Court's work during its first decade was its relative unimportance."[3] Similarly, George Lee Haskins and Herbert A. Johnson comment in their 1981 volume in the Holmes Devise History of the Supreme Court that the Court was a "relatively feeble institution during the 1790s, too unimportant to interest the talents of two men who declined President Adams' offer of the position of Chief Justice, it . . . acquired in . . . a few years' time, and largely under the guiding hand of John Marshall, more power than even the framers of the Constitution may have anticipated."[4] There is also the following observation by Robert G. McCloskey in *The American Supreme Court* (1960), arguably the most important book ever written about the Court:

> It is hard for a student of judicial review to avoid feeling that American constitutional history from 1789 to 1801 was marking time. The great shadow of John Marshall, who became Chief Justice in the latter year, falls across our understanding of that first decade; and it has therefore the quality of a play's opening moments with minor characters exchanging trivialities while they and the audience await the appearance of the star.[5]

There are countless other examples of the pre-Marshall Court being trivialized by law professors, historians, and political scientists.[6] Invariably, scholars point out that Robert H. Harrison never served as an associate justice after he was confirmed, and that William Cushing declined elevation from associate to chief justice. Similarly, Charles C. Pinckney, Edward Rutledge, Alexander Hamilton, and Patrick Henry—significant statesmen in the 1790s—refused to be appointed to the Court, and several men who were appointed resigned to accept other positions. Most notable among the latter group, John Rutledge left the Court after two years to become chief justice of the South Carolina Court of Common Pleas, and John Jay, who spent part of his Supreme Court tenure serving as minister to Great Britain, resigned from the Court to become governor of New York, and later refused reappointment to the Court.

After noting the difficulty of staffing the early Supreme Court, scholars usually mention in passing a few cases, such as *Hayburn's Case* (1792), *Chisholm v. Georgia* (1793), *Ware v. Hylton* (1796), *Hylton v. United States* (1796), and *Calder v. Bull* (1798), and then hurry on to discuss related Marshall Court opinions. While some may hesitate for a moment to address *Chisholm v. Georgia*, those who do typically emphasize that this decision was overturned in 1798 by the Eleventh Amendment. Finally, many scholars cite the absence of a separate Supreme Court building as evidence that the early Court lacked prestige.[7]

There have been scholars, of course, who recognized that the early Court has been neglected. Edward S. Corwin, for one, in his 1919 book about John Marshall, wrote:

> The pioneer work of the [pre-Marshall] Supreme Court in constitutional interpretation has, for all but special students, fallen into something like obscurity owing to the luster of Marshall's achievements and to his habit of deciding cases without much reference to precedent. But these early labors are by no means insignificant, especially since they pointed the way to some of Marshall's most striking decisions.[8]

Unfortunately, Corwin failed in his long and distinguished career to fill this gap in the literature.

A few scholars have begun to challenge the idea that the Supreme Court became important only when John Marshall arrived. The multivolume ongoing project documenting the activity of the early Court edited by Maeva Marcus and others, and Marcus's edited collection of essays on the Judiciary Act of 1789, have been of great assistance in this regard.[9] Also worth noting is William R. Casto's *The Supreme Court in the Early Republic: The Chief Justiceships of John Jay and Oliver Ellsworth* (1995). Casto, who contributes an essay about Oliver Ellsworth in this volume, makes an important contribution with his book by presenting a compelling theory as to why the pre-Marshall Court is often viewed negatively. As he puts it:

> Society in the late twentieth century—particularly political society—is usually viewed primarily in terms of conflicts of values and interests. . . .The abiding theme of the early Supreme Court, however, was precisely to the contrary. The Court sought to support the political branches of the new federal government, not to oppose them.[10]

According to Casto, "Though the justices occasionally resorted to constitutional interpretation, their primary objective was to bolster and consolidate the new federal government." The label of "mediocrity" attached to the pre-Marshall Court, he concludes, "is probably due to the direct conflict between the modern judicial paradigm of conflict and the early Court's paradigm of support."[11]

## *Insights from Biography*

Although a few scholars have begun to pay attention to the pre-Marshall Court,[12] much work remains to be done. One fruitful approach is to examine the contributions pre–Marshall Court justices made as *individuals* to American law and politics. After all, one does not need to subscribe to the psychological and sociological tenets of legal realism to recognize that any court, including the Supreme Court, is first and foremost composed of individuals.[13] The biographical approach to the pre-Marshall Court is particularly appropriate, given that most of that Court's business took place while the justices were riding circuit. *Seriatim: The Supreme Court before John Marshall* was designed with a multiple biographical methodology in mind.

The ten pre–Marshall Court justices (this number excludes the largely unknown Thomas Johnson and Alfred Moore) are worthy of study because of their impressive credentials and active involvement in America's founding. Of the ten, three signed the Declaration of Independence, six were members of the Federal Convention of 1787, and six were prominent members of their state ratifying conventions. Besides these credentials, seven served in the Continental Congress, eight had held prior judicial posts, and all served in state governments in some capacity. Two, Oliver Ellsworth and William Paterson, cowrote the Judiciary Act of 1789, which helped to shape the institution of the Court.

As the first president, George Washington had the unique opportunity to nominate an entire Supreme Court. He took this responsibility seriously and regarded "the due administration of Justice as the strongest cement of good government." Consequently, he sought "the fittest characters to expound the laws and dispense justice."[14]

In his classic study of the political history of the appointment process, Henry J. Abraham identifies seven criteria employed by Washington to choose Supreme Court justices:

> (1) support and advocacy of the Constitution; (2) distinguished service in the Revolution; (3) active participation in the political life of state or nation; (4) prior judicial experience on lower tribunals; (5) either a "favorable reputation with his fellows" or personal ties with Washington himself; (6) geographic suitability; (7) love of country.[15]

The result was a number of impressive appointees. The nation's first Court was composed of John Jay of New York, John Rutledge of South Carolina, William Cushing of Massachusetts, James Wilson of Pennsylvania, John Blair of Virginia, and Robert H. Harrison of Maryland. The original six justices never met together as the Court, however. On his way to the inaugural session, Harrison fell ill, so ill in fact that he resigned his post without ever having sat on the Court. While Harrison's resignation is sometimes used as evidence to indicate that the early Court lacked prestige, it should be noted that his death two months later indicates the severity of his sickness. Harrison was replaced by James Iredell of North Carolina.

In 1791 the Supreme Court lost a second member, John Rutledge, who resigned to become chief justice of the South Carolina Court of Common Pleas. After South Carolinians Charles C. Pinckney and Edward Rutledge had both declined, Washington offered the position to Thomas Johnson of Maryland. Although Johnson accepted, he resigned within two years. William Paterson of New Jersey was then named to succeed Johnson.

Chief Justice John Jay was next to leave the Court, resigning in 1795 after being elected governor of New York. Washington's decision to replace Jay with John Rutledge—who had expressed a desire to return to the Supreme Court as chief justice—led to an embarrassing series of events. Rutledge's was a recess appointment, and during the recess he attacked the Jay Treaty with such vitriol that his confirmation by the Senate was unlikely at best. Indeed, the Federalist-controlled Senate considered Rutledge's assault on the treaty tantamount to treason and rejected his appointment by a vote of 10 to 14. Washington turned to Patrick Henry to fill the center chair, but Henry declined the nomination. William Cushing was then nominated and confirmed as the nation's third chief justice. About a week later, Cushing, citing advanced age and ill health, resigned his promotion and returned to his position as the Court's senior associate justice. Finally, in 1796 Oliver Ellsworth of Connecticut became chief justice, a post he held for a full four years.

The year 1796 was also when John Blair's resignation from the Court became effective. Washington offered Blair's seat to Samuel Chase of Maryland, the converted Antifederalist, who accepted. Two years later James Wilson died in office, becoming the first justice to do so. After John Marshall had declined an invitation to serve as an associate justice, Wilson's seat was filled by his former law student, Bushrod Washington of Virginia.

James Iredell died the following year and was replaced by Alfred Moore, a fellow North Carolinian. Moore served four years on the Court but with little distinction. Finally, in 1800, in a letter sent from France where he was serving as a special envoy, Chief Justice Oliver Ellsworth resigned from the Court. John Adams quickly nominated John Jay, who was confirmed by the Senate. Jay refused to serve, however. The chief justiceship then fell to Adams's secretary of state, John Marshall of Virginia, who has since acquired the reputation as the "greatest" Supreme Court justice in American history.[16]

The difficulty Washington, and to a lesser extent Adams, had in staffing the Supreme Court is stressed by those who dismiss the significance of the pre-Marshall Court. At a minimum, this perspective ignores the hardships faced by the early justices, such as illness and circuit riding.[17] More substantially, it overlooks the important contributions to American law and politics made by the early justices, both on circuit, where most of their judicial business was conducted, and before they arrived at the highest court in the land, where their respective efforts in the founding of the American regime were tremendous.

Scholars have long appreciated the value of studying individual Founders when trying to discern the character of the early American republic. The scores of volumes and papers projects on John Adams, Alexander Hamilton, Thomas Jefferson, James Madison, John Marshall, and George Washington, among others, all testify to this fact. In a real sense, *Seriatim* picks up where Stephen B. Presser left off. Presser, who contributes an essay about Samuel Chase to the present collection, demonstrated in his provocative book, *The Original Misunderstanding: The English, the Americans and the Dialectic of Federalist Jurisprudence* (1991), the value of examining the individual pre–Marshall Court justices—in Presser's case, Chase—for dispelling the myth of Marshall's apotheosis.[18] This said, the point of *Seriatim* is *not* that Marshall was not a force in American law and politics. There is, after all, a difference between revisionism and fiction. Rather, *Seriatim* is designed to put an end to the claim to unequivocal domination by Marshall on early American jurisprudence.

## *John Marshall's Apotheosis*

Recently, I reviewed for the *Journal of American History* two new biographies of John Marshall. Both books, Charles F. Hobson's *The Great Chief Justice: John Marshall and the Rule of Law* (1996) and Jean Edward Smith's *John Marshall: Definer of a Nation* (1996),[19] are welcome additions to scholarship and I say so in my joint review.[20] Unfortunately, however, both books perpetuate the myth that Marshall is "The Father of the Court" and "The Jurist Who Started It All." To make the point more directly, these two books were twice reviewed together prior to my joint review, and the quoted titles to these reviews demonstrate dramatically the impression the books leave on readers.[21] Gordon S. Wood is the author of the review titled "The Father of the Court."[22] If one of the greatest living early American historians can default to clichés about the early Supreme Court, then clearly more work needs to be done on the origins of the Court.

Given the supposition that John Marshall is unduly credited with almost everything significant to spring from the early Supreme Court, the question that must be asked is this: Why is Marshall glorified? The answer to this question is not as clear as one might think. Hobson, editor of *The Papers of John Marshall,* wrote the following response to a query from me in which I speculated that Marshall's apotheosis was the handiwork of Albert J. Beveridge's politically inspired biography of 1916–1919:

> Marshall's greatness was recognized long before Beveridge. At his death in 1835 he had a reputation as a great statesman, if not always free from controversy. John Adams in 1825 wrote to Marshall that it was "the pride of my life that I have given to this nation a Chief Justice equal to Coke or Hale, Holt or Mansfield." John Quincy Adams entered these words in his diary, a few days after Marshall died: "John Marshall . . . was one of the most eminent men that this country has ever produced." Marshall's colleague, Joseph Story, delivered a memorable eulogy of the chief justice that wonderfully captures the essence of Marshall's greatness. Now, it is true that post–Civil War nationalism enhanced Marshall's standing and that Beveridge wrote in that context—attempting to make Marshall into a symbolic hero of Am[erican] nationalism, like Lincoln. Hope this helps.[23]

Help it does. There is, however, a difference between being a great *politician* and a great *judge.** Other scholars offer a far more partisan-oriented account of Marshall's deification than Hobson does. R. Kent Newmyer, the dean of judicial biographers, answers the question as follows:

> The process of glorification was launched with Allan Magruder's worshipful biography in 1890; it gained momentum with the Marshall Day celebration of 1901 (the outcome of which was a three-volume collection of encomiums compiled by John F. Dillon); and it culminated with Albert Beveridge's *The Life of John Marshall* (4 vols., 1916–1919) and Charles Warren's *The Supreme Court in United States History* (2 vols., 1922). With prodigious documentation Beveridge unabashedly celebrated the victory of light (conservative nationalism) over darkness (Jeffersonian states' rights agrarianism). And, by sheer force of emphasis and pervasive romanticism, his work raised Marshall above the Court, depicting him as the epic hero of American nationalism. Warren's history was more scholarly, more bal-

*It is difficult to deny that Marshall was a great politician. Only a great politician could do what Marshall did in *Marbury:* Announce that the Jefferson administration was wrong to withhold the judicial commissions in question and that courts could issue writs to compel public officials to do their prescribed duty—but that the Supreme Court had no power to issue such writs in the case at bar because the portion of the Judiciary Act of 1789 that gave the Court the power to do so was unconstitutional. In short, a showdown with the Jefferson administration was avoided, but Marshall still was able to "reaffirm" the Court's power of judicial review.

anced, and more generous in spreading the glory to include Marshall's colleagues but showed the same preference for conservative nationalism.[24]

Finally, Presser emphasizes—in his typically provocative fashion—more recent events: The need for "liberal" academics to use Marshall's "supposed greatness" to "legitimize" the rash of post-1937 "liberal" Supreme Court decisions. Presser explains:

> "Liberal" court critics since the early 1920s and 1930s had argued that the Supreme Court's job was to accommodate the Constitution to the changing economic and social needs of the country. It seems more than coincidental that at about the time the courts were frustrating implementation of New Deal legislation, scholars began lavishly to praise John Marshall for his famous decisions. . . . Similarly, when liberal academics praised the Warren Court's expansive interpretations of the Bill of Rights and the Fourteenth Amendment to protect the victims of educational, political, and economic discrimination, more volumes appeared apotheosizing Marshall.[25]

Whatever one's position regarding the pedigree of John Marshall's apotheosis, as far as the conventional wisdom is concerned, Marshall still casts a long shadow—an eclipse—across the history of the early Supreme Court. Nowhere is this more apparent than in the debate over the origins of judicial review in America.

## *The "Myth" of Marbury v. Madison (1803)*

Scholars have appreciated for some time that *Marbury v. Madison* was not sewn from whole cloth.[26*] From Sir Edward Coke's opinion in *Dr. Bonham's Case* (1610), to James Otis's speech against the Writs of Assistance (1761), to a series of pre-federal Constitution state-court cases,[27] to *Federalist* no. 78, there exist a host of pre-*Marbury* precedents for judicial review. More to the point, the essays that constitute *Seriatim* reveal that virtually every member of the pre-Marshall Court played an important role in establishing the

*Marshall himself acknowledged as much. See *Marbury v. Madison,* 5 U.S. (1 Cr.) 137, 176 (1803). Moreover, President Jefferson, who came to resent *Marbury,* was not taken aback by the judicial-review aspects of the decision. (Jefferson believed that the Court, as well as the president and Congress, had the right to pass on the constitutionality of matters before it.) Rather, he resented Marshall's obiter dictum that Marbury was entitled to his judicial commission.

Supreme Court's power of judicial review—a power that is synonymous to this day with John Marshall's most famous opinion.[28] Indeed, many of the justices championed judicial review long before they were appointed to the Court. My essay on William Cushing, for example, suggests that even before independence was declared Cushing was charging grand juries in Massachusetts that courts had the authority to declare acts of Parliament unconstitutional, while Wythe Holt describes how John Blair participated in at least three early cases involving judicial review in Virginia. Furthermore, Willis Whichard points out that James Iredell articulated on several occasions before the Constitution went into effect perhaps the most sophisticated argument for judicial review offered during the Founding (an argument with which Marshall was almost certainly familiar).[29] James Haw reveals that, despite fighting hard in the Federal Convention of 1787 to protect the power of state courts, John Rutledge both expected and supported federal judicial review, and William Casto demonstrates that Oliver Ellsworth endorsed the concept of judicial review at the Connecticut ratifying convention.

As sitting justices, the individuals who preceded John Marshall to the Supreme Court continued to advocate judicial review. The best-known examples of this are William Paterson's jury charge in *Van Horne's Lessee v. Dorrance* (1795) and Samuel Chase's jury charge in the trial of James Callender (1800). As Daniel Degnan's essay about Paterson and Presser's about Chase suggest, these jury charges helped to pave the way for public acceptance of judicial review. Similarly, Mark Hall demonstrates in his James Wilson essay that Wilson presented the case for judicial review in his famous law lectures of 1790–1792—lectures that influenced generations of American lawyers. Students of the Court, moreover, are remiss if they fail to appreciate, as Father Degnan and Casto describe in their respective essays, that the Judiciary Act of 1789, which Paterson and Ellsworth cowrote when they were serving in the Senate, authorized federal courts to review decisions from the states' highest courts if they involved certain federal questions.

The justices who composed the Supreme Court before John Marshall did more than simply advocate judicial review, they practiced it. Barely a year had passed since the establishment of the federal courts when Chief Justice John Jay and Associate Justice William Cushing, on circuit, declared several states' laws unconstitutional. There is also

*Ware v. Hylton* (1796), in which Justices Chase, Cushing, Paterson, and Wilson, sitting together as the Supreme Court,[30] struck down a Virginia statute on the ground that it was inconsistent with a federal treaty and, hence, the supremacy clause of the Constitution.[31] Moreover, James Stoner points out in his essay about Bushrod Washington that Washington, who was accused in a widely repeated remark of being little more than a double for Marshall—an accusation that Stoner rejects—asserted in *Cooper v. Telfair* (1800) that the Court possessed the power of judicial review.[32]

The pre–Marshall Court justices exercised judicial review over federal law as well. As Holt's and Hall's essays describe, the first clear occasion in which this occurred was *Hayburn's Case* (1792), wherein Justices James Wilson and John Blair, on circuit, declared the Invalid Pensioners Act of 1792 unconstitutional. The Court as a whole, in the then-unreported *United States v. Yale Todd* (1794), appears to have concurred with Wilson's and Blair's position.[33] Perhaps most important, in *Hylton v. United States* (1796) the Court reviewed a congressional tax on carriages to determine whether the tax was constitutional. The Court concluded that it was, but the justices nevertheless recognized their power to declare otherwise. Indeed, Hall reports that when John Wickham, the counsel for the government, offered at the circuit level to address the issue of judicial review, Justice Wilson told him to sit down and be quiet because the issue had "come before each of the judges in their different circuits, and they all concurred in the opinion" that the Court could declare congressional statutes unconstitutional.

More examples of pre-*Marbury* incidents of judicial review could be discussed,[34] but it should be clear by now that the pre–Marshall Court justices understood the concept of judicial review, that they argued for it, and that they practiced it. There is also abundant evidence that Marshall was both fully aware of and substantially influenced by these early precedents. Presser suggests, for example, that Marshall was in the audience when Samuel Chase delivered his jury charge in the *Callender* trial, and that Marshall later adopted some of Chase's language in his *Marbury* opinion. Similarly, Whichard advises that Marshall's opinion in *Marbury* drew upon Iredell's well-known writings on judicial review. Finally, I surmise in my essay about Cushing that Cushing and/or Paterson probably made Marshall aware of the early Court's precedents on judicial review.

## *An "Interdisciplinary Conversation"*

All of this said, *Seriatim* is important not only because it provides new information about the substantive contributions made to American law and politics by the pre–Marshall Court justices but also because of what the collection says about the method of studying the early American republic. Law, history, and political science are all represented in the collection, and each of these separate disciplines is represented by a diversity of methodological (as well as ideological) viewpoints. By including essays from a variety of methodological perspectives, *Seriatim* aspires to move research on the American Founding in new directions.

The five law professors among the contributors consist of one, Wythe Holt (who also is trained in history), who emphasizes social, political, and economic events; a second, Justice Whichard, who utilizes the descriptive techniques of biography; a third, Daniel Degnan, who employs the doctrinal focus of traditional legal analysis; a fourth, Stephen Presser, who combines the melding of biography, political science, and intellectual history (in the tradition of J. G. A. Pocock) with the fervor of a polemicist; and a fifth, William Casto, who highlights the psychological aspects of individual legal and political behavior. Karl Llewellyn, who long ago urged academic lawyers to employ more social science methods, would be pleased.[35]

Two of the contributors teach primarily in history departments. The first, Sandra VanBurkleo, attempts to locate her subject within the context and languages of his particular historical moment. She identifies relationships between the subject and the prevailing intellectual currents, socioeconomic developments, and political climate of the time, much as Holt does from the legal academy (albeit without Holt's Marxist orientation). The second, James Haw, approaches his justice through the descriptive and narrative method of a "traditional" historian.

Last, but it is to be hoped not least, the three political scientists also approach their justices in diverse ways. Although Mark Hall and James Stoner both utilize the method of political theory, Stoner's Straussian orientation gives his essay a flavor different from that of Hall's. My essay on Cushing is more disparate still: It employs deconstruction as a methodological approach.

In short, the contributors to *Seriatim* are engaged in an "interdisciplinary conversation" in the best sense of that phrase.[36] Although none of the contributors (the editor included) are methodologists, let alone philosophers of science, we all share a commitment to both methodological self-consciousness and methodological pluralism. We value methodological self-consciousness because those who fail to pay attention to method are almost always in the grip of a prevailing methodology. (Here, we are paraphrasing John Maynard Keynes's famous retort that those who dislike theory or claim to do without it are simply in the grip of an older theory.) We value methodological pluralism because a prevailing methodology might not be the "best" methodology, let alone the "perfect" methodology. A comparison between perhaps the two most diametrically opposed methodologies represented in *Seriatim* will illustrate why we take methodology so seriously.[37]

In his chapter on John Rutledge, James Haw employs the methodology of a "traditional historian," writing descriptive, narrative history in relatively narrow terms. More than anything else it is, in the words of Arthur M. Schlesinger, Sr., "the business of the historian to find, collect, classify, and appraise data relating to the past."[38] Haw's essay on Rutledge, with its painstaking attention to archival materials and myriad new discoveries about this controversial member of the pre-Marshall Court, is a testament to the continuing vitality and relevance of good "old-fashioned" history.

By contrast, my chapter on William Cushing employs one of the most popular—and controversial—methodologies of the postmodern age; "namely," deconstruction. Where Haw seeks to provide "new" information about John Rutledge's contributions to American law and politics, I attempt to reverse and resituate the "existing" conceptual priorities upon which the various orderings and evaluations of William Cushing and, consequently, of John Marshall, thrive.

Can students of the early American judiciary learn from deconstruction as well as from traditional history? from political theory as well as from doctrinal legal analysis? from psychology as well as from social, political, and economic considerations? from the melding of biography, political science, and intellectual history as well as from "unadulterated" biography? from a Straussian orientation as well as from a Marxist orientation? We hope the reader will grapple with these questions. A brief preview of the essays that follow may provide some assistance in this regard. The essays, written by *the* leading authorities on the particular justices at issue, appear in the order of the justices' respective appointments to the Supreme Court.

## *The Findings*

Sandra VanBurkleo explores in her essay relationships between John Jay's intellectual "system"—that is, his systematic political and economic philosophies—and his conception of the Supreme Court's role in government. Unlike some of *Seriatim*'s contributors, she challenges the notion that Jay's jurisprudence (and, for that matter, his bench) can best be understood by tightening the links between Jay and Marshall—that is, by rendering the federal judicial experience more continuous and homogenous. That approach, she contends, is unacceptably Whiggish. Jay has to be understood on his own terms, as both a product and an architect of the early phases of the American Revolution. First and foremost a diplomat, Jay had in mind a federal judiciary quite unlike the system refashioned and consolidated by John Marshall after 1801. To draw straight lines between past and present, to rub out strange and abandoned practices, VanBurkleo thinks, is to impoverish the present by eliminating an important part of the republic's past. Thus, she introduces a certain amount of distance between Jay and Marshall: Jay was extremely important—but not as a harbinger of Marshall. Rather, his now mostly archaic vision of federal practice offers ripe opportunities for comparative study and cultural-historical enrichment.

James Haw describes John Rutledge's distinguished career. He was a lawyer, colonial and state legislator, member of the Continental Congress, governor of South Carolina during most of the War of Independence, chancellor and later chief justice of South Carolina, delegate to the Federal Convention of 1787, and associate justice of the Supreme Court of the United States. Haw discusses how at the Constitutional Convention Rutledge advocated a mixed republic in which gentlemen would govern in the public interest, and sought to safeguard the interests of South Carolina. But, Haw suggests, Rutledge was willing to compromise repeatedly to achieve a more effective central government. Rutledge's most important contributions, Haw believes, were chairing the Committee of Detail, and helping to secure the enumeration of congressional powers, the necessary and proper clause, and safeguards for the deep South on the slave trade and taxation of exports.

Haw characterizes Rutledge's judicial philosophy as being quite conservative. Rutledge believed that judges should follow established legal constructions unless the legislature clearly changed them. Occasionally, however, he allowed equitable or political considerations to influence his rulings. His service on the federal bench was too brief to permit any major contribution there, Haw concludes. From 1792 through 1795, his deep mental depression produced erratic behavior that, combined with his outspoken opposition to the Jay Treaty, led the Senate to reject Rutledge's nomination as chief justice in 1795. Consequently, more than any of the justices chronicled in *Seriatim*, the vast majority of Rutledge's contributions to American law and politics occurred independent of his Supreme Court service.

My essay on William Cushing endeavors to disrupt the conventional wisdom that Cushing is but a footnote in the text of American history. Instead of viewing Cushing as the Dan Quayle of the early American republic—in other words, as an intellectual lightweight who rose to power through family and political connections—I argue that Cushing contributed much to American law and politics (perhaps as much as John Marshall).

My deconstruction of William Cushing reveals that he played a leading role in Massachusetts in, among other things, abolishing slavery and securing ratification of the federal Constitution. Cushing also had a great deal to do with the development of judicial review in America and, most importantly, with establishing the "textualist" approach to legal interpretation—an approach for which, like judicial review itself, John Marshall has been given undue credit over the years.

Mark Hall explains in his essay on James Wilson that while many students of the early American republic know about Wilson's extensive contributions to the framing and ratification of the Constitution, few are aware of the quality of his political thought. In fact, Hall argues that once Wilson's political theory is understood, his contributions at the Constitutional Convention and on the Supreme Court fall readily into place.

Hall makes clear that central among Wilson's political ideas was his belief that all individuals possess natural rights that must be protected by government. Contrary to many of his contemporaries, Wilson contended that thoroughly democratic institutions provide the best protection for both minority and majority rights. As a result, he supported the direct, popular election of representatives, senators, and executives. His democratic theory also informed his view of federalism, leading him to be a consistent nationalist. Yet Wilson did not hold a naive faith in the people, as indicated by his support for countermajoritarian checks such as judicial review. Hall attempts to reconcile Wilson's support of these checks with his democratic theory, and ultimately concludes that Wilson was the foremost advocate among the Founders of a strong and democratic government that also protects minority rights.

Wythe Holt characterizes John Blair as a wealthy, well-connected, and influential merchant, planter, legislator, and lawyer from the powerful Tidewater aristocracy who was an important leader of second rank when Virginia joined most of the colonies in the drive for independence. Blair won repute serving on Virginia's highest courts and, as a member of the Constitutional Convention and Virginia's ratification convention, he silently aided the formation of a new government for the new nation.

Holt's essay demonstrates that, as a member of the first Supreme Court, Blair cautiously but steadily in actions and opinions showed himself to be a staunch Federalist and a supporter of the mercantile-oriented, weak new central government, imperiled from within by agrarian and democratic dissent and from without by imperialistic European powers. He was, however, neither a profound writer nor a leader on the Court. But, Holt insists, the proper criterion by which to assess the Court's opinions in the perilous 1790s is their political effectiveness in persuasively upholding the power, authority, and respect of the government while exciting no dismembering discontent; and the proper gauge of its members is their courage and consistency in supporting the new Constitution and its constituted government. On both of these measures, the amiable, safe, conscientious John Blair ranks at the top, Holt concludes, because his clear pronouncements empowering the government were phrased narrowly so as to provoke no animosity, even though he was the only southern justice consistently to support Federalist positions.

Willis Whichard explains that James Iredell came to America as a British official to be the comptroller of customs in Edenton, North Carolina. Iredell studied law under Samuel Johnston, a politically influential lawyer, and acquired the reputation of a superior lawyer. In his most significant case as counsel, Whichard reveals, Iredell advocated the concept of judicial review. He also championed it in a series of sophisticated letters and essays.

Whichard demonstrates how Iredell became a leading essayist for the American cause in the Revolution and a bellwether for the Federalist forces in the effort to ratify the federal Constitution. Iredell answered George Mason's objections, led other literary efforts, and served as floor leader for the Federalist forces at the initial North Carolina ratification convention. When that convention failed to approve the Constitution, Iredell continued his endeavors until a second convention ratified the document. President Washington rewarded Iredell's efforts by appointing him to the Supreme Court. Whichard suggests that the grasp of constitutional questions Iredell displayed in promoting ratification was the foremost reason for the appointment.

Whichard maintains that Iredell's most significant opinion was his dissent in *Chisholm v. Georgia*. In that case Iredell took the position that a citizen of one state could not sue another state. The Eleventh Amendment incorporated Iredell's position into the Constitution. Iredell spent most of his Court years traveling the circuits. He led efforts to terminate or reduce the travel but, Whichard reveals, those efforts were largely to no avail. His work on circuit undermined his health, and he died after a near-decade of service.

Daniel Degnan reminds us that William Paterson was a member of the Constitutional Convention and author of the New Jersey, or small-states, plan. Despite his advocacy of the rights of the smaller states, however, Paterson proved to be a consistent nationalist. As a member of the first Senate, Paterson was a principal coauthor, with Oliver Ellsworth, of the Judiciary Act of 1789. The first nine sections of the act, establishing the federal district and circuit courts, were in Paterson's handwriting.

Paterson served on the Supreme Court from 1793 to 1806 where, Father Degnan argues, his work was a continuation of his work in the convention and the Senate. For Paterson, prize capture on the high seas evoked the plenary power of the national government in foreign affairs. The national power to tax, he believed, was not to be narrowly constrained. State laws were to be tested by the new Constitution, as were state court decisions on the issue. Congress had the power to abolish federal courts (as well as to establish them), although judges would lose their positions. Practical contemporary construction was dispositive.

Perhaps most interesting, Father Degnan suggests, is that Paterson issued in a circuit court case one of the most striking early statements of the doctrine of judicial review: "What is a Constitution? It is the form of government, delineated by the mighty hand of the people, in which certain first principles of fundamental laws are established. . . . [E]very act of the Legislature, repugnant to the Constitution, is absolutely void." To Paterson, Father Degnan concludes, these principles formed a straight line from the Constitutional Convention and the first Senate through the foundations laid by the early Supreme Court.

Was Samuel Chase, the only Supreme Court justice ever to be impeached, a partisan bully unfit to sit on the bench (as his Jeffersonian tormentors insisted), or was he unfairly attacked for seeking to maintain the rule of law when it was under partisan assault (as the defenders at his trial before the Senate maintained)? While most historians are prepared to concede Chase's obvious brilliance, his hair-trigger temper and his obduracy led one recent historian—*Seriatim*'s own William Casto—flatly to declare that Chase's appointment was "one of the most regrettable nominations in the Court's history."

In 1991 Stephen Presser published his book *The Original Misunderstanding*, a summation of fifteen years of work, to argue that Chase should be regarded as one of the greatest of the early Supreme Court justices, and someone who articulated a vision of constitutional law more in keeping with the Framers' original understanding than did John Marshall. Presser's book intrigued historians and academic lawyers, who had quite different responses to his thesis and to Samuel Chase. In his essay in this volume, Presser revisits Chase's contributions to American law and politics, responds to his critics, and explores some of the tensions facing scholars writing legal history.*

*Readers will notice that Presser's essay is structured differently than the others in the book. Because *Seriatim* essentially picks up where Presser left off with his earlier work on Chase, we thought readers might find it interesting to see why Presser did what he did there and what the reaction to his work has been.

William Casto approaches his essay on Oliver Ellsworth as an assault upon anachronistic preconceptions that many scholars have about the Founding generation. Specifically, Casto argues that there is a tendency to emphasize the secular aspects of political life in the early republic and to deemphasize the religious dimensions. Casto also insists that our late-twentieth-century preconceptions of the proper role of judges in political life has distorted our analyses of judicial conduct in the early American republic. The concept of separation of powers and the ideal of judicial aloofness from political controversy have changed substantially over the past twenty years, Casto maintains.[39]

Casto uses Ellsworth as an archetype to illustrate two points. Ellsworth was a thoroughgoing religionist who viewed his public and private activities through the lens of Calvinism. The point is not that Ellsworth's religion caused him to act in different ways—although Casto suspects that it did. Instead, Casto believes that Calvinism was the organizing philosophy of Ellsworth's life and that he and others like him cannot be understood if his faith is marginalized. With respect to his judicial conduct in the early republic, Chief Justice Ellsworth is depicted as one who was deeply involved in the national politics of the late 1790s. Casto believes that Ellsworth viewed himself not so much as a judge but, rather, as an active participant in public life who happened to be a judge.

Finally, in his essay on Bushrod Washington, James Stoner makes a powerful case for viewing Washington as a bridge between the pre-Marshall Court and the more famous Marshall Court. Consequently, Stoner explodes the myth that Washington and Marshall should be viewed, as William Johnson once charged, as "one Judge."

Stoner argues that though Bushrod Washington lived in the shadow of two great men—his uncle George Washington and his friend of fifty years, John Marshall—he was an independent man who left his mark on federal justice and helped make possible the extraordinary unity of the Marshall Court. (This latter achievement is yet another for which Marshall receives undue credit.) Educated in law by George Wythe and James Wilson, distinguishing himself at an early age on the Richmond bar, Washington was appointed to the Court by John Adams in 1798. From the start, his jurisprudence is characterized by respect for legislative authority, a sense of exact justice, and a certain moderation. Stoner makes it clear that although Washington is largely overlooked today, he was a highly respected judge in his own day.

## *A Word Is Worth a Thousand Pictures*

This, then, is what is chronicled in the essays that follow. Before readers are left to enjoy the essays, it might be useful for me to say a few words about why the collection is titled *Seriatim* (Latin for "severally" or "in series").

As judicial process scholars probably know, the practice in English appellate courts is for all of the participating judges to write, and deliver orally, individual opinions explaining their views on a case. This process is known as "seriatim" opinion writing. (The seriatim custom originated in the jury-charge practice of the common-law courts.) Seriatim opinion writing was also the practice used in early American appellate courts—the U.S. Supreme Court included—before, that is, John Marshall became chief justice.

When John Marshall was appointed chief justice in 1801, he put an end to the practice of seriatim opinion writing. Chief Justice Marshall did so because he believed that the Supreme Court's "power and prestige" would be enhanced if it spoke with a "single voice."[40] To that end, Marshall established the practice of a single "opinion of the Court"—almost always signed, at least in the early days of his chief justiceship, by Marshall himself[41]—that would reflect the views of the Court as an institution and be recorded and reported to the public. As with any collaborative product, however, this new practice meant that differences among the justices were adjusted internally and, consequently, hidden from public view. Although this was plainly Marshall's intention, the end of seriatim opinion writing meant that the contributions of individual justices were difficult, if not impossible, to discern. This, we suspect, goes a long way toward explaining why Marshall has come to eclipse in the conventional wisdom the other justices of the early Supreme Court. And this, we believe, is unfortunate.

In short, the collection is titled *Seriatim* for three reasons: (1) because the justices who composed the Supreme Court before John Marshall functioned, for the most part, and spoke, almost always, as individuals, (2) because we aspire to dispel the myth that the early Court became significant only when Marshall arrived, and (3) because we hope to suggest something of the drama in which the pre–Marshall Court justices performed their important duties. To make the point even more directly, a good book title captures the essence of what the author endeavors to accomplish. The title *Seriatim* does that for us.

## NOTES

1. See, for example, Rogers M. Smith, "Political Jurisprudence, The 'New Institutionalism', and the Future of Public Law," *American Political Science Review* 82 (March 1988): 89–108.

2. See, for example, Thomas G. Walker, Lee Epstein, and William J. Dixon, "On the Mysterious Demise of Consensual Norms in the United States Supreme Court," *Journal of Politics* 50 (May 1988): 361–89. See also Byron R. White, "Dear Colleagues" letter, reprinted in 509 U.S.—Part 3 (preliminary print) (1993), vi–vii.

3. Bernard Schwartz, *A History of the Supreme Court* (New York: Oxford University Press, 1993), 33.

4. George Lee Haskins and Herbert A. Johnson, *Foundations of Power: John Marshall, 1801–15* (New York: Macmillan, 1981), 7.

5. Robert G. McCloskey, *The American Supreme Court* (Chicago: University of Chicago Press, 1960), 30. Sanford Levinson updated this classic tome in 1994.

6. See, for example, G. Edward White, *The American Judicial Tradition: Profiles of Leading American Judges*, enlarged ed. (New York: Oxford University Press, 1988), 7–34.

7. See, for example, Carl Brent Swisher, *American Constitutional Development* (Boston: Houghton Mifflin, 1943), 98–101; Fred Rodell, *Nine Men: A Political History of the Supreme Court from 1790 to 1955* (New York: Random House, 1955), 3–72.

Several histories of the Supreme Court are less guilty of trivializing the pre-Marshall Court than are others, but even those works do not examine the contributions of the individual justices in any depth. See generally Julius Goebel, Jr., *Antecedents and Beginnings to 1801* (New York: Macmillan, 1971); Charles Warren, *The Supreme Court in United States History*, rev. ed., vol. 1 (Boston: Little, Brown, 1926), 31–168; David P. Currie, *The Constitution in the Supreme Court: The First Hundred Years, 1789–1888* (Chicago: University of Chicago Press, 1985), 1–58. The increasingly popular encyclopedia-style biographical collections of the Supreme Court are too basic to be of much use to scholars. See, for example, Clare Cushman, ed., *The Supreme Court Justices: Illustrated Biographies, 1789–1993* (Washington, D.C.: CQ Press, 1993); Leon Friedman and Fred I. Israel, eds., *The Justices of the United States Supreme Court: Their Lives and Major Opinions,* rev. ed., 5 vols. (New York: Chelsea House, 1995); Melvin I. Urofsky, ed., *The Supreme Court: A Biographical Dictionary* (New York: Garland, 1994).

8. Edward S. Corwin, *John Marshall and the Constitution: A Chronicle of the Supreme Court* (New Haven: Yale University Press, 1919), 17–18. This insight is especially rare in books about Marshall, which tend to emphasize the inadequacy of the Court that preceded his. See, for example, Albert J. Beveridge, *The Life of John Marshall*, vol. 3 (Boston: Houghton Mifflin, 1919), 120–21; Leonard Baker, *John Marshall: A Life in Law* (New York: Macmillan, 1974), 363–64.

9. Maeva Marcus et al., eds., *The Documentary History of the Supreme Court of the United States, 1789–1800*, 5 vols. to date (New York: Columbia University Press, 1985–); Maeva Marcus, ed., *Origins of the Federal Judiciary: Essays on the Judiciary Act of 1789* (New York: Oxford University Press, 1992). Marcus's *Documentary History* renders largely obsolete George Lankevich's more limited collection. See George J. Lankevich, ed., *The Federal Court, 1787–1801* (Millwood, N.Y.: Associated Faculty Press, 1986).

10. William R. Casto, *The Supreme Court in the Early Republic: The Chief Justiceships of John Jay and Oliver Ellsworth* (Columbia: University of South Carolina Press, 1995), 247.

11. Ibid., 247, 213.

12. In addition to the work of Marcus and the previous and continuing efforts of the contributors to the present volume, see also Stewart Jay, *Most Humble Servants: The Advisory Role of Early Judges* (New Haven: Yale University Press, 1997).

13. See J. W. Peltason, "Supreme Court Biography and the Study of Public Law," in *Essays on the American Constitution: A Commemorative Volume in Honor of Alpheus T. Mason*, ed. Gottfried Dietze (Englewood Cliffs, N.J.: Prentice-Hall, 1964), 215–27.

14. Letter from George Washington to John Rutledge, 29 September 1789, in Marcus, *Documentary History*, vol. 1, 20–21. President Washington wrote similar letters to all his nominees. See James R. Perry, "Supreme Court Appointments, 1789–1801: Criteria, Presidential Style, and the Press of Events," *Journal of the Early Republic* 6 (Winter 1986): 371, 374.

15. Henry J. Abraham, *Justices and Presidents: A Political History of Appointments to the Supreme Court*, 3d ed. (New York: Oxford University Press, 1992), 71–72. For a detailed discussion of Washington's and Adams's appointment processes, see Perry, "Supreme Court Appointments, 1789–1801," 371–410.

16. See, for example, Abraham, *Justices and Presidents*, 81, 412–14.

17. Numerous letters exist from different justices complaining about the onerous duty of circuit riding—especially in the Southern Circuit. See, for example, Marcus, *Documentary History*, vol. 1, 731–32; vol. 2, 126, 132, 288–90, 344; vol. 3, 240.

18. See Stephen B. Presser, *The Original Misunderstanding: The English, the*

*Americans and the Dialectic of Federalist Jurisprudence* (Durham: Carolina Academic Press, 1991).

19. Charles F. Hobson, *The Great Chief Justice: John Marshall and the Rule of Law* (Lawrence: University Press of Kansas, 1996); Jean Edward Smith, *John Marshall: Definer of a Nation* (New York: Henry Holt, 1996).

20. See Scott D. Gerber, Book Review, *Journal of American History* 84 (September 1997): 658–59.

21. See also Herbert A. Johnson, *The Chief Justiceship of John Marshall, 1801–1835* (Columbia: University of South Carolina Press, 1997).

22. Gordon S. Wood, "The Father of the Court," *New Republic*, 17 February 1997, 38–41. See also Mark Miller, "The Jurist Who Started It All," *Wall Street Journal*, 10 December 1996, A20.

23. E-mail letter from Charles F. Hobson to Scott D. Gerber, 29 September 1995 (letter in my possession).

24. R. Kent Newmyer, *The Supreme Court under Marshall and Taney* (Arlington Heights, Ill.: Harlan Davidson, 1968), 20–21. See also letter from William E. Leuchtenburg to Scott D. Gerber, 18 November 1995 ("It is not my impression, though Chuck Hobson should know a good deal more, that Marshall had the reputation he does today in the 19th Century. He was seen then as considerably more of an embattled Federalist and a champion of certain interests.") (letter in my possession).

25. Presser, *The Original Misunderstanding*, 172.

26. See, for example, Gordon S. Wood, "The Origins of Judicial Review," *Suffolk University Law Review* 22 (Winter 1988): 1293–307 (arguing that the origins of judicial review are to be found in the colonial period).

27. The state-court cases are *Josiah Philips's Case* (Va., 1778), *Holmes v. Walton* (N.Y., 1780), *Commonwealth v. Caton* (Va., 1782), *Rutgers v. Waddington* (N.Y., 1784), *The Symsbury Case* (Conn., 1785), *Trevett v. Weeden* (R.I., 1786), and *Bayard v. Singleton* (N.C., 1787). There is considerable debate in the scholarly community about the status of these early cases.

28. See, for example, David G. Barnum, *The Supreme Court and American Democracy* (New York: St. Martin's Press, 1993), 3–9 (emphasizing *Marbury v. Madison*); James Q. Wilson and John J. DiIulio, Jr., *American Government: Institutions and Policies*, 6th ed. (Lexington, Mass.: D. C. Heath, 1995), 420 (same). See also Smith, *John Marshall*, chapter 13. Of course, there have been specific studies of judicial review over the years, particularly by historians, that recognize that *Marbury* has been overemphasized. See, for example, J. M. Sosin, *The Aristocracy of the Long Robe: The Origins of Judicial Review in America* (Westport, Conn.: Greenwood Press, 1989). My point is simply that the conventional wisdom is still to the contrary—and that the role the pre–Marshall Court justices played in the origins of judicial review has been largely overlooked.

29. See also William R. Casto, "James Iredell and the American Origins of Judicial Review," *Connecticut Law Review* 27 (Winter 1995): 329–63.

30. Iredell had been one of the judges in the lower circuit court that adjudicated the case. Consequently, he did not participate in the Supreme Court's decision. He did take the unusual step, however, of reading into the record his thoughts on the matter.

31. Ellsworth, who was not serving on the Supreme Court at the time *Ware* was decided, voiced his agreement with the decision in *Hamilton v. Eaton*, 11 F. Cas. 336, 340 (C.C.D.N.C. 1796).

32. See also the seriatim opinions of Justices Chase, Paterson, and Cushing in *Cooper v. Telfair*, 4 U.S. (4 Dall.) 14, 18–20 (1800), as well as *Pennhallow v. Doane's Administrators*, 3 U.S. (3 Dall.) 54 (1795).

33. *Yale Todd* was cited in *United States v. Ferreira*, 54 U.S. (13 How.) 40 (1851). Maeva Marcus suggests, but does not conclude, that the Supreme Court ruled that Yale Todd's pension was invalid because the judges of the circuit courts wrongly interpreted the statute to allow them to act as commissioners and hear claims. See Maeva Marcus, "Judicial Review in the Early Republic," in *Launching the "Extended Republic": The Federalist Era*, ed. Ronald L. Hoffman (Charlottesville: University Press of Virginia, 1996), 41 n.54. Marcus, in an earlier essay written with Robert Teir, suggests, but again does not conclude, that the Supreme Court in *Yale Todd* declared the statute unconstitutional. See Maeva Marcus and Robert Teir, "*Hayburn's Case*: A Misinterpretation of Precedent," *Wisconsin Law Review* (July-August 1988): 527, 531 n.25.

John Marshall himself—and in *Marbury v. Madison*, no less—made note of another unreported case, *Chandler v. Secretary of War* (1794), in which the Court appears to have invalidated an executive act. See *Marbury v. Madison*, 5 U.S. (1 Cr.) 137, 172 (1803) (discussing the case). Susan Low Bloch and Marcus suggest, but once again do not conclude, that *Chandler* was decided on other than constitutional grounds. See Susan Low Bloch and Maeva Marcus, "John Marshall's Selective Use of History in *Marbury v. Madison*," *Wisconsin Law Review* (March-April 1986): 301, 315 n.54. But see Gordon E. Sherman, "The Case of John Chandler v. The Secretary of War," *Yale Law Journal* 14 (May 1905): 431, 437 (arguing that *Chandler* was decided on constitutional grounds). Bloch and Marcus maintain that Marshall manipulated precedents such as *Chandler* to get his desired political result in *Marbury*. See Bloch and Marcus, "John Marshall's Selective Use of History in *Marbury v. Madison*," 301–37.

34. For more, see Marcus, "Judicial Review in the Early Republic," 25–53.

35. See Karl Llewellyn, "Legal Tradition and Social Science Method—A Realist's Critique," in *Essays on Research in the Social Sciences*, ed. Leverett S. Lyon, Isador Lubin, Lewis Meriam, and Philip G. Wright (Washington, D.C.: Brookings Institution, 1931; repr., Port Washington, N.Y.: Kennikat, 1968), 89–120.

36. This phrase was coined by historian Peter S. Onuf in a refreshing essay

criticizing his fellow historians of the American Founding for attempting to defend history against "alien disciplines." See Peter S. Onuf, "Reflections on the Founding: Constitutional Historiography in Bicentennial Perspective," *William and Mary Quarterly* 46 (April 1989): 341–75.

37. On the importance of methodology in legal history, see G. Edward White, *Intervention and Detachment: Essays in Legal History and Jurisprudence* (New York: Oxford University Press, 1994).

38. Arthur M. Schlesinger, "History: Mistress and Handmaid," in Lyon et al., *Essays on Research in the Social Sciences*, 139.

39. Here, readers will be reminded of the thesis of Casto's superb tome, *The Supreme Court in the Early Republic*.

40. Henry J. Abraham, *The Judicial Process: An Introductory Analysis of the Courts of the United States, England, and France*, 6th ed. (New York: Oxford University Press, 1993), 199.

41. Haskins and Johnson make an interesting case for the possibility that the opinion of the Court was delivered, but not necessarily written, by the senior justice who participated in the case. Given that Marshall was both chief justice and rarely absent, this tended to be Marshall. See Haskins and Johnson, *Foundations of Power*, 382–87 (discussing this subject, as well as the more general subject of the transition from seriatim opinion writing to institutional opinion writing). Casto maintains that Marshall merely solidified a custom—using institutional rather than seriatim opinions—that Ellsworth initiated during his chief justiceship. See Casto, *The Supreme Court in the Early Republic*, 110–11.

*Chapter 2*

# "Honour, Justice, and Interest"
## *John Jay's Republican Politics and Statesmanship on the Federal Bench*

*Sandra Frances VanBurkleo*

In 1779, at the height of the Deane controversy, Richard Henry Lee pronounced John Jay a "Tory friend" and "Mercantile Abettor" masquerading as a republican.[1] Lee's remarks were unusually sharp. But a good many others harbored similar reservations and, in the rarefied atmosphere of American Revolution studies, such criticisms die hard. Scholars expect a great deal of founding fathers, and Jay consistently falls short of the mark. As a result, readers find one-dimensional caricatures of Jay's political thought, values, and objectives that merely perpetuate or deny the allegations of eighteenth-century critics. David Hackett Fischer, for example, once sketched a nostalgic, slightly pathetic "conservative idealist" permanently flawed by King's College monarchism and by yearnings for a bygone ancien régime. In this rendition, Jay rejected his own historical moment, devolving with James Kent and George Cabot into an Old Guard reactionary. Others describe an abrasive "realist" from New York more taken with the China trade than with Blackstone or Locke, for whom political and legal discourse functioned mainly as window dressing. And Richard Morris, after decades of invaluable research and editing, essentially turned the stereotype on its head. Transformed into a relatively affable patriot and closet democrat roughly equal in stature to John Mar-

An earlier version of this essay appeared under the same title in *Journal of the Early Republic* 4 (Fall 1984): 239–74. Portions are reprinted by permission. The author wishes to thank Edward M. Wise for valuable editorial help.

shall,[2] Morris's Jay steadily advanced the American cause by means of shrewd diplomacy and by presciently anticipating the Marshall Court's economic nationalism as well as its pivotal victory in *Marbury* v. *Madison*.[3]

Put differently, political and constitutional historians—unlike foreign relations scholars, who have managed to avoid interpretive extremes[4]—cling to time-honored caricatures of a bored, boring, and often incompetent chief justice and an insubstantial Supreme Court between 1789 and 1795. To some extent, this unflattering portrait originates in the fact of a limited body of personal writing, an unforthcoming man behind the pen, and a cryptic legal record: at critical moments, the historical record simply falls silent. But two additional factors shape the narrative: lawyer-historians bring exacting technical and practical standards to bear on Jay's law practice and management of the high court, in the process reinforcing traditional skepticism; and scholars trained in history greatly prefer John Marshall (or, for that matter, the more pragmatic Hamilton and Madison), if only because Marshall's charmingly darned stockings and chats with the newsboy play better on the lecture circuit than do Jay's starched cuffs and mannered grand jury charges. For these and other reasons, constitutional historians have been content to dismiss Jay's tenure as an embarrassing lapse in an otherwise distinguished common-law tradition.

Among constitutional historians, the long Marshallian shadow has been particularly damaging. Jay most assuredly was not Marshall; Morris's views aside, historians have yet to forgive him for failing to be affable, flexible, and devoted to the Supreme Court for its own sake. Jay was undeniably cantankerous in dealings with legislators. His informal advisory opinions and open partisanship seem to flout the idea of an autonomous, apolitical federal judiciary, and his brusque departure for diplomacy in 1794 without first resigning the chief justiceship annoys even Morris. Most important, Jay did not secure the all-important review power around which Marshall fashioned a recognizably modern, uniquely American appellate practice after the "midnight judges" episode, in the process insulating the Court from the more egregious inroads of what Jay called "political grubs."[5]

Hence, scholars typically portray the Jay Court as the Marshall Court writ small—a primitive, amorphous prelude to the durable consolidations pursued after Jefferson's election. Within this Whiggish framework, Jay's aspirations as chief justice have been deduced not from reconstructions of his intellect but from the use made by nineteenth-century jurists of Jay Court decisions. Historians imply, in other words, that Jay must have intended to lay foundations for whatever the high court finally became, and failed miserably. Robert McCloskey, for instance, compares the Court before 1801 to a "play's opening moments with minor characters exchanging trivialities," candidly conceding that the "great shadow of John Marshall . . . falls across our understanding." Charles Haines once pointed to "unpromising beginnings"; a classic textbook treats the years before Marshall's arrival in four pages. And Morris basically employs the same yardstick, arguing success and doctrinal kindredness in the place of failure and pale imitation. Had Jay accepted John Adams's invitation to return to the Court in 1801, he concludes, Marshall's finest state papers "would very probably have been written by Jay, whose views Marshall so completely shared."[6]

Yet John Jay's views were entirely his own, molded before all else by the exigencies of revolution. When Washington signed Jay's commission as chief justice of the United States in September 1789, the republic was situated differently and more precariously than it would be a dozen years later. Economic distress seemed to portend the nation's early demise, especially in competition with deeply skeptical European empires. A theoretically promising frame of government was untried; vague constitutional language surrounding the Court's role in governance—made more explosive with the addition of contested sections in the 1789 Judiciary and Process Acts—invited Anti-Federalists to dismantle what Washington called the "keystone" of federalism.[7]

Indeed, criticisms often seem to be well founded. Before 1795, the Supreme Court's caseload was thin, its members frustrated and disconsolate, and what Jay called its "Facilities of usage and Habit" mostly unspecified. Without immediate institutional antecedents, the entire federal judiciary lacked legitimacy and came to be humiliated all too easily by congressional adoption of the punitive Eleventh Amendment in 1798.[8] The chief justice, moreover, has been dismissed as a "trifling" student of domestic law whose court escaped mediocrity (when it did) largely because James Wilson and other imaginative associates shared the bench. Again, when measured against modern standards, such charges seem plausible. Jay produced no scholarship more extensive than grand jury charges and brief *Federalist* essays. His apprenticeship and private practice were relatively insubstantial, and his judicial experience in New York before 1789 was fleeting.[9]

But appearances mislead. Jay's vision of the Supreme Court's role in government differed in several respects from modern conceptions of the institution's role in federated government. This is exactly as it ought to be. Unlike Marshall, Jay superintended a wholly untested judiciary, supported only in part by colonial antecedents. His chief justiceship, moreover, coincided with a particularly volatile phase of revolutionary process—the period immediately after formal adoption of a contested (some thought illegal) frame of government. In addition, Jay's intellectual and professional inclinations, while well suited to the day and to his own conception of judicial responsibility, were sweepingly internationalist (in Morris's view, "continental")[10] rather than inward turning or provincial, philosophic rather than lawyerly, organic and hegemonic rather than mechanical and pluralist. Within his elegant, symmetry-seeking intellectual "system," Jay merged High Federalist legalism and political conservatism with free-trading economic liberalism; for this rigidly principled man, and for many of his friends, conservative republicanism and Smithian political economy coexisted quite peaceably, bound together by an encompassing framework of moralizing, stabilizing public law. This collection of unfamiliar associations surely represents not a watered-down prelude to grandeur but an *alternative* jurisprudential scheme bound up tightly in the reality of an unfinished, highly unstable revolution.

## *The Road to Reluctant Patriotism*

John Jay's youth prefigured the man. The eldest son of the wealthy Peter and Mary Van Cortlandt Jay, whose ancestry was partly Huguenot, John followed the path dictated by his parents' lofty position within the New York mercantile community. After private tutoring, he entered King's College (now Columbia University) to study the classics, natural science, public law, philosophy, and political economy. Jay came to the law in his final year at the college, and then (as was customary among gentlemen) primarily as preparation for public service. He graduated with honors and took up an apprenticeship (again, as was customary) with the eminent New York City attorney

Benjamin Kissam; as assistant to chief clerk Lindley Murray, he soon chafed under piles of tedious copy work. When city lawyers struck in support of the Stamp Act protest in 1765, Jay happily fled to the family estate in Rye, New York. There, he buried himself in philosophy, public law, and the classics; two years later, King's College rewarded these efforts with a master of arts degree.

By all reports, Jay was a successful lawyer. In 1766, two years after his return to Kissam's office, he gained admission to the New York bar and opened a New York City law office with his schoolmate Robert Livingston, Jr. Jay leavened work with upper-class diversions: debating clubs, the exclusive Dancing Assembly, and conservative state political groups. In 1769, he accepted his first public office as a commissioner charged with settling a New York–New Jersey boundary dispute; five years later, Jay's bright professional and social prospects allowed marriage to the wellborn Sarah (or Sally) Van Brugh Livingston.

But, even as the couple exchanged vows, American cities rumbled with rebellious talk about the Intolerable Acts and George III's abrogations of his coronation oath. Jay initially resisted independence; he helped formulate the conciliatory Olive Branch Petition of 1774 and seriously considered expatriation as an alternative to treason. But, by 1775, the ever-louder transatlantic screaming match about both the constitutional status of the colonies and the merits of an Anglo-American economic partnership exerted a powerful attraction. Jay, after all, held advanced degrees in political economy and public law, including the law of nations; he feared, too, that the crown no longer could protect colonial trade and property. Intellectual challenges aside, familial and class interests—responsible only in part for Jay's nervousness about imminent public disorder[11]—led him to remain in the New World.

Jay served the cause initially in state political groups and then in the First and Second Continental Congresses. For the moment, he suspended his half-buried Calvinism and deep-seated skepticism about republican faith in voluntarism and perfectibility: perhaps Americans *were* capable of self-government. During these tumultuous years, he even parted ways occasionally with moderating colleagues in the New York congressional delegation: his championship of the Galloway Plan for colonial economic unification, for instance, as well as his strident support for nonimportation agreements as a member of New

York's radical Committee of Sixty, set him sharply apart from many of his friends. At the same time, he sat on state Committees of Correspondence and Safety, synchronizing intracolonial protests and providing a semblance of government as the British magistracy collapsed. Jay helped draft the New York state constitution; until 1779, he also served (erratically and without distinction) as chief justice of the New York superior court. Only a few days after he arrived in Philadelphia to serve as a New York delegate to the general government, members of the new Congress elected Jay president of that body. Shortly afterward, he became minister plenipotentiary to Spain; a scant three years later, he went to Europe with four other commissioners to negotiate what would become the Paris Peace Treaty with Great Britain.

These were traumatic experiences. Almost at once, Jay concluded that his original, gloomy assessment of the republican character—and, more generally, American prospects for success within a decentralized confederation—had been appallingly accurate. As a weak quasi-executive in Congress, Jay helplessly presided over what he took to be the disintegration of the confederation. Where other men saw growing pains, Jay perceived moral decay and the loss of security in liberty. Americans engaged in the invention of modern political parties and in a celebration of nascent capitalism were entirely aware of the divisive, self-interested quality of their activities; Clintonians and other "modern men" regularly pointed to an emerging polity and economy accessible to Everyman. Jay detected what Gordon Wood might call an "assault on aristocracy"[12] and its traditional monopoly of public culture. Everywhere, republicans seemed to embrace or tolerate moral degeneracy, demagoguery, disdain for law, extreme "levelling," disastrous logjams in Congress, the fettering of diplomats, drifts of worthless paper currency, and tooth-and-nail competition among the states for trading privileges. In Europe, Jay personally guaranteed repayment of war loans; privately, he despaired of society's capacity for virtue and Congress's ability to navigate the rapids between independence and nationhood. How could diplomats persuade Europeans of republican integrity, he wondered, when the people's representatives embraced ignoble, self-destructive practices and policies?

Thus, scholars have ample ground to contend that Jay, well before the ink dried on the Judiciary and Process Acts, steadily rowed against the republican current, or at least against the democratizing, socially transformative part of that current. Jay was keenly aware of instabilities lurking in those "soft ambiguous moments"[13] after ratification. In his own words, the problem at hand was to discover, within legal and political limits, how the new federal judiciary—and especially the Supreme Court—might best provide "due support to the national government" in pursuit of "great and obvious principles of sound policy."[14] Because the main task was *establishment* rather than expansion or innovation, Jay's understanding of such terms as "due support" or "great and obvious principles" merits close attention. How did he imagine proper relations between polity, economy, and law? Toward what ends did the new federal government move, and through whom? How might the high court advance those ends most effectively?

## *Jay's Political Economy and Jurisprudence in the Crucible of Revolution*

Jay's political and jurisprudential "system" blended an extremely conservative domestic politics with liberal economic theory, the latter very narrowly construed. With Adam Smith and other political economists, Jay conceived of liberalism primarily as a blueprint for stable, global commercial development, predicated upon the existence of moral domestic societies in advance of economic exchange.[15] He also distinguished between political citizenship as defined by individual nations and the broader, more significant membership of Americans and Europeans in a transnational economic community. To facilitate the emergence of a harmonious "band of brethren" in North America, Jay urged internal centralization, reliance upon a few enlightened statesmen, and strict attention to federal law—the embodiment of reason and divine morality—in order to secure both forms of citizenship against the evils inherent in all people. Without these safeguards, Jay predicted swift decline into the immorality and greed so "natural" in human societies.[16]

Imbedded in Jay's political thought was a stinging critique of the basic tenets of Revolutionary idealism. These disagreements, which Jay pressed steadfastly from the Revolution's earliest moments through retirement, originated in an unusually bleak and remarkably static assessment of human nature. His expressions of doubt about perfectibility, and then about the merits of voluntarism or adherence to the popular will, vacillated between moderation and stridency with changing circumstances. During "Seasons of general Heat Tumult and Fermentation" such as wartime or diplomatic crises, his anxieties intensified; his views softened appreciably with the prospect of a strengthened "national Head" after 1787. But shifting colorations barely masked an essential, unremitting gloom about the motives of politicized Americans and about "democratical" experimentation in an untutored postcolonial society wrenched too suddenly—that is, in violation of the laws of natural social development—from British imperial moorings.[17]

Jay's existential depression flowed partly from pietism. A devoted Anglican, he nevertheless remained conscious for a lifetime of his family's Huguenot origins; indeed, his notorious admiration of Great Britain reflected considerable gratitude that his forebears had been provided "an Assylum." Old Testament and apocalyptic imagery punctuated his prose, alongside pointed analogies between public and private salvation or states of grace. Jay also participated actively in religious and antislavery societies, for the persistence of slavery—an "inconsistent . . . unjust and, perhaps, impious" blemish upon supposed libertarians—powerfully reinforced the conviction that civic virtue could only be "drawn to a point," after which improvement was unlikely.[18]

Only a handful escaped Jay's obloquy, and common folk, to whom he frequently imputed bestial qualities, were the least favored of all. As early as 1777, he had been alarmed by a potentially savage "Public," admonishing his friend Gouverneur Morris to send soothing "Paragraphs" to colleagues serving on the New York Council of Safety for mass distribution: "The People suspect the worst [when] . . . we say Nothing. Their Curiosity must be constantly gratified, or they will be uneasy." Similarly, Jay admired Pennsylvania's experiments with manufactures to alleviate unemployment and unrest, on the ground that bread and abundant work might keep ordinary citizens "easy and Quiet." When "Fellow Mortals are busy and well fed," Jay theorized, "they forget to complain."[19]

By the mid-1790s, Jay had dispensed with rhetorical caution. Steely resignation replaced the relatively benign assertion that man was a "degraded creature," or that humankind was guided more by "conveniences than by principles." No longer would he entertain fantasies about an "age of reason, prior to the millennium"; nor would he "believe one word of" the "modern" suggestion that appetite could be subordinated to "right reason." In 1797, Jay was consoled by the knowledge that "every scourge of every kind by which nations are punished"—perhaps the same "Evils inseparable from Humanity" identified some twenty years before—were under the "control of a wise and benevolent Sovereign." When Judge Peters hinted in 1815 that the people always meant well, Jay wasted little ink: "The word *people*, you know, applies to all the individual inhabitants of a country." The portion that "mean well never was, nor until the millennium will be, considerable."[20]

Also by the mid-1790s, Jay routinely divided the polity into "Politicians" and "Citizens." The former encompassed legislative demagogues, "pharisaical patriots," and the "lower Class of Mankind" who blindly followed these charlatans toward Jacobinism.[21] "Citizens," on the other hand, included sober, contemplative statesmen who refused to contrive "a shoe that would fit every foot," as well as that small portion of the electorate with courage enough to support them. Virtue was inborn: some men possessed it from birth, others did not. And those who did not sometimes pretended otherwise, posing as statesmen in legislative chambers. Jay's conclusions were essentially genetic: the "improper arts" of assemblymen reflected the fact that "creatures will act according to their nature, and it would be absurd to expect that a man who is not upright, will act like one who is."[22]

With politicians, Jay was unsparing. These were "men raised from low Degrees . . . rendered giddy by Elevation," who typically consulted "prevailing fashions" rather than "the utility of their goods to those who are to wear them." Worse, pernicious "levelling principles" and self-serving campaign promises spawned violence after the French example. Jay therefore hoped to circumscribe the influence of "men without Character [or] Fortune" until virtue had been disseminated more broadly through education and exposure to law, or until a centralized government might be perfected.[23] With the possibility of a new Constitution after 1787, Jay speculated about gradual improvement among politicians over several generations. Ultimately, however, he resigned himself to a succession of barbarians whose "artifices," pandering, and "irascible passions" would be contained for a time through the "strenuous efforts of the wise." Only in another world might "all books and histories and errors . . . be consumed," and "truth . . . rise and prevail and be immortal."[24]

Unfortunately, wisdom was a scarce resource, and typically the special province of executives or jurists who came to office without popular election. Jay associated political debts and localism with incompetence: the further removed a man might be from his constituency, the less likely corruption or pettiness. The fact of election thus aroused the New Yorker's suspicions, while nomination assuaged them; and federal appointees were less tainted and more gifted than their counterparts in the states by virtue of selection from an expanded pool. It followed that the general government would be "more wise, systematical, and judicious" than local governments, for there would be no "want of proper persons." Unsullied by the "*necessity of the Case*," this self-selecting "elect" somehow had to retain what Edward Rutledge called "the Staff' until Americans demonstrated "whether they could govern themselves." At stake was republican survival, and Jay was worried. The same sensitivities that separated the wise from mere politicians also encouraged disillusionment in the face of public abuse, for the "Residue," as Jay dubbed the majority, rarely mustered "Honesty or Spirit enough openly to defend unpopular Merit," thereby routing talented but weary statesmen.[25]

From this pessimistic bedrock, Jay's posture toward Britain and his restrictive domestic politics followed logically and inexorably. In fact, both were little more than an elaboration of a favorite maxim: "Fortitude founded on Resignation." His reluctant but diligent patriotism, for example, originated less in a firm preference for independence than in perceptions of an intractable emergency in political economy. Jay had preferred British citizenship at least through 1775, despite serious misgivings about the empire's performance. His shift to the cause, while facilitated by deeper association through marriage with the Livingston family, crystallized primarily with mounting evidence of the crown's inability to protect distant property and to guarantee trade—the "great and weighty reasons" underlying all political unions.[26]

Yet these decisions did not alter Jay's fascination with British civilization or with imperial governance. While drafting the Olive Branch Petition, he yearned for a speedy restoration of peace without "further Effusion of Blood," confessing that he would be "hurt" by the destruction of England and by loss of access to "the Prosperity of the

Empire now rent by unnatural Convulsions."[27] A decade after independence, he still urged Americans to preserve cultural and trading channels established during long centuries of British tutelage. The crown's ability to suppress provincial violence through centralization fascinated him,[28] and he fretted constantly about exclusion from the world's most extensive commercial network, eagerly anticipating a "liberal Alliance" with Londoners. The rebellion and its stormy aftermath, he thought, were unseemly escalations of a necessary squabble between parent and talented child. Even in the throes of war, Jay contemplated a return to British domination "with Horror" and would "risque all for Independence"; but that point settled, he encouraged the swift extension of "advantageous commercial Terms."[29]

Years later, John Adams complained that the Revolution had not been sustained by "such characters" as Jay and the Morrises—those irksome New Yorkers who castigated the public's potential for "virtue" and so cast doubt upon the Revolution's main engines. He was both right and wrong. Jay certainly deplored the creation of a decentralized commonwealth guided by unfettered congressional "politicians" and by emasculated executive departments—a structure dangerously dependent upon the "public" metamorphosing instantly into "citizens." He detected mischief in the notion that most Americans would sacrifice short-term gain for the greater good, and more than a little French romance in "levelling." More important, he dreaded the construction of an isolated, introverted new imperial economy, tied fatally to collective decision making and to an unrealizable, undesirable self-sufficiency.[30]

In short, while Jay disagreed with most of the assumptions and strategies propelling Revolutionary politics, he did not reject the possibility that independent republican citizens might behave virtuously. He denied only the universality of virtue in the "Public" and thus its reflection in the minds and labors of legislators. In Jay's estimation, virtue resided mainly in a very few statesmen then held in check by the new Congress, which dramatically reduced its value to society. Criticisms were urgent: if pie-eyed republican schemes prevailed, unity and prosperity—the fundamental "objects" of nationhood—would be sabotaged.[31]

Jay's "first wish" for the new nation was domestic unification—an internal, primarily political object. Unity was basic and altogether critical; without it, property and persons might never be secure. At the same time, unity was only a first step onto the world stage, and so a penultimate object en route to Jay's ultimate goal: prosperity. Jay knew that a disunited nation would be denied membership in a global community, having failed to achieve the "character of ONE GREAT NATION." And the structure best suited to unity's achievement and maintenance, given republican imperfections, was a "strong government" of decisive federal institutions and laws "ably administered" by a wise minority.[32]

These sentiments emerged as early as 1776 in response to wartime disorders: the need for "good and well ordered Governments" to prevent "that Anarchy which already too much prevails," he told Alexander McDougall, must be "inculcated." But "Anarchy" persisted after independence; and the Confederacy, Jay feared, was a sorry plan indeed. In 1777, he allowed only that the general government "augurs well," wanly conceding that an indifferent constitution was "better than none." As atomization seemed to continue, Jay's anxieties proliferated. He began to calculate the odds for and against complete collapse, grimly anticipating which "Parties and Factions will arise, to what Objects be directed, . . . and who will be the victims." His frustrations deepened appreciably while negotiating the peace for an unhelpful Congress and as secretary for foreign affairs after 1783. Chaos at home plainly threatened the safety and tranquility of New World citizens. But it also marked republicans as unreliable and violent. The mark of Cain, in turn, introduced untenable disadvantages in dealings with Europeans, with whom Americans were obliged to compete on the high seas, and from whom the republic absolutely required grants of respect and legal standing.[33]

This fresh awareness of diplomatic complexity, combined with Jay's considerable disdain for legislators, soon produced brutal denunciations of congressional bickering and immobilization. The secretary's complaints were legion: he decried the states' "impatience of government," which encompassed local resistance to congressional taxation; an insatiable rage for property in the face of national hardship; and a reckless "desire of equality in all things." Jay also deplored government's failure to prevent Indian attacks, chronic absenteeism in Congress, procrastination over debts, and the absence of a "continental, national spirit." Pointing to an empty treasury "though the country abounds in resources," he bemoaned "disappointment to our creditors [and] disgrace to our country"—conditions that spoke to the "want of good government to guard good faith and punish violations."[34]

The origins of public apathy toward unification, Jay argued in 1788, were cultural. Americans had agreed to a confederation more "paternal and persuasive than coersive and efficient" after centuries of colonial dependency, during which affairs of state such as war, peace, and commerce had been "managed for us and not by us." Republicans therefore responded to crisis times with passivity and ignorance. What might be done? Durable unification, Jay explained, typically proceeded from "constitutional coersion, or . . . the dictates of reason." The former was unavailable, and Americans in their present condition were deaf to reason. Stopgap strategies seemed equally futile: even a unifying war would be lost at the hands of congressmen whose honor and authority decayed almost daily. Within this "wonderful system of government," Jay told fellow New Yorkers, "almost every national object . . . [is] unprovided for."[35] The secretary sensed "some crisis"; he was "uneasy and apprehensive; more so than during the war." And Shays's Rebellion was a terrifying omen: "The insurrection in Massachusetts is suppressed," he fussed, "but the spirit of it exists."[36]

Jay toyed with the idea of constitutional reform—a grant of necessary powers so that Congress might better regulate commerce and "general concerns"—but quickly fastened upon a more drastic remedy. Unification, as well as the liberation of the nation's "ablest men" from legislative constraints, could not be achieved within a defective frame of government; no amount of tinkering would save the day. The single most glaring defect was the "great mistake" of a multifunctional Congress bent upon reducing "big men into little ones." Powers to make and execute law, Jay admonished Jefferson, should never be vested in "one and the same body of men," not only because confusion would eventuate but also because legislators could hide behind one another. Whenever assemblies divide "blame and credit," he explained, "too little falls on each man."[37]

Nor should a reorganized Congress be granted decisive power in pursuit of crucial "objects of state." In 1776, Edward Rutledge wanted to allow "no more Power than what's absolutely necessary" in order to retain executive autonomy; Jay pursued the same strategy in a different context. Otherwise, he later explained, the "executive business of sovereignty" would be "but feebly done."[38] With other

Federalists, Jay recommended a departmental system of government composed of three formal branches. Quite separately, though, he imagined two competing blocs of power—an informal coalition of executives and judges pitted against legislative excess. Laws then would be "expounded in one sense and executed in the same manner," allowing the United States to move along "uniform principles of policy." Collaborators, in other words, could "harmonize, assimilate, and protect the several parts," guaranteeing "mutual participation in commerce, navigation, and citizenship."[39]

For Jay and other High Federalists, anarchical decay was far more likely than despotism or ministerial tyranny; indeed, he might have welcomed a parliamentary arrangement with properly autonomous ministries. Jay may well have associated executive license with royal prerogative, and modeled his informal alliance after customary relations between the King-in-Parliament and the courts at Westminster; whatever the case might be, he lacked the patience and taste for further experimentation, particularly with legislators at the helm. "The most perfect Constitutions, the best Governments, and the wisest Laws are vain," Jay told grand jurymen in 1790, "unless well administered and well obeyed." Time and again, Jay made clear, often in tropes borrowed from English law practice, that adherence to the rule of law ensured freedom: fidelity to law was not "unfriendly to Liberty," or at least to "that Liberty which is really inestimable. [O]n the Contrary, nothing but a strong Government of Laws, irresistably bearing down arbitrary power & Licenciousness can defend it against those two formidable Enemies. Let it be remembered," he added for good measure,

> that civil Liberty consists not in a Right to every Man to do just what he pleases—but it consists in an equal Right to all the Citizens to have, enjoy, and to do, in peace Security and without Molestation, whatever the equal and constitutional laws . . . admit to be consistent with the public Good.

A scant three years later, in the emergency atmosphere accompanying Washington's Neutrality Proclamation, Jay made the point a bit differently, contending that reliance upon law necessarily increased when men claimed extraordinary freedom.

> The more free the people are, the more strong and efficient ought their Governm[en]t to be; and for this plain Reason, that it is a more arduous Task

> to make and keep up the Fences of Law & Justice about twenty Rights than about five or six; & because it is more difficult to fence against & restrain men who are unfettered, than men who are in Yokes & Chains.[40]

Jay augmented this judge-led, law-bound "balance of power" against popular and congressional licentiousness with harsh circumscription of state power—a scheme reminiscent of the old New Jersey Plan.[41] Again inspired by British practice, Jay conceived of the states as extraordinarily weak administrative fictions existing at federal pleasure. As he told Adams, "I would have them [states] considered . . . in the same light in which counties stand to the States," as constitutionally dependent "districts to facilitate the purposes of domestic order and good government." Adamantly opposed to the creation of new states—whether through subdivision or in frontier areas where "white savages" compared unfavorably with "tawny ones"—Jay even recommended that key state officials be nominated by the general government. These choices spoke to law enforcement that, he thought, would not "always accord or be consistent" without strength at the center, as much from the "variety of independent courts" as from "different local laws and interests." Jay similarly applauded the construction of centralized courts as a hedge against "[l]aws dictated by the Spirit of the Times not the Spirit of Justice."[42]

Zeal for constitutional revision (and for expanded prerogative powers for agents of the executive branch) increased dramatically wherever Jay perceived a threat to diplomatic efforts. Prosperity—his ultimate "object of state"—required confrontations with ancient, well-defended imperial powers, and successful interaction was doomed, he knew, without at least the appearance of internal harmony. Jay was obsessed with Congress's dubious respectability in Europe and persuaded as well that circumstances could only deteriorate, for experienced mercantilists were not obliged to deal with upstart republicans inhabiting an unstable polity. Jay feared that Americans would soon wave "FAREWELL, A LONG FAREWELL" to unrealized prosperity, and that friendly nations then willing to embrace a "great and powerful" America would be forced to retreat. "Whatever may be our situation," he warned in a *Federalist* essay, "whether firmly united . . . or split into a number of confederacies, certain it is, that foreign nations will know and view it exactly as it is; and they will act towards us accordingly[.]"

> If they see that our national government is efficient and well regulated . . . our resources and finances discreetly managed—our credit re-established—our people . . . united, they will be much more disposed to cultivate our friendship. . . . [I]f they find us destitute of an effectual government . . . what a poor, pitiful figure will America make in their eyes!

And, when he finally addressed republican grand juries on the Eastern Circuit in 1790, Jay hammered away—rather obsessively, given the nature of the cases pending—at the perils of bad faith in foreign affairs, notably (but not only) in meeting treaty obligations.[43]

These preoccupations reflected Jay's unhappy years as a diplomat-statesman. While laboring after 1781 to secure peace with Britain, he had been nettled and occasionally mortified by Congress's poor credit and shoddy intelligence procedures, but his exertions in the foreign affairs office between 1783 and 1789 were frustrated more directly and constantly.[44] International agreements, he insisted, should be negotiated only by private statesmen guided by conscience and by the sterling principles of international law. "Large assemblies," said Jay, "often misunderstand . . . the obligations of character, honour, and dignity, and will collectively do or omit things which individual gentlemen in private capacities would not approve." Congress was public, raucous, and sluggish; diplomacy required discretion and "immediate despatch." And transient lawmakers were ill qualified for the "attainment of those great objects" that had to be "steadily contemplated in all their relations and circumstances." To relegate foreign policy to petty politicians hounded by voters and limited by their own character was to court economic and diplomatic disaster. On one occasion, Jay sarcastically announced that, if forced to choose, he preferred the "Enterprise, Activity and Industry of private Adventurers" to the "Lukewarmness of Assemblies," for "Public Virtue" was "not so active as private Love of Gain."[45]

The term "lukewarmness" captured several complaints about legislative lassitude, the majority's unaccountable fascination with disclosure, and the myopic quality of congressional economic policy. It mattered little whether shortcomings flowed from human frailties or the clumsiness of political process; Europeans saw only the consequences and would be alienated accordingly. Here, Jay again offered pointed analogies between public and private morality. Fraud, rudeness, and insolence, he counseled, would not only *"degrade* and *dis-*

*grace* nations & Individuals, but also *expose* them to Hostility & insult." National "indiscretions," he wrote in an uncommonly frank jury-charge draft, "have given Occasion to many Wars." On the other side, fair dealing and a harmonious polity encouraged peace and prosperity. Indeed, among the just causes of war, Jay listed treaty violations, which he associated with French influence, craven state governments, and, by 1795, indebted speculators who preferred "spoil and plunder" to "patient industry and honest gains."[46]

Jay particularly fulminated against violations of the Definitive Treaty with Britain and of the compacts supporting Revolutionary War debts. His own promises underpinned many such agreements. Of greater moment, however, were national "honour, justice, and interest." Time and again, he advocated broader powers of "coersion" so that administrators and judges might enforce these "most salutary and constitutional objects." Jay also pleaded for a moratorium upon new loans until old debts had been cleared. He chided Congress for its inattention to the obligations of nationhood, as opposed to the more pleasurable rights and privileges.[47] With Washington, he suspected that disadvantageous political entanglements flowed inevitably from dependence upon the "charity of our friends" and the "mercy of our enemies"; in 1793, he feared as well that the "Man or the Nation who eludes the payment of Debts, ceases to be worthy of further Credit."[48]

If lingering debts threatened healthy relations with the French and Dutch, violations of the Paris Peace Treaty directly affected an Anglo-American rapprochement. The president's alarm paralleled Jay's: "If you tell the Legislature they have violated the treaty of peace," he wrote, "they will laugh in your face. What, then, is to be done?" Jay chose moral and political instruction. Treaties, he said in various ways, were "only another name for a bargain." State evasions of lawful debts had not surprised Jay. As early as 1783, he predicted that designing debtors would try to undermine the treaty's unpopular fourth article, which promised payment for wartime contracts or confiscations of Loyalist property. But continued belligerence now partook "more of vengeance than of justice," Jay argued, fattening state coffers at the expense of the nation's long-term interests.[49]

Jay therefore joined other Federalists in the struggle against obstructionism in the states, simultaneously apologizing to friends in Europe. In 1786, Lafayette learned of Congress's regrettable disarray; Jay also assured Britain's Lord Lansdowne, from whom Jay begged abundant "good nature," that constitutional lethargy and the lack of "temper and liberality" among republicans would be remedied swiftly by honorable men.[50] The secretary campaigned tirelessly against "discriminations inconsistent with the treaty of peace" through which worthy men had been deprived of citizenship and property. After 1789, these efforts continued from the bench. Repeating his warnings about obligations and duties, Chief Justice Jay admonished Americans to abide by "treaties Conventions, and the like compacts." Just as "in private Life a fair and legal Contract between two Men, cannot be annulled nor altered by either without the Consent of the other, so neither can Treaties between Nations." By 1794, he had begun to discourage British acquaintances from investments in American enterprise. New sequestration measures, he told them, theoretically were "improper" and therefore unlikely, but when pressed for assurances, he "declined to give any."[51]

Stern exhortations about public morality, political harmony, and "effective Power" in the hands of statesmen coexisted with equally fervent pleas for liberalized trading relations. Jay's prescription for the nation's economy, which superficially resembled James Wilson's Commonwealth of Nations fantasy,[52] rested upon sophisticated, shrewd analyses of the strategic weaknesses of the United States and of its "natural wealth, value, and resources." Economic success seemed to depend entirely upon "break[ing] the ice" with England. With Wilson, Adams, and others, Jay envisioned a "base system"[53] of reciprocal trade agreements—first with Britain's competitors, whose friendship was strategically useful in the struggle against British mercantilism, if a limited avenue to great wealth, and then with England itself. Jay probably hoped, too, that public mobilization around the prospect of collective financial gain might spur unification, should political tactics fail.[54]

Jay distinguished, then, between undesirable dependencies accompanying the status of debtor—which he dubbed "dependence for friendship," and which necessitated a very dangerous form of gratitude—and mutual respect between autonomous trading partners. This healthy dependency was couched, not coincidentally, in the equalizing tropes of contract law. Jay clearly saw the republic's glaring military and financial inequality; legal fiction shielded statesmen and traders alike, facilitating independence "in the most extensive sense." Americans could be "honest and grateful to our allies," Jay noted wryly, "but . . . think for ourselves."[55] Early agreements with France, Spain, or Russia served as a tempting carrot to dangle before the British crown while Americans exploited distant ports in relative safety. It was in the "interest of all Europe," Jay advised the Spanish, to join republicans in "breaking down the exorbitant power" of an empire he openly lionized and just as plainly wished to befriend, cutting the "sinews" of British monopoly power while maximizing unequaled access to world markets.[56]

Well before the Paris peace, Jay had rejected the related notions of self-sufficiency and protectionism, perceiving that economic isolation and the mindless replication of an Old World empire provided false security. By 1783, these insights fed mounting concern and irritation. When Benjamin Vaughan and others resisted a "nugatory" reciprocity during the peace negotiations while also defending a favorable balance of trade for the British, Jay rather haplessly threatened an opposing navigation act. Two years later, his fears had not diminished. The English "expect much from the trade of America," he wrote Adams, yet "put it out of our power to pay. . . . I wish most sincerely that credit was at an end." Reciprocity and direct exchange, he speculated, would defuse belligerence between nations with shared interests: "one cannot enrich herself without enriching the other," creating a peaceable "natural connexion."[57]

These "connexions" further allowed an undercapitalized America to evolve industrial capacities, without contrivance or frenzy, on firm agrarian foundations. Jay distrusted "unnatural" preoccupations among Hamiltonians and others with domestic manufactures. Having laboriously calculated population increases, agricultural production, wage levels, and land availability in Europe and North America, he concluded, with many other economists,[58] that the New World enjoyed significant advantages in agriculture that laborers recognized and would pursue. Hence, Jay foresaw several generations of small farmers primarily in an ever-expanding "*Northern Hive*" exchanging foodstuffs and other staples for capital-intensive European goods. "So great is the extent of country," he expounded, "and so inviting to settlers, that labor will very long remain too dear to admit of considerable manufactures."

> . . . [W]hen the poor . . . gain affluence by tilling the earth, they will refuse the scanty earnings which manufacturers . . . offer them. [Thus] exports

> from America will consist of raw materials which other nations will [process] at a cheaper rate . . . [yielding for] the American States . . . *actual wealth.*[59]

Put differently, internal unification combined with "natural" agrarianism promised reconciliation with Britain and prosperity in the place of crippling indebtedness.[60] Jay's correspondents in the Old Country frequently empathized. Lansdowne thought that his countrymen should be "deeply interested" in America's "prosperity and reputation"; and Jay heaped praise upon these "large and liberal views" that applied to the "future as well as the present . . . interests of the nation."[61] Significantly, Jay also contemplated a universal "fellow citizenship" for republicans and Europeans alike, in the process elevating economic community over its political counterpart. How greatly would it "redound to the happiness as well as honour of all civilized people," he suggested, "were they to consider and treat each other like fellow-citizens; each nation governing itself as it pleases, but each admitting others to a perfect freedom of commerce." Toward that end, he cautioned Jefferson against perpetuating "ancient prejudice" in agreements with France—the "fencing" and "guarding" so characteristic of mercantilism—hoping instead that "all the commercial privileges" of Frenchmen might be exchanged for their American equivalents. From the vantage point of illegitimate revolutionaries, these were useful, canny suggestions. But they also betrayed Jay's dogged internationalism—a frame of reference not shared entirely by proponents of a self-regenerating Fortress America.[62]

## *The Supreme Court as Diplomatic and Moral Umpire*

While awaiting Jefferson's return from France in 1789, Jay served simultaneously as secretary of state and chief justice of the United States. This professional dualism was both circumstantial and characteristic, for Jay the jurist was primarily and inseparably a diplomatist. Historians of the Jay Court often decry these bifurcated interests and credentials, but Washington found them uniquely compatible with American needs and priorities in 1789.[63] From Jay's point of view, the new Supreme Court seemed a peculiarly inviting forum for the cultivation of domestic unity, equitable trade relations, and a working alliance between executives and judges. The chief justice's experience and prejudices had convinced him that "nations and Individuals injure their essential Interests in proportion as they deviate from order." He therefore eagerly pursued "form . . . strength order and harmony" (in 1793, he called it "national Regularity") through rigorous exercise of the Court's relatively uncontested original and exclusive jurisdictions. Few strategies held as much promise for the realization of a "due Distribution of Justice."[64]

Before 1789, Jay had argued repeatedly that a "due Distribution" required cooperation between executives and jurists, whether through a council of revision, as in New York,[65] or, to borrow George Washington's term, through the well-orchestrated "Interpretation and Execution" of federal laws. Consultation surely strengthened the authority of a few good men against throngs of legislators, and coordination in advance of public action prevented potentially damaging impressions of indecision or disagreement in high places. But enlightened statesmanship for Jay also implied a certain freedom from structural constraints. The ends of governance, after all, transcended momentary political assignment; institutional attachments were vehicles toward those ends, not objects in themselves as legislators might have it. The autonomy of gentlemen-lawyers and executive agents therefore was essential, and their curtailment or confinement treacherous.[66]

For these reasons, Jay freely provided informal advice to kindred spirits throughout his federal judicial career while staunchly denying a formal advisory role for the Court itself. He also abruptly and freely abandoned the bench when he perceived that national "objects" were best pursued elsewhere. Jay's advisory offerings ranged broadly, reflecting his eclectic expertise. In 1789 and 1790, for instance, Washington asked for assessments of the "real situation" in foreign affairs, the state of the judiciary, and general matters. Hamilton similarly requested and received advice on numerous subjects: congressional powers in Indian relations, trading rights, fortress and post-road construction, currency regulation, the legality of local commercial laws, and the propriety of an executive proclamation during Pennsylvania's Whiskey Rebellion. On the other hand, Jay steadfastly refused to bulldoze formal boundaries between federal departments: in a 1792 New York circuit court hearing on a writ of mandamus in *Hayburn's Case*, to give the best-known example, he defended the separation of powers by refusing to allow federal courts to pass judgment, as an act of

Congress seemed to require, on claims of invalid pensioners; the decision (reinforced in 1794, to give one example among several, by suggestive language in *Glass* v. *The Sloop Betsy*) eased the way for later, strident attempts to claim an implied power to evaluate acts of Congress for constitutionality.[67]

Jay's decision to accept a special diplomatic assignment in 1794 capped several years of increasing frustration. The "essential interests" of the United States, as Jay defined them in 1793, coincided neatly with two aspects of federal law: the Constitution, case law, and acts of Congress that shaped "the Conduct of the Citizens relative to our own nation & people," and the law of nations treating behavior "relative to foreign Nations & their Subjects."[68] Indeed, without law's presence, Jay could not have supported free trade. At every juncture, legal principle ordered and moralized an otherwise anarchic marketplace. The chief justice fixed his fondest hopes upon this convergence of object and federal jurisdiction. At long last, statesmen possessed formidable tools toward unification and prosperity—even without the more elusive, politically explosive implied review powers. Leaders could establish this new machinery with dispatch and move from strength thereafter; in Jay's words, "Order usually succeeds Confusion" within adequate structures.[69]

Or so he hoped. Jay cautioned Hamilton against excessive force during the debt-assumption controversy: the less panic and noise, the better. Victory over unruly republicans demanded stealthy "exertion"; neither violence nor passive "reflection" would do. The federal plan, after all, mirrored the "design of Providence"; political heresy could be defeated legally and elegantly by simply enforcing new rules and shoring up contested or poorly articulated jurisdictions, including a federal common law of crime.[70] While riding circuit, Jay doggedly instructed untutored jurymen in the rudiments of citizenship and effective government. And he was heartened by early acquiescence to federal judicial authority in Rhode Island, New York, and elsewhere in scattered but politically charged disputes involving the Paris treaty and admiralty jurisdiction.[71]

A direct statement about the subordination of states to the nation, however, awaited the Jay Court's confrontation with Georgia after 1792 in the fateful *Chisholm* v. *Georgia*. The circumstances underlying the debacle are well known: Chisholm, a Carolinian and the executor of one Farquhar, sought state performance of a Revolutionary

War contract through the Court's original diversity jurisdiction—that is, the jurisdiction granted federal courts whenever noncitizens sued states. And Georgia returned the summons, claiming sovereign immunity from federal process. Unfortunately, the concept of state suability in federal courts was no less controversial in 1792–1793 than it had been before passage of the 1789 Judiciary Act.[72] On its face, the situation plainly addressed whether Jay's "first wish" might be achieved through federal law: if "national Regularity" resulted from "Attention and Obedience to those Rules and principles of Conduct which Reason indicates and which Morality and Wisdom prescribe," then Georgia's refusal to appear subverted Jay's plan for unification spearheaded by federal executives and judges.[73]

Jay's associates behaved predictably. All except James Iredell confirmed Georgia's subordination to the nation, declaring the venerable doctrine of sovereign immunity inappropriate in a republic. With James Wilson, Attorney General Edmund Randolph articulated a vision of the states as administrative fictions that coincided almost perfectly with Jay's sentiments. In a curiously wistful, nonlegalistic opinion, the chief justice had only to agree. Said Randolph, the United States was no longer a "Government of supplication"; and the states, given increased national "energy," were merely "assemblages of . . . individuals" liable to process and to "diminutions of sovereignty, at least equal to the making of them defendants." Would not the nation be useless if a "pleasure to obey or transgress with impunity should be substituted in the place of . . . laws"?[74]

But, for Jay, *Chisholm*'s significance extended beyond these questions. At issue was Georgia's constitutional right to resist federal judicial power *in a dispute involving the Paris peace*, and thus to invite renewed conflict with Britain and fresh castigation of Americans in Europe. As went the sanctity of treaties, Jay feared, so went the republic's reputation.

In 1792, the Court also heard arguments in *Brailsford* v. *Georgia*, a suit in equity involving sequestered Loyalist property. The amount had become the object of an injunction, and, against the advice of his colleagues, Jay urged a continuance of the restraining order so that Georgia's voluntary presence in *Brailsford* might be exploited in *Chisholm*. Both Randolph and Jay perceived connections between state suability and abrogations of the Paris peace through permanent sequestration and renunciation. The attorney general, for instance, referred suggestively in *Chisholm* to the fearsome implications of immunity for public safety. "The Federal head cannot remain unmoved," he opined,

> amidst these shocks to the public harmony. Are not peace and concord among the states two of the great ends of the Constitution? To be consistent, [my] opponents . . . must say, that a state may not be sued by a foreigner.—What? Shall the tranquility of our country be at the mercy of every State? . . . [Why] may not the measure be the same, when the citizen of another State is the complainant?

Did not the immunity doctrine lose "half of its force" when Georgia willingly and crassly appeared in *Brailsford*—that is, when the state benefited from an appearance?[75]

Jay's opinion leaves little doubt that, in his estimation, the Georgia cases went beyond garden-variety disagreements about federal and state power, ultimately reaching both of his "objects." Before 1789, he recalled, the confederated states became "amenable to the law of nations," and it was "their interest as well as their duty" to be so constrained. Amazingly, Americans still resisted the moral and political imperatives of nationhood—notably, their collective responsibility to harmonize and elevate the "conduct of each state, relative to the law of nations, and the performance of treaties." Rather against hope, Jay wished that the "State of Society were so far improved, and the Science of Government [so perfected] that the whole nation could in the peaceable course of law, be compelled to do justice." But, in 1793, such improvement seemed increasingly remote. Jay could only repeat that obedience, uniformity, and scrupulosity were fundamental to republican survival—that they were "*wise . . . honest* [and] *useful.*"[76]

The outcry after *Chisholm* and the related march toward constitutional limitation completely shattered Jay's ever-diminishing faith in the high court's political and diplomatic utility. In December 1792, the Georgia assembly had resolved not to be bound by an unfavorable court ruling; when the decision came down, a grand jury formally presented a grievance to Governor Telfair, who in turn urged passage of a statute (adopted two weeks later) affirming the state's sovereign immunity. On March 18, Massachusetts lawmakers in special session commenced a drive to secure congressional adoption of what would become the Eleventh Amendment, making it impossible for federal marshals and judges to summon states as defendants. Virginia condemned Jay for attacking state sovereignty; Georgians toyed with hanging federal officers, should they again try to force a state appearance.

State concerns were not groundless. If allowed to stand, *Chisholm* probably rendered depleted state treasuries vulnerable to the claims of war suppliers and Loyalist "traitors"; it was plain, too, that Jay hoped to force several states to eat humble pie. On February 20, 1793, process had been returned and the state ordered to appear at the next term in *Oswald* v. *New York*. At virtually the same moment, the high court awarded a subpoena in *Grayson et al.* v. *Virginia*; five months later, when federal judges granted William Vassal (a Loyalist victim of the Massachusetts confiscation statute) a subpoena, Governor Hancock delivered a speech warning his countrymen of the perils of runaway judicial federalism.

Hence, the flood of anti-Court sentiment leading to constitutional amendment. Jay had little trouble finding the door: with his Court effectively closed after 1793 to the resolution of European financial claims, he quickly transferred his efforts into personal diplomacy and eventually into support for a mixed international commission. In the year of his exit, the chief justice had been able in *The Sloop Betsy* to decry France's use of its American consul as a prize agent, thereby shoring up the precarious United States claim of sovereignty, and his dissent on circuit in *Ware* v. *Hylton* (well before the 1796 Supreme Court ruling on the case) anticipated the Ellsworth Court's affirmation of the republic's obligation to abide by the terms of treaties. But such opportunities were few and, in the wake of *Chisholm*, the political lesson was painfully clear: "objects of state" were not yet "far beyond the reach" of licentious men.

Jay's resignation thus symbolized keen disappointment, and, from the point of view of his colleagues marooned on a sinking federal bench, the situation could only get worse. On February 14, 1798, when the Eleventh Amendment took effect, the Supreme Court clerk, David Caldwell, spread over the minute book a pathetic list of cases (including, perhaps ironically, the nettlesome *Brailsford*) dismissed or discontinued for want of jurisdiction.[77] Had the bench been "on its proper footing," Jay later explained, "there is no public Station that I should prefer. . . . It accords with my Turn of mind, my Education and my Habits." Given Jay's priorities, however, the high court was useless, especially when confronted with multiple or contrary visions of what the polity ought to look like—an eventuality for which Jay, unlike the author of *Federalist No. 10,* made inadequate provision.[78]

Plainly, Jay's "turn of mind" did not lie with the relatively tedious, incremental creation of a tradition in domestic law, with political process, or with the construction of judicial state papers; indeed, he may well have assumed that a Court operating under rules largely borrowed from King's Bench should issue English-style, nonexpository opinions. Whatever the case might have been, Jay's mind gravitated toward "systems" and far-reaching "objects," not to the relatively staid, circumscribed world of legal research and writing. Arguably, he also had developed a taste for the spotlight, which federal courts rarely attracted. For these and other reasons, he finally branded the federal judiciary a "defective" department without sufficient "energy, weight and dignity" to provide that "due support" upon which the republic's future seemed to depend.[79]

After 1794, Jay resolved anew "to see things as . . . they are, to estimate them aright, and to act accordingly"—a reassertion of "Fortitude founded on Resignation." He then pressed his position on the debt question relentlessly through diplomacy. Apparently neither Jay nor Washington perceived conflict between service as a "private gentleman" on diplomatic assignment and as chief justice: the envoyship to Jay was simply a necessary, if personally inconvenient, exercise of duty and expertise. The president granted his envoy virtually a free hand with unpaid debts. Jay, he recalled, had been "personally conversant" with negotiators in Paris, served as foreign affairs secretary, and witnessed "what has passed in our [federal] courts" respecting confiscated property. Few men could claim so much.[80]

And fewer still were so determined. England, Jay warned, would surely "insist that British debts, so far as injured by lawful impediments, should be *repaired* by the United States, by decision of mutual commissioners." He expected disapprobation, without which he would have been "agreeably disappointed"; he also hoped to ease his conscience. "Should the treaty prove . . . beneficial," he announced, "justice will *finally* be done. If not, be it so—my mind is at ease." In a revealing letter, Jay (who had been nominated in absentia by New York Federalists to run for governor) told Randolph that the debt-related Sixth Article addressed "that justice and equity which judicial proceedings may, on trial, be found incapable of affording," for a neutral commission could do "exactly what is right." Anxiety and anger shared the stage with Jay's conscience: as the contest over the Jay Treaty raged in Congress, and on the eve of his election to the New York governorship, he marveled at the insatiable appetites of scoundrels in legislative chambers, worrying aloud in a letter to his old friend Washington that rejection of the treaty would again "put the United States in the wrong," damaging "honour, engagements, and important interests"—among them, the "*further extension* of commerce."[81]

## *The Judge as Arbiter of "The Common Good"*

How should scholars characterize Jay's republican politics and statesmanship? First, the nation's first chief justice was not reactionary, crassly self-interested, or politically liberal in any modern sense. John Jay despised pluralism. He was neither fluent in nor comfortable with the language of "rights." With Joseph Story and other conservative legalists, he emphasized duties and obligations; but, more clearly in Jay than in others, the law of contract in its several manifestations (private, constitutional, and international) organized his legal and political consciousness, sometimes to the exclusion of all else. In 1793, to give one example, he told Chesapeake freeholders that, while republicans were "governed only by Laws . . . of our own making," those laws represented "Rules for regulating the Conduct of Individuals, and are established according to, & in pursuance of that Contract, which each Citizen has made with the Rest, and all with each. He is not a good Citizen," said Jay emphatically, "who violates his Contract with Society; and when Society execute their laws, they do no more than what is necessary to constrain Individuals to perform that Contract, on the due operation and observance of which [t]he common Good & welfare of the Community depends." Toward what ends did this contract—the embodiment of the old English right to law—aspire? Its "object," said Jay, was to "secure to every man what belongs to him as a member of the nation, and by increasing the common Stock of Prosperity, to augment the Value of his Share in it. Most essentially therefore is it the Duty and Interest of us all, that the Laws be observed and irresistably executed."[82]

For Jay, then, the rule of law was a "Fence" between civilization and barbarism, a mighty engine capable of instilling a divine spark in ordinary men, a guarantor of liberty as entrepreneurs scrambled after wealth, and the scaffolding around which Americans would erect a national reputation and lasting prosperity. Jay did not devolve suddenly into political cynicism in the mid-1780s, as did a good many other Federalists. Instead, he was consistently "stiff in his self-righteousness,"[83] disdainful of what Ralph Lerner has called "the New-Model Man,"[84] and suspicious of republican enchantments with mediocrity, majoritarianism, and publicity. A consummate diplomatist, Jay neglected his own art with legislators and adversaries. He feared unruly commoners and nervously charted the course of Jacobinism in Europe, assiduously guarding the prerogatives of the "best Men" who alone could rescue America from its "present Condition." And Jay no doubt lacked a fluid political imagination; amidst a revolution jerry-built from bits and pieces of British legalism, Lockean liberalism, Whig oppositionism, and post–Great Awakening Protestantism, he moved primarily from ancient history, political economy, the law of nations, and scripture—choices that betray a certain remoteness from the society at hand.[85]

Jay's grim view of human nature underlay all that he believed and became: for most of his life, he rejected the presumption of goodness (or at least human perfectibility) from which political liberalism proceeds. Lindley Murray said of the young Jay that he had been notable for "strong reasoning powers, comprehensive views, indefatigable application, and uncommon firmness of mind"; nowhere did Murray note Jay's optimism, empathy, or great good humor. In midlife, and partly in response to the trauma of revolution, Jay's intellectual proclivities crystallized into a sophisticated but rigidly legalistic variant of republicanism rooted firmly in existential despair and staunchly opposed to the twin doctrines of perfectibility and voluntarism. Few of the Founders preferred greater distance from the "Public," devalued the general will so completely, and stressed the perils of lawlessness so constantly. In the end, Jay even distrusted himself, handing over prosperity, his ultimate object, to God and international law—the closest approximation of godly wisdom available to humankind—for safekeeping. "[W]ho made the Laws of Nations?" he asked rhetorically in the year of the Georgia cases. "The answer is *he* from whose *will* proceed all moral Obligations, and which *will* is made known to us by Reason or Revelation." At home, unification behind a supreme man-made law might suffice, but, in dealings with Europeans, where traders and politians might succumb to temptation or where public displays of dirty laundry might lead to war, there would be "no Judge but the great Judge of all."[86]

In eighteenth-century understandings, these were eminently conservative ideas, but they were not precisely reactionary. While Jay preferred Court to country politics, his "system" fell easily within the broad spectrum of Revolutionary discourse. Unlike Old Guard curmudgeons, Jay found republican forms plausible, if regrettably optimistic and poorly implemented. And, unlike Hamilton, Jay fulsomely embraced important elements of economic liberalism, championing free trade and agrarianism as avenues to national standing and wealth. By 1776, he had embraced the necessity of independence—grudgingly, to be sure, and no doubt as much to conserve wealth as to advance republican liberty, but nonetheless irrevocably. Thereafter, by articulating contrary "objects," tactics, and institutional arrangements among peers far more responsive in 1787 than earlier, Jay became a constructive participant in revolutionary change and the embodiment of the marriage—apparent in a good many Founders—between free-trading liberalism and political corporatism, the whole made safe for wayward republicans with lavish doses of law.

Jay's emphasis upon global commerce and "independence for friendship" as a main object of domestic unification differed appreciably from Marshall's priorities; to a great extent, the federal judiciary rose to power after 1800 by turning inward, away from Europe and the law of nations toward the American hinterland and bodies of domestic law. Jay proposed a "comprehensive"[87] rather than introspective system of politics and law—an organic whole conspiring slowly and fitfully under law toward a collective, ultimately global state of grace. Jay hoped, too, that this homogenizing process would be supervised by wise, wellborn statesmen. To both domestic and international spheres, he assigned separate allegiances and "objects." But these memberships and goals were unequally weighted and intricately joined: at every turn, domestic political economy supported its more important international counterpart. The sheer delicacy of this balancing act generated considerable apprehension in Jay: "It cannot be too strongly impressed on the Minds of us all," he tautly instructed several grand juries in 1790, "how greatly our individual Prosperity depends on our national Prosperity; and how greatly our national

Prosperity depends on a well organized vigorous Government, ruling by wise and equal Laws, faithfully executed."[88]

The particular urgencies underlying these remarks had diminished appreciably by 1801, but, in 1789, no agenda seemed to touch the public good more directly. Jay's plan therefore represented more than the selfish agitations of an Empire State capitalist. To ignore economic and strategic weaknesses, Jay thought, was to invite Jacob's bad use of Esau's weakened condition,[89] for brave assertions about a republic's inevitable prosperity strained hard against history and against a very thorny reality. To Jay's mind, an omnipresent law ensured moral judgment and moral action among republicans predisposed as a group to selfishness, licentiousness, and evil: when Alexander Hamilton advocated manipulation of election returns in 1800 to defeat Thomas Jefferson, Jay quietly wrote off both Hamilton and Federalism. Better to sacrifice party and individuals than to leave high moral ground.[90]

To modern eyes, Jay's values can seem outmoded and reprehensible. These reactions, however, often reflect impatience with failed imagination—to make matters worse, on the losing side of history. Scholars know how the story came out, and so tend to demonstrate "the inevitability of the evolution they describe."[91] Federalists like Jay and Marshall indeed shared a uniform vocabulary of legalism and nationalism. But the meanings, shadings, and priorities conveyed through language necessarily varied according to the speaker and his context. Jay clearly infused such terms as "nation" or "federal law" with meanings that reflected his own intellect, experience, and reading of republican circumstance.

As Morris once noted, a campaign to secure controversial review powers in the 1790s would have been foolhardy; on circuit, moreover, Jay's colleagues quietly and steadily hammered away at the possibility, carrying the idea of judicial purview over congressional acts as far as political opponents allowed it to be carried.[92] For the Court itself, Jay mostly had in mind other objectives. More pressing by far was national establishment within reliable, respected structures—labors for which Jay's "turn of mind," broad interests, and nonspecialized statecraft were especially well adapted. In the absence of a guiding "Light of Experience," Jay's colleagues hammered out rules and procedures appropriate to an unrealized appellate practice—a thankless task if ever there was one. Simultaneously, the chief justice tried to solidify an alliance with the executive branch, fearing with Hamilton that a bench with "neither Force nor Will, but merely judgment" would soon collapse.[93] He also explored the Court's potential as an agency of "honour, justice, and interest" against incipient evil. Laboring to sensitize republicans to the perils of their chosen form of government, he concluded by 1794 that citizens still refused a very difficult but critical discipline, and that he could not secure a permanent state of grace for his countrymen through federal courts. Privately, he awaited the millennium; as a statesman, he pursued "great and obvious principles" elsewhere.

Arguably, these ideas constitute an alternative conception of ideal relations between polity, economy, and law rather than a prelude to modernism. Scholars may rightly decide that Jay lacked genius and political generosity, that he was a poor excuse for an appellate judge, and that his "system" was too fragile and too tightly bound to context to wear well. But similar complaints have not prevented engagement with the likes of Roger Taney or Chancellor James Kent, whose ambiguities and illiberalism have been absorbed, if not entirely forgiven. And, in the decade after ratification, Jay's professional style—so much a part of an oracular tradition in judgeship[94]—was common enough.

More important, and scholarly approval aside, meaningful comparisons with later practice depend upon an initial grant of seriousness. The desire to provide consistent standards through law against which republicans might measure moral progress, for example, or the idea that political work transcends constituencies and institutions, both give pause. At the least, John Jay's vision increases the distance between 1789 and 1801, clarifying and complicating our understanding of how the third branch came to occupy modern ground. Even Jay's champion, Richard Morris, saw clearly that Jay was a product (as are we all) of his historical moment; he only failed to see that, in a cultural and perhaps social-psychological sense, Marshall's moment was light years removed from the terrors and thrills of 1789. Said Morris in 1967, John Jay's "tireless effort to endow the national government with energy, capacity, and scope . . . attest to his vision, courage, and tenacity. It remained for others to spell out the safeguards for individual liberties and the limitation on national power . . . essential to the maintenance of a democratic society."[95]

NOTES

1. Quoted in Gordon Wood, *The Creation of the American Republic* (Chapel Hill 1969), 420.

2. David Hackett Fischer, *The Revolution of American Conservatism* (New York 1965), 7–10, esp. 8. See also George Pellew, *John Jay* (Boston 1890); Merrill Jensen, *The New Nation* (New York 1950), 13–14, 365–366, and passim; Frank Monaghan, *John Jay, Defender of Liberty* (New York and Indianapolis 1935); Gottfried Dietze, *The Federalist* (Baltimore 1960), 105–111; Jack Rakove, *The Beginnings of National Politics* (Baltimore 1979), 53–56; the biographical sketch in Donald L. Smith, *John Jay: Founder of a State and Nation* (New York 1968); Herbert Johnson, *John Jay, 1745–1829* (Albany, N.Y. 1970), and "John Jay: Lawyer in a Time of Transition, 1764–1775," *University of Pennsylvania Law Review*, 124 (May 1976), 1260–1292. See also the biographical detail in commentaries of William Jay in *The Life of John Jay: Selections from His Correspondence and Miscellaneous Papers* (2 vols., New York 1833), esp. Vol. I, 1–68, a collection that William overzealously edited to protect his father's reputation, and in Richard B. Morris's introduction to *John Jay, The Making of a Revolutionary: Unpublished Papers, 1745–1780* (2 vols., New York 1975), Vol. I, 1–26, cited hereafter as Morris, *Unpublished Papers*. Among Morris's interpretive works are *John Jay, the Nation, and the Court* (Boston 1967); *The Peacemakers* (New York 1965); *Seven Who Shaped Our Destiny* (New York 1973), ch. 5; "The John Jay Court: An Intimate Profile," *Journal of Contemporary Law*, 5 (Spring 1979), 163–179; "The American Revolution Comes to John Jay," in Jacob Judd and Irwin Polishook, eds., *Aspects of Early New York Society and Politics* (Tarrytown, N.Y. 1974), 96–117; and the more recent (and slightly less positive) account, "John Jay: Aristocrat as Nationalist," in Morris, *Witnesses at the Creation: Hamilton, Madison, Jay, and the Constitution* (New York 1985). Milton Klein accurately summarized scholarly attitudes in his review of Morris's edition of Jay's papers, *American Journal of Legal History*, 21 (Oct. 1977), 365–369. See also Morris's *Forging of the Union, 1781–1789* (New York 1987), in which he weaves John Jay as a diplomatist and statesman into the fabric of the framing decade far more persuasively than in earlier, somewhat strained accounts. See also Sandra VanBurkleo, "John Jay," in Melvin Urofsky, ed., *Supreme Court Justices: A Biographical Dictionary* (Westport, Conn. 1995), 263–269.

3. On the power to review acts of Congress, see *Marbury* v. *Madison*, 1 Cranch 137 (1803). See also Robert Lowry Clinton, *Marbury v. Madison and Judicial Review* (Lawrence, Kans. 1989), and Sylvia Snowiss, *Judicial Review and the Law of the Constitution* (New Haven 1990).

4. For negative, positive, and compromise positions, see Samuel Bemis, *Jay's Treaty: A Study in Commerce and Diplomacy* (New York 1923); Morris, *Peacemakers*; and Jerald Combs, *The Jay Treaty* (Berkeley 1970). Alexander De-

Conde's *Entangling Alliances* (Durham, N.C. 1958) supplies additional detail about Jay's diplomatic career.

5. Jay to Judge Lowell, Feb. 29, 1796, in Henry P. Johnston, ed., *The Correspondence and Public Papers of John Jay* (4 vols., New York 1891), IV, 204–205. Hereafter cited as Johnston, *Jay Papers*. The expectation of modern attitudes toward separation of powers and professional specialization leads Morris to argue that Jay's failure to resign was a well-intended "lapse" that provided a dangerous precedent for "overstepping" separation of powers; *John Jay*, 92–93. Morris's edition of unpublished papers, unlike Johnston's old edition, preserves the original spelling, punctuation, and capitalization, but it does not include all of Jay's writings. Few attempts have been made here to reconcile differing editorial practices. Where possible, I rely on the transcriptions in Maeva Marcus et al., eds., *Documentary History of the United States Supreme Court, 1789–1800* (5 vols. to date, New York 1985–). Cited hereafter as Marcus, *Documentary History*.

6. Robert McCloskey, *The American Supreme Court* (Chicago 1960), 30; Charles Grove Haines, *The Role of the Supreme Court in American Government and Politics, 1789–1835* (New York 1960), 124; Alfred Kelly, Winfred Harbison, and Herman Belz, *The American Constitution* (6th ed., New York 1983), 164–167; and Morris, *John Jay*, 69. See also Morris, "Intimate Profile," wherein Jay is portrayed as a typical "nationalist chief justice" who sought review powers without adequate support. He also links Jay's views on judicial autonomy to Marshall's, primarily because of Jay's resistance to formal advice in *Hayburn's Case* and *Sloop Betsy*, 2 Dallas 409 (1792), Jay and Associate Justices to Washington, July 20, 1793, in Johnston, *Jay Papers*, III, 486–489. On formal parallels between Jay and Marshall in the use of syllogism or nationalist language, see Morris, *John Jay*, 56–60, 70, 102, or G. Edward White, *The American Judicial Tradition* (New York 1976), 25, 27–30.

7. George Washington to Jay, Oct. 5, 1789, in Johnston, *Jay Papers*, III, at 378.

8. Charge to the Grand Jury of the Circuit Court for the District of New York, April 12, 1790, in Marcus, *Documentary History*, II, 27. On the Eleventh Amendment, see William Guthrie, "The Eleventh Article of Amendment to the Constitution of the United States," *Columbia Law Review*, 8 (Mar. 1908), 183–207, which should be read alongside Clyde Jacobs's more sensitive *The Eleventh Amendment and Sovereign Immunity* (Westport, Conn. 1972), and compared with Julius Goebel, *History of the Supreme Court of the United States: Antecedents and Beginnings to 1801* (New York 1971), esp. 736–741, which is hostile to Jay. See also Jacobs, "Prelude to Amendment: The States Before the Court," *American Journal of Legal History*, 12 (Jan. 1968), 19–40, and Louis Jaffe, "Suits Against Governments and Officers: Sovereign Immunity," *Harvard Law Review*, 77 (Nov. 1963), 1–39.

9. Goebel, *History of the Supreme Court*, 552 and 729–733, also credits Jay

with initiating the "lamentable standards of American judicial historiography." On Jay's *Federalist* contributions and the acknowledgment among contemporaries of diplomatic expertise, see Douglass Adair, "The Authorship of the Disputed Federalist Papers," *William and Mary Quarterly*, 1 (Jan. 1944), 97–122, (Apr. 1944), 235–264, esp. 246. For Washington's acknowledgment, see Instructions as Envoy Extraordinary, 1794, in Johnston, ed., *Jay Papers*, IV, 14.

10. Morris, *John Jay*, 100.

11. I attribute Jay's unremitting anxiety about the character of "the people out of doors" as much to Calvinism as to class; others disagree, though no one (me included) has pursued this question rigorously.

12. Gordon Wood, *The Radicalism of the American Revolution* (New York 1992), 271. Interestingly, Wood seems to attribute the old gentry's decline—at least in the North—to capitalist expansion and (possibly) to the triumph of middling over monied classes: "With the weakening and disappearance of older forms of patronage, with the expansion of commerce and the fluctuating redistributions of wealth, with the spread of paper money and the widening commercial opportunities for plain and 'middling' men everywhere, the gentry's position in northern society became more and more anachronistic." Ibid.

13. Bernard Bailyn, *Education in the Forming of American Society* (New York 1960), 14. Legal scholars too often consider that the Revolution ended with ratification, which helps explain unhistorical readings of judicial motivations before 1801. For the periodization of Revolutionary process adopted here, see John Howe, "Republican Thought and the Political Violence of the 1790's," *American Quarterly*, 19 (Summer 1967), 147–165.

14. Jay to John Adams, Jan. 2, 1801, in Johnston, ed., *Jay Papers*, IV, 285.

15. On relationships between Smith's economic and moral philosophy, see Donald Winch, *Adam Smith's Politics* (Cambridge, Eng. 1978), or Robert Nisbet, *History of the Idea of Progress* (New York 1980), esp. 187–193, arguing that Smith's precept of "natural liberty" in the marketplace arises as easily from "prepolitical social bonds" as from an "invisible hand" divorced from the polity.

16. Federalist Nos. 2 and 4, in Jacob E. Cooke, ed., *The Federalist* (Middletown, Conn. 1961), 9, 22. Hereafter cited as Cooke, *Federalist.*

17. Jay to Washington, Apr. 21, 1779, in Morris, *Unpublished Papers,* I, 586–587.

18. Jay to Gouverneur Morris, Apr. 29, 1778, ibid., 476; Jay to Richard Price, Sept. 27, 1785, Jay to Washington, June 27, 1786, in Johnston, *Jay Papers*, III, 168–169, 205. Also see Jay to R. Lushington, Mar. 15, 1786, ibid., 185–186; or Jay to Robert Livingston and Morris, Apr. 29, 1777, and to Egbert Benson, Sept. 18, 1780, in Morris, *Unpublished Papers,* I, 401, 823. Jay's religiosity is never disputed; e.g., Morris, *John Jay*, 12, 86.

19. Jay to Morris, July 21, 1777, Jay to Alexander McDougall, Dec. 23,

1775, in Morris, *Unpublished Papers,* I, 423, 213. In addition, see Jay to Washington, Apr. 22, 1779, and to Sarah Jay, June 22, 1775, ibid., 586, 154.

20. Jay to Washington, Sept. 21, 1788, in Johnston, *Jay Papers,* III, 360; Jay to Lindley Murray, Aug. 22, 1794, to William Vaughan, May 26, 1796, to Benjamin Rush, Mar. 22, 1797, and to Judge Peters, Mar. 14, 1815, ibid., IV, 52, 215–216, 226, 387. With other Federalists, Jay advocated popular sovereignty while distinguishing between legal and social equality, and so could say that, while republicans were intractibly unequal in social terms, the "only source of just authority" was *"the People";* Jay to Washington, Jan. 7, 1787, ibid., III, 229. For "Evils inseparable from Humanity," see Jay to Sarah Jay, Mar. 25, 1777, in Morris, *Unpublished Papers, I,* 382.

21. Federalist No. 2, in Cooke, *Federalist,* 8; Edward Rutledge to Jay, June 29, 1776, and Jay's reply, July 6, 1776, in Morris, *Unpublished Papers, I,* 281, 281n, wherein he says Rutledge's ideas "parallel" his own; Jay to Judge Peters, Mar. 14, 1815, in Johnston, *Jay Papers*, IV, 387. On Jacobinism, see, e.g., Jay to Washington, March 6, 1795, ibid., 162–171.

22. Jay to William Vaughan, May 26, 1796, and to Washington, Feb. 25, 1795, Johnston, *Jay Papers*, IV, 216, 161.

23. Jay to Washington, Apr. 21, 1779, and Rutledge to Jay, June 29, 1776, in Morris, *Unpublished Papers,* I, 586, 281; and Jay to Francis Hopkinson, Mar. 29, 1786, in Johnston, *Papers*, III, 187–188. In the same vein, see Rutledge to Jay, Dec. 25, 1778, Jay to Morris, Apr. 29, 1778, in Morris, *Unpublished Papers*, I, 516, 475; and Jay to Washington, Jan. 7, 1787, in Johnston, *Jay Papers*, III, 227.

24. Jay to Judge Lowell, Feb. 29, 1796, to Peter Van Schaack, July 28, 1812, and to Washington, Feb. 25, 1795, in Johnston, *Jay Papers*, IV, 204, 361, 161.

25. Federalist Nos. 2 and 3, in Cooke, *Federalist,* 11–12, 15, 17; Jay to Washington, Sept. 21, 1788, in Johnston, *Jay Papers*, III, 361; Rutledge to Jay, June 29, 1776, Jay to Philip Schuyler, Dec. 11, 1777, and New York Convention to John Hancock [July 10], 1776, in Morris, *Unpublished Papers,* I, 281, 453, 291.

26. Jay to Sarah Jay, Mar. 25, 1777, in Morris, *Unpublished Papers*, I, 382, and Federalist No. 2, in Cooke, *Federalist,* 12. On "resignation" and "duty," see also Jay to Robert Livingston, Jan. 6, 1776, in Morris, *Unpublished Papers, I,* 223; Jay to Sarah Jay, Apr. 15, 1794, and to Lindley Murray, Aug. 22, 1794, in Johnston, *Jay Papers*, IV, 3, 51.

27. Proofs that the Colonies Do Not Aim at Independence [after Dec. 11, 1775], and Jay to Alexander McDougall, Oct. 17, 1775, in Morris, *Unpublished Papers*, I, 199, 172. On "lasting Union," see Jay to John Vardill, Sept. 24, 1774, and Draft of the Olive Branch Petition, June 1775, ibid., 137, 152–154, urging unification to secure "Harmony . . . Wealth and Power."

28. See, e.g., Federalist No. 5, in Cooke, *Federalist,* 23–24.

29. Jay to Morris, Apr. 29, 1778, in Morris, *Unpublished Papers*, I,

475–476. Morris characterizes Jay more positively as a "prudent revolutionary"; *John Jay*, 3.

30. See Wood, *Creation,* 419–421, where New Yorkers' criticisms are virtually equated with self-interest.

31. For national "objects," see Federalist Nos. 2 and 3, in Cooke, *Federalist,* 12–15. Jay also associated unity with safety.

32. Jay to Judge Lowell, May 10, 1785, and to Washington, June 27, 1786, in Johnston, *Jay Papers*, III, 143, 205. For the Lowell letter capitalizations, see William Jay's commentary in *Letters of John Jay*, I, 190, and Frank Monaghan's discussion of Johnston's version, *John Jay*, 282, 454 at note 6.

33. Jay to Alexander McDougall, Apr. 11, 1776, to James Duane, Dec. 14, 1777, and to Washington, Apr. 21, 1779, in Morris, *Unpublished Papers*, I, 254, 454, 586. In the last, Jay scratched out a phrase suggesting that the people lacked "wisdom." The best source for details about Jay's difficulties with Congress after 1783 remains Johnston, *Jay Papers*, III, 104–378; on difficulties before then, see Morris, *Peacemakers*, passim. Misgivings about collective decision making in maritime or economic affairs emerged early. See, e.g., Jay to Washington, Apr. 26, 1779, in Morris, *Unpublished Papers*, I, 587–588.

34. Jay to Governor Livingston, July 19, 1783, to Thomas Jefferson, Oct. 27, 1786, to Adams, Feb. 21, 1787, and to Jefferson, Nov. 3, 1787, in Johnston, *Jay Papers*, III, 55, 212, 235, 260. On congressional absenteeism, see Jay to Jefferson, Jan. 9, 1786, and to Jacob Read, Dec. 12, 1786, ibid., 178, 222.

35. Report to Congress on a Joint Letter from Adams and Jefferson, May 29, 1786, and Address to the People of the State of New York, Spring 1788, ibid., 198–199, 298–301.

36. Jay to Washington, June 27, 1786, and to Jefferson, Apr. 24, 1787, ibid., 204, 244. On rebellion and feeble government, see Jay to Adams, Nov. 1, 1786, to William Carmichael, Jan. 4, 1787, and to Jefferson, Feb. 9, 1787, ibid., 214, 225, 232.

37. Jay to Governor Livingston, July 19, 1783, to Adams, Feb. 21, 1787, to Washington, Jan. 7, 1787, and to William Vaughan, May 26, 1796, ibid., III, 55, 234, 227; IV, 216. Also see Jay to Jefferson, Aug. 18, 1786, ibid., III, 210–211.

38. Rutledge to Jay, June 29, Nov. 24, 1776, in Morris, *Unpublished Papers*, I, 281, 322; Jay to Washington, Jan. 7, 1787, in Johnston, *Jay Papers*, III, 227.

39. Here, Jay echoed other High Federalists. See, e.g., Jay to Jefferson, Aug. 18, 1786, in Johnston, *Jay Papers*, III, 210–211, and Gordon Wood's discussion of competing conceptions of "worthiness," constitutional decay, and separation of powers, in *Creation*, 471–518. But see also Jay's extreme recommendations to Washington, Jan. 7, 1787, in Johnston, *Jay Papers*, III, 227, concerning life tenure for senators and annual election for House members, presumably to conserve wisdom and rout out demagoguery. On collaboration, advisory councils, and the

royal prerogative, see Federalist No. 4, in Cooke, *Federalist*, 20; Address to the People of the State of New York, Spring 1788, and Jay to the Chevalier de Bourgoing, Aug. 29, 1788, and to Washington, Jan. 7, 1787, in Johnston, *Jay Papers*, III, 316, 355–356, 227.

40. Charge to the Grand Jury of the Circuit Court for the District of New York, April 12, 1790, and Charge to the Grand Jury of the Circuit Court for the District of Virginia [Richmond], May 22, 1793, in Marcus, *Documentary History*, II, 28, 30, 390. On crown-court relations, see J. H. Baker, *Introduction to English Legal History* (London 1971), 39–50, or S. F. C. Milsom, *Historical Foundations of the Common Law* (London 1969), 74–87. Charles Warren tied Jay's notion of cooperation to partisan politics, *The Supreme Court in United States History* (2 vols., Boston 1926), I, 85–112. On mixed and departmental government, see Wood, *Creation*, 197–256. Part of Jay's preference for British forms sprang from hatred of the "former arbitrary government" of France, which was "dreadful"; his vision of vigorous executive and judicial power included strict adherence among statesmen to the rule of law. See Jay to Robert Goodloe Harper, Jan. 19, 1796, in Johnston, *Jay Papers*, IV, 200–201. See also Federalist No. 3, in Cooke, *Federalist*, 15.

41. Wood, *Creation*, 159, 472–473; Martin Diamond, "What the Framers Meant by Federalism," in Robert Goldwin, ed., *A Nation Of States* (Chicago 1974), 31–33; and Jay's allusion to Washington, Mar. 16, 1786, Johnston, *Jay Papers*, III, 186–187.

42. Jay to Washington, Jan. 7, 1787, to Adams, Oct. 14, 1785, to Jefferson, Dec. 14, 1786, to James Lowell, May 10, 1785, and to Adams, May 4, 1786, in Johnston, *Jay Papers*, III, 228, 172, 224, 143, 195; Federalist No. 3, in Cooke, *Federalist*, 15; and Jay to Washington, Apr. 21, 1779, in Morris, *Unpublished Papers*, 586.

43. Federalist Nos. 2 and 4, in Cooke, *Federalist*, 13, 22–23; Charge to the Grand Jury of the Circuit Court for the District of New York, April 12, 1790, in Marcus, *Documentary History*, II, as at 29. See also Jay's Address to the People of the State of New York, Spring 1788, asserting that disorder "alienated the minds of men everywhere . . . from republican forms"; Jay to Washington, Jan. 7, 1787; to Adams, July 4, 1787, suggesting authority strong enough to ensure "national security and respectability"; and Report to Congress on a Joint Letter from Adams and Jefferson, May 29, 1786, regretting that problems of the United States were "common conversation in Europe." Johnston, *Jay Papers*, 394, 313–315, 319, 228, 248, 198.

44. Morris, *Peacemakers*, passim.

45. Jay to Washington, Jan. 7, 1787, in Johnston, *Jay Papers*, III, 226–227; Federalist No. 64 [63], in Cooke, *Federalist*, 434; Jay speaking before Congress, in Wood, *Creation*, 96.

46. Draft of John Jay's Charge to the Grand Jury of the Circuit Court for the

District of Virginia [before April 22, 1793], in Marcus, *Documentary History*, II, 362 (much of which was muted in the final version delivered in Richmond, ibid., 380–391); Jay to James Duane, Sept. 16, 1795, in Johnston, *Jay Papers*, IV, 193; Federalist No. 3, in Cooke, *Federalist*, 14. For late-life musings about an immutable moral law "given by the Sovereign" and mutable "ordinances" that could not contradict God's law, see Jay to John Murray, Jr., Apr. 15, 1818, in Johnston, *Jay Papers*, IV, 403–419. This Calvinist framework comported well with his favored "individual-nation" analogy, which in turn was reinforced by readings in natural law and the law of nations. For the imagery couched in religious language, see Jay to Rev. Dr. Thatcher, May 26, 1796, ibid., III, 481, and IV, 215.

47. Jay to Jefferson, July 14, 1786, in Johnston, *Jay Papers*, III, 207. On indebtedness, see Report to Congress on a Joint Letter from Adams and Jefferson, May 29, 1786, and Jay to Jefferson, Dec. 14, 1786, ibid., 198, 223. On Jay's involvement in early agreements, see Jay to Floridablanca, June 22, 1780, and John Adams, Extract from a Journal, Nov. 3, 10, 1782, in Jared Sparks, ed., *Diplomatic Correspondence of the American Revolution* (12 vols., Boston 1830), VI, 465–466, 468–470, VII, 325.

48. Draft of John Jay's Charge to the Grand Jury at . . . Virginia [before April 22, 1793], in Marcus, *Documentary History*, II, 360; Letter to Congress incorporating a letter to the Count de Vergennes, Sept. 22, 1780, in Sparks, *Diplomatic Correspondence*, VII, 384.

49. Jay to Governor Livingston, July 19, 1783, and Washington to Jay, Aug. 15, 1786, in Johnston, *Jay Papers*, III, 55, 209; and Federalist No. 64 [63], in Cooke, *Federalist*, 437. The Definitive Treaty of Peace is reprinted in Morris, *Peacemakers*, 461–465. See also John Adams's parallel sentiments, Extract from a Journal, Nov. 10, 1782, in Sparks, *Diplomatic Correspondence*, VI, 473. On sequestration, see Goebel, *History of the Supreme Court*, 722–759, or Morris, *John Jay*, 73–102.

50. Jay to the Marquis de Lafayette, June 16, 1786, and to Lord Lansdowne, Apr. 20, 1786, but also see Jay to Lansdowne, Apr. 16, 1786, in Johnston, *Jay Papers*, III, 192, 202, 190.

51. Jay to Adams, Feb. 21, 1787, ibid., III, 234–235, IV, 140; Charge to the Grand Jury of the Circuit Court for the District of New York, April 12, 1790, in Marcus, *Documentary History*, II, 29; Jay to Edmund Randolph, Nov. 19, 1794, in Johnston, *Jay Papers*, IV, 140. Active on revolutionary committees of safety, Jay did not sanction Loyalism, yet he was troubled by harsh treatment of men of merit. See Jay to Adams, Sept. 6, 1785, ibid., III, 166.

52. Jay's papers do not confirm a direct Wilsonian influence, but the two served together in Congress and on the high court. Although Wilson's assumptions were more "democratical" than Jay's, structural similarities in the arguments of the two men are striking, as is a shared belief that the law of nations em-

bodied divinity. See Arnaud Leavelle, "James Wilson and the Relation of the Scottish Metaphysics to American Political Thought," *Political Science Quarterly*, 57 (Sept. 1942), 394–410; Mary Delahanty, *The Integrationist Philosophy of James Wilson* (Millwood, N.Y. 1978); Charles Smith, *James Wilson, Founding Father, 1742–1798* (Chapel Hill 1956); Robert McCloskey, ed., *The Works of James Wilson* (2 vols., Cambridge, Mass. 1967).

53. John Adams, Extract from a Journal, Nov. 3, 1782, in Sparks, *Diplomatic Correspondence*, VI, 466.

54. Jay to Washington, Mar. 6, 1795, in Johnston, *Jay Papers*, IV, 170, or Jay's Letter to Congress, Nov. 6, 1780, in Sparks, *Diplomatic Corrrespondence*, VII, 358. On revolutionary diplomatic theory, see Gregg Lint, "The American Revolution and the Law of Nations, 1776–1789," *Diplomatic History*, 1 (Winter 1977), 20–34, which identifies "enlightened" thought but not shrewdness, and J. H. Hutson, "Intellectual Foundations of Early American Diplomacy," ibid., 1–19.

55. Jay to William Greene, Mar. 4, 1783, in Johnston, *Jay Papers*, III, 33; Adams to Robert Livingston, Oct. 31, 1782, quoting Jay and agreeing with "sentiments and systems"; Sparks, *Diplomatic Correspondence*, VI, 437, 473–474.

56. Letter to Congress, 1780, in Sparks, *Diplomatic Correspondence*, VII, 247, 272–274. On unity against Britain, see Jay to Lafayette, July 15, 1785; on long-term economic prospects, see Jay to Jefferson, Apr. 24, 1788, and to Adams, Sept. 5, 1785; on China, see Jay to President of Congress, Jan. 20, 1786; in Johnston, *Jay Papers*, III, 161, 165, 180, 326–327.

57. Jay to Benjamin Vaughan, Mar. 28, 1783, to Adams, Sept. 6, 1785, and to Jefferson, Jan. 9, 1786, Feb. 9, 1787, in Johnston, *Jay Papers*, III, 34–35, 165, 178–179, 231–233; Letter to Congress, 1780, in Sparks, *Diplomatic Correspondence*, VII, 275–276.

58. Useful studies of political economy include J. E. Crowley, *This Sheba, Self* (Baltimore 1974); Drew McCoy, *The Elusive Republic* (Chapel Hill 1980); Merrill Peterson, "Thomas Jefferson and Commercial Policy, 1783–1793," *William and Mary Quarterly*, 22 (Oct. 1965), 584–610; Joyce Appleby, "The Social Origins of American Revolutionary Ideology," *Journal of American History*, 64 (Mar. 1978), 935–958; John R. Nelson, Jr., "Alexander Hamilton and American Manufacturing: A Reexamination," ibid., 65 (Mar. 1979), 971–995; Drew McCoy, "Republicanism and American Foreign Policy: James Madison and the Political Economy of Commercial Discrimination, 1789 to 1794," *William and Mary Quarterly*, 31 (1974), 633–646; Ralph Lerner, "Commerce and Character: The Anglo-American as a New-Model Man," *William and Mary Quarterly*, 26 (1979), 3–26; Joyce Appleby, *Capitalism and a New Social Order: The Republican Vision of the 1790s* (New York 1984); Cathy Matson and Peter Onuf, *A Union of Interests: Political and Economic Thought in Revolutionary America* (Lawrence, Kans. 1990); and, for intersections between commercial and interna-

tional law, Peter Onuf and Nicholas Onuf, *Federal Union, Modern World: The Law of Nations in an Age of Revolutions* (Madison, Wis. 1993).

59. Federalist No. 5, in Cooke, *Federalist*, 26, and Letter to the President of Congress, May 26, 1780, in Sparks, *Diplomatic Correspondence*, VII, 247.

60. Interestingly, Jay's agrarianism seems to have lacked the moral preoccupations so much a part of republican agrarianism. He imagined wealth production, not seedbeds of republican virtue, although he would not have objected to the latter. See generally McCoy, *Elusive Republic*, and (for a later period) John Ashworth, *Agrarians and Aristocrats: Party Political Ideology in the United States, 1837–1846* (London 1983). On this score, Jay was every inch the modernist.

61. Lansdowne to Jay, Sept 4, 1785, and Jay to Lansdowne, Apr. 20, 1786, in Johnston, *Jay Papers*, III, 189, 193. See also Jay to Jefferson, Apr. 24, 1788, ibid., 326–327.

62. Jay to Lansdowne, Apr. 20, 1786, to Jefferson, Apr. 24, 1788; to Lafayette, Apr. 26, 1788; and Address to the People of the State of New York, Spring 1788; ibid., 193–194, 314, 327–328. Additionally, see Federalist Nos. 3 and 4, in Cooke, *Federalist*, passim.

63. Washington to Jay, Oct. 5, 1789, and Instructions to Envoy Extraordinary, May 6, 1794, in Johnston, *Jay Papers*, III, 378–379, IV, 14.

64. Draft of John Jay's Charge to the Grand Jury of the Circuit Court for the District of Virginia [before Apr. 22, 1793], in Marcus, *Documentary History*, II, 359; Jay to Washington, Apr. 21, 1779, and Jay to John Vardill, May 23, 1774, in Morris, *Unpublished Papers*, 587, 131. Before 1798, federal courts possessed original and exclusive jurisdiction in suits to which the United States was party, in admiralty, in suits touching consuls and ministers, and in litigation between states or a state and noncitizens. See Goebel, *History of the Supreme Court*, 552–721.

65. Morris, *John Jay*, 12. Jay's support for this council has been viewed as evidence of his eagerness to garner implied powers of review, but an advisory role is conceptually distinct from the ability to negate congressional legislation after the fact.

66. George Washington to the Justices of the Supreme Court, Apr. 3, 1790, in Marcus, *Documentary History*, II, 21.

67. Washington to Jay, June [?], 1789, Nov. 19, 1790; Jay to Washington, Nov. 13, 1790, to Alexander Hamilton, Nov. 28, 1790; and Hamilton to Jay Sept. 3, 1792, in Johnston, *Jay Papers*, III, 369, 409, 405–408, 410, 446–447. See also Jay's draft of Washington's neutrality proclamation, ibid., 474–477.

68. John Jay's Draft of the Charge to the Grand Jury of . . . Virginia [before Apr. 22, 1793], in Marcus, *Documentary History*, II, 360.

69. Jay to George Read, Dec. 12, 1786, an unpublished letter quoted in Morris, *John Jay*, 26–27.

70. Judge-made criminal law exercised at the federal level held obvious appeal for Jay, whose vision of a stable polity depended upon swift punishment of wayward citizens, particularly when they threatened lawful government. In addition, Jay had tried crimes against government while serving on New York's Committee of Safety (a job that he found distasteful), and held forth at length in grand jury charges after 1790 as to how and why the republic might enforce criminal sanctions. A recent study of Jay's last reported case, *U.S.* v. *Joseph Ravara*, confirms his interest in this murky jurisdiction; see John Gordon III, "*United States* v. *Joseph Ravara*: 'Presumptuous Evidence', 'Too Many Lawyers', and a Federal Common Law of Crime," in Maeva Marcus, ed., *Origins of the Federal Judiciary: Essays on the Judiciary Act of 1789* (New York 1992), 106–172.

71. Ibid.; Jay to Washington, Jan. 7, 1787, in Johnston, *Jay Papers*, III, 226. Early rulings included *Oswald* v. *New York*, 2 Dallas 401, 415 (1792, 1793), or *Van Staphorst* v. *Maryland,* 2 Dallas 401, 402 (1792, 1793). The Court's docket is described in Goebel, *History of the Supreme Court*, appendices, and (more usefully and painstakingly) in Marcus, *Documentary History*, I, Part 1 ("Appointments and Proceedings"). On the importance of circuits as vehicles for instruction about the new federation, and also as a focus for judicial energies before 1795, see Ralph Lerner, "The Supreme Court as Republican Schoolmaster," in Philip B. Kurland, ed., *Supreme Court Review* (Chicago 1967), 127–180.

72. *Chisholm* v. *Georgia*, 2 Dallas 419 (1793). See also Doyle Mathis, "*Chisholm* v. *Georgia*: Background and Settlement," *Journal of American History*, 54 (June 1967), 19–29, correcting factual errors in earlier accounts. On the Judiciary Act and its contested sections, see essays and bibliography in Marcus, *Origins of the Federal Judiciary*, and Wilfred Ritz, *Rewriting the History of the Judiciary Act of 1789: Exposing Myths, Challenging Premises, and Using New Evidence*, ed. Wythe Holt and L. H. LaRue (Norman 1990).

73. Jay to James Lowell, May 10, 1785; Draft of John Jay's Charge to the Grand Jury of . . . Virginia [before Apr. 22, 1793], in Marcus, *Documentary History*, II, 359–360. On Jay's involvement with Oswald, Van Staphorst, and other creditors, see Harold Syrett, ed., *Papers of Alexander Hamilton* (26 vols., New York 1961–1979), VI, 567–569; and John Adams's description of meetings, Extract from a Journal, October 31 through November 15, 1782, in Sparks, *Diplomatic Correspondence*, VII, 465–475.

74. *Chisholm* v. *Georgia*, 2 Dallas 419, 422–423 (1793). At 424–425, Randolph argues that states exist only for "domestic purposes." For the politics underlying James Iredell's dissent, see Jeff Fordham, "Iredell's Dissent in *Chisholm* v. *Georgia*: Its Political Significance," *North Carolina Historical Review*, 8 (Apr. 1931), 155–167.

75. *Georgia* v. *Brailsford*, 2 Dallas 402, 415 (1792, 1793), and *Chisholm* v. *Georgia*, 2 Dallas 419, 422–425, 473–474 (1793). The long-continued *Brailsford* case reappeared on the Supreme Court docket in 1798 to be dismissed in light of

the Eleventh Amendment; see note 77. On *Brailsford* as a struggle mainly against judicial nationalism, see Haines, *Role of the Supreme Court*, 93–104; and on Georgia's several high court encounters, see Doyle Mathis, "Georgia before the Supreme Court," *American Journal of Legal History*, 12 (Apr. 1968), 112–121.

76. *Chisholm* v. *Georgia*, 2 Dallas 409, 478–479 (1793).

77. Marcus, *Documentary History*, I, Part 1, 304–305.

78. Federalist No. 64 [63], in Cooke, *Federalist*, 437, and Jay to Washington, Apr. 30, 1794, in Marcus, *Documentary History*, I, Part 2, 747.

79. Jay to Adams, Jan. 2, 1801, in Johnston, *Jay Papers*, IV, 285. Unlike Madison, Jay could not relinquish the ideal of organic homogeneity achieved through law, eschewing what Gordon Wood calls "mechanical devices and institutional contrivances" through which Federalists supposedly hoped to contain revolutionary "social forces," without a clear object in mind beyond containment; Wood, *Creation*, 428, 475–476. For Jay, law encompassed both substance and structure; the law of nations especially carried within it virtually flawless principles that, if heeded, eventually would make public morality actual and universal. Thus, while law served hegemonic purposes, Jay's system also was organic and educative—and, in its way, progressive; he could not embrace the notion of machinery imposed for its own sake without abandoning the possibility of social redemption. This impasse may explain his existential despair after 1795.

80. Instructions as Envoy Extraordinary, May 6, 1794, and Jay to Lindley Murray, Aug. 22, 1794, in Johnston, *Jay Papers*, IV, 14, 51. See also Jay to John Hartley, Jan. 8, 1795, and, on resignation and duty, Jay to Sarah Jay, Apr. 15, 1794, ibid., 3, 153. The notion that statesmen's work might be limited to labor undertaken within particular institutions had not yet taken hold, even among proponents of departmentalized government; into the 1790s, Jefferson and others did the same thing, holding political and diplomatic posts at the same moment.

81. Jay to Washington, Aug. 5, 1794, to Rufus King, Nov. 19, 1794, to Edmund Randolph, Nov. 19, 1794, and to Washington, Mar. 6, 1795, ibid., IV, 45, 136, 140, 170–171. On treaty negotiations, see Combs, *Jay Treaty*, esp. his discussion of the mixed commission, 151–155.

82. Charge to the Grand Jury of the Circuit Court for the District of Virginia [Richmond], May 22, 1793, in Marcus, *Documentary History*, II, 390–391.

83. Fischer, *Revolution in American Conservatism*, 10.

84. Ralph Lerner, "Commerce and Character: The Anglo-American as a New-Model Man," *William and Mary Quarterly*, 26 (1979), 3–26.

85. Jay to George Read, 1786, quoted in Morris, *John Jay*, 27. On republicanism and Federalist objects in 1787, see early discussions (and, in some cases, texts epitomizing the so-called "republican synthesis") such as Wood, *Creation*; Bernard Bailyn, *Ideological Origins of the American Revolution* (Cambridge,

Mass. 1967); the long introduction in Jack Greene, ed., *Reinterpretation of the American Revolution* (New York 1968); two classic articles by Robert Shalhope, "Toward a Republican Synthesis: The Emergence of an Understanding of Republicanism in American Historiography," *William and Mary Quarterly*, 29 (Jan. 1972), 49–80, and "Republicanism and Early American Historiography," ibid., 39 (Apr. 1982), 334–356; John Murrin, "The Great Inversion, or Court versus Country . . . ," in J. G. A. Pocock, ed., *Three British Revolutions: 1641, 1688, 1776* (Princeton 1988); and a special issue of the *American Quarterly* (Fall 1985), ed. Joyce Appleby. For recent attempts to marry republican and liberal discourses, to declare them irreconcilably divorced, or to pronounce republicanism an outmoded idea, see Milton Klein et al., eds., *The Republican Synthesis Revisited: Essays in Honor of George Athan Billias* (Worcester, Mass. 1992); Isaac Kramnick, *Republicanism and Bourgeois Radicalism: Political Ideology in Late Eighteenth-Century England and America* (Ithaca 1990), esp. ch. 9; Joyce Appleby, *Liberalism and Republicanism in the Historical Imagination* (Cambridge, Mass. 1992); Scott Douglas Gerber, *To Secure These Rights: The Declaration of Independence and Constitutional Interpretation* (New York 1995), Part I; and (for allegations of bankruptcy) Daniel Rodgers, "Republicanism: The Career of a Concept," *Journal of American History*, 79 (1992), 11–38. These works also contain extensive bibliographic information.

86. Draft of John Jay's Charge to the Grand Jury at . . . Virginia [before Apr. 22 1793], in Marcus, *Documentary History*, II, 361–362. Cf. Stephen Presser, "A Tale of Two Judges," *Northwestern University Law Review*, 73 (Mar.-Apr. 1978), 48–52.

87. Federalist No. 2, in Cooke, *Federalist*, 8.

88. John Jay's Charge to the Grand Jury of the Circuit Court for the District of New York, Apr. 12, 1790, in Marcus, *Documentary History*, II, 30. Jay delivered essentially the same charge on circuit in Massachusetts, Connecticut, and other eastern states.

89. Letter to Congress, Sept. 22, 1780, in Sparks, *Diplomatic Correspondence*, 384.

90. For a brief account of the episode, see Morris, *John Jay*, 100–101.

91. John Noonan, Jr., *Persons and Masks of the Law* (New York 1976), 163. On Whiggish representation in legal-historical studies, see Robert Gordon, "Recent Trends in Legal Historiography," *Law Library Journal*, 69 (Nov. 1976), 462–468, esp. 465; "Introduction," *Law and Society Review*, 10 (Fall 1975), 9–55; and "Historicism in Legal Scholarship," *Yale Law Journal*, 90 (Apr. 1981), 1017–1059. See also Harry Scheiber's odd suggestion that constitutional history, unlike its private law counterpart, has been more or less impervious to criticism; "American Constitutional History and the New Legal History: Complementary Themes in Two Modes," *Journal of American History*, 68 (Sept. 1981), 337–350. For additional essays, see Kermit Hall, ed., *United States Constitutional and*

*Legal History,* Vol. I, *Main Themes in U.S. Constitutional and Legal History* (New York 1987).

92. Morris, *John Jay*, 86. The Court's cumulative experience on circuit with the review question can be tracked fairly easily in Marcus, *Documentary History*, II, "The Justices on Circuit." On this question and others, the *Documentary History* is indispensable.

93. John Jay's Charge to the Grand Jury of the Circuit Court for the District of New York, Apr. 12, 1790, in Marcus, *Documentary History*, II, 27; and Alexander Hamilton, Federalist No. 78, in Cooke, *Federalist*, 523. On procedural innovation, see Goebel's decidedly unappreciative *History of the Supreme Court*, passim.

94. White, *American Judicial Tradition*, 2–3.

95. Morris, *John Jay*, 102.

*Chapter 3*

# John Rutledge

## *Distinction and Declension*

*James Haw*

John Rutledge was a tall and imposing figure. His long, powdered hair ran back from a large forehead that set off his "dark piercing eyes, and firm mouth." An aloof, dignified bearing revealed the pride of a South Carolina lowcountry (coastal plain) aristocrat. Normally polite and courteous, Rutledge had a temper and could lash out in anger. One French commentator characterized Rutledge in 1788, with some exaggeration, as "the most eloquent man in the United States, but also the proudest and most imperious."[1]

On the South Carolina bench, Chancellor Rutledge personified authority. "Though ordinarily patient and always impartial, his temper sometimes took fire, and broke out without much check. . . . 'Court, jury, and audience quailed before him, when he assumed his gubernatorial air.'" Rutledge had a thorough knowledge of the law, but his greatest asset as a jurist was his ability quickly to grasp all the questions and implications raised by a complex case, put them in proper perspective, and penetrate to the heart of the issue.[2]

This facile mind was joined to an ardent, uneasy temperament. Rutledge made up his mind rapidly and preferred quick, decisive action.[3] He grew impatient with prolonged debate. Rutledge's oratory reflected his personality. He was a speaker whose torrent of vehement rhetoric rushed his listeners along to the desired conclusion. Charles Cotesworth Pinckney described Rutledge's speech as "strong and argumentative, and remarkable for close reasoning."[4]

If John Rutledge was a proud aristocrat, his gentility was of the freshly minted colonial variety. His English ancestors had settled in Ireland in the seventeenth century.[5] An uncle, lawyer Andrew Rutledge, emigrated to South Carolina around 1730 or 1731. He quickly achieved professional success, married a wealthy widow, and won election to the Commons House of Assembly. He rose to leadership of the country party, which defended the interests of the colony in clashes with the royal governor, and attained the post of speaker. Andrew's brother, Dr. John Rutledge, followed him to Charleston a few years later and also achieved prominence in the Commons House. In 1738 the doctor married his brother's fourteen-year-old stepdaughter, Sarah Hext, who was heiress to a sizeable fortune. The first of their seven children, John Rutledge, was born in 1739.[6]

Rutledge began his education at home and with tutors, then turned at an early age to the law. His legal education started in his Uncle Andrew's office and continued under prominent attorney James Parsons after Andrew Rutledge died in 1755. He then attended the Middle Temple in London and gained admission to the South Carolina bar in January 1761.[7]

Professional success came quickly. Rutledge handled more civil suits than any other lawyer in South Carolina's Court of Common Pleas during the period 1761–1774. He was equally successful in the colony's other courts. Estimates of Rutledge's legal income during these years range from £1,000 to more than £2,000 sterling per annum, a level that few American colonists achieved in any occupation. The proceeds of his plantations added to his fortune, but land speculation and family responsibilities to his brothers drained his resources. In 1763 he married Elizabeth Grimké, with whom he had eight children who survived infancy.[8]

Rutledge served in the Commons House of Assembly from 1761 to 1775. As early as 1762 he emerged as a leader of the country party.[9] A firm defender of local rights and legislative prerogatives, Rutledge opposed the Stamp, Townshend, and Tea Acts in the legislature, the Stamp Act Congress, public meetings, and the courts, but was not involved in extralegal crowd activity. Like most Americans before 1774, he believed that Britain should regulate colonial trade and make broad policy for the empire but should not tax the colonies or interfere in their local affairs.

Rutledge considered the extension of vice-admiralty jurisdiction in the colonies "the most enormous of any [grievance] Whatever." He spoke from personal experience, having been an attorney for Henry Laurens in several celebrated cases in 1767 and 1768 that resulted from "customs racketeering" by venal crown officers. Rutledge won the suits in which he was involved and successfully sued a customs officer for damages in one of them.[10]

Rutledge was among South Carolina's representatives to the First Continental Congress in 1774. Though firm in defense of colonial rights, he wanted to avoid placing unnecessary obstacles in the way of reconciliation with Britain. Events caused Rutledge to support more radical measures at the Second Continental Congress in 1775, but he continued to hope for reconciliation. He apparently rejected Parliament's power over the colonies completely by May 1775, acknowledging only the king's authority. By October, the dissolution of the colonial government in South Carolina, and rising chaos there and elsewhere, caused him to advocate new, temporary governments based on the people. Having secured Congress's consent, he left Philadelphia to lay the resolution before South Carolina's Second Provincial Congress.[11] When that body met in February 1776, Rutledge served on the drafting committee that wrote the new state constitution. The nineteenth-century historian George Van Santvoord credited him with primary responsibility for creating the document. There is, however, no contemporary evidence of his (or anyone else's) contribution beyond the fact that he wrote the preamble. Rutledge ultimately accepted independence as a necessity but remained a reluctant rebel to the last.[12]

In the meantime, the new General Assembly had elected Rutledge president of South Carolina. Highlights of his administration were successful defenses of Charleston against a British attack from the sea in June 1776, and of the frontier against the Cherokee.[13] Rutledge resigned as president in March 1778, in protest against the legislature's approval of a new state constitution. His principal objections were to the elimination of the president's veto, and to direct popular election of state senators by parish and district, instead of having the lower house choose them at large. These changes, he feared, would alter a mixed government too much in the direction of democracy. Though Rutledge did not detail his objections to democracy, he probably shared a common contemporary view that turbulence, injustice, and susceptibility to the wiles of demagogues had frequently resulted from that form of government in the past. In any case, he did not want to give the upcountry (piedmont) increased influence in state government at the expense of Charleston and the lowcountry.[14]

Rutledge's fall from power was brief. Britain shifted the brunt of its North American war effort to the South late in 1778, overrunning much of Georgia. The legislature returned Rutledge to the governorship in February 1779, hoping that his leadership could preserve the state from invasion as it had in 1776.[15] This time, though, local and Continental military resources were insufficient to resist the increased British pressure. Charleston and the southern Continental Army surrendered after a siege in May 1780.[16]

Governor Rutledge reluctantly had left the city in April, just before the British ring around Charleston tightened. The Continental commander, General Benjamin Lincoln, persuaded him to go in order to organize reinforcements for the relief of the city and to preserve the state government's existence if Charleston fell. The legislature had earlier armed the executive with broad powers to do what was "necessary to secure the peace, safety, and happiness of this State" until the legislators could meet again.[17] Hence Rutledge was able to act as a one-man government of South Carolina while the state was under British occupation.

Rutledge made two trips to Philadelphia in 1780 and 1781 to solicit aid from Congress for the southern theater.[18] He spent the rest of that period with the restored southern Continental Army, reviving his state's militia and trying to supply it and the Continentals. In the summer and fall of 1781, as American forces regained control of most of his state, Rutledge began to reestablish state government. The culmination of his efforts was the election of a new legislature that met at Jacksonborough in January 1782. There Rutledge, who was constitutionally ineligible for another term, relinquished his office.[19]

The Jacksonborough assembly elected Rutledge to Congress, where he served until November 1783. The major issues that he dealt with in Congress were finance, support for the army, and peace terms. Rutledge was especially determined that the United States must have a western boundary on the Mississippi River. He distrusted France, believing correctly that the French favored a line farther east.[20]

Rutledge remained in South Carolina for the next three and a half years. He declined congressional appointments to a special court to decide a Massachusetts–New York boundary dispute, and as minister to the Netherlands.[21] Gout and a serious illness during the war had permanently impaired his health.[22] Moreover, he needed to turn his attention to his personal affairs, sadly neglected in a decade of full-time public service.

Rutledge's plantations, like those of other South Carolinians, had suffered considerable damage during the war. Rebuilding required a substantial investment; Rutledge incurred increased debt. Crops were poor through 1785, and prices suffered from the disruption of old trading patterns.[23] Rutledge's income was further diminished by his not resuming the practice of law. Instead he became one of the judges of the new state Court of Chancery, which exercised equity jurisdiction, mainly involving wills and estates. Unable to rebuild his fortune but continuing to live in a gentleman's style, Rutledge was in deep financial trouble by the late 1780s.[24]

In the South Carolina House of Representatives, Rutledge and his allies were hard pressed to preserve the political dominance of low-country gentlemen. Artisans, mechanics, and some merchants in Charleston unsuccessfully challenged aristocratic domination of the state as contrary to republican principles. The growing upcountry populace demanded legislative reapportionment and removal of the state capital to the interior, achieving the latter but making only modest gains related to the former. Rutledge was critical of the paper-money and debt-relief schemes that the legislature adopted to assuage popular discontent and to save prominent planters and small farmers alike from bankruptcy.[25]

Thus Rutledge had firsthand knowledge of the problems that his state and nation faced in the 1780s. As wartime governor, he experienced the difficulties that resulted from the inability of Congress to raise men and money for the war effort. As a result, he saw the need for a central government capable of providing for the national defense. He became convinced that Congress needed some power to tax. The economic difficulties of the 1780s, both in South Carolina and in the other states, made him and his state willing to give Congress the power to regulate trade in order to counter British commercial restrictions, but only if South Carolina's interests were protected by requiring a two-thirds majority on trade issues and by prohibiting congressional interference with the slave trade. Upcountry discontent, challenges to deferential politics and to lowcountry dominance in

South Carolina, and paper-money and debt-relief schemes portended ill for the future of the republic. John Rutledge probably shared his brother Edward's fear that Shays's Rebellion threatened "a general distribution of property." Gentlemen, Edward Rutledge warned, must rouse themselves "to support the central government."[26] John Rutledge accepted election to the Philadelphia convention of 1787 in the belief that the future of the new nation hung in the balance.

## *The Constitutional Convention*

John Rutledge's role at the Constitutional Convention reflected a political outlook grounded in traditional Anglo-American Whig thinking, adapted to the circumstances of the South Carolina lowcountry gentry. Rutledge's extant writings contain no explanation in any detail of his political ideas. There are only a few brief, general comments reflecting his political theory before 1787. It is clear, though, that in the 1760s he shared the Whig view that the British constitution had reached a high degree of perfection, its excellence resting on a balance of power between King, Lords, and Commons. After independence he advocated a continuation of the principle of balance between branches of governments in a republican political order. In 1778 he wrote that the purpose of government was the people's good, and that form of government was best which made the people most happy. His own preference at that time was for a "compounded or mixed" republic rather than "a simple democracy, or one verging towards it," at the state level. Democracy was at first glance an attractive theory, he noted, but "its effects have been found arbitrary, severe and destructive."[27] To Rutledge, a mixed or balanced republic at the state level implied a strong, independent executive; a legislature of two houses, the upper house more independent of public opinion than the lower; an independent judiciary; and a deferential political order that enabled gentlemen to lead. Balance also included protection for the major interests in society; in a South Carolina context, protection especially for the minority interests of lowcountry planters and merchants. Rutledge adapted these basic concepts to the national level in his view of a proper central government for the United States.

The mix of qualities that Rutledge wanted in the national legislature was "Honesty" in the lower house, "Ability" and experience in the upper.[28] That formula, as applied in state governments, generally implied popular election of at least the lower house, but Rutledge unsuccessfully opposed popular election of either house of the national legislature. The South Carolina delegates at first wanted the state legislatures to elect the lower house, which would then choose the upper house from nominees submitted by the state legislatures. After the convention opted for popular election of the lower house, the delegates moved unsuccessfully that the states be allowed to determine the method of electing the House of Representatives, permitting indirect election in those states that so desired. Rutledge argued that the state legislatures would choose more "proper characters" than the people, and there was no difference in principle. "It was the same thing to act by oneself, and to act by another." This position reflected Rutledge's alarm at the poor performance of overly democratic state governments in the 1780s, and his desire that national legislators be gentlemen of property and ability removed from the pressures of public opinion. For the same reason, he also advocated property qualifications for office and opposed salaries.[29]

However the legislators were chosen, Rutledge and his South Carolina colleagues supported proportional representation of the states in both houses of the national legislature. How to determine the proportion was important to them, since South Carolina was only the seventh largest state in total population, and the ninth in free population, according to the census of 1790.[30] These figures were of course unknown to the delegates, but they had a general idea of the states' relative standing. Very much aware that the Carolinas and Georgia had regional interests in slavery, the slave trade, and commerce to protect, Rutledge worked for a formula that would give the southernmost states as much representation as possible.

Rutledge at first endorsed representation in proportion to the states' "comparative importance," then fought repeatedly for a formula based on state quotas of the national government's expenses or on national taxes paid. "Property was certainly the principal object of Society," he remarked. The theory that wealth and property deserved consideration in representation was widespread in eighteenth-century America, but it had taken especially deep root in the South Carolina lowcountry. The state constitution of 1778 based representation on a combination of population and wealth. That formula gave the lowcountry a majority in the legislature despite the upcountry's growing majority in population. Not fully articulated as of 1787, this low-country view of representation apparently assumed that property deserved special protection; that the major property interests—planters, merchants, lawyers—deserved a share of power that would protect each interest in an equipoise that theoretically promoted harmony and the good of the whole; and that those who supplied the bulk of the tax money for the state's defense and welfare deserved commensurate representation. The deep South was a numerical minority in the United States with special interests to protect, as was the lowcountry in South Carolina. Rutledge and his colleagues at the convention therefore advocated a familiar representation formula for familiar purposes. In the end, they settled for representation based on population, including three-fifths of the slaves.[31] Since slaves were a form of wealth, they found that provision an acceptable compromise, though they were not entirely pleased with it.

Proportional representation in both houses was unacceptable to many delegates from the smaller states. Rutledge was elected to the committee that devised the Great Compromise on representation. He urged "the indispensable necessity of a representation from the states *according to their numbers and wealth*," and was unhappy with the committee's report: proportional representation in the lower house, an equal vote for each state in the upper house, and a provision that money bills must originate in the former and could not be amended in the latter.[32]

Rutledge continued to oppose the Great Compromise on the floor of the convention. He argued again for representation based on wealth, or wealth and population combined. He expressed fear that new, poorer western states could gain a majority in a lower house based solely on population. Again, this argument reflected attitudes formed in lowcountry-upcountry conflicts in South Carolina. As for the Great Compromise's provision regarding money bills, Rutledge believed that it was of no advantage, based "on a blind adherence to the British model" and productive only of conflict in his experience in South Carolina.[33]

The South Carolina delegates voted against the Great Compromise but accepted it once it was adopted. When Virginia's Edmund Randolph and others expressed dissatisfaction and some spoke of adjourning, Rutledge urged that the convention must go on. "Altho' we could not do what we thought best, in itself, we ought to do something" rather than "abandon every thing to hazard." Defects in the plan could be remedied later.[34]

Rutledge favored vesting the executive power in one person. "A single man would feel the greatest responsibility and administer the public affairs best." He first suggested that the upper house of the national legislature alone should choose the executive, a doubly refined choice that would ensure ability, wisdom, and independence from direct pressures of public opinion. Probably, too, Rutledge concurred in his state's initial preference that the executive have a relatively short term and be eligible for reelection. The convention, however, decided that the executive should be chosen by both houses of the national legislature for a seven-year term, and be ineligible to succeed himself. Rutledge supported this arrangement from then on, and opposed the electoral college. He also wanted the executive to have sole responsibility for vetoing bills. The proposal to join the Supreme Court justices with the president in a council of revision to exercise the veto was, he thought, improper. "The Judges ought never to give their opinion on a law till it comes before them."[35]

Rutledge wanted a more restricted federal judiciary than the convention ultimately created. He favored only a single Supreme Court, arguing that inferior federal courts were "an unnecessary encroachment on the jurisdiction of the States." State courts should "decide in all cases in the first instance"; appeals to the Supreme Court would protect the national government's authority. Given that power, though, the judges must be independent. Rutledge opposed a motion to allow the president to remove federal judges from office upon the application of both houses of the national legislature. That would be improper "if the Supreme Court is to judge between the U. S. and particular States." It would influence the judges unduly to favor national power.[36]

Rutledge believed that the powers of the new government, though substantially broadened, should be enumerated. He did not like the sweeping general grant of authority originally contained in the Virginia Plan. Nor was he happy with the proposal that the national legislature be empowered to veto unconstitutional state laws. Rutledge eventually got satisfaction on both points. He successfully advocated replacing the latter provision with one that made the Constitution enforceable as the supreme law of the land. And, as chairman of the Committee of Detail, Rutledge had an important hand in substituting enumerated powers, plus the necessary and proper clause, for the virtually unlimited authority given to Congress in the Virginia Plan.[37]

In general, Rutledge's conception of federalism thus envisioned a central government of enhanced but limited powers, reserving all other powers to the states or the people. His opposition to lower federal courts indicates that he did not want to extend the central government's authority beyond what he believed experience had proven necessary. But there was some room for implied powers in his thinking. He considered a constitutional provision guaranteeing the states against foreign and domestic violence unnecessary. It was "involved in the nature of the thing," he commented, that Congress "had the authority . . . to co-operate with any State in subduing a rebellion."[38]

Chairing the Committee of Detail also gave Rutledge an opportunity to protect his state's particular interests in slaves and commerce against a northern majority in Congress. The committee's report provided that Congress could not abolish or tax the slave trade. A two-thirds majority would be required for passage of navigation acts, and exports could not be taxed at all. These concessions to the lower South proved too much for the majority of the convention to accept. When some delegates spoke against slavery, Rutledge denied that the slave trade raised any issues of "Religion and humanity." It was purely a matter of interest, he maintained. "If the Northern States consult their interest, they will not oppose the increase of Slaves, which will increase the commodities of which they will become the carriers." The southernmost states, he predicted, would not ratify the new constitution "unless their right to import slaves be untouched."[39] Like most South Carolinians, Rutledge was unaffected by the growing opposition to slavery in the northern states and the upper South. He saw slaves simply as productive assets and sources of wealth.

Ultimately, though, Rutledge supported a compromise on these issues. The convention agreed that Congress could prohibit slave importation after 1808, and could tax it up to ten dollars per slave in the meantime. It deleted the two-thirds majority for passage of navigation acts while retaining the prohibition of export taxes. Rutledge remarked that it was important to reopen the British West Indies to American trade, "and a navigation Act was necessary to obtain it. . . . As we are laying the foundation for a great empire, we ought to take a permanent view of the subject and not look at the present moment only."[40]

Rutledge also sought to advance his state's interests by advocating appointment of a committee to consider assumption of state debts by the national government. That was both right and necessary, he argued, since state debts had been "contracted in the common defense," and the states were yielding import duties—"the only sure source of revenue"—to the central government. South Carolina was struggling with a large war debt and stood to gain greatly from this proposal. But, though the convention adopted Rutledge's motion, no constitutional provision resulted.[41]

The final Constitution did not entirely please Rutledge, but he considered it a vast improvement on the Articles of Confederation. His own contribution at the convention was substantial. Two authorities have concluded that only four or five delegates played a greater role at Philadelphia than Rutledge, though several others contributed as much.[42] Rutledge spoke frequently in the debates and was chosen for five committees. His effective chairmanship of the Committee of Detail, his important role in securing the enumeration of congressional powers, the necessary and proper clause, the supremacy clause, and safeguards for the deep South on the slave trade and taxation of exports rank among his more conspicuous contributions to the Constitution. Not the least of his contributions was his frequent role as compromiser, both in word and by force of example. Often Rutledge did not get what he wanted, but he remained satisfied enough to make and urge concessions in the overriding interest of a more effective central government. The one partial exception was Rutledge's strong opposition to the Great Compromise. Once it was adopted, though, Rutledge exerted his influence to calm discontents and ensure a successful conclusion.

When the South Carolina legislature considered the Constitution in January 1788, Rutledge spoke in defense of the provision including treaties in the supreme law of the land. He remarked that the Articles of Confederation were "demonstrably . . . not worth a farthing," while the new system promised a bright future for South Carolina and the nation. As a delegate to the state ratifying convention, Rutledge defended the strength of the Constitution's safeguards against abuses of power by officeholders and argued that rotation in office was unnecessary and undesirable. The convention ratified by a vote of 149 to 73.[43]

## *Later Life and Judicial Career*

When the Constitution took effect, President George Washington offered his old and esteemed friend John Rutledge the senior associate justiceship of the United States Supreme Court in September 1789.[44] Rutledge later said that only Washington's complimentary personal letter, which appealed to his patriotic duty, induced him to resign as chancellor of South Carolina and accept the appointment. Privately, he was disgruntled that he had not been offered the chief justiceship. Rutledge believed that his own legal knowledge and experience gave him a better claim to head the high court than Washington's choice, John Jay.[45] His lack of enthusiasm for the job, combined with his poor health and the rigors of travel on circuit, as well as for sessions of the high court, explains why Rutledge remained on the Court for only a year and a half.

Rutledge made no significant contributions to the Court's work during his short tenure as associate justice. He did not attend its February term in either 1790 or 1791. Rutledge did make the trip to New York for the August 1790 term, but he suffered a painful attack of gout in the capital that prevented his presence at the brief two-day session. Since the Court heard no cases in any of its first three terms, Rutledge's absence was not of vital importance.[46]

Rutledge and Justice James Iredell were assigned to the Southern Circuit—the Carolinas and Georgia—in 1790. They held the first sessions of the Circuit Court in South Carolina and Georgia in the spring of 1790, but the North Carolina court had not yet been organized. Rutledge attended the fall session of the Circuit Court only in South Carolina. He arrived in Savannah for the Georgia session five days late, to find that the district judge had also been absent and Iredell had adjourned the court. Another severe attack of gout prevented him from going on to New Bern for the North Carolina session. The sessions that were held in 1790 were occupied with admitting attorneys and establishing rules of procedure. Like the other early justices, Rutledge, Iredell, and the district court judges who sat with them adopted the rules of the state courts where they met. They went beyond their colleagues in adopting the same principle for equity proceedings as well. No cases were decided on the Southern Circuit during Rutledge's tenure.[47]

Rutledge was involved in one incident of potential importance during his brief stint on the Court. In the fall of 1790, he was one of three justices who granted Robert Morris's request for a writ of certiorari to transfer a suit to which Morris was a party from the North Carolina Superior Court to the U.S. Circuit Court. The case arose from a dispute between Morris and some of his former partners—citizens of a different state—over financial responsibility for a ship that the British had captured during the War for Independence. The justices' action revived Antifederalist fears that the Constitution imperiled state sovereignty by extending federal jurisdiction. Certiorari was by common-law definition an order from a superior to an inferior court based on the latter's presumably improper or biased activity. North Carolinians in general, and Antifederalists elsewhere, could not accept either the inferiority of the highest state court to the U.S. Circuit Court or the implication of impropriety. The North Carolina Superior Court refused to obey the order, denying that the federal courts had any authority in the matter, and the state legislature approved that stand. The federal judges, now unsure of their ground, did not press the issue, and a clash that might have damaged the national judiciary was avoided.[48] Rutledge's action in granting the writ seems inconsistent with his desire at the Constitutional Convention to limit federal jurisdiction. Perhaps he had changed his mind, or perhaps he believed that the Constitution and the Judiciary Act of 1789 authorized the writ and he therefore felt compelled to grant it.

Rutledge resigned from the Supreme Court in March 1791 to become chief justice of the South Carolina Court of Common Pleas and General Sessions.[49] Most of the cases that that court heard were routine. Nevertheless, Rutledge's recorded opinions as chief justice provide some insight into his judicial philosophy.

Rutledge's jurisprudence was rooted in a deep respect for English legal tradition, instilled during his legal education. He wrote in 1769 that Coke's *Institutes* were "almost the foundation of our law," and found Blackstone "useful."[50] Rutledge's judicial opinions generally followed statute law, common law, and precedent. He believed that the courts must follow established legal constructions. Changes in the law were the business of legislatures, and legislators should clearly stipulate any changes that they wanted to make. Rutledge expressed this philosophy in a case involving the order in which the debts of an insolvent estate should be paid. Specifically, were notes of hand in the same category with bonds, or did they fall under the heading of other debts? Rutledge, delivering the unanimous decision of the court, ruled that a conversation among several representatives was inadmissible as evidence of the legislature's intent. "If we once admit of suppositions," Rutledge wrote, "we may suppose anything" about legislative intent; "and one judge may suppose one thing, and another judge another thing. We have no rule to govern us, but, construing the act according to the legal and technical meaning, we stand on firm ground." "The legal and technical meaning" of an act depended on its clear wording and on precedent. "It is of great consequence to every free country, that the laws should be fixed and settled; and that when they are so, and generally known and understood, that they should not be changed by implication, or otherwise than by a clear, express and positive declaration of the will of the legislature." The same philosophy underlay Rutledge's ruling that South Carolina's debt-installment law did not alter the principle of "the common law or statute of frauds" that a judgment for debt was for the whole amount, not just the installments due at the time of the judgment.[51]

*State v. Washington*, Rutledge's first case as chief justice, occasioned perhaps the best extant display of his technical virtuosity in the law. He delivered the court's opinion upholding a conviction for forgery of a state indent and receipt, which had been appealed on the grounds of technical deficiency in the wording of the indictment. The appellant also alleged that indents and receipts were not writings obligatory within the scope of the applicable law. Rutledge's unusually lengthy opinion was notable for its close and detailed reasoning on the technical issues and its careful application of common law and precedent. He also emphasized that the jury was the judge of fact—including, in this case, the intent to defraud—and the court could not question the jury's decision on matters of fact.[52]

A few of Rutledge's rulings departed from his usual judicial philosophy. He occasionally decided exceptional cases on the basis of equity or practical political considerations. There was, for example, the case of a slave woman who was allowed to find her own employment and keep her earnings after paying her owner a fixed sum. When the woman used her money to buy a slave girl in order to set her free, the woman's master claimed ownership of the girl. Legally, he argued, a slave's property belonged to her master. Rutledge instructed the jury that the master had received the stipulated income from his slave woman. He was entitled to no more, and the jury should not "do such manifest violence to so singular and extraordinary an act of benevolence." His instructions rested on principles of equity, which counsel for the defense had argued should override the letter of the law in this case.[53] Though Rutledge never questioned the legitimacy of slavery—indeed, he fought hard to protect it during the Federal Convention of 1787—he could apparently be touched on occasion by manifest injustice to an individual slave.

Political considerations influenced Rutledge when a former Loyalist sought a new trial to regain ownership of a slave taken and sold by patriot militia under what the militia termed "Sumter's law" during the war. Twice before, judges had given jury charges favoring the Loyalist, and twice juries had returned contrary verdicts in an apparent display of bias against Tories. The court granted the motion for a third trial, but Rutledge dissented. "As this was a dispute about property taken during the war, it was best that there should be an end of it," he remarked.[54] The War for Independence in South Carolina had included a bitter civil war between patriots and Loyalists, especially in 1780 and 1781, that left lasting enmities among many of the state's citizens. Rutledge believed it prudent to let this case rest.

Rutledge's life outside the courtroom in the early 1790s became emotionally troubled. He sank into a depression so deep as to produce erratic and sometimes deranged behavior. His emotional problems apparently became serious after two deaths in 1792. On April 22 Rutledge's mother, Sarah Hext Rutledge, passed away at sixty-eight. Some six weeks later, on June 6, his wife, Elizabeth, died after a brief illness.[55]

Rutledge was a "remarkably domestic" man who found his greatest pleasure "at his own fireside." The loss in quick succession of the two most important women in his life, especially his wife's sudden passing, was a terrible blow to him. Rutledge withdrew into lengthy periods of silent, solitary mourning. According to Ralph Izard, "After the death of his Wife, his mind was frequently so much deranged, as to be in a great measure deprived of his senses."[56]

Bereavement was not the only source of Rutledge's depression. His physical health remained shaky, and his financial situation continued to deteriorate. He realized that his debts were unpayable and all of his property would likely be lost. His eldest son, John Rutledge, Jr., and his brothers, Edward and Hugh Rutledge, became deeply involved by assuming obligations for his debts. Much of Rutledge's property went to John Jr. and Edward in the 1790s to compensate them for their assistance, perhaps to the dismay of other creditors. But it was not enough.[57] In or before March 1795, Rutledge executed a deed of trust that gave Hugh Rutledge and John Rutledge, Jr., the power to receive his income and sell his remaining property, using the proceeds to pay his debts and reimburse the son for payments he had made for his father. Rutledge almost immediately regretted the deed, but the trust remained in effect at least into 1797.[58] To be so dependent on his family was a serious blow to the personal morale of this proud aristocrat.

In his depression, Rutledge's behavior became erratic. Charlestonian William Read referred in 1795 to Rutledge's "mad frollicks and inconsistent conduct." It also was reported at that time that "several Grand Juries" had presented Rutledge "for what they thought Misconduct or at least Negligence of his Duty." The presentments of which evidence survives, though, were for tardiness, not conduct on the bench.[59] As far as can be determined from the limited extant evidence, Rutledge was a capable chief justice of South Carolina despite his emotional problems outside court. Indeed, that post of honor and responsibility was one of the few things that sustained a degree of personal morale for him.

By June 1795, Rutledge had learned that a position of greater honor and responsibility would soon be vacant. John Jay had been elected governor of New York, which would require him to resign as chief justice of the United States. Rutledge wrote to George Washington to inform the president that he was available for the post he had desired six years earlier. He still wanted it to cap his career, erase his previous disappointment, and boost his morale. Rutledge was not unaware of the strain that the job would impose on his ailing physique, but a 1793 revision of the Judiciary Act of 1789 that required each justice to ride circuit only once a year instead of twice allowed him to hope that he would be able to perform the requisite duties.[60]

Washington received Rutledge's letter and Jay's resignation on the same day: June 30, 1795. Apparently unaware of Rutledge's emotional problems, the president immediately appointed him chief justice.[61] It was a recess appointment, the Senate having recently adjourned until December.

Before adjourning, on June 24, the Senate ratified the treaty that Jay had brought back from Britain earlier in the year. The vote was 20 to 10, following strict party lines. When the treaty's previously secret terms became public, there was a strong and widespread negative reaction to an agreement that many considered one-sided and damaging to the interests and honor of the United States. The Rutledge brothers, who had been strongly anti-British since the War for Independence, were among the leaders of public protest against the treaty in South Carolina.

After several days of crowd demonstrations in the streets of Charleston, Rutledge made an impassioned speech against the treaty at a public meeting on July 16. He probably had not yet learned of his appointment to the chief justiceship. Having denounced the treaty in the strongest terms, Rutledge angrily declaimed that "he had rather the President should die, dearly as he loves him, than he should sign that treaty."[62]

The speech, made in the context of disorderly public protests, shocked Federalists and contributed greatly to a rising opposition to Rutledge's confirmation as chief justice. Hitherto seen as a reliable Federalist, Rutledge was suddenly tied in Federalist minds to a chain of threats running from the Genet affair, the Democratic-Republican Societies, and the Whiskey Rebellion to the current Democratic-Republican challenge over the Jay Treaty. "C[hief] Justices," wrote John Adams, "must not go to illegal Meetings and become popular orators in favour of Sedition, nor inflame the popular discontents which are ill founded, nor propagate Disunion, Division, Contention, and delusion among the People."[63]

This politically motivated opposition strengthened objections to Rutledge that already had arisen from questions about his character and competence. It was reported widely, and apparently with considerable truth, that Rutledge was "deranged in his mind," frequently drunk, indecorous in public, and unethical in his financial dealings. If true, these reports alone disqualified him for high office in the opinion of men like Alexander Hamilton.[64] Federalists believed that an experimental new government needed gentlemen of influence, character, and ability in positions of leadership to help it survive challenges from a disorderly populace infected with French revolutionary ideas. Rutledge shared the Federalist belief in elite leadership, but Federalists saw his conduct as a betrayal of them and of his own principles. Political opposition to the nomination and doubts about Rutledge's personal fitness to serve were inseparably intertwined. Rutledge's derangement, some Federalists thought, explained his Jay Treaty speech, and "the crazy speech" proved his mental incapacity.[65]

Despite the controversy swirling around him, Rutledge behaved with dignity when he went to Philadelphia to preside as interim chief justice over the August term of the Supreme Court. He participated in two decisions, both involving the legality of ship seizures by French privateers. In *Talbot v. Jansen*, Rutledge concurred with a unanimous Court in invalidating the capture of a Dutch ship by what was ruled to be an American vessel fraudulently operating as a French privateer. The ship, he ruled, was illegally fitted out in the United States, and its prize was taken in violation of international law and of United States treaty obligations to Holland. The decision supported Washington administration neutrality policy that French privateers could not be fitted out and manned in U.S. ports. In *United States v. Peters*, he delivered the majority decision that a French privateer could not be detained in a United States port by order of a federal court to answer for the legality of a seizure made on the high seas and taken to a French port. The trial of prizes and application of international law in such a case lay exclusively with French courts.[66] These cases contributed to the definition of United States maritime and neutrality law.

Rutledge continued to behave circumspectly through the fall of 1795 as the controversy over his nomination mounted. He would not recant his opposition to the Jay Treaty, but he kept quiet and lived "very much retired" until he embarked on his fall tour of the Southern Circuit. He participated in fifteen decisions, mostly involving ship seizures, at the Charleston session of the Court from October 26 to November 5. Despite poor health, he journeyed on to Augusta, Georgia, but could do no business there because the district judge was absent, the clerk had died, and the records were not available. Rutledge then set out for Raleigh, North Carolina, the last stop on the circuit. On November 21, a few hours after he left Evans Tavern on Lynch's Creek, he became too ill to go on. After recuperating for a while at Evans's, he headed for home.[67]

This experience forced Rutledge to face the fact that he was not physically equal to the demands of Supreme Court service. That realization gave a final, crushing blow to his already depressed spirits. He had lost his wife, his mother, much of his property, and control over what property remained. Already dependent on his brothers and eldest son, he faced the prospective loss of all of his property and with it the remnants of the personal independence that eighteenth-century gentlemen so highly valued. The public attacks on his character had badly damaged his reputation, and his confirmation as chief justice was very much in doubt. Now he knew that he could not do the job in any case. The proud aristocrat concluded that he had no reason to live. He attempted suicide by drowning at Camden on the way home. Rutledge's family watched him closely to prevent another suicide attempt, but they were not vigilant enough. On December 26 or 27, he left home before dawn and again tried to drown himself in the Ashley River. Blacks working nearby rescued him despite his protests.[68]

After this second failure to take his own life, Rutledge became calm and rational. On December 28, 1795, he resigned as chief justice, stating that he had found his health "totally unequal to the discharge of the duties of the Office." He apparently had not yet learned that the Senate had rejected his nomination by a vote of 14 to 10 on December 15. It was a straight party-line vote that reproduced the alignment on the Jay Treaty, except for the Federalist senator Jacob Read of South Carolina, who voted to confirm Rutledge in the belief that his rejection would badly damage the Federalist Party in his state.[69] Doubts about Rutledge's personal fitness to serve and political considerations were both important to the outcome—and inextricably linked—but the vote suggests that the political factor was the stronger one.

The Senate's vote was significant as a reflection of party conflict and ideology in the 1790s. Its importance for the subsequent history of the Supreme Court is debatable. One scholar has argued that had Rutledge been confirmed, and had he remained in office until his death in 1800, Oliver Ellsworth would not have been chief justice in the late 1790s, and the timing of Rutledge's death would have made John Marshall's appointment as his successor unlikely.[70] That conclusion is questionable. If in fact Rutledge resigned before learning of the Senate's vote on his confirmation, the outcome of that vote was irrelevant to the subsequent personnel of the Court. Washington would have had to appoint a new chief justice early in 1796 even if Rutledge's nomination had been confirmed. Presumably, the result would have been the same, and subsequent judicial history would have been unaffected. Whether or not Rutledge would have resigned for health reasons if there had been no opposition to his confirmation is, of course, another question.

Rutledge remained rational after his 1795 suicide attempts. He lived in seclusion for more than two years, preoccupied with his debts for at least part of that period. At some time after August 1797, he resumed control of his own financial affairs. In May 1798 he suddenly returned to society in a burst of high spirits. Rutledge's improved mood did not reflect a change in his fortunes. Between 1798 and 1800, forty-one judgments for debt were entered against him in the Charleston District Court of Common Pleas. But locally, at least, his name continued to command respect. He was elected to the state House of Representatives in a December 1798 special election to fill a vacancy from Charleston. He died on July 18, 1800.[71]

## *Conclusion*

John Rutledge's major contribution to the constitutional history of the United States was his significant role at the Philadelphia convention of 1787. As chairman of the Committee of Detail, he had much to do with the enumeration of Congress's powers and insertion of the necessary and proper clause. He fought, with partial success, to secure the interests of the southernmost states on slavery, the slave trade, and commercial matters. He had an important hand in securing the Constitution's supremacy clause. His willingness to compromise his desires helped to ensure the success of the convention.

Rutledge decided no cases during his service as associate justice of the United States Supreme Court in 1790 and 1791. His contribution during that period was to help open and organize the Circuit Court in South Carolina and Georgia. As interim chief justice in 1795, Rutledge participated in two cases, both involving ship seizures. Although his role was not pivotal, his opinions helped define United States law on neutrality and maritime issues, and supported the Washington administration's neutrality policy.

The best expositions of Rutledge's judicial philosophy were contained in his opinions on the South Carolina bench. There his jurisprudence reflected adherence to common law, statute law, and precedent. Established legal constructions, he believed, should be upheld; the courts should leave legal innovation to legislators, in the belief that fixed and known laws were important to liberty. Together with his role at the Federal Convention of 1787, Rutledge's greatest services came in the Continental and Confederation Congresses, and in all three branches of colonial and state government. His two terms as wartime chief executive of South Carolina stand out among his contributions at the state level. History has generally given him due credit for his achievements.

## NOTES

1. Helen Kohn Hennig, *Great South Carolinians; From Colonial Days to the Confederate War* (Chapel Hill: University of North Carolina Press, 1940; reprint, Freeport, N.Y.: Books for Libraries, 1970), 123–24; Henry Flanders, *The Lives and Times of the Chief Justices of the Supreme Court of the United States*, vol. 1 (Philadelphia: T. & J. W. Johnson & Co., 1881), 477–78, 481; Liste des Membres et Officiers du Congres, 1788, Max Farrand, ed., *The Records of the Federal Convention of 1787*, rev. ed., 4 vols. (New Haven: Yale University Press, 1940), 3:238.

2. Flanders, *Lives of Chief Justices*, 1:600–601; David Ramsay, *The History of South Carolina, from Its First Settlement in 1670, to the Year 1808*, 2 vols. (Charleston, S.C.: David Longworth, 1809), 2:271.

3. Flanders, *Lives of Chief Justices*, 1:478.

4. Alexander Garden, *Anecdotes of the Revolutionary War . . .* (Charleston, S.C.: A. E. Walker, 1822), 176; Charles Fraser, *Reminiscences of Charleston . . .* (Charleston, S.C.: Garnier & Co., 1854), 71.

5. Notes from Anna Wells Rutledge, Aug. 4, 1977, Rutledge file, genealogical materials, South Carolina Historical Society, Charleston (hereafter SCHS); Ramsay, *History of South Carolina*, 2:269.

6. Walter B. Edgar and N. Louise Bailey, *Biographical Directory of the South Carolina House of Representatives*, vol. 2 (Columbia: University of South Carolina Press, 1977), 571–73, 576–77; Colonial Plats, 1:305, South Carolina Department of Archives and History, Columbia (hereafter SCAr); Robert Johnson to Peter Lehup, Oct. 29, 1732, quoted in Hoyt P. Canady, Jr., *Gentlemen of the Bar: Lawyers in Colonial South Carolina* (New York: Garland Publishing, 1987), 298; wills of Hugh Hext, Will Book 3:12–15, and of Sarah Fenwick, Will Book 2:55–57, Probate Court, Charleston County Courthouse, Charleston, S.C.

7. Hennig, *Great South Carolinians*, 109; Flanders, *Lives of Chief Justices*, 1:436; Canady, *Gentlemen of Bar*, 182; Edgar and Bailey, *Biographical Directory*, 2:578.

8. Judgment Rolls, Court of Common Pleas, SCAr; Ramsay, *History of South Carolina*, 2:269; Canady, *Gentlemen of Bar*, 272, 274, 276–78, 291; "Journal of Josiah Quincy, Junior, 1773," *Massachusetts Historical Society Proceedings* 49

(1915–1916): 446–47; Mabel L. Webber, "Dr. John Rutledge and His Descendants," *South Carolina Historical & Genealogical Magazine* 31 (1930): 17–19; Edgar and Bailey, *Biographical Directory*, 2:578.

9. Edgar and Bailey, *Biographical Directory*, 2:580–81; Jack P. Greene, *The Quest for Power; The Lower Houses of Assembly in the Southern Royal Colonies, 1689–1776* (Chapel Hill: University of North Carolina Press for the Institute of Early American History and Culture, 1963), 485; Commons House of Assembly Journals, 1761–1775, SCAr.

10. Silas Deane, Diary, [Oct. 5, 1774], Paul H. Smith, ed., *Letters of Delegates to Congress, 1774–1789*, 22 vols. to date (Washington, D.C.: Library of Congress, 1976–), 1:144; Oliver M. Dickerson, *The Navigation Acts and the American Revolution* (Philadelphia: University of Pennsylvania Press, 1951), 208–26; Philip M. Hamer et al., *The Papers of Henry Laurens*, 13 vols. to date (Columbia: University of South Carolina Press for the South Carolina Historical Society, 1968–), 5: 283–84, 396–400, 464, 679–80, 722–23; 6:5n, 31, 295–383, 400, 455–567; 7:96; *South Carolina Gazette* (Charleston), Sept. 7, 21, 1767, July 11, 18, 1768.

11. James Haw, "The Rutledges, the Continental Congress, and Independence," *South Carolina Historical Magazine* 94 (1993): 233–43.

12. Ibid., 243, 249; Feb. 11, 1776, William Edwin Hemphill and Wylma Anne Waites, eds., *Extracts from the Journals of the Provincial Congresses of South Carolina, 1775–1776* (Columbia: South Carolina Archives Department, 1960), 185; George Van Santvoord, *Sketches of the Lives and Judicial Services of the Chief-Justices of the Supreme Court of the United States* (New York: Charles Scribner, 1854), 110; Draft of Temporary Constitution, Mar. 26, 1776, South Carolina Papers, South Caroliniana Library, University of South Carolina, Columbia.

13. Henry Lumpkin, *From Savannah to Yorktown: The American Revolution in the South* (Columbia: University of South Carolina Press, 1981), 10–26; William Moultrie, *Memoirs of the American Revolution . . .*, vol. 2 (New York: David Longworth, 1802; reprint, New York: Arno Press, 1968), 282–84.

14. David Ramsay, *The History of the Revolution of South-Carolina, from a British Province to an Independent State*, vol. 1 (Trenton, N.J.: Isaac Collins, 1785), 132–38; Jerome J. Nadelhaft, *The Disorders of War: The Revolution in South Carolina* (Orono: University of Maine at Orono Press, 1981), 38.

15. *South Carolina & American General Gazette* (Charleston), Feb. 11, 1779.

16. Lumpkin, *Savannah to Yorktown*, 41–49.

17. Moultrie, *Memoirs*, 2:105; James Duane to George Washington, May 9, 1780, Smith, ed., *Letters of Delegates*, 15:97–98; William Edwin Hemphill, Wylma Anne Waites, and Nicholas Olsberg, eds., *Journals of the General Assem-*

*bly and House of Representatives, 1776–1780* (Columbia: University of South Carolina Press for the South Carolina Department of Archives and History, 1970), 252, 268.

18. J. Rutledge to Horatio Gates, July 4, 1780, Gates Papers, New York Historical Society, and to S. C. Delegates in Congress, Mar. 8, 1781, "Letters of John Rutledge," annotated by Joseph W. Barnwell, *South Carolina Historical & Genealogical Magazine* 18 (1917): 135–36.

19. The sources on Rutledge's activities in 1780 and 1781 are too numerous and scattered to detail here. They are fully documented in my book *John and Edward Rutledge of South Carolina* (Athens: University of Georgia Press, 1997).

20. A. S. Salley, ed., *Journal of the House of Representatives of South Carolina, January 8, 1782–February 26, 1782* (Columbia: Historical Commission of South Carolina, 1916), 38. The principal sources on Rutledge's congressional service are Worthington Chauncey Ford, ed., *Journals of the Continental Congress, 1774–1789*, 34 vols. (Washington, D.C.: Government Printing Office, 1904–1937), vols. 22–24, and Smith, ed., *Letters of Delegates*, vol. 19.

21. Ford, ed., *Journals of Congress*, 27:710, 29:497; Richard Henry Lee to J. Rutledge, Jan. 24, 1785, J. Rutledge to President of Congress, Mar. 26, Aug. 1, 1785, Papers of the Continental Congress, National Archives, Washington, D.C.

22. Nathanael Greene to Henry Lee, Aug. 19, 1781, in Henry Lee, *The Campaign of 1781 in the Carolinas . . .* (Philadelphia: n. p., 1824; reprint, Chicago: Quadrangle Books, 1962), appendix, xvi; John Sandford Dart to Thomas Sumter, Sep. 14, 1781, Thomas Sumter Papers, Library of Congress, Washington, D.C.; Van Santvoord, *Sketches of Chief-Justices*, 187; J. Rutledge to Jacob Read, [Jan. 26, 1783], Edmund C. Burnett, ed., *Letters of Members of the Continental Congress*, 10 vols. (Washington, D.C.: Carnegie Institution, 1921–1936; reprint, Gloucester, Mass.: Peter Smith, 1963), 7:200.

23. Reports of Senate Committee, Dec. 17, 1791, and House Committee, Dec. 13, 1791, on Petition of J. Rutledge, General Assembly Papers, ser. 4, 1791, no. 24, 60, SCAr; Edward Rutledge to John Rutledge, Jr., Nov. 1, 1797, John Rutledge Jr. Papers, Duke University, Durham, N.C.; Charles Gregg Singer, *South Carolina in the Confederation* (Philadelphia: University of Pennsylvania Press, 1941), 14, 17–20, 22, 24.

24. Van Santvoord, *Sketches of Chief-Justices*, 152–53; Liste des Membres et Officiers du Congres, 1788, Farrand, ed., *Records*, 3:238.

25. The best source on the 1780s is Nadelhaft, *Disorders of War*. For Rutledge's role, see the published journals of the House of Representatives and the Charleston newspapers for the period.

26. Lark Emerson Adams and Rosa Stoney Lumpkin, eds., *Journals of the House of Representatives, 1785–1786* (Columbia: University of South Carolina Press for the South Carolina Department of Archives and History, 1979), 349, 370, 382–83, 396, 398; Nadelhaft, *Disorders of War*, 174; *Charleston Evening*

*Gazette*, Oct. 5, 1785, Feb. 8, 1786; E. Rutledge to Jeremiah Wadsworth, Oct. 21, 1786, cited in Richard Brent Clow, "Edward Rutledge of South Carolina, 1749–1800: Unproclaimed Statesman" (Ph. D. diss., University of Georgia, 1976), 228–29.

27. J. Rutledge to E. Rutledge, July 30, 1769, in Rev. J. Adams, *Laws of Success and Failure in Life . . .* (Charleston, S.C.: A. E. Miller, 1833), 51; Ramsay, *History of Revolution of South Carolina*, 1:136–37; Speech of J. Rutledge, Mar. 5, 1778, Christopher Gadsden Papers, South Caroliniana Library, University of South Carolina.

28. James H. Hutson, ed., *Supplement to Max Farrand's The Records of the Federal Convention of 1787* (New Haven: Yale University Press, 1987), 109; Farrand, ed., *Records*, 2:279.

29. Farrand, ed., *Records*, 1:50, 52, 130–32, 353–54, 359, 364–65, 216, 392, 420, 426–27, 2:249, 251; Hutson, ed., *Supplement*, 71.

30. Carl Van Doren, *The Great Rehearsal; The Story of the Making and Ratifying of the Constitution of the United States* (New York: Viking, 1948), 16 n.

31. Farrand, ed., *Records*, 1:163, 192–93, 196, 201, 534, 536–37, 582, 586.

32. Ibid., 509, 516, 522–23.

33. Ibid., 534, 571, 582, 2:279–80.

34. Ibid., 1:549, 2:13–15, 17–20.

35. Ibid., 1:65, 68–69, 79, 81, 88, 230, 2:22–24, 50–51, 57, 61–62, 64, 66, 68, 70–71, 80, 97, 116–18, 121–22, 511.

36. Ibid., 1:119, 124–25, 2:428.

37. Ibid., 1:53–54, 164, 168, 2:17, 22, 24, 28, 95, 97, 181–83, 390–91.

38. Ibid., 2:48.

39. Ibid., 2:183, 364, 373.

40. Ibid., 366, 374, 396, 408, 446–49, 452.

41. Ibid., 322, 324, 327.

42. Clinton Rossiter, *1787: The Grand Convention* (New York: Macmillan, 1966), 247–49; Max Farrand, *The Framing of the Constitution of the United States* (New Haven: Yale University Press, 1913), 196–99.

43. David Ramsay to Benjamin Rush, Feb. 17, 1788, Robert L. Brunhouse, ed., "David Ramsay on the Ratification of the Constitution in South Carolina, 1787–1788," *Journal of Southern History* 9 (1948): 553; Jonathan Elliot, ed., *The Debates in the Several State Conventions on the Adoption of the Federal Constitution . . .*, 2nd ed., vol. 4 (Philadelphia: J. D. Lippincott, 1888; reprint, New York: Burt Franklin, 1974), 267–68, 311–12; *City Gazette* (Charleston), May 20, 21, 16, 1788.

44. Washington to J. Rutledge, Sept. 29, 1789, Maeva Marcus and James R. Perry, eds., *The Documentary History of the Supreme Court of the United States, 1789–1800*, 5 vols. to date (New York: Columbia University Press, 1985–), 1:20 (hereafter *DHSC*).

45. Rutledge to Washington, Oct. 27, 1789, June 12, 1795, *DHSC*, 1:22, 94–95. For his resignation as chancellor, J. Rutledge to Gov. Charles Pinckney, Dec. 17, 1789, General Assembly Papers, ser. 6, no. 512, SCAr.

46. Fine minutes of Supreme Court, 1790–1791, James Iredell to John Jay, William Cushing, and James Wilson, Feb. 11, 1791, and Richard Nichols Harison to Robert Morris, Sept. 7, 1790, *DHSC*, 1:171–91, 2:132, 87; William Loughton Smith to E. Rutledge, July 30, 1790, William Loughton Smith Papers, SCHS.

47. Minute books, U.S. Circuit Courts for N.C., S.C., Ga., Federal Record Center, East Point, Ga.; *City Gazette*, Oct. 26, 29, 1790; J. Iredell to Hannah Iredell, Oct. 30, 1790, *DHSC*, 2:103–4; Julius Goebel, Jr., *The Oliver Wendell Holmes Devise History of the Supreme Court of the United States: Antecedents and Beginnings to 1801* (New York: Macmillan, 1971), 580–81.

48. Wythe Holt and James R. Perry, "Writs and Rights, 'clashings and animosities': The First Confrontation between Federal and State Jurisdictions," *Law and History Review* 7 (1989): 89–120.

49. Rutledge to Washington, Mar. 5, 1791, *DHSC*, 1:23.

50. J. Rutledge to E. Rutledge, July 30, 1769, Adams, *Laws of Success*, 51.

51. *Executors of Rippon v. Executors of Townsend* (1795), *Tucker v. Lowndes* (1791), Elihu Hall Bay, *Reports of Cases Argued and Determined in the Superior Courts of Law in the State of South Carolina, since the Revolution*, vol. 1 (New York: I. Riley, 1809), 445, 213–14.

52. *State v. Washington* (1791), 1 Bay 120.

53. *The Guardian of Sally, a Negro, v. Beatty* (1792), 1 Bay 260.

54. *Administrators of Moore v. Cherry* (1792), 1 Bay 269.

55. Webber, "Dr. John Rutledge," 15, 18; *City Gazette*, Apr. 27, 1792; Smith to E. Rutledge, Feb. 13, 1792, George C. Rogers, ed., "The Letters of William Loughton Smith to Edward Rutledge, June 6, 1789 to April 28, 1794," *South Carolina Historical Magazine* 69 (1968): 236; Flanders, *Lives of Chief Justices*, 1:628.

56. Flanders, *Lives of Chief Justices*, 1:628, 631; Mary Bray Wheeler and Genon Hickerson Neblett, *Chosen Exile: The Life and Times of Septima Sexta Middleton Rutledge, American Cultural Pioneer* (Nashville: Rutledge Hill Press, 1980), 18, 33; Izard to Read, Nov. 17, 1795, *DHSC*, 1:807.

57. J. Rutledge, Jr., memorandum, May 1797, and E. Rutledge to J. Rutledge, Jr., Apr. 24, 1794, John Rutledge Jr. Papers, Duke University; Charleston County Court of Equity Bills, 1803, no. 29, SCAr.

58. Account of J. Rutledge with J. Rutledge, Jr., n. d., with J. Rutledge, Jr.'s notation, May 1797, and J. Rutledge, Jr., memo and statement of accounts, May 1797, John Rutledge, Jr. Papers, Duke University.

59. William Read to J. Read, July 27, 1795, Read Family Correspondence, SCHS; J. Adams to Abigail Adams, Dec. 21, 1795, *DHSC*, 1:816; for references

to presentments, John C. Meleney, *The Public Life of Aedanus Burke: Revolutionary Republican in Post Revolutionary South Carolina* (Columbia: University of South Carolina Press, 1989), 245, and John Belton O'Neall, *Biographical Sketches of the Bench and Bar of South Carolina*, vol. 1 (Charleston, S.C.: S. G. Courtney & Co., 1859), 26–27.

60. J. Rutledge to Washington, June 12, 1795, *DHSC*, 1:94–95; Charles Warren, *The Supreme Court in United States History*, rev. ed., vol. 1 (Boston: Little, Brown, 1937), 89.

61. Washington to J. Rutledge, July 1, 1795, *DHSC*, 1:96–97.

62. George S. McCowan, Jr., "Chief Justice John Rutledge and the Jay Treaty," *South Carolina Historical & Genealogical Magazine* 62 (1961): 13–14; Flanders, *Lives of Chief Justices*, 1:633; W. Read to J. Read, July 21, 1795, Read Family Correspondence, SCHS; *South Carolina State Gazette* (Charleston), July 17, 1795, *DHSC*, 1:765–67.

It is not entirely clear when Rutledge learned of his appointment. Leon Friedman, "John Rutledge," in Leon Friedman and Fred L. Israel, eds., *The Justices of the United States Supreme Court, 1789–1969: Their Lives and Major Opinions*, vol. 1 (New York: R. R. Bowker, 1969), 45, calculates that Rutledge should have heard of the appointment before the speech. Edmund Randolph to Washington, July 29, 1795, *DHSC*, 1:773, agreed. Warren, *Supreme Court*, 1:129, states that Rutledge received his commission on July 24, after the speech. W. Read to J. Read, July 21 and 27, 1795, Read Family Correspondence, SCHS, supports Warren. Read commented on the speech in both letters but reacted to the appointment only in the second one.

63. J. Adams to A. Adams, Dec. 17, 1795, *DHSC*, 1:813.

64. Randolph to Washington, July 25, 1795, William Vans Murray to James McHenry, Dec. 24, 1795, Stephen Higginson to Timothy Pickering, Aug. 29, 1795, J. Adams to A. Adams, Dec. 21, 1795, A. Adams to John Quincy Adams, Nov. 29, 1795, *Columbian Centinel* (Boston), Aug. 26, 1795, *Aurora* (Philadelphia), Oct. 20, 1795, Alexander Hamilton to Rufus King, Dec. 14, 1795, ibid., 772, 817, 793, 816, 819, 784–86, 804–5, 811–12.

65. William Bradford, Jr., to Hamilton, Aug. 4, 1795, Randolph to Washington, July 29, 1795, ibid., 775, 773.

66. Pierce Butler to Aedanus Burke, Oct. 10, 1795, Pierce Butler Letterbook, 1794–1822, Historical Society of Pennsylvania, Philadelphia; Flanders, *Lives of Chief Justices*, 1:640; *United States v. Peters* (1795) and *Talbot v. Jansen* (1795), A. J. Dallas, *Reports of Cases Ruled and Adjudged in the Several Courts of the United States . . .*, 2nd ed., vol. 3 (New York: Banks Publishing Co., 1899), 121, 131; William R. Casto, *The Supreme Court in the Early Republic: The Chief Justiceships of John Jay and Oliver Ellsworth* (Columbia: University of South Carolina Press, 1995), 77, 113.

67. W. Read to J. Read, Sep. 10, Nov. 25, 1795, Read Family Correspon-

dence, SCHS; *City Gazette*, Nov. 6, 1795; Minutes, U.S. Circuit Court for S.C., Federal Record Center, East Point, Ga.; J. Rutledge to Washington, Dec. 28, 1795, *Aurora*, Dec. 23, 1795, *DHSC*, 3:84–86, 1:810.

68. J. Adams to A. Adams, Dec. 21, 1795, W. Read to J. Read, Dec. 29, 1795, *Columbian Centinel*, Jan. 6, 1796, Robert Lindsay to Samuel Johnson, Jan. 13, 1796, *Federal Gazette* (Baltimore), Jan. 8, 1796, *Aurora*, Feb. 3, 1796, *DHSC*, 1:816, 820–21, 824, 831, 822, 826.

69. W. Read to J. Read, Dec. 29, 1795, J. Rutledge to Washington, Dec. 28, 1795, Senate Executive Journal, Dec. 15, 1795, ibid., 820, 100, 98–99.

70. Warren, *Supreme Court*, 1:139.

71. W. Read to J. Read, Aug. 19, 1796, Read Family Correspondence, SCHS; W. Smith to King, July 23, 1796, quoted in George C. Rogers, Jr., *Evolution of a Federalist: William Loughton Smith of Charleston (1758–1812)* (Columbia: University of South Carolina Press, 1962), 288; E. Rutledge to Henry Middleton Rutledge, Nov. 1, 1796, Dreer Collection, Historical Society of Pennsylvania; J. Rutledge, Jr. to Robert Smith, Apr. 1, 1798, Mar. 4, 1800, and Frederick Rutledge to J. Rutledge, Jr., Mar. 21, 1800, John Rutledge, Jr. Papers, Southern Historical Collection, University of North Carolina, Chapel Hill; J. Iredell to H. Iredell, May 8, 11–12, 18, 1798, *DHSC*, 3:263–65, 272–73; Judgment Rolls, 1798–1800, Charleston District Court of Common Pleas, SCAr; *City Gazette*, Dec. 10, 11, 12, 1798, July 24, 1800.

*Chapter 4*

# Deconstructing William Cushing

*Scott Douglas Gerber*

## *Structuralism: The Dan Quayle of the Early American Republic*

### Encyclopedia-Style Biographical Entry

William Cushing was born on March 1, 1732, in Scituate, Massachusetts, into one of the oldest and most powerful families in the colony. His maternal grandfather, Josiah Cotton, was a county judge and member of the General Court, as well as a grandson of the Reverend John Cotton, the theological giant of seventeenth-century Massachusetts. On his father's side, the family descended from Matthew Cushing, who settled in Hingham, Massachusetts, in 1638, and was ancestor of Thomas, Caleb, and Luther S. Cushing. William Cushing's grandfather and father both served as members of the Governor's Council and of the Superior Court of Judicature, the highest court in the province. Cushing graduated from Harvard College in

I like to think of this essay as an exercise in "small 'd'" deconstruction. What I mean by that is the essay attempts to reverse and resituate the existing conceptual priorities upon which the various orderings and evaluations of William Cushing thrive without forcing the reader to endure yet another exercise in postmodern criticism with its attendant—often impenetrable—jargon. I thank Jim Miclot, John Osborn, Scott Roulier, Mary Ann Tetreault, and Bill Weaver, each of whom is skilled in the methodology of postmodern theory, for their help in this regard. Thanks also to Todd Ellinwood for his research assistance, to Mark Hall for his twice reading the essay, to George Billias for his suggestions about historiography, to Bill Casto for his thoughts on textualism, and to Donald Dewey and Herb Johnson for their strong support. For an example of the variety of deconstruction I attempt here, see Mary Ann Tetreault, "Deconstructing the Other: Teaching Politics of the Middle East," *PS: Political Science & Politics* 29 (December 1996): 696–700.

1751, studied law in the office of a distinguished Boston attorney, and was admitted to the bar in 1755.

After practicing law briefly in his hometown of Scituate, Cushing relocated to Pownalborough (now Dresden) in the district of Maine. Before the move, he was commissioned as justice of the peace and judge of probates for newly-created Lincoln County. As one commentator succinctly puts it, "From this modest beginning developed a judicial career of a full half century's span, which was to include service in nine separate judicial positions and embrace the cause of justice for the British Crown, a Revolutionary province, a free Commonwealth, and finally, the United States."[1] Why a man from so prominent a family would choose to bury himself in the frontier is unclear. Cushing's critics maintain that it was because he was not very bright. His supporters suggest that it had more to do with his desire to make a reputation of his own.[2]

Cushing returned from Maine in 1771. The occasion for his return was his father's retirement from the Massachusetts Superior Court of Judicature and William's selection, through his father's influence, as successor. William Cushing was to serve on the various incarnations of the high court of Massachusetts from 1772 until his appointment to the U.S. Supreme Court in 1789.

William Cushing was the third justice appointed by President George Washington to the original U.S. Supreme Court. Generally speaking, Cushing was regarded as the senior associate justice. John Rutledge was appointed first after Chief Justice John Jay, but Rutledge never attended a formal session of the Court (though he did participate from his lodging in various administrative matters dealt with by the Court and ride circuit). During Jay's absence in England in the years 1794 and 1795, Cushing served as acting-chief justice. After Jay's resignation and the Senate's rejection of Rutledge, Cushing was nominated and unanimously confirmed as chief justice. Cushing held the chief justiceship for about a week in 1796 before he decided to resign the center chair for health reasons and resume his position as senior associate justice.[3]

## The Conventional Wisdom about William Cushing

Surprisingly little has been written about William Cushing. In view of the significant contributions Cushing made to American law and politics throughout his many years of public life, the term "surprisingly little" is applicable.

The conventional wisdom about William Cushing is largely negative in outlook. John D. Cushing (no relation), author of the most comprehensive study of William Cushing to date, concludes in his 1959 Ph.D. dissertation that Cushing's impressive resume was more the product of family and political connections than of merit.[4] As far as Cushing's modest place in history is concerned, this same scholar maintains, "If the maxim 'As you sow, also shall you reap' is valid, it appears from all available evidence that posterity has placed Cushing in his rightful place in history, or close to it."[5]

Others share this unfavorable view of Cushing. Donald O. Dewey opens his brief essay in Melvin I. Urofsky's edited collection, *The Supreme Court Justices: A Biographical Dictionary*, with the unflattering pronouncement that "William Cushing served longer with minimal effect than any of the fourteen Supreme Court justices whose terms overlapped his."[6] Herbert Alan Johnson expresses an equally negative opinion of Cushing when he writes, "Throughout his life Cushing was unsure of the law; decision for him was thus a consultative rather than a deliberative process."[7]

Still other scholars insinuate Cushing was either a dullard throughout the course of his entire life—one story that is repeated in almost all the biographical accounts is how Cushing allegedly was so bored at the Massachusetts Constitutional Convention of 1779 he resorted to making a list of materials he would need for a new suit[8]—or at least "somewhat senile" during much of his tenure on the U.S. Supreme Court.[9] With respect to Cushing's interest in fabric, it is quite a leap of logic to conclude that because he took a moment to jot down a description of a suit of clothes he found attractive, he was uninterested in the affairs of state. The more reasonable supposition is that Cushing's *fifty years* of public service signified a *considerable* interest in public affairs.

As far as Cushing's being "somewhat senile" during much of his tenure on the U.S. Supreme Court is concerned, this charge is also suspect. There is, after all, a difference between being old and sometimes ill—as Cushing undoubtedly was—and being insane or "somewhat senile." A careful reading of the summary accounts of Cushing's life reveals that the disparaging statements about Cushing's faculties are supported by little else than Justice William Johnson's assertion in an

1822 letter to Thomas Jefferson that "Cushing was incompetent, Chase could not be got to think or write—Paterson was a slow man and willingly declined the Trouble, and the other two [Marshall and Washington] . . . are commonly estimated as one Judge."[10] What is never mentioned is the fact that Justice Johnson was a Democratic-Republican, whereas Justice Cushing (and the other justices attacked by Johnson) was a Federalist.[11] Consequently, one reasonably may question Justice Johnson's objectivity as far as his evaluation of Justice Cushing (and his colleagues) is concerned. Frankly, the Democratic-Republican leadership's well-known animosity toward the Federalist-controlled federal judiciary, coupled with the vitriolic tone of Justice Johnson's letter, makes it difficult to take Justice Johnson's characterization seriously.

There have been a few favorable appraisals of William Cushing.[12] Unfortunately, such appraisals are dated and generally neglected. The more one looks in depth at Cushing's career, however, the more one becomes impressed. This essay offers a fresh look at William Cushing by actually examining his record rather than simply repeating what other scholars have said before. The more one reads the increasingly popular encyclopedia-style biographical collections of Supreme Court justices, the more one realizes the essayists merely repeat—rephrase, but nevertheless repeat—what other essayists have stated in previous collections.[*] Succinctly put, there must be reasons that preeminent Founders such as John Adams and George Washington held William Cushing in high regard for nearly fifty years.[13**]

*Cushing fares no better outside the biographical encyclopedias. For example, Frank H. Easterbrook states he would have added Cushing to David P. Currie's list of the "most insignificant" justices ever to serve on the Supreme Court, but for Cushing's *declining* the chief justiceship. Easterbrook writes: "[Cushing's] single fortunate act of declining the [chief justice] post disqualifies him from being Most Insignificant: had Cushing taken the job, John Marshall never would have become Chief Justice, and we would be living in a much changed nation." Frank H. Easterbrook, "The Most Insignificant Justice: Further Evidence," *University of Chicago Law Review* 50 (Spring 1983): 481, 484 n.11. See generally David P. Currie, "The Most Insignificant Justice: A Preliminary Inquiry," ibid., 466–80. If Easterbrook seems to believe that Cushing did little more than open the door for John Marshall, R. Kent Newmyer, in an otherwise superb biography, appears to suggest that Cushing's most important accomplishment was dying so the nation could have Joseph Story. See R. Kent Newmyer, *Supreme Court Justice Joseph Story: Statesman of the Old Republic* (Chapel Hill: University of North Carolina Press, 1985), 70, 87, 99, 407 n.81.

**John Marshall also thought highly of Cushing. A June 29, 1807, letter—the time when critics allege Cushing was "somewhat senile"—finds Marshall soliciting Cushing's ad-

## Deconstruction: A Force in American Law and Politics

### Ratifying the Constitution

William Cushing was not among the delegates who met in Philadelphia during the summer of 1787 to frame a new form of government for the United States of America. However, even Cushing's critics acknowledge he played a significant role in securing ratification of the Constitution in Massachusetts.[14] Given that Massachusetts was one of the most important states in the Union and that ratification by the commonwealth was far from certain,[15] this was a major contribution indeed. Cushing helped secure ratification in two principal ways: (1) through a series of grand jury charges that were designed to educate the public about the need for a new form of government, and (2) by presiding over most of the ratifying convention sessions, which were held in Boston in January of 1788.

As chief justice of Massachusetts, Cushing was in a unique position to apprise the public of the need to ratify the proposed Constitution. A series of well-received grand jury charges delivered shortly before the ratifying convention assembled found Cushing making a passionate case for ratification. The following charge is representative of Cushing's position on this defining question of the day:

> It seems to be agreed that the Confederation is weak, without powers—totally inadequate to all great national purposes—unable to uphold the union—to protect the country—to pay any part of the public debt or even the interest—that commerce is in a wretched situation, unregulated, unprotected, unproductive of revenue—that all the world are become our carriers, except that we ourselves are in a good manner excluded; ship-building and navigation in a good manner cease;—while . . . our carpenters and . . . honest seamen on the coast, with men of numerous other trades and businesses dependant upon those now be still for want of employ; in short the interest of all classes of men . . . is essentially afflicted from the ocean to the wilderness.[16]

vice on several technical aspects of Aaron Burr's treason trial. Whether Marshall sought the advice of his other Supreme Court colleagues is unclear. Marshall's letter to Cushing suggests, however, that the chief justice limited his requests for advice to Cushing and Bushrod Washington. See Letter from John Marshall to William Cushing, 29 June 1807, in Charles F. Hobson, ed., *The Papers of John Marshall*, vol. 7 (Chapel Hill: University of North Carolina Press, 1993), 60–62. I thank Chuck Hobson for bringing this letter to my attention.

In short, Cushing, like most Federalists at the time, saw ratification of the Constitution as the best way, perhaps the only way, to ensure a stable and effective Union.[17] And for Cushing, as for most Federalists, the most important difference between the proposed Constitution and the existing Articles of Confederation was the authority Congress would enjoy under the new form of government to exercise on its own accord all powers that were necessary—but no more powers than were necessary—to the legislative function. This point was the centerpiece of Cushing's grand jury charges.[18]

Turning to the Massachusetts ratifying convention, John Hancock, then governor of Massachusetts, was elected president of that important body. Cushing was elected vice president. Given that Hancock, one of the most notorious "finger-in-the-wind" politicians of his day, was overtaken with his nearly chronic "political gout,"[19] Cushing presided over most of the convention's proceedings. As chair of the proceedings, it was not Cushing's place to take part in the debate. His grand jury charges were widely known, however, and hence his views were apparent to all who did participate. Perhaps even more critically, the prestige of Cushing's office as chief justice and his proficient stewardship of the proceedings helped achieve a majority, albeit a narrow one, in favor of ratification.

One of the most illuminating documents for discerning Cushing's views on the Constitution is what is described as "Justice Cushing's Undelivered Speech on the Federal Constitution."[20] It is not clear why Cushing refrained from delivering it. The leading authority on the matter, William O'Brien, suggests that Cushing was pressured by Hancock to suppress the speech. By late January a group of leading Massachusetts Federalists had managed to persuade—or, better yet, to "bribe"—Hancock to come to the convention. Father O'Brien's colorful description of what likely transpired next is worth quoting at length:

> Upon this sudden development, Cushing, relieved of his chafing duties as presiding officer, felt that he could with perfect propriety give full voice to his own convictions and air in public his long pent-up emotions. Filled with his subject, he did not take very long to compose a formal address. It may be surmised, however, that Hancock did not relish the thought that another major speech besides his own was to be given by the vice-president of the convention at one of its closing sessions. Vain as he is reputed to have been, the governor must have taken singular delight in the dramatic role in which he had been cast: a stricken man rising from a sick bed, coming before a di-

vided convention, with galleries packed, peacemaker and conciliator, the expectation of the Federalists, yet a bearer of balm for their aggrieved opponents. He must have demonstrated ill humor at the prospect of sharing such a spotlight with another.[21]

## Cushing's Thoughts on Government

Although Cushing chose not to deliver his speech in support of the Constitution, the manuscript nevertheless sheds considerable light on his thoughts on government. Cushing opened the speech by informing his (prospective) audience that he would be concentrating on the "principal objections" to the proposed Constitution.[22] The first of the objections he addressed was the question of annual versus biennial elections for members of Congress. Delegate Samuel Thompson expressed this objection in particularly dramatic fashion. "O my country!" exclaimed Thompson, "never give up your annual elections; young men, never give up your jewel!"[23]

For Cushing, this objection was nothing but a distraction. That is to say, what the people really needed to be concerned about, Cushing believed, was whether they themselves were sufficiently virtuous to keep the governors in their place—regardless of how long a particular term of office might be. "Boundaries and barriers upon paper are of no consequence," Cushing observed, "if [the] people are not properly watchful of their liberties. Rulers and Representatives may overleap two years, as well and as easy as one."[24]

What is intriguing about Cushing's argument is not the substance of it—the "parchment barriers" theme was rehearsed by many of Cushing's contemporaries—but what it says about Cushing's ability to get to the heart of the matter. Unlike most of his peers, Cushing did not fill his public addresses with seemingly unending references to history and philosophy. And this was not because he was unfamiliar with those references. Indeed, Cushing was a voracious reader, so much so that during his circuit travels his wife would read to him from books he kept in special receptacles he had designed for his carriage.[25] As will be discussed below, Cushing approached the questions that came before him as a U.S. Supreme Court justice in the same straightforward manner.

The absence of a bill of rights from the proposed Constitution was of great concern to many delegates to the Massachusetts ratifying convention. Cushing's speech indicates that he did not share this concern. In fact, the speech reveals that Cushing was prepared to offer the standard Federalist response to the call for a bill of rights.[26] As Cushing phrased it:

> The fact is (and it is a selfevident proposition)—we retain all that we do not part with . . . —going upon this . . . ground . . . no authority could be exercised over the people, but such as should be expressly granted by them, which in my opinion is better and safer than any Bill of Rights, that the wisest mortal can draw up by attempting a particular enumeration of all rights.[27]

Cushing skillfully discussed a variety of other controversial topics in his speech—from the "necessary and proper clause," to Congress's power to suspend the writ of habeas corpus, to the separation of powers. His argument against term limits for members of Congress is worth singling out, however.

The Massachusetts ratifying convention was not immune from the concern raised in many states about the proposed elimination of the Articles of Confederation provision on mandatory rotation in office. For instance, Charles Turner thought rotation in the lower house necessary "to guard against the deep arts of popular men."[28] Cushing could not have disagreed more with his fellow delegate from Scituate. He explained:

> A rotation in Congress has been held up as necessary:—that is when a person has been in office a certain period; the people, however they may trust in his experience ability and integrity shall not have a right to choose him for a certain other period:—This I think would be an open downright abridgment of the peoples liberties and right of election—and a bold stroke for any Constitution makers to attempt; besides that it might prove dangerous to the *Commonwealth* in being obliged to bring in, new and unexperienced men, perhaps in all hazardous moment, a time of war, to conduct the affairs of State, instead of their tried and faithful Servants, whom they wish to choose. Let the people, as it is their right, judge for themselves in this matter.[29]

Put directly, Cushing opposed term limits because the people already had the *power* to limit terms—and to do so more severely than could any formal requirement of rotation in office. More important, Cushing insisted that the people had the *right* to reelect representatives with whom they were satisfied, and that it was often in the best interests of the political community that they did so.

Like almost all the leading figures of the American Founding, William Cushing was a political leader, not a political philosopher. Consequently, he never wrote a systematic treatise on political theory.[30] Evidence exists, however, that provides insight into Cushing's political theory. Most notably, this is in the form of the grand jury charges he delivered while on circuit as a U.S. Supreme Court justice. As Ralph Lerner explains in his classic article on the subject, the justices often used their grand jury charges to instruct the public on the basic purpose of politics.[31] Cushing's charges are consistent with Lerner's thesis.

Cushing's charge of November 7, 1794, in Providence is the most detailed of his charges uncovered to date. His opening remarks about the purpose and nature of government are so helpful in understanding his political theory that they are worth quoting at length:

> The great end of government, you know, is peace and protection; peace with nations, protection against foreign force:—peace and order within; protection of individuals, of all classes of men, whether poor or rich, in the undisturbed enjoyment of their just rights, which are comprehended under a few, but important words—*security of person and property*, or, if you please, *rights of man*. Hence government involves in it a sacred regard to the principles of justice, and to all moral obligations. . . .
>
> Where people are not permitted to enjoy these blessings, *security of person and property*, unmolested, there is tyranny, whether it arises from monarchy, aristocracy, or a mob. Where all men are equally and promptly protected in the free exercise of these rights, there is liberty and equality;—liberty, to do whatever just laws made by a free representative allow; equality, that is, as to right of protection respecting the great objects of life, liberty and property, when not forfeited to the state by criminal conduct; respecting property, which a man has fairly and honestly obtained—not that which is unrighteously taken or forced from another;—not equality in regard to quantity; for that seldom, if ever, can happen, owing, under providence, to the infinitely various faculties and diligence of different individuals;—not a right for the indolent to rob the laborious—to share equally the fruits of the virtuous industry of others; such ideas being founded in extravagance of enthusiasm and delusion, or in downright dishonesty and depravity of mind—subversive of the first principles of justice, and the great ends of society.[32]

As this quotation suggests, Cushing had the outlook of a classical liberal on government—one he articulated with a straightforward, but nonetheless learned, voice.[33] Indeed, Cushing's contemporaries held his grand jury charges in extremely high esteem. Abigail Adams, for one, thought so highly of Cushing's charge on the Alien and Sedition Act that she urged her husband, John, then president, to publish the charge alongside copies of the act.[34] Consequently, it seems curious, to say the least, to cast aspersions upon Cushing's abilities without taking his grand jury charges into account. Unfortunately, Cushing's present-day critics never mention, let alone discuss, his grand jury charges.

## Inventing Textualism

William Cushing's critics focus most of their attention on the opinions he wrote as a U.S. Supreme Court justice. The two stock criticisms are (1) Cushing did not author many opinions on the Supreme Court, and (2) those opinions he did author are superficial. With respect to the first criticism, David R. Warrington reports in *The Oxford Companion to the Supreme Court of the United States* that Cushing's "age and his increasingly ill-health, coupled with the rigors of circuit riding, so taxed his strength that he wrote only 19 opinions."[35] Similar statements are repeated in virtually all the biographical accounts of Cushing's life.[36] Other than underscoring the repetitive nature of most biographical encyclopedias, these statements tell us little. Nay, more, they are misleading. A fresh look at the record reveals that Cushing wrote as many opinions as the other members of the pre-Marshall Court. Admittedly, the number is not great, but this is because the Supreme Court had a light docket in its early years. Consequently, the thinly-veiled attempts to characterize William Cushing as not much more than judicial deadwood are without foundation.*

*By the time the Supreme Court had begun to hear a significant number of cases, John Marshall had assumed the center chair. Two related changes in the inner workings of the Court meant that only Marshall authored many opinions during the formative years of his chief justiceship (which is when Cushing served with him): (1) the practice of seriatim opinion writing came to an end, and (2) the "opinions of the Court" were almost always written (or at least signed and delivered) by the chief justice. See George Lee Haskins and Herbert A. Johnson, *Foundations of Power: John Marshall, 1801–15* (New York: Macmillan, 1981), 382–87. The Ellsworth Court (1796–1800) relied heavily upon per curiam disposition of cases, which also reduced the number of opportunities Cushing had to write opin-

When one turns from the quantity of Cushing's opinions to their quality, Cushing does not fare any better at the hands of his critics. David P. Currie, for one, asserts, "Cushing wrote pedestrian opinions that added little."[37] A glance at Currie's footnote reveals, however, that he, too, appears to be relying heavily upon what other critics have said before. His footnote reads: "*See* G. Haskins & H. Johnson *supra* note 7, at 87, noting John Dickinson's contemporaneous view that Cushing added nothing to his brethren's exposition of the law."[38]

But why cannot the argument be reversed? In other words, why not point out that the opinions of the *other justices* added little to *Cushing's* exposition of the law? No one ever considers this possibility. Similarly, critics never mention that, as senior associate justice, Cushing was obliged to speak last—a procedural nuance that almost certainly influenced the level of detail in his opinions. Most important, a careful examination of Currie's tome discloses that the comments he offers about the quality of the opinions in individual cases often amount to little more than a series of throwaway lines like "Paterson, Wilson, and Cushing issued forgettable opinions confined almost entirely to the interpretation of the treaty"[39] and "most of the Justices had nothing meaningful to say."[40] This is assertion, not analysis—something, ironically enough, Cushing's critics accuse *Cushing* of.[41] As now will be seen, many of Cushing's opinions are insightful;** they simply are not adorned with the myriad references to history and philosophy contained in the opinions of his colleagues. In brief, Cushing's *style* was different from his brethren's: Like his ratifying convention speech on behalf of the Constitution, Cushing cut to the heart of the matter. Some might consider this a virtue, rather than a vice. In fact, it is not unfair to say that Cushing was one of the earliest—and most

ions. See William R. Casto, *The Supreme Court in the Early Republic: The Chief Justiceships of John Jay and Oliver Ellsworth* (Columbia: University of South Carolina Press, 1995), 110–11.

**Some critics of Cushing's opinion writing go so far as to deny Cushing credit for quality opinions that bear his name! See, for example, Haskins and Johnson, *Foundations of Power*, 384 (insisting "the quality of [Cushing's] opinion in *M'Ilvaine v. Coxe's Lessee* [1805] lead[s] one to question the commonly accepted assumption that *delivery* of a majority opinion implied *authorship* of the opinion"). In fairness to the always fair-minded Johnson, he advises this author that "seniority also raises the question if Marshall wrote all the opinions *he* delivered, particularly after Story joined the Court in 1812." Letter from Herbert A. Johnson, 6 December 1995 (copy in my possession).

consistent—proponents of a school of legal interpretation known today as "textualism."[42]

*Chisholm v. Georgia* (1793), *Hylton v. United States* (1796), *Ware v. Hylton* (1796), and *Calder v. Bull* (1798) are generally regarded as the most important Supreme Court cases of the 1790s.[43] Cushing did not participate in *Hylton* and his *Calder* opinion as reported by Alexander Dallas is only two sentences long. Consequently, *Chisholm* and *Ware* will be used to illustrate Cushing's approach to legal interpretation.

*Chisholm v. Georgia* (1793)[44] was the first full-scale constitutional law decision by the Supreme Court. At issue was whether a citizen of one state, South Carolina, could bring suit in federal court against another state, Georgia. The subject matter of the suit was a sizeable debt that the state of Georgia had incurred in purchasing military supplies from Chisholm's testator.

The first of the opinions was James Iredell's—the only justice among the five to reject the view that a state may be sued by a citizen of another state.[45] Iredell is highly regarded by modern students of the pre-Marshall Court.[46] His opinion in *Chisholm*, however, was more appropriate for the halls of Congress than it was for a court of law. That is to say, Iredell ignored the plain words of the Constitution to press for a desired political result.[47] Most notably, Iredell ignored the second paragraph of Article III, section 2, which states that in cases "in which a state shall be a party the Supreme Court shall have original jurisdiction." Iredell emphasized instead the Judiciary Act of 1789, essentially arguing that the Court's jurisdiction was not self-executing and that Congress had not executed it in that, or any other, statute. It took Iredell twenty-one pages in Dallas's *Reports* to reach this conclusion, about half of which was devoted to a discussion of the law and practice of England. The point of the latter discussion seems to have been that the Court was bound by the common law relative to suits against sovereigns.

If Iredell's opinion was better suited for the halls of Congress, James Wilson's was more appropriate for the ivory towers of academe.[48] Although Mark D. Hall contends that Wilson "wrote the most memorable and theoretically interesting seriatim opinion,"[49] much of that opinion was superfluous. Indeed, Wilson spent most of his thirteen pages off-point, ranging far and wide over history and the basic concepts of sovereignty, the state, and man's relation to the state. He invoked Reid, Bacon, Cicero, William the Conqueror, the Ephori of Sparta, Homer, Demosthenes, Louis XIV, Bracton, and the author of the *Mirror of Justice*. Wilson's purpose was to show that in the United States the people are sovereign. Consequently, the state of Georgia could be sued. Almost lost among Wilson's elaborate discussion was the Constitution itself. In fact, Wilson devoted only a few lines of his opinion to the document he was charged with interpreting. When he did turn to the Constitution, he found the answer to the question before the Court readily available. He concluded the fact that Georgia could be sued in federal court "rests not upon the legitimate result of fair and conclusive deduction from the constitution: it is confirmed, beyond all doubt, by direct and explicit declaration of the constitution itself."

Chief Justice John Jay's opinion also contained elaborate references to history and philosophy.[50] For instance, Jay devoted a sizeable portion of his opinion to comparing the differences of the feudal governments of Europe with governments by compact. It was not until the end of his opinion that the chief justice, like the other members of the majority, concluded that the Constitution's express reference to federal jurisdiction over suits involving states made Georgia amenable to suit by a citizen of South Carolina.

The opinions of John Blair and William Cushing in the *Chisholm* case have been called, among other things, "unimaginative."[51] It is more accurate to say they stayed on point. Blair began his opinion with a subtle expression of disapproval of the rambling opinions of Iredell, Wilson, and Jay: Blair said he would pass over the "various European confederations. . . . The Constitution of the United States is the only fountain from which I shall draw."[52] Blair was true to his word. In fact, he needed but three pages to decide the case, and his decision was based on a plain reading of the words of the Constitution.

William Cushing's opinion was similar to Blair's in both tone and method. He, too, began by saying, "the point turns not upon the law or practice of England, . . . nor upon the law of any other country whatever" and he, too, emphasized the words of the Constitution.[53] Put simply, Cushing's opinion is a straightforward example of textual analysis. To Cushing, the clause in question, "between a state and citizens of another state," needed to be read in conjunction with the clause that immediately preceded it, "to controversies between two or more states"—a clause that plainly envisioned the state as a defendant. If any exception was intended in the suability of a state, Cushing insisted, it would have been written into the Constitution. Cushing drove this point home by explaining that another clause in the relevant section subjected foreign states to suit in federal court by American citizens. Thus, the "sovereignty" argument was of no avail, Cushing concluded, unless one accepted the improbable argument that the clause meant "we may touch foreign sovereigns but not our own."

The editors of the *Documentary History of the Supreme Court* perceptively note that *Chisholm* "involved an issue that continues to haunt constitutional jurisprudence to this day: what weight was to be given the plain meaning of the text against the intent of its authors and ratifiers insofar as that could be determined."[54] Cushing chose the textualist route, but that does not make his opinion "unimaginative" or, more disparagingly, he himself "unsure of the law" or "simple." Indeed, Cushing demonstrated in *Chisholm* itself that he well understood that questions of political philosophy often underlaid cases that came before the Supreme Court. As Cushing put it eloquently: "The rights of individuals and the justice due them, are as dear and precious as those of the states. Indeed the latter are founded upon the former; and the great end and object of them must be to secure and support the rights of individuals, or else vain is government."

*Ware v. Hylton* (1796)[55] found the Supreme Court confronting the problem of state legislation during the American Revolution that confiscated the obligations Americans owed to British merchants. Under the Treaty of Paris of 1783, which the Constitution adopted as part of the supreme law of the land, "creditors . . . shall meet with no lawful impediment to the recovery . . . of all bona fide debts heretofore contracted." The issue before the Court was whether the ratification of the Constitution repealed *ab initio* a 1777 Virginia statute by which citizens of Virginia discharged their debts by paying the amount owed to British merchants into the state treasury.

Samuel Chase's opinion,[56] which at twenty-five pages was the longest of the five opinions reported by Alexander Dallas, is characterized by modern commentators as "something of a *tour de force*."[57] Like Iredell's, Wilson's, and Jay's in *Chisholm*, however, much of Chase's opinion was superfluous. For instance, he spent a good third of his opinion describing the elements of the defendants' claim—and then declared that the description amounted to nothing. After many fits and starts, Chase turned to the language of the treaty itself. "On the best investigation I have been able to give the 4th article of the treaty," Chase wrote, ". . . I am satisfied that the words, in their natural import, and common use, give a recovery to the *British* creditor from his original *debtor* of the debt contracted *before* the treaty, notwithstanding the payment thereof into the public treasuries, or loan offices, under the authority of any State law." In short, Chase concluded that the plain language of the treaty supported the creditor's claim: He simply took an eternity to reach this conclusion.

As in *Chisholm*, James Iredell appeared to forget in *Ware* the difference between a politician and a judge. Iredell had been one of the judges in the lower circuit court who adjudicated the case. Consequently, it was not appropriate for him to participate in the appeal before the Supreme Court. Nevertheless, Iredell decided, with his brethren's acquiescence,[58] to read into the record his thoughts on the matter. At twenty-four pages in length, Iredell's thoughts were considerable.[59] They were also an unambiguous exercise in result-oriented jurisprudence. No matter what the plain language of the treaty said, Iredell—the pre-Marshall Court's most fervent guardian of states' rights[60]—was going to find a way to uphold the state law. The manner by which Iredell accomplished his aim was to offer a strained reading of the treaty's language. As Iredell awkwardly phrased it: "When these general words, therefore, can comprehend so many cases, all reasonable objects of the article, I cannot think, I am compelled, as a judge, and therefore, I ought not to do so, to say, that the general words of this article shall extinguish private as well as public rights." Put more simply, Iredell concluded that the treaty did not pertain to private parties.

Cushing's modern-day critics dismiss his *Ware* opinion out-of-hand. William Paterson and James Wilson fare no better. Julius Goebel, for instance, contends, "For what the Justices (Paterson, Wilson, and Cushing) who concurred in Chase's conclusion had to offer, they might as well have let his opinion stand as that of the Court."[61] David Currie basically repeats Goebel's contention, albeit in more caustic language. "Paterson, Wilson, and Cushing issued forgettable opinions confined almost entirely to the interpretation of the treaty,"

Currie declares.[62] What the critics fail to mention, however, is that the question before the Court was what the *treaty said*. Consequently, it is odd, to say the least, to criticize Cushing and the others for doing precisely what the Court was charged with doing.

Cushing's two-and-a-half-page opinion in *Ware* was a workmanlike exercise in textualism,[63] just as his opinion in *Chisholm* had been. For Cushing, the "great question" was the "fourth article of the treaty." And to him, "the plain and obvious" meaning of the treaty was to "nullify, *ab initio*," all laws that frustrated a creditor's right or remedy against his original debtor. There was nothing fancy about Cushing's opinion, but there did not need to be. This is not to say that Cushing was unaware of the possible unfairness of forcing a debtor to pay his debt twice (once to the state treasury and a second time to the creditor). On this point, Cushing invoked a well-settled rule of textual construction; namely, "As to the rule respecting odious constructions; that takes place where the meaning is doubtful, not where it is clear, as I think it is, in this case." Here again we see that while Cushing tended to boil down to the bone the question before the Court, he was sensitive to the principles that underlaid that question.[64]

Jurisprudence scholars recognize that there are a variety of methodologies available for interpreting the law, generally, and the Constitution, specifically. Philip Bobbitt in his *Constitutional Fate* discusses six types of "constitutional argument": historical, textual, doctrinal, prudential, structural, and ethical.[65] Scholars disagree about what the prevailing approach to interpretation was among early American judges and lawyers.[66] Cushing's opinions in *Chisholm v. Georgia* and *Ware v. Hylton* indicate that he took a textualist approach to the law.[67] In fact, Cushing was one of the earliest—and most consistent—proponents of textualism.[68] Cushing's present-day critics call his approach "simple" and "unimaginative," but they manage to overlook the fact that even the more "flashy" members of the Court almost always returned to the text to decide the case—albeit after ranging far and wide over everything tangentially relevant. To reiterate, Cushing's *style* was different from his brethren's. It was not necessarily "worse," and it might even have been "better" because it was easier to understand and thereby easier to follow.[69] It also is worth mentioning that Cushing's textualism—like textualism generally—evidences deference to the lawmakers who framed or legislated the particular law under consideration. Such deference was squarely within the jurisprudential mainstream of Cushing's time.[70*]

## Establishing Judicial Review

William Cushing made other contributions to American law and politics as well, not the least of which was the role he played in the development of judicial review. To date, Cushing has received almost no credit in this regard. A still compelling essay written by F. W. Grinnell in 1917 offers three explanations for why this might be so:

> First, the habit of looking for a precedent, rather than a principle, has led men to rely on Chief Justice Marshall's opinion in *Marbury v. Madison;* although he himself looked for the principle without worrying about the precedents. Second and third, the combined forces of Anti-Federalist "politics" on one side, and the American tendency to self-glorification on the other, stepped in and asserted that it was exclusively an American idea invented by Chief Justice Marshall. The fact that there were few printed law reports before 1803 when *Marbury v. Madison* was decided helped this myth. Recent researches have uncovered a mass of buried information showing that the principle was neither exclusively American nor invented by Marshall.[71]

Although through these "researches" scholars have come to realize that judicial review was not "invented" by John Marshall, the credit Marshall receives for the development of the doctrine still eclipses all others to this day. From basic textbooks on American government,[72] to more advanced treatises on the judicial process,[73] judicial review remains synonymous in the literature with Marshall's opinion for the Court in *Marbury v. Madison* (1803). Indeed, recent revisionist accounts of the origins of judicial review, most often written by historians, continue to use *Marbury* as the point of departure.[74]

*One further point about Cushing's textualism is worth noting, if only because it illustrates well how the broader text of American legal history has been misread over the years. The misreading in question is the credit John Marshall receives for almost everything important to come from the early Supreme Court. The clearest example of this as far as textualism is concerned is Leslie Friedman Goldstein, *In Defense of the Text: Democracy and Constitutional Theory* (Savage, Md.: Rowman and Littlefield, 1991). In her book, Goldstein credits Marshall with being the founder of the "textualist tradition." Not one word is said about Cushing. Marshall might have been a textualist—and a talented one at that—but Cushing was employing the methodology long before Marshall came on the scene.

Cushing's contributions to the development of judicial review in America were considerable. For instance, even before independence was declared Cushing was charging grand juries in Massachusetts that courts had the authority to declare acts of Parliament unconstitutional.[75] As far as Cushing's service on the federal bench is concerned, a strong argument can be made that Cushing and Jay, on circuit, were the first members of the Supreme Court to employ judicial review—over state and federal legislation alike. The sporadic nature of case reporting during the early days of the federal judiciary makes it unwise to declare unequivocally that Cushing and Jay were "first," but the available evidence points in this direction. Newspaper accounts suggest that Cushing and Jay held state laws unconstitutional in April and May of 1791 and in June of 1792.[76] These same two circuit justices (together with district judge Duane) "upheld" a federal law in April of 1792, but they nevertheless recognized the power of the federal courts to declare acts of Congress unconstitutional.[77]* There is also *Cooper v. Telfair*, a case brought before the entire Supreme Court in 1800, in which Cushing declared, "I am of the opinion[] that this court has the same[] power that a court of Georgia would possess[] to declare the law void."[78] Last, but far from least, a careful reading of *Marbury* itself reveals that Marshall relied heavily upon the Court's 1794 decision *Chandler v. Secretary of War*, which many scholars now believe declared a congressional statute unconstitutional. Since no official report of *Chandler* existed, it is likely Marshall was made aware of this precedent by Cushing and/or Paterson, the only justices who served on the Court in both cases.[79]

*They "upheld" the statute—the Invalid Pensioners Act—by interpreting it as an offer of a *nonjudicial* commissionership, which they each were free to accept or reject. Maeva Marcus maintains that the New York Circuit was issuing an advisory opinion only, because it "did not have an actual case before [it]." Unfortunately, Marcus provides no substantial evidence for this proposition. See Maeva Marcus, "Judicial Review in the Early Republic," in *Launching the "Extended Republic": The Federalist Era*, ed. Ronald L. Hoffman (Charlottesville: University Press of Virginia, 1996), 38 n.45 (citing an April 10, 1792, letter to President Washington asking that the president forward to Congress the circuit's April 5, 1792, opinion). The letter is also printed in *Hayburn's Case*, 2 U.S. (2 Dall.) 409, 410 n. (1792). Father O'Brien maintains, by contrast, "claimants appeared before [Cushing and Jay] while on circuit in New York." William O'Brien, "The Pre-Marshall Court and the Role of William Cushing," *Massachusetts Law Quarterly* 43 (March 1958): 52, 57. Marcus does not mention Father O'Brien's reading of the case. See also Max Farrand, "The First Hayburn Case," *American Historical Review* 13 (January 1908): 281–85.

## Abolishing Slavery

No assessment of William Cushing's contributions to American law and politics would be complete without discussing his role in the abolition of slavery in Massachusetts.* In fact, Robert M. Cover, in *Justice Accused: Antislavery and the Judicial Process,* describes a case in which William Cushing, then the Massachusetts chief justice, participated as the first case in the United States to confront the institution of slavery as a matter of constitutional law.[80] That case—which has been called "the most famous slave case[] in America prior to the Dred Scott decision"[81]—was actually a series of cases now known as the Quock Walker Case.

The complex series of cases began in 1781 as civil actions (in which Cushing did not participate) for the assault and battery a master, Jennison, allegedly perpetrated on his runaway slave, Walker, and on another man, Caldwell, who sheltered Walker. Jennison's defense was that he was merely attempting to recover his property, a runaway slave. Walker and Caldwell countered that Walker could not be a slave because the 1780 Massachusetts Constitution abolished slavery. Article I read:

> All men are born free and equal, and have certain natural, essential, and unalienable rights; among which may be reckoned the right of enjoying and defending their lives and liberties; that of acquiring, possessing, and protecting property. . . .

The civil actions resulted in inconsistent verdicts: Jennison was found liable for beating Walker, but Caldwell was found liable for enticing Walker to flee. As the civil actions worked their way through the appeals process, a criminal indictment was brought against Jennison for assault and battery. The criminal case went to trial in 1783, and it was this trial that resulted in a famous jury charge issued by Cushing. It is important here to point out that in

*A less momentous contribution is worth mentioning as well: the role Cushing played in changing the practice by which lawyers are admitted to the U.S. Supreme Court bar. When Chief Justice Jay presided, which was most of the time, he insisted that the attorney general be an integral part of the admissions process. When Cushing presided, by contrast, he permitted lawyers to be admitted on the motion of a current member of the bar. Cushing's less formal approach became the norm. See James R. Perry and James M. Buchanan, "Admission to the Supreme Court Bar, 1790–1800: A Case Study of Institutional Change," *Supreme Court Historical Society Yearbook* (1983): 10–18.

Massachusetts at the time all judicial cases, including appeals, were tried before a jury.

In charging the jury, Cushing discussed "the doctrine of slavery and the right of Christians to hold Africans in perpetual servitude, and selling and treating them as we do horses and cattle." He acknowledged that such a practice had been common, but while the laws of the province had tolerated it, no act had ever expressly permitted or established the institution of slavery. He described slavery as a "usage" that had grown out of European custom, and had come to be regarded as legal in America chiefly because the British government had established regulations governing the slave trade. The remaining portion of Cushing's famous charge should be quoted in full:

> But whatever usages formerly prevailed or slid in upon us by the example of others on the subject, they can no longer exist. Sentiments more favorable to the natural rights of mankind, and to that innate desire for liberty which heaven, without regard to complexion or shape, has planted in the human breast—have prevailed since the glorious struggle for our rights began. And these sentiments led the framers of our constitution of government—by which the people of this commonwealth have solemnly bound themselves to each other—to declare—*that all men are born free and equal;* and that *every subject is entitled to liberty*, and to have it guarded by the laws as well as his life and property. In short, without resorting to implication in constructing the constitution, slavery is in my judgement as effectively abolished as it can be by the granting of rights and privileges wholly incompatible and repugnant to its existence. The court are therefore fully of the opinion that perpetual servitude can no longer be tolerated in our government, and that liberty can only be forfeited by some criminal conduct or relinquished by personal consent or contract. And it is therefore unnecessary to consider whether the promises of freedom to Quaco, on the part of his master and mistress, amounted to a manumission or not. The Deft must be found guilty as the facts charged are not controverted.[82]

Cushing's charge to the jury—which exemplifies both his textualism and his appreciation that political philosophy underlaid legal texts—is unambiguous: The jurors had to consider slavery to have been abolished by the state's constitution and they therefore had to convict Jennison of the crime for which he was accused. Unfortunately, the role this charge played in abolishing slavery in the commonwealth is not as clear as the charge itself. Indeed, Cover aptly notes that the question of which case actually abolished slavery in

Massachusetts "has become a historians's perennial football."[83] At last count, there are no fewer than six articles—all of which are well researched and well argued—devoted to the Quock Walker Case,[84] and the case is also mentioned in all the biographical sketches of Cushing's life.

While this essay cannot presume to put an end to the controversy over the Quock Walker Case, a middle-ground position between arguing that Cushing played *no* role in the abolition of slavery in Massachusetts and that he played the *definitive* role is possible. That position is that slavery was a dying institution in the Commonwealth of Massachusetts in the eighteenth century—witness, for example, the "free and equal" clause in the Massachusetts Constitution of 1780—but Cushing's prestige as chief justice and the forceful and unambiguous temper of his jury charge put the final nail in the coffin, at least as far as permanent residents were concerned.[85] Cushing was, after all, held in high regard in the commonwealth and the jury charge he delivered in Quock Walker was widely reported.

## *Conclusion: Is God Dead?*[*]

Poststructuralism is often described as the most important intellectual movement in the postmodern age. History, however, has proved far less receptive to its influence than have philosophy, literature, and law.[86] This essay has attempted to "deconstruct" William Cushing, one of the original members of the U.S. Supreme Court appointed by President George Washington. In essence, what I have endeavored to do is disrupt the conventional wisdom that William Cushing is but a footnote in the text of American history. For too long William Cushing has been credited with little more than traveling in an elegant carriage, having a strange interest in fabric, and wearing a funny wig.[87]

The deconstruction of early American legal and political history need not proceed by random doubt or generalized skepticism. The

*Nietzsche, of course, coined the phrase "God is dead." See Friedrich Wilhelm Nietzsche, *Thus Spoke Zarathustra: A Book for Everyone and No One*, trans. R. J. Hollingdale (Baltimore: Penguin Books, 1969), 2–3. The conventional wisdom in history is that John Marshall is "The Father of the Court." See, for example, Gordon S. Wood, "The Father of the Court," *New Republic*, 17 February 1997, 38–41. The conventional wisdom in philosophy is that Nietzsche is the "father" of postmodernism.

only thing I have aspired to "destroy" is the claim to unequivocal domination by John Marshall on early American jurisprudence. In short, my objective has been to expose the fallacy of excluding other members of the early Supreme Court—specifically, here, William Cushing—from significance. Cushing may not have "ratified" the Constitution, "invented" textualism, "established" judicial review, or "abolished" slavery, but he deserves as much credit for these things as Marshall does. John Marshall may have been a force in American law and politics,[88] but William Cushing contributed his fair share as well.*

## NOTES

1. John D. Cushing, "A Revolutionary Conservative: The Public Life of William Cushing, 1732–1810," unpublished doctoral dissertation, Clark University, 1960, 13.

2. George J. Lankevich, ed., *The Federal Court, 1787–1801* (Millwood, N.Y.: Associated Faculty Press, 1986), 242–43. See generally John M. Murrin, "Anglicizing an American Colony: The Transformation of Provincial Massachusetts," unpublished doctoral dissertation, Yale University, 1967 (pointing out that in the colonial era young men had to prove themselves and did not immediately step into important positions unless they had some connection with the crown).

3. See Henry Flanders, *The Lives and Times of the Chief Justices of the Supreme Court of the United States*, vol. 2 (Philadelphia: T. and J. W. Johnson, 1881), 46.

4. See generally Cushing, "A Revolutionary Conservative." Only slightly more than six pages of John Cushing's 337-page Ph.D. dissertation pertain to William Cushing's U.S. Supreme Court service. Given that John Cushing is largely responsible for the conventional wisdom about William Cushing—i.e., the more recent assessments of William Cushing (abbreviated though they may be) track John Cushing's dissertation research and conclusions—it should not be surprising to learn that William Cushing's U.S. Supreme Court service is viewed negatively by John Cushing. See, for example, ibid., 327 ("As acting Chief Jus-

*Donald Dewey advises that those who find this last paragraph "a bit excessive" should "welcome it as an appealing bit of nyah nyah bravado in behalf of an associate justice who will never be ranked among the greats, but is deserving of better treatment than he has had." Letter from Donald O. Dewey, 13(?) December 1995 (copy in my possession). Perhaps it also shows that Peter S. Onuf is correct: history should not be the exclusive province of historians. See Peter S. Onuf, "Reflections on the Founding: Constitutional Historiography in Bicentennial Perspective," *William and Mary Quarterly* 46 (April 1989): 341–75 (criticizing his fellow historians of the American Founding for attempting to defend history against "alien disciplines").

tice Cushing did nothing to distinguish himself. Neither did he do anything to win lasting fame as an associate justice or as a judge of the United States Circuit Court").

5. Ibid., 336.

6. Donald O. Dewey, "William Cushing," in *The Supreme Court: A Biographical Dictionary*, ed. Melvin I. Urofsky (New York: Garland, 1994), 127.

7. Herbert Alan Johnson, "William Cushing," in *The Justices of the United States Supreme Court: Their Lives and Major Opinions*, ed. Leon Friedman and Fred I. Israel, rev. ed., vol. 2 (New York: Chelsea House, 1995), 41, 45.

8. See, for example, ibid., 44; Clare Cushman, "William Cushing," in *The Supreme Court Justices: Illustrated Biographies, 1789–1993*, ed. Clare Cushman (Washington, D.C.: CQ Press, 1993), 11, 14.

9. Charles Warren, *The Supreme Court in United States History*, rev. ed., vol. 2 (Boston: Little, Brown, 1926), 400.

10. Quoted in George Lee Haskins and Herbert A. Johnson, *Foundations of Power: John Marshall, 1801–15* (New York: Macmillan, 1981), 382.

11. See Henry J. Abraham, *Justices and Presidents: A Political History of Appointments to the Supreme Court*, 3d ed. (New York: Oxford University Press, 1992), 420.

12. Most notable in this regard is a series of articles written in the late 1950s and early 1960s by William O'Brien. The book to which those articles were supposed to lead never came to fruition. See also Arthur P. Rugg, "William Cushing," *Yale Law Journal* 30 (November 1920): 128–44.

13. The profound esteem in which Cushing was held by Adams and Washington is evidenced by, among other things, Adams's lobbying to get Cushing appointed chief justice of Massachusetts and Washington's nominating Cushing to the U.S. Supreme Court (and later, to be chief justice).

14. See, for example, Cushing, "A Revolutionary Conservative," 314; Johnson, "William Cushing," 49.

15. The final vote for ratification was 187 to 168. A series of letters between James Madison and George Washington reveals the depth of concern among leading Federalists about whether ratification efforts in Massachusetts would succeed. See William O'Brien, "Justice Cushing's Undelivered Speech on the Federal Constitution," *William and Mary Quarterly* 15 (January 1958): 74, 75–76 (discussing the letters).

16. Quoted in Cushing, "A Revolutionary Conservative," 312.

17. Of course, not all Federalists who supported the Constitution became Hamiltonian Federalists after the Constitution went into effect.

18. See ibid., 313.

19. O'Brien, "Justice Cushing's Undelivered Speech," 74–75.

20. Ibid., 74.

21. Ibid., 78–79.

22. Quoted in ibid., 80. Cushing's speech is reprinted in Father O'Brien's article. All references are from that article.

23. Quoted in Samuel B. Harding, *The Contest over the Ratification of the Federal Constitution in the State of Massachusetts* (New York: Longmans, Green, 1896; repr., New York: Da Capo Press, 1970), 69.

24. Quoted in O'Brien, "Justice Cushing's Undelivered Speech," 81. Cushing made a similar argument when defending the respective terms of office for senators and the president. He also insisted that these longer terms would provide stability for the government, something he believed was in "the interest of the people and the security of their liberties." Ibid., 84.

25. See, for example, Cushman, "William Cushing," 13.

26. See James Wilson, "Speech on the Federal Constitution, delivered in Philadelphia," 6 October 1787, in *Pamphlets on the Constitution of the United States*, ed. Paul L. Ford (Brooklyn: 1888; repr., New York: Da Capo Press, 1968), 115, 156; James Madison, "Speech in the Virginia Convention," 25 June 1788, in *The Writings of James Madison*, ed. Gaillard Hunt, vol. 5 (New York: Putnam's Sons, 1900–10), 231; *The Federalist* No. 84 (Alexander Hamilton), ed. Clinton Rossiter (New York: New American Library, 1961), 513.

27. Quoted in O'Brien, "Justice Cushing's Undelivered Speech," 83. At the end of his speech Cushing offered some support for Hancock's specific proposals for amendments to the Constitution. The tepid nature of Cushing's support suggests he was speaking to the proposals because Hancock's sponsorship of them required him to say at least something in their behalf.

28. Quoted in Harding, *The Contest over the Ratification of the Federal Constitution in the State of Massachusetts*, 70.

29. Quoted in O'Brien, "Justice Cushing's Undelivered Speech," 85.

30. *The Federalist* is about as close as one can get to identifying a political theory treatise written during the American Founding. Scholars have long understood, however, that those essays must be read with a full awareness of their underlying objective: to convince the people of New York, and to a lesser extent, the other states, to ratify the Constitution. The purest attempts at political philosophizing during the American Founding were probably John Adams's *A Defense of the Constitutions of Government of the United States of America* (1787) and James Wilson's "Lectures on Law" (1790–1792).

31. Ralph Lerner, "The Supreme Court as Republican Schoolmaster," in *1967 Supreme Court Review*, ed. Philip B. Kurland (Chicago: University of Chicago Press, 1967), 127–80.

32. William Cushing's Charge to the Grand Jury of the Circuit for the District of Rhode Island, 7 November 1794, in *Documentary History of the Supreme Court of the United States, 1789–1800*, ed. Maeva Marcus et al., vol. 2 (New York: Columbia University Press, 1985–), 491, 491–92.

33. The grand jury charges Cushing delivered as a Massachusetts judge were

similar in both style and substance to those he delivered as a U.S. Supreme Court justice. For instance, a grand jury charge delivered at the height of the debate over the ratification of the Massachusetts Constitution of 1780 found Cushing reminding his audience that the purpose of any proper government was to render security to the individual; to secure "the peaceable and quiet enjoyment of those rights which are not necessarily given up to some body of men, by entering into society for the good of the whole—that the rich and powerful may not oppress or Tyrannize the weak and the indigent." Quoted in Cushing, "A Revolutionary Conservative," 158.

34. See Letter from Abigail Adams to John Adams, 21 December 1798, in Marcus, *Documentary History of the Supreme Court*, vol. 3, 317.

35. David R. Warrington, *The Oxford Companion to the Supreme Court of the United States*, ed. Kermit L. Hall (New York: Oxford University Press, 1992), 213, 214. Cushing actually wrote eighteen opinions as a Supreme Court justice. The nineteenth was issued as a circuit court judge. See *M'Donough v. Dannery*, 3 U.S. (3 Dall.) 188 (1796). Of the three cases in which Cushing participated on circuit that were appealed to the Supreme Court, two were reversed. See *Bingham v. Cabot*, 3 U.S. (3 Dall.) 19 (1795); *United States v. Schooner Peggy*, 5 U.S. (1 Cr.) 103 (1801). However, the Court, in an opinion by Chief Justice Marshall, maintained that *Schooner Peggy* was "rightful" when Cushing decided it, and only a subsequent change in the law made it impossible to affirm his circuit judgment. The fact that so few of Cushing's circuit cases were appealed speaks well of Cushing's handling of them.

36. See, for example, Cushman, "William Cushing," 14; Dewey, "William Cushing," 127; Johnson, "William Cushing," 50.

37. David P. Currie, *The Constitution in the Supreme Court: The First Hundred Years, 1789–1888* (Chicago: University of Chicago Press, 1985), 58.

38. Ibid., 58 n.8.

39. Ibid., 37 (discussing *Ware v. Hylton*).

40. Ibid., 41.

41. See, for example, Dewey, "William Cushing," 127 (negatively characterizing Cushing's opinions as "simple").

42. See generally Leslie Friedman Goldstein, *In Defense of the Text: Democracy and Constitutional Theory* (Savage, Md.: Rowman and Littlefield, 1991).

43. See, for example, Bernard Schwartz, *A History of the Supreme Court* (New York: Oxford University Press, 1993), chapter 1.

44. 2 U.S. (2 Dall.) 419 (1793).

45. 2 U.S. (2 Dall.) at 429–50 (Iredell, J., dissenting).

46. See, for example, Currie, *The Constitution in the Supreme Court*, 57 ("As far as the individual Justices are concerned, Paterson and Iredell seem the most impressive"); William R. Casto, *The Supreme Court in the Early Republic: The Chief Justiceships of John Jay and Oliver Ellsworth* (Columbia: University of

South Carolina Press, 1995), 250 ("Paterson and Iredell stood head and shoulders above their fellows").

47. The quick passage of the Eleventh Amendment indicates Iredell's political instincts were correct.

48. 2 U.S. (2 Dall.) at 453–66 (Wilson, J.).

49. Mark D. Hall, "James Wilson: Democratic Theorist and Supreme Court Justice," in this volume.

50. 2 U.S. (2 Dall.) at 469–79 (Jay, C.J.).

51. Casto, *The Supreme Court in the Early Republic*, 192.

52. 2 U.S. (2 Dall.) at 453, 454 (Blair, J.).

53. 2 U.S. (2 Dall.) at 466–69 (Cushing, J.).

54. Marcus, *Documentary History of the Supreme Court*, vol. 5, 127.

55. 3 U.S. (3 Dall.) 199 (1796).

56. 3 U.S. (3 Dall.) at 220–45 (Chase, J.).

57. Julius Goebel, Jr., *History of the Supreme Court of the United States: Antecedents and Beginnings to 1801* (New York: Macmillan, 1971), 751. See also James Haw, Francis F. Beirne, Rosamond R. Beirne, and R. Samuel Jett, *Stormy Patriot: The Life of Samuel Chase* (Baltimore: Maryland Historical Society, 1980), 180 (quoting Goebel).

58. Judicial recusal ethics were apparently more flexible during the Court's formative years than they are now. Herbert Alan Johnson, "John Marshall's Chief Justiceship," Speech to the Supreme Court Historical Society, 9 April 1997, Washington, D.C.

59. 3 U.S. (3 Dall.) at 256–80 (Iredell, J.).

60. See Christopher T. Graebe, "The Federalism of James Iredell in Historical Context," *North Carolina Law Review* 69 (November 1990): 251–72.

61. Goebel, *Antecedents and Beginnings to 1801,* 753.

62. Currie, *The Constitution in the Supreme Court*, 37.

63. 3 U.S. (3 Dall.) at 281–84 (Cushing, J.).

64. Paterson's opinion was a bit more unfocused than Cushing's, but he, too, emphasized that "The phraseology made use of leaves in my mind no room to hesitate as to the intention of the parties. The terms are unequivocal and universal in their signification, and obviously point to and comprehend all creditors, and all debtors, previously to the 3d of September, 1783." 3 U.S. (3 Dall.) at 245–56. Unlike his elaborate opinion in *Chisholm*, Wilson's opinion in *Ware* was concise to the point of abruptness, as Wilson himself acknowledged when he began by saying, "I shall be concise in delivering my opinion, as it depends on a few plain principles." Wilson, too, emphasized the text. He wrote: "It is impossible, by any glossary, or argument, to make words more perspicuous, more conclusive, than by a bare recital." 3 U.S. (3 Dall.) at 281.

65. Philip Bobbitt, *Constitutional Fate: Theory of the Constitution* (New

York: Oxford University Press, 1992). See also Michael J. Gerhardt and Thomas D. Rowe, Jr., *Constitutional Theory: Arguments and Perspectives* (Charlottesville, Va.: Michie, 1993).

66. Compare Scott Douglas Gerber, *To Secure These Rights: The Declaration of Independence and Constitutional Interpretation* (New York: New York University Press, 1995) with Christopher Wolfe, *The Rise of Modern Judicial Review: From Constitutional Interpretation to Judge-Made Law* (New York: Basic Books, 1986).

67. Other opinions Cushing wrote on the Supreme Court indicate likewise. See, for example, *Fowler v. Lindsey*, 3 U.S. (3 Dall.) 410, 414 (1799). Cushing employed a textualist approach on the state bench as well. See Cushing, "A Revolutionary Conservative," 165–77, especially 176 ("In every instance, it appears that Cushing's [Massachusetts high court opinions] were possessed of the same literal conservatism that marked his entire judicial career").

68. There are a number of definitions of textualism, but Bobbitt's is as good as any. Bobbitt defines textual argument as "argument that is drawn from a consideration of the present sense of the words of the provision." Bobbitt, *Constitutional Fate*, 7.

69. For an analogous interpretation of the implementation and compliance problems that have developed because of modern Supreme Court justices' inability to stay on point, see David M. O'Brien, *Storm Center: The Supreme Court in American Politics*, 3d ed. (New York: W. W. Norton, 1993), 346.

70. See, for example, Sylvia Snowiss, *Judicial Review and the Law of the Constitution* (New Haven: Yale University Press, 1990).

71. F. W. Grinnell, "The Anti-Slavery Decisions of 1781 and 1783 and the History of the Duty of the Court in Regard to Unconstitutional Legislation," *Massachusetts Law Quarterly* 2 (May 1917): 437, 442.

72. See, for example, James Q. Wilson and John J. DiIulio, Jr., *American Government: Institutions and Policies*, 6th ed. (Lexington, Mass.: D. C. Heath, 1995), 420.

73. See, for example, David G. Barnum, *The Supreme Court and American Democracy* (New York: St. Martin's Press, 1993), 3–9.

74. See, for example, J. M. Sosin, *The Aristocracy of the Long Robe: The Origins of Judicial Review in America* (Westport, Conn.: Greenwood Press, 1989); Gordon S. Wood, "The Origins of Judicial Review," *Suffolk University Law Review* 22 (Winter 1988): 1293–1307.

75. See Letter from William Cushing to John Adams, 20 May 1776, in *Papers of John Adams*, ed. Robert J. Taylor, vol. 4 (Cambridge: Harvard University Press, Belknap Press, 1979), 199. See also Rugg, "William Cushing," 144 ("The towering form of Marshall has dominated the domain of national constitutional law[,] [b]ut Cushing had been interpreting the great constitution of Massachu-

setts for nearly ten years before the Constitution of the United States was ratified").

76. The April 1791 case voided, pursuant to the supremacy clause of the federal Constitution, a Connecticut statute that conflicted with a provision in the Treaty of Peace with Great Britain ratified in 1783. That case is chronicled in *Connecticut Courant*, May 12, 1791, p. 3; *Massachusetts Spy*, August 25, 1791, p. 3, and July 14, 1791; *Boston Gazette*, July 4, 1791; *Columbian Centinel*, June 29, 1791. The May 1791 case, *Barnes v. West*, struck down a Rhode Island legal tender law as inconsistent with the "gold and silver" clause of section X of the federal Constitution. That case is documented in *Providence Gazette*, June 25, 1791 and July 9, 1791. The June 1792 case, *Champion and Dickason v. Casey*, invoked the contracts clause and adjudged another Rhode Island prodebtor statute unconstitutional. That case is described in *Salem Gazette*, June 26, 1792; *Columbian Centinel*, June 20, 1792; *New York Daily Advertiser*, June 22, 1792; *Providence Gazette*, June 16, 1792. See generally William O'Brien, "The Pre-Marshall Court and the Role of William Cushing," *Massachusetts Law Quarterly* 43 (March 1958): 52, 54 (discussing the cases).

77. See *Hayburn's Case*, 2 U.S. (2 Dall.) 409, 410 n. (1792) (reporting the April 5, 1792, New York circuit opinion of Jay, Cushing, and District Judge Duane). Justices Wilson and Blair, and District Judge Peters declared the statute—the Invalid Pensioners Act—unconstitutional seven days later in the Pennsylvania Circuit, which marked the first time an act of Congress was nullified by a federal court. See ibid., 411–12 n.

78. 4 U.S. (4 Dall.) 14, 20 (1800) (Cushing, J.).

79. See Gordon E. Sherman, "The Case of John Chandler v. The Secretary of War," *Yale Law Journal* 14 (May 1905): 431, 437. See generally *Marbury v. Madison*, 5 U.S. (1 Cr.) 137, 172 (1803) (discussing the case). Susan Low Bloch and Maeva Marcus suggest, but do not conclude, that *Chandler* was decided on other than constitutional grounds. See Susan Low Bloch and Maeva Marcus, "John Marshall's Selective Use of History in *Marbury v. Madison*," *Wisconsin Law Review* (March-April 1986): 301, 315 n.54. I prefer Sherman's reading of the case, which is also Marshall's. Bloch and Marcus accuse Marshall of manipulating a series of precedents to get a desired political result. See generally ibid., 301–37. Bloch and Marcus's article, despite occasionally reading as impenetrably as do most deconstruction articles, is must reading for any student of the early Court. See also Maeva Marcus and Robert Teir, "*Hayburn's Case*: A Misinterpretation of Precedent," *Wisconsin Law Review* (July-August 1988): 527–46.

80. See Robert M. Cover, *Justice Accused: Antislavery and the Judicial Process* (New Haven: Yale University Press, 1975), 8, 43–50.

81. Robert M. Spector, "The Quock Walker Cases (1781–83)—Slavery, Its

Abolition and Negro Citizenship in Early Massachusetts," *Journal of Negro History* 53 (January 1968): 12.

82. Quoted in John D. Cushing, "The Cushing Court and the Abolition of Slavery in Massachusetts: More Notes on the 'Quock Walker Case,'" *American Journal of Legal History* 5 (April 1961): 118, 132–33 (printing for the first time what is evidently the final version of Cushing's jury charge).

83. Cover, *Justice Accused*, 44.

84. See Cushing, "The Cushing Court and the Abolition of Slavery in Massachusetts," 118–44; Grinnell, "The Anti-Slavery Decisions of 1781 and 1783," 437–41; William O'Brien, "Did the Jennison Case Outlaw Slavery in Massachusetts?," *William and Mary Quarterly* 17 (April 1960): 219–41; Spector, "The Quock Walker Cases (1781–83)," 12–32; Elaine MacEacheren, "Emancipation of Slavery in Massachusetts: A Reexamination, 1770–1790," *Journal of Negro History* 55 (October 1970): 289–306; Arthur Zilversmit, "Quok Walker, Mumbet, and the Abolition of Slavery in Massachusetts," *William and Mary Quarterly* 25 (October 1968): 614–24.

85. The status of slaves in transit and nonresident runaway slaves was not before the high court of Massachusetts in Cushing's day. Those issues were addressed by Chief Justice Lemuel Shaw's court in the nineteenth century. See Leonard W. Levy, *The Law of the Commonwealth and Chief Justice Shaw* (Cambridge: Harvard University Press, 1957), 59–108.

86. See generally Saul Cornell, "Early American History in a Postmodern Age," *William and Mary Quarterly* 50 (April 1993): 329–41.

87. A story that is reported in the biographical accounts of Cushing's life with almost as much frequency as the story about his making a list of materials he would need for a new suit is one about how Cushing was the last American judge to wear the full-bottomed English judicial wig.

88. Marshall's contributions are well summarized by Johnson: (1) establishing the "opinion of the Court" as the major vehicle for announcing the Court's decisions; (2) insisting upon "collegial decorum" among the justices; and (3) encouraging the justices to share expertise, to work together for the good of the Court, and to be sensitive to the abilities and limitations of their brethren. Johnson, Speech to the Supreme Court Historical Society. See generally Herbert A. Johnson, *The Chief Justiceship of John Marshall, 1801–1835* (Columbia: University of South Carolina Press, 1997).

*Chapter 5*

# James Wilson
## *Democratic Theorist and Supreme Court Justice*

*Mark D. Hall*

James Wilson (1742–1798) is perhaps the most underrated Founding Father. He was one of six men to sign both the Declaration of Independence and the Constitution of the United States, and his influence on the latter was second only to James Madison's. Wilson played a central role in the ratifying debates as well, and he also was the moving force behind the Pennsylvania Constitution of 1790. As a law professor and U.S. Supreme Court justice, Wilson produced some of the period's most profound commentary on the Constitution and American law.

Despite Wilson's many historic contributions and the high quality of his political thought, he has been largely overlooked by political scientists, historians, and academic lawyers alike. Although most students of the early American republic are aware of Wilson and his role in the framing and ratification of the federal Constitution, few realize the sophistication of his thought or the scope of his contributions. This is evidenced, in part, by the lack of scholarship about Wilson.[1] My essay attempts to fill this void in the literature by demonstrating that Wilson had a sophisticated political theory that strongly influenced his significant role in the creation of the American regime.

## *A Quick Rise to Prominence*

James Wilson was born in Carskerdo, Scotland in 1742, the son of a lower-middle-class farmer. Dedicated to the ministry at birth, Wilson received an uncommonly good education, which culminated in his winning a scholarship to the University of St. Andrews. However, after four years of undergraduate work and one year of divinity school, he was forced to withdraw from the university upon the death of his father.[2] By the time Wilson's brothers were old enough to take care of themselves and their mother, Wilson decided against continuing his studies and emigrated to America to seek fame and fortune.

Wilson arrived in New York in the fall of 1765 and immediately moved to Pennsylvania, where a letter of recommendation helped him to receive an appointment as a tutor at the College of Philadelphia. Although Wilson did well there, he was much too ambitious to remain in the academy. Instead, he applied to read law under one of Pennsylvania's most prominent lawyers, John Dickinson.

After studying under Dickinson for several years, Wilson opened his own private law practice, first in Carlisle and later in Philadelphia. Wilson promptly won a number of important cases—some in which he represented his adopted state. A first-rate legal reputation thereby was secured.[3] An indication of the high regard in which Wilson's legal abilities were held is George Washington's willingness to pay Wilson one hundred guineas to accept his nephew Bushrod as a law student. Bushrod, aware that this fee was well above the going rate, begged his uncle to allow him to study elsewhere, but Washington was convinced of Wilson's superior ability as a lawyer and insisted upon him. Bushrod was evidently well served by this arrangement, as indicated by his own successful legal career and eventual appointment to Wilson's seat on the U.S. Supreme Court.[4]

Wilson also was recognized internationally. For instance, in 1779 Conrad-Alexandre Gérard bestowed upon Wilson the great honor of appointing him France's advocate-general in America. The appointment was confirmed by Louis XVI in 1781, and Wilson held the post until 1783, when he resigned because the French monarch was unwilling to pay the high fees he required. Ultimately, Louis XVI paid Wilson 10,000 livres for his services.[5]

Wilson maintained an active law practice until his appointment to the U.S. Supreme Court in 1790, but from the start of the Revolutionary War until his death he spent the largest portion of his time engaged in affairs of state. In 1774 Wilson joined Carlisle's Committee of Correspondence and shortly thereafter was elected a deputy to the July 15 meeting of Pennsylvania leaders. Although Wilson was not selected to go to the first Continental Congress, he was recognized as a rising star on the political scene with the publication of his 1774 pamphlet, "Considerations on the Nature and Extent of the Legislative Authority of the British Parliament."[6] In this pamphlet Wilson provided the first public argument for why the "legislative authority of the British Parliament over the colonies [should be] denied *in every instant*."[7]

Wilson was able to put his theory of resistance into practice when in May 1775 he was elected to the Second Continental Congress. After making several important contributions to the debate over independence, he cast the deciding vote in the Pennsylvania delegation, and thus switched the delegation's vote and allowed the Declaration of Independence to be unanimously adopted. Wilson then turned to the task of regime building, first by opposing what he considered to be dangerous aspects of Pennsylvania's radical constitution of 1776 and then by serving in Congress under the Articles of Confederation.[8]

Wilson's principled stands in both state and national politics led him to offend just about every American. Pennsylvania's aristocrats could not understand Wilson's consistent support for fully democratic institutions, while commoners and radical democrats never comprehended his advocacy of separated powers and checks and balances. Wilson's support for the latter, when combined with his defense of several local merchants accused of treason, contributed to his reputation as an enemy of democracy.[9] Opposition to Wilson reached its zenith in October 1779, when a mob descended upon Wilson and his allies. After a short gun battle the mob was chased off, but the "Attack on Fort Wilson," as the incident became known, exacerbated the view that Wilson was an enemy of democracy—a view that has lasted in some circles to this day.[10]

## *Democratic Theorist of the American Founding*

James Wilson's greatest contributions to the American republic were made in the Federal Convention of 1787. Among the few delegates to attend the convention from start to finish, Wilson participated in all of the most important proceedings. He spoke more times (168) than any other member, save Gouverneur Morris, and he often responded to the most serious attacks on the concept of a strong and democratic national government. Indeed, scholars as varied in their interpretations of the American Founding as Samuel Beer, James Bryce, Max Farrand, Ralph Ketcham, Adrienne Koch, Robert McCloskey, and Clinton Rossiter agree that Wilson was second only to James Madison, and was perhaps on a par with him, in terms of influence on the framing of the Constitution.[11]

Wilson's contributions to the debates at the Federal Convention of 1787 were numerous and detailed. The best way to approach them is not to review the story of the entire convention but instead to outline Wilson's political theory and then explore its practical consequences. Once the framework of Wilson's political theory is understood, his activities at the convention and, indeed, during his entire political career, fall readily into place.

Central to Wilson's political theory was his view of morality. He followed Richard Hooker, who in turn borrowed from St. Thomas Aquinas, and adhered to a traditional Christian conception of natural law.[12] Wilson added to this tradition by his insistence that the natural rights of individuals are firmly based on this law, and that any human law that violates natural rights is void.[13] Rights play so important a part in Wilson's political theory that he argued that their protection is the "primary and principal object in the institution of government."[14]

In his famous law lectures of 1790–1792 Wilson provided a detailed discussion of the rights governments must protect. Central among these are the rights of individuals to safety, property, character, and liberty.[15] Wilson had a fairly expansive view of the latter concept. In his judgment, liberty includes freedom of religion and the right to "think, to speak, to write, and to publish freely."[16] Wilson also maintained that all members of society should be equally protected by law because law is based upon moral principles, not popular opinion. And in a statement that foreshadowed John Stuart Mill's *On Liberty*, Wilson declared: "On one side, indeed, there stands a single individual: on the other side, perhaps, there stand millions: but right is weighed by principle; it is not estimated by numbers."[17]

What sort of government would best protect rights? Because Wilson believed that people could know natural law through their moral senses, and because he had a relatively optimistic view of human nature, he concluded that majority rule is the best way to make human laws.[18] Consequently, he embraced the concept of popular sovereignty, and argued that all legitimate governments must be based directly on the will of the people. His position is best illustrated through his most famous metaphor:

> The pyramid of government—and a republican government may well receive that beautiful and solid form—should be raised to a dignified altitude, but its foundations must, of consequence, be broad, and strong, and deep. The authority, the interests, and the affections of the people at large are the only foundation, on which a superstructure, proposed to be at once durable and magnificent, can be rationally erected.[19]

Every aspect of government, therefore, must be founded upon the authority of the people. Their consent, he taught, is the "sole legitimate principle of obedience to human laws."[20]

Wilson's views about popular sovereignty led him to be the most democratic member of the convention. From the convention's opening days, Wilson advocated the direct, popular election of both representatives and senators.[21] To ensure that the base of his pyramid was as broad as possible, he successfully fought the inclusion in the Constitution of a property qualification for suffrage.[22] For the same reason he argued that because people, not states, are the basis of representation, members of both houses ought to be elected from proportionally-sized districts.[23] More radical still, he moved that the executive should be directly elected by the people.[24] While some of his proposals were not adopted, Wilson was instrumental in making the Constitution as democratic as it was, and he successfully kept the door open so that it could become more democratic in the future.[25]

For all his democratic idealism, Wilson was aware of the danger of tyranny by the majority. He recognized that people are "imperfect" and that they suddenly may "become inflamed by mutual imitation and example" and do irrational or immoral things that they normally would not do.[26] To prevent this, he supported the Constitution's system of separated powers and checks and balances. He reasoned that these mechanisms would divide power and make both minority and majority tyranny difficult.

Wilson supported a number of devices that he thought would check the will of an errant majority. These included a six-year term for senators and an executive veto.[27] His most interesting checks, however, involved the judiciary. Early in the convention he supported Madison's Council of Revision, which consisted of the executive and "a convenient number of the judiciary."[28] The council would have had an absolute veto over legislative acts. Madison's proposal was eventually rejected, but Wilson did not give up on efforts to strengthen the judiciary.

Wilson was convinced that the Supreme Court needed to be independent from the other institutions of the national government. He therefore adamantly opposed the Virginia plan's provision that the legislature appoint the justices.[29] He also fought his old mentor John Dickinson's proposal that judges be easily removable, and he supported the constitutional prohibition against lowering their salaries.[30] After Wilson helped to form a largely independent Supreme Court, he proceeded to argue for a system of lower federal courts. He eventually agreed to the compromise of giving Congress the power to create lower federal courts in the future.[31]

Not only did Wilson support an independent Supreme Court, he intended it to have the power of judicial review.[32] He most clearly expressed this expectation in his law lectures, where he maintained that a bad law might be vetoed by the executive and that it is "subject also to another given degree of control by the judiciary department, whenever the laws, though in fact passed, are found to be contradictory to the constitution."[33]

The Supreme Court is in a particularly good position to check Congress, Wilson insisted, because the justices are well trained in complex legal matters and are insulated from popular passions.[34] Wilson later showed that he was serious about this proposition when he led a circuit court in *Hayburn's Case* (1792) in refusing to comply with an unconstitutional act of Congress.

Was Wilson's support for checks like judicial review inconsistent with his democratic theory? Elsewhere I argue in detail that it was not, but here I can merely suggest a solution.[35] Wilson made it clear that he did not expect countermajoritarian checks to be used often. About judicial review, for instance, he wrote that "laws may be unjust, may be unwise, may be dangerous, may be destructive; and yet not be so unconstitutional as to justify the judges in refusing to give them effect."[36] He also argued for judicial self-restraint. A judge, Wilson contended, should "remember, that his duty and his business is, not to make the law, but to interpret and apply it."[37]

Wilson did not believe that the Supreme Court would use its power to thwart the majority on many issues. Instead, he thought the Court would use the power of judicial review only rarely: to strike down blatantly unconstitutional or unjust laws. For Wilson, countermajoritarian checks like judicial review are at best temporary injunctions for preventing majorities from acting out of "passions" and "prejudices" that are "inflamed by mutual imitation and example."[38] In the final analysis the Court cannot prevent the people from passing a law, but this is as it should be because the people are best able to create just laws. The purpose of checks like judicial review is not, then, to make policy but to restrain improper or unjust laws until the people recognize them as such and correct them.

Wilson's democratic views greatly influenced his theory of federalism. While partisans of the states or the national government argued (and argue) about which is sovereign, Wilson presented the truly democratic view of the subject. For Wilson, only the people are sovereign, and once this principle is settled

> the consequence is that they may take from the subordinate governments powers with which they have hitherto trusted them, and place those powers in the general government, if it is thought that there they will be productive of more good. They can distribute one portion of power to the more contracted circle called state governments: they can furnish another proportion to the government of the United States. Who will undertake to say as a state officer that the people may not give to the general government what powers and for what purpose they please? how come it sir, that these state governments dictate to their superiors?—to the majesty of the people.[39]

In America the people decided to split the power of government between the states and the nation. Of course the difficulty with this approach is deciding which powers belong to the states and which belong to the nation. Wilson taught that the "general principle" that should be used to draw "a line between the national and the individual governments of the states" is that

> whatever object was confined in its nature and operation to a particular State, ought to be subject to the separate governments of the States; but

> whatever in its nature and operation extended beyond a particular State, ought to be comprehended within the federal jurisdiction.[40]

Wilson attempted to put this principle into practice when, as a member of the Committee of Detail, he played a key role in drafting Article One, Section Eight of the Constitution.[41]

Wilson believed that the scope of the national government was limited to powers enumerated in the Constitution. It is true that he supported the necessary and proper clause. But he thought implied powers must be closely connected to enumerated powers—they were not a license to do anything.[42] Powers not given to the national government are reserved to the people, who may or may not chose to give them to the states.[43]

Wilson so strongly believed that the national government was limited to enumerated powers that he opposed the addition of a bill of rights to the Constitution. Why, for example, add a statement that Congress cannot restrict the liberty of the press if Congress has no power over the press? Furthermore, Wilson insisted, a bill of rights would be dangerous because if any rights are left out it might be assumed that they are not retained by the people.[44]

Wilson was not so naive as to think that an enumeration of Congress's powers would prevent conflicts from arising between the states and the nation. In fact, he warned George Washington in 1791 that "the most intricate and the most delicate questions in our national jurisprudence will arise in running the line between the authority of the national government and that of the several states."[45] To prevent these conflicts from arising, Wilson thought the national government should commission him to prepare a digest of the laws of the United States to work out the parameters of each government's powers. Washington liked Wilson's codification project and encouraged him to pursue it. The project ultimately was abandoned at the urging of Attorney General Edmund Randolph, who considered the task to be beyond any one man.[46]

Wilson did not rely on his codification project alone. He believed that ultimately the national government must judge for itself the proper application of its powers. Initially, this belief led him to support Madison's proposal that the national legislature have the power to veto state laws.[47] Wilson supported this proposal not because he wanted Congress to examine every state law and strike down those it did not like. Rather, he considered the congressional veto to be primarily a form of self-defense against encroachments by the states into matters of national jurisdiction.

When it became clear that a congressional veto over state laws was not going to be adopted, Wilson helped to develop an acceptable alternative. As a driving force behind the Committee of Detail, Wilson deserves considerable credit for the supremacy clause of the Constitution. This clause, he eventually was able to convince his ally Madison, was a reasonable alternative to the congressional veto, for it guaranteed that federal laws, made pursuant to the Constitution, would be the supreme law of the land.[48]

Of course the question still remained: Who decides whether a particular federal law is constitutional, and therefore supreme? Wilson thought that this task belonged to the Supreme Court. He noted that in this institution the

> "judicial power of the United States is vested" by the "people," who "ordained and established" the constitution. The business and the design of the judicial power is, to administer justice according to the law of the land. . . . When the question occurs—What is the law of the land? it [the judiciary] must also decide this question.[49]

Hence Wilson concluded that the Supreme Court had the power to resolve all disputes involving federalism, subject only to the ultimate power of the people themselves.

The above pages outline James Wilson's contributions to the creation of a strong and democratic national government that protects individual rights. It is interesting to note how closely America's current constitutional system resembles the one he envisioned. Early in the nineteenth century states began to make some of the suffrage reforms that Wilson advocated. By the twentieth century his proposal that senators be elected by the people had become enshrined in the Constitution, and his "chimerical" idea that the president be elected by the people has become the political practice, if not the constitutional rule. It was at this time as well that the Supreme Court began to exercise its power to check the other institutions of government and protect individual and minority rights to the extent Wilson conceived. In 1964, for instance, the Court effectuated one of Wilson's most important ideals when it applied the principle of one-person, one-vote to the U.S. House of Representatives. Indeed, Justice Hugo Black's opinion for the Court cited Wilson's law lectures on this point.[50]

## *Leader in the Ratification Debate*

From the Constitutional Convention Wilson proceeded to the Pennsylvania ratifying convention where, as the only member to attend both, he became the leader of the proratification forces. He began his defense of the Constitution with his famous "State House Yard Speech," given in Philadelphia on October 6, 1787. There Wilson promoted the benefits of the Constitution and responded to several of the main Antifederalist attacks.[51] Most significantly, as noted above, he defended the absence of a bill of rights from the Constitution.

Wilson was the first member of the Federal Convention to defend the Constitution publicly. He did his job so well that Pennsylvania became the second state, and the first large one, to ratify the Constitution. Because of his success, Federalists throughout the country enlisted his aid in their own ratification efforts. George Washington, for instance, sent a copy of Wilson's "State House Yard Speech" to a friend, and noted that

> the enclosed *Advertiser* contains a speech of Mr. Wilson's, as able, candid, and honest member as was in the convention, which will place most of Colonel Mason's objections in their true point of light, I send it to you. The republication of it, if you can get it done, will be serviceable at this juncture.[52]

By December 29, 1787, the speech had been reprinted in 34 newspapers in twelve states.[53] In addition, it was published in pamphlet form and circulated throughout the nation. It was so important, Bernard Bailyn insists, that "in the 'transient circumstances' of the time it was not so much the *Federalist* papers that captured most people's imaginations as James Wilson's speech of October 6, 1787, the most famous, to some the most notorious, federalist statement of the time."[54] Many defenders of the Constitution in other states referred to the speech for ammunition in their own ratification battles.[55] It soon became, in Gordon Wood's words, "the basis of all Federalist thinking."[56]

As his final act of constitution making, Wilson was pleased to lead Pennsylvania in disposing of its constitution of 1776. The Pennsylvania constitutional convention of 1789–1790 commenced with Wilson, the Federalist leader, and William Findley, the leader of the western radicals, agreeing to renounce the old constitution and begin debating a new draft constitution Wilson wrote. In the draft Wilson provided for a government based firmly on the will of the people but limited through a strong system of separated powers. Ironically, Wilson, who often had been labeled an aristocrat, broke with his old allies and joined the western democrats on several issues. Most significant, he led the fight for the direct, popular election of representatives, state senators, and the governor.[57] Wilson's contributions to the Pennsylvania Constitution of 1790 are noteworthy for present purposes insofar as they demonstrate that he did not argue for democratic institutions at the Federal Convention simply because he was from a large state.

### *U.S. Supreme Court Justice*

After the Constitution was ratified, Wilson thought he deserved a position in the new national government. Accordingly, he wrote to President Washington and suggested that he be appointed chief justice of the United States.[58] Washington responded coolly, writing: "To you, my dear Sir, and others who know me, I presume it will be unnecessary for me to say that I have entered upon my office without the constraint of a single *engagement*."[59] Eventually, however, Wilson was appointed and confirmed as an associate justice of the first Supreme Court. From this position he was to play an important role in the formation of American law. Although he participated in fewer than two dozen cases, he left his mark in a variety of ways.

One of the most significant decisions by Wilson as a Supreme Court justice is also one of the most overlooked. In 1792 Congress passed the Invalid Pensioners Act, which provided federal assistance to veterans injured in the Revolutionary War. It also required federal circuit court judges to determine whether individuals who claimed benefits were eligible for them. The judges' decisions were subject to final approval by the secretary of war and Congress. The first case arose in the New York Circuit, where Chief Justice John Jay and Associate Justice William Cushing were presiding with District Judge James Duane. These judges informed Congress that they had problems with this duty, but that they would perform it out of respect for the legislators and the pensioners.[60]

When a case arose in the Pennsylvania Circuit, Justices Wilson and John Blair, along with District Judge Richard Peters, refused to accept the pensioner's case. Under Wilson's leadership the justices and the judge wrote a letter to President Washington in which they argued that reviewing invalid pensioners' claims was not a judicial function and, more important, that it violated the principle of separation of powers because the secretary of war and Congress had the final say. They refused to hear the claim.[61]

In response to the letter, Attorney General Edmund Randolph applied to the Supreme Court for a writ of mandamus requiring the circuit court judges to perform their duty. Fortunately for John Marshall's reputation, the full Court did not have to rule on the matter. Before the justices could act, Congress altered the offending legislation and mooted the case.

Because the Supreme Court never issued an official opinion, *Hayburn's Case* (1792) is often overlooked by students of the judicial process.[62] But it is fair to consider the case to be, in Hayburn's words, the "first instance in which a court of justice has declared a law of Congress unconstitutional."[63] James Madison evidently agreed with this assessment, as indicated by a letter to Richard Henry Lee in which Madison commented that the circuit court judges in Pennsylvania had pronounced the act "unconstitutional and void."[64] Similarly, St. George Tucker, in his 1803 "republicanized" edition of Blackstone's Commentaries, cited *Hayburn's Case* as evidence that the judiciary has the duty to void an unconstitutional act of Congress.[65] Thus, eleven years before *Marbury v. Madison* (1803) the justices, led by Wilson, were engaging in judicial review of federal legislation.

Without a doubt, Wilson's most significant opinion came in the 1793 case *Chisholm v. Georgia*.[66] The case arose when Chisholm, the executor of the estate of a Loyalist, sued Georgia for payment of a debt incurred during the Revolutionary War. Georgia officials claimed that, as a sovereign, Georgia could not be sued. The state officials recognized that to submit Georgia to the jurisdiction of the federal courts would strike a major blow to state sovereignty. This concern had been repeatedly raised by the Antifederalists, who had argued in many of the ratifying conventions that individuals would be able to sue states as states.[67]

In *Chisholm* the Antifederalists' worst nightmare seemed to come true: the Supreme Court ruled four to one against Georgia. Wilson joined the majority and wrote the most memorable and theoretically interesting of the seriatim opinions. He moved far beyond the simple legal question and concluded that the case was not primarily about jurisdiction but instead concerned the question whether "the people of the United States form a Nation?"[68]

Wilson provided an elaborate answer to this question. As he was wont to do, he began with an examination of the relevant jurisprudential issues. He opened with a quote from Thomas Reid about the importance of language. Language is important because imprecise words can lead to bad political theory. For instance, people often misuse the terms "state" and "sovereign." To define these terms, Wilson returned to first principles and reminded his audience that people are "fearfully and wonderfully made," and that they are endowed by their "Creator" with "dignity." A state, on the other hand, is but an "inferior contrivance of man." While a state is certainly "useful and valuable," the people should never forget that a state exists to serve them, not vice versa.[69]

Wilson built on this distinction, and informed his readers that the people always retain their power of original sovereignty. While the people may vest aspects of this sovereignty in states, this is merely sovereignty of a "derivative" nature. It is therefore inaccurate to speak of a "sovereign state," for only the people are sovereign. Wilson thereby looked at the issue from the perspective of the Union and decreed that the people as a whole—including the citizens of Georgia—created the Constitution. Consequently, "as to the purposes of the Union . . . Georgia is NOT a sovereign State."[70]

On the basis of "general jurisprudence," Wilson concluded that Georgia is not a sovereign state and that it has a duty to fulfill its contracts. Although Wilson probably was tempted to rest his decision on these theoretical grounds, he proceeded to examine a number of precedents that supported his proposition that governments could be sued. Wilson admitted that in England this had not been the case since the Norman Conquest. Yet under the Saxon government, rulers were subject to the law. Similarly, he pointed to several Greek and Spanish precedents that seemed to support his position.

Given that the sovereign people can grant the national government whatever powers they choose, the only question that remained was whether they did indeed give the Supreme Court jurisdiction over state governments.[71] To answer this question Wilson finally turned to Article III, Section 2 of the Constitution, where it states that the judicial power "shall extend to controversies, between a state and citizens of another state."[72] Clearly, Wilson contended, this provision shows that the people gave the Supreme Court the jurisdiction to hear cases like Chisholm's. Georgia therefore must submit to the will of the sovereign people and subject itself to the jurisdiction of the Court.[73]

Wilson's opinion has been criticized—including in this collection—for being unnecessarily complex.[74] It is true that Wilson could have forgone the theoretical discussion and simply turned to the text of the Constitution. But Wilson recognized the power of language and ideas. He firmly believed that popular sovereignty was the foundation upon which the American system of government was based. Consequently, he wanted to attack head-on—and in detail—the notion of state sovereignty, which he correctly perceived could tear the nation apart.

Americans were not yet willing to embrace Wilson's views on sovereignty. Indeed, states' rights advocates moved quickly to pass a constitutional amendment to reverse *Chisholm*. Unfortunately, there are no records of Wilson's reaction to the Eleventh Amendment. One reasonably may presume, however, that Wilson would have considered the Eleventh Amendment unwise because it allowed states to judge themselves. That said, Wilson undoubtedly would have accepted the amendment because he supported the power of the people to change the Constitution as they saw fit.

Wilson played a role in two other important early Supreme Court decisions involving federalism. In *Hylton v. U.S.* (1796), he concurred with the Court that Congress's uniform tax on carriages was not a direct tax and was therefore constitutional.[75] Wilson did not write an opinion because the Court upheld the ruling he made on circuit. The case significantly strengthened the ability of the new national government to raise revenue by upholding a key element of Alexander Hamilton's plan for rescuing the finances of the fledgling republic. The mere acceptance of this case also implied that the justices believed that the Court had the power to strike down acts of Congress. In fact, when Wilson was presiding over the circuit court arguments in the case, he told the government's counsel that the justices were of the opinion that federal courts could strike down congressional legislation as unconstitutional.[76]

In *Ware v. Hylton* (1796), Wilson held that the national government's treaty-making power takes precedence over state law. Specifically, the 1783 treaty with Great Britain, which required repayment of prewar debts to British citizens, preempted a 1777 Virginia law that effectively abolished those debts.[77] Wilson was tempted to make this ruling solely on the basis of the "law of nations," but he ultimately joined the rest of the Court in declaring that the supremacy clause operated retroactively. An important precedent concerning the supremacy of federal law thereby was established.[78]

Throughout his legal career Wilson evidenced a profound commitment to the idea that law must be based on the will of the people. He challenged, for instance, the conventional wisdom that juries should judge only facts. Instead, Wilson proposed that in at least some instances they should be able to judge law as well. In his first charge to a federal grand jury, Wilson stated that

> it may seem, at first view, to be somewhat extra-ordinary that twelve men, untutored in the study of jurisprudence, should be the ultimate interpreters of the law, with a power to overrule the directions of the Judges who have made it the subject of their long and elaborate researches, and have been raised to the seat of judgment for their professional abilities and skill.[79]

Wilson believed that a jury could decide both facts and laws because it is serving as a representative of society.[80] Jurors therefore may choose to reject a judge's instructions on a point of law, even though a judge is better trained in law than they are. For Wilson, when it comes to principles of right and justice, the common person is able to know truth as well as—if not better than—the trained expert.[81]

Wilson respected juries because he felt they represent the will of the people. For a similar reason he cherished the common law.[82] Indeed, Wilson declared that "every lovely feature [of common law] beams consent."[83] Common law is one of the most democratic of all types of law because people have agreed to it and have participated in its development throughout the ages.[84] As he did with democracy, Wilson supported common law not as an end in itself but because it is an important means by which natural law can be known.[85]

This was not to say, however, that common law is perfect. Wilson recognized that it contained errors, and he criticized aspects of it throughout his law lectures.[86] But, like society, common law is in a state of progression because its "authority rests on reception, approbation, custom, long and established. The same principles, which establish it, change, enlarge, improve, and repeal it."[87]

Wilson taught that in addition to providing a good rule of justice, common law is practical. Among its other benefits, it can help define terms and fill in gaps not covered by statutory law.[88] Further, common law is of such "vast importance" that "by it, the proceedings and decisions of courts of justice are regulated and directed."[89] Because common law is complex and important, he encouraged lawyers to specialize in it.[90]

One of the most pressing unsettled legal issues in the new republic was the extent to which common law should be accepted by American courts, particularly federal courts.[91] Antifederalists generally opposed a federal common law because they feared it would increase the power of the national government. Wilson joined many of his Federalist colleagues in arguing that common law, insofar as it is not in conflict with the Constitution or federal statutory law, should be accepted by federal courts. His most important contributions in this regard were his grand jury charges in the United States circuit court cases of Gideon Henfield and Joseph Ravara.

In July 1793, Gideon Henfield was charged before a grand jury with, among other things, engaging in acts hostile to nations at peace with the United States by seizing a British ship. No statute explicitly forbade Henfield's activities, but Wilson argued that the common law is the basis of jurisprudence in America, that American common law, like English common law, incorporated the law of nations, and that Americans are therefore liable for violations of common law.[92] Although to the great rejoicing of the Antifederalists the jury acquitted Henfield, Wilson's charge contributed to the eventual, though short-lived, acceptance of common law claims by the federal courts.[93]

Wilson also played a role in the prosecution of Joseph Ravara, consul-general of the Republic of Genoa. Ravara was indicted by a grand jury, with Supreme Court Justices Wilson and James Iredell and District Judge Richard Peters presiding, for "sending anonymous and threatening letters to Mr. Hammond, the British Minister, Mr. Holland, a citizen of Philadelphia, and several other persons, with a view to extort money."[94] Because this case was poorly reported, scholars long have debated the exact nature of the charges.[95] Recent scholarship has shown that both the prosecutors and the defense attorneys understood that the central charge was based on common law.[96] Ravara was found guilty, but he was pardoned by President Washington for diplomatic reasons. The case is significant because it was the first time a person was convicted in a federal court for violating the common law, and because Wilson was again at the forefront of the action.

As mentioned above, Antifederalists did not want the federal courts to have jurisdiction in common-law cases because it would strengthen the power of the national government. As a Federalist, Wilson did not share this concern. Rather, he was so enamored of the democratic character of the common law that he felt it necessary for courts to use it if they are to make just decisions. Because the common law stems from the custom of many people over many years, it was, in Wilson's mind, similar to natural law. Thus he joined the Federalists in advocating federal common-law jurisdiction not because he wanted to expand the power of the national government but, rather, because he believed common law to be extremely democratic, and therefore an excellent approximation of natural law.[97]

Perhaps Wilson's most important contribution to American jurisprudence took place off the bench. From 1790 to 1792 he found time to teach law at the College of Philadelphia. There, Wilson presented the first set of lectures on American constitutional law.[98] The significance of Wilson's lectures is indicated by the audience that attended his inaugural address, which included

> the President of the United States, with his lady—also the Vice-President, and both houses of Congress, the President and both houses of the Legislature of Pennsylvania, together with a great number of ladies and gentlemen . . . the whole comprising a most brilliant and respectable audience.[99]

Wilson's lectures are important for the present discussion because he believed law should be "studied and practiced as a science founded in principle [not] followed as a trade depending merely upon precedent."[100] Consequently, Wilson spent most of his time focusing on philosophical matters, especially those that pertained to morality, epistemology, metaphysics, and politics. He thought that once these foundations of jurisprudence were mastered, students then could learn what he termed "the retail business of law."[101]

This is not to say, however, that Wilson did not discuss mundane legal matters. His lectures progressed naturally from abstract political theory to more concrete constitutional issues, such as the powers of Congress, the president, and the Court. He also examined state and local governments, relatively uninteresting offices like sheriff and coroner included. He lectured on specific crimes against individuals and property as well, and the punishments associated with those crimes. Yet even when Wilson discussed the most banal of subjects he was careful to return as often as possible to the first principles of American jurisprudence.

It is unfortunate that Wilson delivered only half of his planned lectures. Although he had written all of them, several are in outline form. Wilson eventually hoped to complete and revise his lectures and thereby provide the definitive account of American law. Even without these revisions, however, Wilson's lectures have been described accurately as among the most systematic and theoretically interesting studies of the Constitution and American law articulated by a Founder.[102]

Wilson's writings illustrate his great faith in "the science of politics."[103] He believed that political science was in its infancy, and that the greatest discoveries lay ahead.[104] He attempted to contribute to this progress through his investigation of the fundamental principles of law and politics. And unlike many political thinkers, Wilson attempted to apply the knowledge he gained through study to real political problems.

## *A Sad End to a Still Important Life*

Wilson spent an ever-increasing amount of time during the later years of his life trying to manage his business affairs. He had borrowed heavily to speculate in western lands and was fighting constantly to meet bills and to borrow more money for further investments. In 1797 an economic downturn devastated the overleveraged Wilson, along with many other prominent men—including Robert Morris, the "Financier of the Revolution" and at one point the richest man in America.[105] Unable to find assistance to meet the variety of notes coming due, Wilson was forced to flee from his creditors. Thrown into jail on two separate occasions, he spent his final days hiding from creditors in a tavern in Edenton, North Carolina, the hometown of Justice

Iredell. Here, with his wife by his side, Wilson contracted malaria and died on August 21, 1798.[106] He was buried with little ceremony on the estate of Mrs. Iredell's father.[107]

Perhaps it is as a result of his early, ignoble death that James Wilson is not better known today. Because he died at a relatively young age he was unable to complete his law lectures and law digests. Yet Wilson is worthy of study because his sophisticated and innovative political theory informed his many important contributions to the creation of the American republic. As this essay has endeavored to show, Wilson was instrumental in supporting and reconciling some of the best ideas of his (and our) day: popular sovereignty, majority rule, and minority rights. The tension remains between these ideas, which means that Wilson should be regarded not only as an influential historical figure but as someone who can inform current debate.

## NOTES

1. There is one good biography of Wilson, and several scholars have published interesting but narrow articles about his political theory. No work, however, provides a systematic account of Wilson's political and legal philosophy. I attempt to do so in *The Political and Legal Philosophy of James Wilson (1742–1798)* (Columbia: University of Missouri Press, 1997), from which the present essay is adapted.

The good biography of Wilson is Charles Page Smith, *James Wilson: Founding Father* (Chapel Hill: University of North Carolina Press, 1956). Geoffrey Seed provides a nice summary of Wilson's political ideas in *James Wilson* (Millwood, N.Y.: KTO Press, 1978). Additional scholarship about Wilson is cited throughout the present essay.

2. Most nineteenth- and early-twentieth-century scholarship about Wilson holds that Wilson studied at the University of Edinburgh and that of Glasgow, as well as at St. Andrews. There is little evidence to support these claims.

3. The most important of these cases was the 1782 dispute between Pennsylvania and Connecticut over the Wyoming Valley. The case in question was argued in Trenton, New Jersey, before a tribunal formed under Article IX of the Articles of Confederation. Wilson's presentation convinced the judges of Pennsylvania's rightful claim to the land. Significantly, Connecticut acquiesced to the decision, which marked the first time a dispute between states had been settled under the auspices of the national government. The successful culmination of this lawsuit likely inspired Wilson's later support for a strong federal judiciary. See Seed, *James Wilson*, 185; Smith, *James Wilson*, 170–76.

4. Bushrod Washington to Bird Wilson, 26 October 1822, in James Wilson Papers, Historical Society of Pennsylvania, Philadelphia.

5. See The Burton Alva Konkle Papers, Swarthmore University, vol. III, esp. 81a.

6. In *The Works of James Wilson*, ed. Robert G. McCloskey (Cambridge: Harvard University Press, 1967), 721–46 (hereafter cited as *Works*). Wilson wrote the pamphlet in 1768. He refrained from publishing it at that time because he considered it to be too radical.

7. Ibid., 721 (emphasis in original). On the pamphlet's significance, see Bernard Bailyn, *The Ideological Origins of the American Revolution*, enlarged ed. (Cambridge: Harvard University Press, 1992), 225.

8. On Wilson and the Pennsylvania Constitution of 1776, see Gordon S. Wood, *The Creation of the American Republic, 1776–1787* (Chapel Hill: University of North Carolina Press, 1969), 137–40, 244–51; John Paul Selsam, *The Pennsylvania Constitution of 1776: A Study of Revolutionary Democracy* (Philadelphia: University of Pennsylvania Press, 1936). On Wilson's role in the Continental Congress, see Edmund Cody Burnett, *The Continental Congress* (New York: Macmillan, 1941); Merrill Jensen, *The Articles of Confederation: An Interpretation of the Social-Constitutional History of the American Revolution, 1774–1781* (1940; repr., Madison: University of Wisconsin Press, 1962).

9. Wilson's participation in these trials had important implications for American treason law. There is good reason to believe, Charles Smith proposes, that Wilson was the primary advocate of the treason clause of the federal Constitution, which requires, among other things, two witnesses to the same overt act of treason. Smith, *James Wilson*, 116–28. See also William Hurst, "Treason in the United States," *Harvard Law Review* 58 (1944): 404.

10. For twentieth-century scholars who continued to view Wilson as an enemy of democracy, see especially Merrill Jensen, review of Charles Page Smith, *James Wilson: Founding Father*, *Pennsylvania Magazine of History and Biography* 80 (1956): 521–23; Jensen, *The Articles of Confederation*, 92, 240; Gustavus Myers, *History of the Supreme Court of the United States* (Chicago: Charles H. Kerr, 1925), 151–96.

11. Samuel Beer, *To Make a Nation: A Rediscovery of American Federalism* (Cambridge: Harvard University Press, 1993), 360; James Bryce, "James Wilson: An Appreciation," *Pennsylvania Magazine of History and Biography* 60 (1936): 360; Max Farrand, *The Framing of the Constitution of the United States* (New Haven: Yale University Press, 1913), 197; Ralph Ketcham, *James Madison: A Biography* (New York: Macmillan, 1970), 229; Adrienne Koch, ed., *Notes of the Debates in the Federal Convention of 1787* (New York: W. W. Norton, 1987), xii; Robert G. McCloskey, "James Wilson," in *The Justices of the United States Supreme Court: Their Lives and Major Opinions*, ed. Leon Friedman and Fred Israel (New York: Chelsea House, 1969), I:79; Clinton

Rossiter, *1787: The Grand Convention* (New York: W. W. Norton, 1966), 247–48.

12. See *Works*, 123–25. Compare St. Thomas Aquinas, *Summa Theologica*, Q. 90–95; Richard Hooker, *Of the Laws of Ecclesiastical Polity*, book I of *The Works of that Learned and Judicious Divine, Mr. Richard Hooker*, ed. R. W. Church and F. P. Paget (Oxford: Clarendon Press, 1888).

Many modern scholars neglect or reject the Christian foundation of Wilson's natural law theory. This is most obvious in Roderick M. Hills, "The Reconciliation of Law and Liberty in James Wilson," *Harvard Journal of Law and Public Policy* 12 (1989): 891–940. For a contrary view, see Randolph G. Adams, *Selected Political Essays of James Wilson* (New York: Alfred A. Knopf, 1930), 7–8; McCloskey, *Works*, 38. William F. Obering, *The Philosophy of Law of James Wilson* (Washington, D.C.: Catholic University of America Press, 1938), is the best of several neoscholastic works on Wilson that take Wilson's natural-law theory seriously.

13. *Works*, 124, 329, 589, 617, 722. Wilson did not make the sorts of distinctions between terms like "natural law," "natural right," and "natural rights" that some modern scholars make. See generally Scott Douglas Gerber, *To Secure These Rights: The Declaration of Independence and Constitutional Interpretation* (New York: New York University Press, 1995), 106 n.*.

14. *Works*, 585, 592–93. It is true, as Barry Alan Shain points out, that Wilson, like most Founders, would have rejected the excessively individualistic view of rights held by many modern Americans. Yet Wilson's view of rights was more liberal and less communal than Shain claims. For Wilson's position, see ibid., 585–610. For Shain's argument, see Barry Alan Shain, *The Myth of American Individualism: The Protestant Origins of American Political Thought* (Princeton: Princeton University Press, 1994).

15. *Works*, 592–93.

16. Ibid., 71, 104, 579.

17. Ibid., 577. Compare John Stuart Mill, *On Liberty* (London: Everyman's Library, 1972), 85.

18. See generally *Works*, 126–47, 197–246, 369–98. For an extended discussion of this issue, see Mark D. Hall, "The Wilsonian Dilemma" (paper presented at the Annual Meeting of the Southern Political Science Association, Savannah, Georgia, 5 November 1994) (paper in my possession).

Wilson's moral sense theory and view of human nature were influenced by the Scottish Enlightenment, especially Thomas Reid. Compare Thomas Reid, *Essays on the Intellectual Powers of the Human Mind* (London: Thomas Tegg, 1827), 276, 353, 355, with *Works*, 213, 136. See also Arnaud B. Leavelle, "James Wilson and the Relation of the Scottish Metaphysics to American Political Thought," *Political Science Quarterly* 57 (1942): 394–410. Morton White argues in *Science and Sentiment in America* (New York: Oxford University Press, 1972) that Wilson was primarily influenced by David Hume.

Wilson's view of human nature, while optimistic, was not naive. He recognized that individuals have free wills and therefore can know the good but refuse to pursue it. On this subject, see especially *Works*, 199, 211, 385. Gordon S. Wood suggests in *The Radicalism of the American Revolution* (New York: Alfred A. Knopf, 1991), 239–40, that Wilson's position was not uncommon during the American Founding.

19. *Works*, 403, 875. See also Max Farrand, ed., *The Records of the Federal Convention of 1787*, rev. ed. (New Haven: Yale University Press, 1937), I:49.

20. *Works*, 180, 77. On these issues Wilson largely followed the social contract theorists, especially John Locke. Wilson was particularly influenced by Locke's view of sovereignty. Compare John Locke, *Two Treatises of Government*, ed. Peter Laslett (Cambridge: Cambridge University Press, 1988), 367.

21. Farrand, *Records*, I:52, 132, 151.

22. Wilson believed that every person "whose circumstances do not render him necessarily dependent on the will of another, should possess a vote in electing" representatives. Unlike many of the delegates, Wilson did not think property ownership was necessary to be independent. *Works*, 407–8, 84, 313, 411, 605, 725; Farrand, *Records*, II:201.

23. Farrand, *Records*, I:488, 495.

24. Ibid., I:69, II:30, 56, 103, 106. Even though the Convention rejected this proposal, Wilson still played an important role in shaping the presidency. See Robert E. DiClerico, "James Wilson's Presidency," *Presidential Studies Quarterly* 17 (1987): 301–17; Daniel J. McCarthy, "James Wilson and the Creation of the Presidency," *Presidential Studies Quarterly* 17 (1987): 689–96.

25. Wilson also opposed restrictions on officeholding, those based on age, country of origin, length of residence, and length of time in office included. Farrand, *Records*, I:375; II:151, 201, 230–31, 237, 268, 272.

Recent scholarship about Wilson has focused on the extent to which he thought participation in democratic institutions would help create more virtuous citizens. See Beer, *To Make a Nation*, 341–78; Stephen A. Conrad, "Polite Foundation: Citizenship and Common Sense in James Wilson's Republican Theory," in *1984 Supreme Court Review*, ed. Philip B. Kurland (Chicago: University of Chicago Press, 1984), 359–88; Stephen A. Conrad "Metaphor and Imagination in James Wilson's Theory of Federal Union," *Law and Social Inquiry* 13 (1988): 3–70; Jennifer Nedelsky, *Private Property and the Limits of American Constitutionalism: The Madisonian Framework and Its Legacy* (Chicago: University of Chicago Press, 1990), 96–140.

26. *Works*, 158, 289–91.

27. Farrand, *Records*, I:94–100, 421, 426; *Works*, 328–30, 341, 391,

416–17. Wilson also played an important role in the creation of the contract and guarantee clauses.

28. Farrand, *Records*, I:95.

29. Ibid., 119.

30. Ibid., II:428–29; *Works*, 297.

31. Farrand, *Records*, I:120, 124–28.

32. Ibid., I:104, II:73.

33. *Works*, 300. Wilson arguably supported the idea that judges could strike down laws that violate natural law. See ibid., 329; John Bach McMaster and Frederick D. Stone, eds., *Pennsylvania and the Federal Constitution, 1787–1788* (Philadelphia: Historical Society of Pennsylvania, 1888; repr., New York: Da Capo Press, 1970), 340–43, 354.

34. Farrand, *Records*, II:73.

35. For more, see Hall, "The Wilsonian Dilemma."

36. Farrand, *Records*, II:73.

37. *Works*, 502.

38. Ibid., 291.

39. McMaster and Stone, *Pennsylvania*, 302; *Works*, 401–2. For excellent discussions of the relationship between Wilson's theories of sovereignty and federalism, see Beer, *To Make a Nation*, 317–25; George M. Dennison, "The 'Revolutionary Principle': Ideology and Constitutionalism in the Thought of James Wilson," *Review of Politics* 39 (1977): 157–91.

40. McMaster and Stone, *Pennsylvania*, 223; *Works*, 764.

41. See Rossiter, *1787*, 200–209.

42. *Works*, 264, 433–35, 824–40; Farrand, *Records*, II:616. Wilson made an argument for implied powers under the Articles of Confederation in his essay "Considerations on the Bank of North America." *Works*, 829. Ralph Rossum contends that Wilson's theory of implied powers "went beyond the 'implied powers' doctrine of *McCulloch v. Maryland* (1819) and fully anticipated the 'inherent powers' doctrine of such twentieth century decisions as *Missouri v. Holland* (1920) and *United States v. Curtis Wright* (1936)." Ralph A. Rossum, "James Wilson and the 'Pyramid of Government'," *Political Science Reviewer* 6 (1976): 115.

43. *Works*, 264; McMaster and Stone, *Pennsylvania*, 143.

44. McMaster and Stone, *Pennsylvania*, 143–45, 253–54. For further discussion of Wilson's views of the Bill of Rights, see Hadley Arkes, *Beyond the Constitution* (Princeton: Princeton University Press, 1990), 58–80. Wilson's position contributed to the adoption of the Ninth Amendment.

45. James Wilson to George Washington, 31 December 1791, in Konkle MSS, II:421.

46. Edmund Randolph to George Washington, 21 January 1792, in Konkle MSS, VI:326–27. See also Perry Miller, *The Life of the Mind in America, From*

*the Revolution to the Civil War* (New York: Harcourt, Brace, and World, 1965), 239–49.

47. Farrand, *Records*, II:391.

48. Ibid., II:168–69. See also Ketcham, *James Madison*, 228–29, 302; Rossiter, *1787*, 197, 208, 214.

49. *Works*, 329–30, 296–97, 300, 497, 502.

50. *Wesberry v. Sanders*, 376 U.S. 1, 17 (1964).

51. McMaster and Stone, *Pennsylvania*, 143–49. Robert Rutland suggests that, although Wilson did not mention it by name, a substantial portion of his speech was aimed at discrediting George Mason's "Objections to this Constitutional Government." Robert A. Rutland, ed., *The Papers of George Mason* (Chapel Hill: University of North Carolina Press, 1970), III:1002, 991–99.

52. George Washington to David Stuart, 17 October 1787, in *The Writings of George Washington*, ed. Jared Sparks (Boston: Russell, 1835), IX:271, 357; Konkle MSS, II:349.

53. John P. Kaminski and Gaspare J. Saladino, eds., *The Documentary History of the Ratification of the Constitution* (Madison: State Historical Society of Wisconsin, 1981), XIII:344.

54. Bailyn, *Ideological Origins*, 328.

55. James Madison, to name the most prominent example, adopted Wilson's defense of the absence of a bill of rights. James Madison, "Speech in the Virginia Ratifying Convention," 25 June 1788, in *The Writings of James Madison*, ed. Gaillard Hunt (New York: Putnam's Sons, 1900–1910), V:231. In New York, Alexander Hamilton also utilized Wilson's argument. See *The Federalist Papers*, ed. Clinton Rossiter (New York: New American Library, 1961), No. 84:510–20. See generally Herbert J. Storing, *What the Anti-Federalists Were For* (Chicago: University of Chicago Press, 1981), 65–67; Benjamin F. Wright, *American Interpretations of Natural Law* (Cambridge: Harvard University Press, 1931), 140.

56. Wood, *The Creation of the American Republic*, 530, 539–40.

57. *Works*, 781–84; Seed, *James Wilson*, 131–37. See also Robert L. Brunhouse, *The Counter-Revolution in Pennsylvania, 1776–1790* (Harrisburg: Pennsylvania Historical Commission, 1942; repr., New York: Octagon Books, 1971).

58. James Wilson to George Washington, 21 April 1789, in Konkle MSS, II:372–73. This letter is reprinted in Maeva Marcus and James R. Perry, eds., *The Documentary History of the Supreme Court of the United States, 1789–1800* (New York: Columbia University Press, 1985), I:612–13. For more about Wilson's appointment, see ibid., 44–53, 613–14. Wilson also expected to be appointed chief justice upon the retirement of John Jay, both before and after the Senate rejected John Rutledge. Yet by this time Wilson's financial problems made that appointment unthinkable.

59. George Washington to James Wilson, quoted in Smith, *James Wilson*, 304 (emphasis in original). Washington's cool reply may be attributed to, at least in

part, Wilson's being a leader of Pennsylvania's presidential electors. Perhaps Washington did not want to raise an appearance of impropriety by "rewarding" Wilson's support for Washington's election. See Konkle MSS, II:364; Gordon Den Booer, ed., *The Documentary History of the First Federal Elections, 1788–1790* (Madison: University of Wisconsin Press, 1989), IV:164–65, 167; Lucian Alexander, "James Wilson, Nation Builder," *Green Bag* 19 (1907): 271.

60. John Jay, William Cushing, and James Duane to George Washington, in *Hayburn's Case*, 2 U.S. (2 Dall.) 410 (1792). In the unreported case of *United States v. Yale Todd* (1794) the Court stated that Jay, Cushing, and Duane acted inappropriately. The Court also may have declared the Invalid Pensioners Act unconstitutional.

61. James Wilson, John Blair, and Richard Peters to George Washington, in *Hayburn's Case*, 2 U.S. (2 Dall.) 411–12 (1792).

62. Christopher Wolfe, for instance, mentions neither Wilson nor *Hayburn's Case* in his *The Rise of Modern Judicial Review* (New York: Basic Books, 1986).

63. Quoted in Max Farrand, "The First Hayburn Case, 1792," *American Historical Review* 13 (1907–1908): 284.

64. James Madison to Richard Henry Lee, 15 April 1792, quoted in Maeva Marcus and Robert Teir, "Hayburn's Case: A Misinterpretation of Precedent," *Wisconsin Law Review* (1988): 527, 531.

65. St. George Tucker, ed., *Blackstone's Commentaries*, vol. I, part I (Philadelphia: Birch and Small, 1803), Appendix:5.

66. 2 U.S. (2 Dall.) 419 (1793).

67. Storing, *What the Anti-Federalists Were For*, 50.

68. 2 U.S. (2 Dall.) at 453.

69. Ibid., 455. William Casto agrees that Wilson's natural-law jurisprudence played an important role in his opinion. Casto also maintains that under modern standards of judicial conduct, Wilson should have recused himself from the case because of its implications for litigation over the Indiana Company, a company in which Wilson owned stock. Yet by eighteenth-century standards Wilson's participation was not inappropriate. See William R. Casto, *The Supreme Court in the Early Republic: The Chief Justiceships of John Jay and Oliver Ellsworth* (Columbia: University of South Carolina Press, 1995), 192–95.

70. 2 U.S. (2 Dall.) at 457.

71. Ibid., 461–64.

72. Ibid., 457–58, 463, 465 (quoting the Constitution).

73. Ibid., 464–66.

74. See Scott Douglas Gerber, "Deconstructing William Cushing," in this volume. See also William R. Davie to James Iredell, 12 June 1793, in *Life and Correspondence of James Iredell*, ed. Griffith J. McRee (1857; repr., New York: Peter Smith, 1949), II:382.

75. 3 U.S. (3 Dall.) 171 (1796).

76. See Casto, *The Supreme Court*, 215.

77. 3 U.S. (3 Dall.) 199 (1796).

78. Ibid., 281. Wilson joined unanimous Supreme Court decisions in *Georgia v. Brailsford*, 2 U.S. (2 Dall.) 402 (1792) and *Glass v. The Sloop Betsy*, 3 U.S. (3 Dall.) 6 (1794) that also helped strengthen the power of the national government.

79. Marcus, *Documentary History*, II:39. Wilson repeated this claim verbatim in his law lectures. See *Works*, 541. Wilson did not hesitate to use his position as a judge to educate the public. See, for example, his jury charges in Marcus, *Documentary History*, II:33–45, 142–53, 197–204, 396–404, 414–23. See generally Ralph Lerner, "The Supreme Court as Republican Schoolmaster," *1967 Supreme Court Review*, ed. Philip B. Kurland (Chicago: University of Chicago Press, 1967), 127–80.

80. Marcus, *Documentary History*, II:40; *Works*, 507–09, 524, 528–29, 540–42. See generally Shannon Stimson, "'A Jury of the Country': Common Sense Philosophy and the Jurisprudence of James Wilson," in *Scotland and America in the Age of the Enlightenment*, ed. Richard B. Sher and Jeffrey R. Smitten (Princeton: Princeton University Press, 1990), 193–208.

81. Wilson seemed to leave open the door for a judge to order a new trial if the jury erred to a significant degree. *Works*, 541–42. In addition, Wilson's dissent in *Wiscart v. D'Auchy*, 3 U.S. (3 Dall.) 321, 324–27 (1796) supported the power of the Supreme Court to rule on facts as well as law when reviewing equity and admiralty decisions. Wilson's argument was based primarily upon the Judiciary Act of 1789, which he read as not making an exception to the Court's appellate jurisdiction. Intriguingly, although Wilson appeared willing to admit that Congress could make exceptions to the Court's appellate jurisdiction, in dictum in *Wiscart* he suggested that "if a positive restriction existed by law, it would, in my judgement, be superseded by the superior authority of the constitutional provision." Ibid., 325. It is not certain what Wilson meant by this, but he likely was arguing that Congress could not limit the Court's appellate jurisdiction in at least some areas of law.

It should be noted that Wilson was attacked in the Pennsylvania ratifying convention for being against the right to trial by jury in civil cases. Wilson responded to this attack by noting that although he was for the right to trial by jury in almost every case, the delegates at the Federal Convention believed that state laws varied on the matter so much that it would be disruptive to include anything about it in the Constitution. McMaster and Stone, *Pennsylvania*, 403–5.

82. *Works*, 122, 183.

83. Ibid., 182.

84. Ibid., 122, 335.

85. Gary McDowell confuses the relation between consent and common law, at least in Wilson's legal theory, when he writes that "Americans had begun to offer a new foundation for the common law. No longer seen to rest on the old nat-

ural-law foundation, the common law was viewed as resting on consent expressed in the form of custom and continued usage." Gary L. McDowell, *Equity and the Constitution: The Supreme Court, Equitable Relief, and Public Policy* (Chicago: University of Chicago Press, 1982), 54. For further discussion of this issue, see J. C. D. Clark, *The Language of Liberty, 1660–1832* (Cambridge: Cambridge University Press, 1994), 93–110, and the literature cited therein.

86. See, for example, *Works*, 647, 818–19. Wilson also recognized that common law could be misused by unscrupulous lawyers. Ibid., 562.

87. Ibid., 353, 564.

88. Ibid., 811–15.

89. Ibid., 182.

90. Ibid., 560–61. Wilson also maintained that every citizen should have at least an elementary knowledge of common law. Ibid., 69–96, 559.

91. Maeva Marcus and Natalie Wexler, "The Judiciary Act of 1789: Political Compromise or Constitutional Interpretation?" in *Origins of the Federal Judiciary: Essays on the Judiciary Act of 1789*, ed. Maeva Marcus (New York: Oxford University Press, 1992), 14, 28.

92. William Casto notes that Wilson made a similar argument as a special prosecutor in the De Longchamps Affair. See Casto, *The Supreme Court*, 131–32.

93. Marcus, *Documentary History*, II:414–23. Thomas Jefferson, then secretary of state, endorsed Wilson's view that Henfield could, and should, be indicted. For further discussion, see Stephen B. Presser, *The Original Misunderstanding: The English, the Americans and the Dialectic of Federalist Jurisprudence* (Durham: Carolina Academic Press, 1991), 67–74; Stewart Jay, "Origins of Federal Common Law," parts I and II, *University of Pennsylvania Law Review* 133 (1985): 1003–1115, 1231–1333; Kathryn Preyer, "Jurisdiction to Punish: Federal Authority, Federalism, and the Common Law of Crimes in the Early Republic," *Law and History Review* 4 (1986): 223–65. The Court reversed itself in the early nineteenth century and rejected common-law jurisdiction. See *United States v. Hudson and Goodwin*, 11 U.S. (7 Cr.) 32 (1812); *United States v. Coolidge*, 14 U.S. (1 Wheat.) 415 (1816).

94. *United States v. Joseph Ravara*, 2 U.S. (2 Dall.) 297 (1793). The "several other persons" mentioned in the charge were George Washington.

95. See, for example, Albert J. Beveridge, *The Life of John Marshall* (Boston: Houghton Mifflin, 1919), III:24–26; Peter Stephen Du Ponceau, *A Dissertation on the Nature and Extent of the Jurisdiction of the Courts of the United States* (Philadelphia: A. Small, 1824); Julius Goebel, Jr., *History of the Supreme Court of the United States: Antecedents and Beginnings to 1801* (New York: Macmillan, 1971), 627; Preyer, "Jurisdiction to Punish," 223.

96. John D. Gordon III, "*United States v. Joseph Ravara:* 'Presumptuous Evidence,' 'Too Many Lawyers,' and a Federal Common Law Crime," in Marcus, *Origins of the Federal Judiciary*, 106–72.

97. Presser, *The Original Misunderstanding*, 71. William Obering stressed that Wilson's conception of the common law was "guided by the philosophy of the Schoolmen. . . ." Although this is an exaggeration, Wilson clearly believed that the common law is a way to know the natural law and that it is closely connected with religion. In his law lectures, Wilson noted that "Christianity is a part of the common law." See William F. Obering, "Our Constitutional Origins," *Thought* 12 (1937): 617; *Works*, 671.

For a different view of Wilson's approach to the common law, see Stephen A. Conrad, "James Wilson's 'Assimilation of the Common-Law Mind,'" *Northwestern University Law Review* 84 (1989): 186–219, esp. 195, 198–99. Conrad argues that Wilson's main concern about the common law was the reconciliation of its reliance on tradition with the Revolution's principle of consent. While there is much to admire in Conrad's essay, he errs by ignoring Wilson's position that common law is a means by which natural law can be known.

98. George Wythe, professor of law at The College of William and Mary from 1779 until 1791, is regarded as America's first law professor. Wilson is a close second, however, and he was the first to lecture systematically about the Constitution.

99. *Pennsylvania Packet* and *Daily Advertiser*, 25 December 1790, Philadelphia, quoted in Conrad, "Polite Foundation," 374.

100. *Works*, 564.

101. Ibid., 397–98. Wilson cared about legal history as well. Indeed, he repeatedly referred to law as a "historical science," and he spent a good deal of time tracing the origin and history of different legal concepts. This activity fit into his conception of law as a science insofar as he was using history to investigate the fundamental principles of law. If precedents agreed with these principles, Wilson was happy to use them. If they did not, he was willing to abandon precedent in favor of "good" law. Ibid., 350, 356, 384, 562–65.

102. McCloskey, "James Wilson," 91; Wright, *American Interpretations of Natural Law*, 281.

103. *Works*, 785.

104. Ibid., 784–85, 562–65.

105. Wilson's attorney, Joseph Thomas, "who had been universally thought an honest man," was discovered at this time to have "absconded, after having defrauded among others some of his most intimate friends." To avoid prosecution, Thomas abandoned his pregnant wife and fled with his clients' money. It is unclear to what degree Thomas was responsible for Wilson's financial collapse, but his flight in the midst of Wilson's troubles could not have helped matters. James Iredell to Mrs. Iredell, 6 August 1798, in McRee, *Life and Correspondence of James Iredell*, II:533–34.

106. Because of a mistake made by the federal government, Wilson's date of death is occasionally given as 28 August 1798. It actually was 21 August 1798,

as recorded by Wilson's friend James Iredell. James Iredell to Miss Gray, 25 Aug. 1798, ibid., 534.

107. In 1906 Wilson's remains were reburied with great ceremony in Philadelphia. See David W. Maxey, "The Translation of James Wilson," *Journal of Supreme Court History* (1990): 29–43.

## Chapter 6

# John Blair
## *"A Safe and Conscientious Judge"*

*Wythe Holt*

> "John Blair, . . . while not a man of the first order of ability, was a safe and conscientious judge. He acted an important part in the history of the country both before and after the American Revolution."[1]
>
> "This court is truly willing to make any voluntary sacrifice for the attainment of so desirable an object as the establishment of courts, which by the expeditious administration of justice, will not only give that relief to suffering creditors, which has already been too long withheld from them, but contribute much to the increase of industry, and improvement of the morals of the people."[2]

It is an honor and a privilege for my work to be included in a volume contributed to by such distinguished and knowledgeable scholars of such diverse backgrounds and approaches. It is a warm pleasure to have as fellow contributors my graduate school roommate, Jim Haw, and my good friends and coworkers in the tiny field of early American federal court history, Steve Presser, Sandra VanBurkleo, and Bill Casto. I have benefited greatly from readings of the prior version of this piece, with astute comments ranging from "cutting edge" to "cutting block" made by Scott Gerber, Brent Tarter, Jim Haw, Bill Casto, my history colleague Forrest McDonald, and my law colleagues Norman Stein and Martha Morgan. This piece is dedicated to Bill Casto, for without his steadfast encouragement, his staunch friendship, and his helpful knowledge and insights it would not have been completed.

Financial assistance to support the extensive research project upon which this piece has been based has been provided most kindly by my colleague and Dean, Ken Randall, and by the University of Alabama School of Law, and I am deeply thankful.

I have kept spelling, punctuation usage, and grammar in the fashion of my 1790s sources when quoting from them, as best I am able, though our age has lost much of the habit of colorful and poignant phrasing to say nothing of punctuation diversity, so that I have not always been successful.

## *Lawyer, Jurist, and Politician in Virginia's Ruling Class*

### Education and Social Relations

Prosperity during the 1750s and 1760s greatly increased the wealth both of the planters and merchants of tidewater Virginia and of the small but able group of lawyers who were their allies and helpmates. Generally in solid political control of the colony, they became ever more assertive, and eventually, using the language of republican political ideology, began to seek independence from the taxation, from the restrictions upon their trade, and from the paternalistic political control exercised by a remote and increasingly mercantilistic royal government in Great Britain.[3] Precisely to this manor born was John Blair, in Williamsburg, the colonial capital, in November 1732.

Blair's family was wealthy and well connected. His great-uncle James Blair had been for nearly five decades the political despot of the colony, personally causing the dismissal of two royal governors, acting as governor himself on one occasion, for fifty years both founding president of The College of William and Mary and member of the governor's Council. John Blair's father, for whom he was named, was for more than four decades the colony's deputy auditor-general, was a member of the Council for a quarter century, and was four times acting governor. Moreover, John Blair *pere* obtained 100,000 acres of land in what is now West Virginia, owned plantations, sat on the Williamsburg city court, and was a partner in a prosperous mercantile firm.[4]

Blair graduated with honors from William and Mary in 1754. Tall, with a generous forehead, blue eyes, red hair, and a gentle disposition, Blair used his family wealth to study law in the Middle Temple in London. In late December of 1756, in Edinburgh, he married his Scottish second cousin Jean Blair, a quiet, sickly, and perhaps mentally afflicted person to whom he became deeply devoted. After he was called to the bar in May 1757, he returned to Virginia.[5]

Blair immediately began practice before the General Court, Virginia's highest court, which sat only in Williamsburg. Virginia in 1748 had required its lawyers to choose either county court or General Court practice. Most opted for the sixty-odd county courts where the local gentry sat as justices of the peace; there old-style informality and gentry dignity prevailed over mercantile efficiency and, at times, mercantile justice. Only a few were able to make the journeys or the sophisticated arguments, or afford the lengthy apprenticeship, required of the General Court bar. "Fewer than twelve Virginians actually attended the Inns, received a call to the bar, and returned to actual legal practice before 1776," and all, like Blair, became leaders of the General Court bar. Others rose from the petty gentry, such as Edmund Pendleton, George Wythe, Patrick Henry, and Thomas Jefferson. Blair was no spellbinding orator like Henry, nor deeply persuasive like Pendleton, being "without that ease in speech, which sometimes gives currency to dross," but he was clear-minded, thorough, learned, and well connected, and he soon gained a respectable share of the business.[6]

Blair also started to take his place in Virginia's social and political order. He began a six-year stint as bursar of the College of William and Mary in 1760. He was selected as the college's representative in the House of Burgesses in 1765, and, despite his very junior status, was chosen for important posts in 1766 and 1768. He was appointed Clerk of the Council in 1770 (resigning from Burgesses and leaving the active practice of law). And he received his father's place as deputy auditor-general and stepped into that octogenarian's shoes in the mercantile business upon his death the following year. Blair's rise to social eminence was also signaled by his becoming the first grand master of Virginia Masons, serving from 1778 to 1784.[7]

## Emergence of the Republic of Virginia

Blair, Pendleton, Wythe, and the rest of the tidewater elite had opposed as premature Henry's shocking defiance of British authority embodied in his 1765 Stamp Act Resolutions, which passed the House of Burgesses by one vote. However, "[a]s events led to separation from Great Britain, Blair sided with those merchants and landowners who favored independence." In May 1769 he presided over the House's adoption of an address strongly condemning Parliament, and when the House was dissolved in 1769 and again in 1770, Blair joined with other merchant and planter leaders to draft the first nonimportation agreements. The dangers of an elite revolt, and the lie at the heart of American democracy, became momentarily apparent when, upon the sudden flight of the royal Governor Dunmore to his ships in May

1775, Blair on behalf of the Council was compelled to reassure the common people that "odious distinctions" between elites and others were now cast aside, and that the councillors were really the "watchful Guardians of the Rights of the People" rather than intent on preserving their own distinct interest.[8]

Virginians now met frequently in Convention, at first as a temporary government. The Convention named Blair one of the three judges of a newly created admiralty court, in January 1776. The following May the Convention created a new Declaration of Rights and Constitution for a colony that now formally declared its independence from the crown, with Blair among the twenty-eight members of the committee that wrote the two documents. There is no record that Blair made any contribution, ideological or political, to these novel, momentous republican instruments that proved inspiring models to many other rebels around the world. He was, however, chosen to be one of the members of the new Council.[9]

Thomas Jefferson's chief contribution to the new structure of government was its judiciary. The trial and appellate jurisdiction of the old General Court was split into three new courts, equity jurisdiction being placed in a Court of Chancery, admiralty in a reconstituted Admiralty Court, and common-law civil and criminal jurisdiction in a fresh General Court. A Court of Appeals, composed of the eleven judges who sat in the other three courts, was created to supervise all three, primarily on important issues of law. All judges had tenure during good behavior. Despite the new Constitution's insistence upon separation of powers and the independence of the judges, prohibiting them from holding office in the other branches, John Blair, who on January 23, 1778, was elected one of the first judges of the new General Court by joint ballot of the two houses of the legislature, did not resign from the Council until February 28.[10]

## Eminence as a Virginia Judge

Having become chief justice of the General Court in 1779, Blair was, in November 1780, elevated to the Court of Chancery. There he joined Edmund Pendleton and George Wythe, perhaps the two most celebrated and competent state court judges of their time. Moreover, both had been lawyers of renown before the Revolution; both had long been leaders in Virginia politics; both had served with great distinction in a Continental Congress full of capable men; both were well known for their political philosophies, Pendleton for his cautious conservatism, Wythe as an independent-minded if intensely learned proponent of Enlightenment republicanism; and both remained revered elders as Virginia achieved nationhood and then joined the new United States. Blair paled in comparison, as perhaps would other judicial contemporaries, and he never achieved any distinction we notice today during their nine years together on the bench.

Yet George Washington, Thomas Jefferson, and Joseph Jones (Blair's predecessor as General Court chief justice) mentioned the three—and no others—when anticipating which Virginians might grace the United States's first Supreme Court in 1789, or, in Jefferson's case, ruminating about the ability of strong judges to enforce constitutional rights in the teeth of majoritarian clamor.[11] Blair's eminence is inexplicable in the apolitical modern language of judicial competence. He was, however, a sturdy, wealthy gentleman of the highest social standing, whose mildness excited no animosity, whose judicial opinions were clear and sound, and who had shown that he could be counted on to support the prevailing order. Blair lived in a time when law was not thought to be sharply separated from politics, and when judges considered themselves and were considered part of the government, so his connections and his loyalty to class and calling go a long way toward providing an understanding of his reputation.

Only four notable opinions that John Blair wrote or joined as a state court judge have come down to us: *Commonwealth v. Caton* (1782), *Commonwealth v. Posey* (1787), the Judges' Remonstrance (1788), and the Judges' Resignation (1789).[12] All four, decided by the Court of Appeals, are of the first rank in importance, since they are among the earliest treatments by judges of their role in a republic.

In *Posey*, the whole court except Wythe and one other judge found a respected, pre-Revolutionary English judicial interpretation of an even more ancient English statute to be automatically binding upon them just as though it were part of the statute. Wythe dissented irately, because, as historian Robert Kirtland has shown, he believed such an ancient foreign judicial decision was not binding; an emerging positivist in outlook, Wythe wanted to look at the reason of the law, and to be able to change poor or outdated judge-made rules. Blair's opinion epitomized the staid, natural-law position of the majority: "If it were a new case, I should be at no loss to decide in favor of the prisoner. But the decision in *Powlter's case*, has prevailed so long, that it must be submitted to; and the authority of it . . . cannot now be shaken." Blair, and the majority, were unable to join Wythe in imagining that law could be judge-made. Rather, law arose from the imperceptible consent of the people, over the ages, to those opinions about the law that had been consistently expressed by and accepted by legislators, judges, learned treatise writers, and members of the bar: mortals did not have the power to alter it, after such a time, except by positive act of the people's elected representatives.[13]

The other three decisions are among the earliest judicial discussions of judicial review. *Caton* involved the alleged pardon of three loyalist Virginians who had been convicted of treason. The state constitution seemed to say that only the House of Delegates had the power of pardon, while a statute required the concurrence of both the House and the Senate in any pardon. The House had given pardon, but the Senate refused to concur. The Court of Appeals heard the prisoners' claim that the statute violated the constitution. Only Wythe and James Mercer of the eight judges who sat claimed the power of judicial review. Mercer boldly declared the statute unconstitutional. Wythe in dictum resoundingly defended judicial review as flowing from the separation of powers, giving the people a recourse where the legislature had overstepped its bounds as laid down in the constitution. But he actually joined most of the rest of the court in a tortured construction of the constitution that eliminated any conflict with the act. They then found the act proper and denied the appeal. Blair did not speak at length, expressly "wa[i]v[ing] the question upon the power of the Court to declare an anti-constitutional Act of Assembly void, since the Treason law was not so." Only one of the judges denied this power of judges to declare a statute void.[14]

Blair's caution disappeared, however, when the issue next arose. Essentially, ever since popular inability to repay debts owed to British merchants had closed Virginia's courts for four years in 1774, trial court dockets had been almost hopelessly clogged, primarily with debt cases. Especially choked were the county courts, where delay was a debtor's best friend; many of the genteel justices were in debt. Relief schemes revolved around having the professional (and more creditor-oriented) upper-court Virginia judges ride circuit through the hinterlands. This produced much opposition from the powerful county courts during the depressed 1780s, but finally in October 1787 the General Assembly added four judges to the General Court and required the fifteen Court of Appeals judges to travel around the state holding court in eighteen districts. In an opinion penned by Pendleton and entered on the record without benefit of litigants or argument, the Court of Appeals unanimously held the scheme unconstitutional, since it had more than doubled their duties without any increase in salary. Separation of powers demanded that the legislature not be "at liberty to compel a resignation by reducing salaries to a copper, or by making it a part of the official duty to become hewers of wood, and drawers of water."[15] Instead of calling the judges on the carpet, the legislature accepted judicial review and wrote another law, establishing a new stationary Court of Appeals (to which Blair and Pendleton were immediately elected) and confining judicial traveling to the enlarged General Court. Although judicial duties had again been increased without extra pay, this time the judges acquiesced because they wanted to "give that relief to suffering creditors, which has already been too long withheld from them." However, in another advisory opinion by Pendleton they unanimously held the new act unconstitutional too, as "incompatible with their independence" because it terminated the old Court of Appeals although its judges should have been "secure in the enjoyment of their office."[16]

Without comment on their momentous import, Blair joined in these opinions tending to protect republican courts from any oversight by republican legislatures, while at the same time allowing the former, though unelected, to sit as unreviewable censors of the latter. Though Pendleton had raised the issue of whether judicial censorship might overstep the same separation-of-powers bounds the judges had laid down for the legislature, abstract issues of proper popular governance did not trouble the bench because the judges had been reared in a natural-law culture that understood their role as finding a law the people had already consented to (which the legislature had disobeyed), rather than exercising political will. Moreover, they were members of a ruling elite with little concern for democratic republicanism. Judicial review itself was not controversial in Virginia, and Blair, as usual, accepted the views of his social peers and eminent judicial colleagues.[17]

## *A Federalist National Security Court*

### Blair as Constitution Maker

John Blair served but a short time on the new Court of Appeals, for nine months later one of his friends wrote to his niece, "I suppose you have heard of your Uncle Blairs appointment—he sets out for New york in Jan'y." George Washington, now president of a reconstituted United States that Blair had helped to create, had named his old friend to the new United States Supreme Court.[18]

Blair had (with his fellow chancellor Wythe) been a delegate to the Constitutional Convention, where Madison recorded him as making no speeches. Though in caucus he had opposed Madison on the issues of a multiple executive and legislative election of the executive, he signed the finished document. He then sat in Virginia's Ratification Convention. While Pendleton chaired the body and spoke in favor, and Wythe both served as chair of the Committee of the Whole (where all the debate was done) and moved for adoption, once again we find that, in the succinct words of James Monroe, "Blair said nothing, but was for it." It is likely that many delegates in both august assemblies agreed with Georgia's Constitutional Convention delegate William Pierce that "his good sense, sound judgment, and excellent principles overbalanced any oratorical deficiency," for Blair's work shaping and promoting the Constitution must have been done, in the tradition of gentry politics, in the halls, at church, and at the dining table.[19] Blair had made a definite choice, however, for on the Supreme Court and even afterward he continued to prove himself a strong supporter of the new government.

### The Embattled United States

A stronger federal government had been created because of the fears held largely by those citizens—by no means a majority—who supported it.[20] The fears had both foreign and domestic sources. The United States was weak and surrounded by the colonial territories of powerful European nations desirous of further aggrandizing themselves, suspicious of both its republican experiment and any chances of success it might have, and, in the case of Great Britain, smarting under recent defeat, contemptuous, and hoping to give its former colonies a comeuppance. Internally, some poor crop years, a decade-long depression, plus the astonished unwillingness of established seaboard elites to share power with the ordinary farmers and artisans who had actually fought the Revolution had created internecine squabbling, intermittent revenue collection, and frequent control of legislatures by anticommercial soft-money forces that issued paper money and enacted other debt-avoidance measures. Flare-ups of farm folk, artisans, and wage workers culminated in Shays's Rebellion in New England—a serious revolt not finally subdued until after the Constitutional Convention assembled.

A procommercial, prodevelopmental thread tied together those members of the elites who wished to reestablish the nation upon a stronger, more centralized basis. Both the ability to exercise armed might either in self-defense or in internal policing, and any permanent enlargement of the government meant that the national government must be given power over its own revenue. The ability to recruit naval aid by arming merchantmen as privateers, which in turn meant the ability to protect a revenue-producing merchant marine, implied the protection of prizes captured in war. Above all, in an increasingly trade-conscious and commodity-desirous world, to gain stability meant borrowing from European sources to finance trade, to stimulate manufactures, and to begin the development of the huge trans-Allegheny territories, the mere acquisition of which had already stimulated a competitive froth of land speculation amongst elites. Borrowing meant establishing credit. This in turn meant, as with any Third World country today, elimination of soft-money and other debtor-favoring practices, and neutralization of localistic and anticommercial juries. It also meant a better debt-payback record than existed with regard both to the huge and largely unpaid debts incurred by both states and the federal government in winning independence, and to the millions of dollars' worth of debts owing from planters and farmers to English and Scottish merchants left unpaid at the onset of the Revolution and still mostly unpaid in 1787, because of lingering anti-British hostility plus the generally depressed circumstances. Policing meant criminal law; revenue protection meant the establishment of revenue jurisdiction; prize meant admiralty jurisdiction; and the neutralization of localism meant the establishment of independent federal courts with appropriate jurisdiction.

The Constitutional Convention (as interpreted by William Casto) did precisely this, establishing a well-articulated system of federal courts with admiralty (including revenue) jurisdiction, jurisdiction over suits between citizens of different states (diversity) and suits brought by aliens (alienage), and jurisdiction over states as defendants. Federal judges were given independence through life tenure and a guarantee against diminution of their salaries. "Federal-question" jurisdiction was granted over cases arising both under treaties—most importantly the 1783 Peace Treaty, which guaranteed repayment of the prewar British debts in pounds sterling (a guarantee the states had widely ignored)—and under the Constitution, because most expected the federal courts to find state (and national) laws in conflict with the Constitution to be void. States were forbidden to impair contracts (debts) or to make anything but gold and silver a legal tender. The federal government, in addition, was allowed to have a military, to raise revenue (largely through import duties), and to control all commerce.

The Judiciary Act of 1789 completed the picture, setting up exclusive federal criminal jurisdiction and establishing a resident federal district judge in each state to hear revenue and prize cases. Circuit courts (comprised of two itinerant Supreme Court judges and the local district judge) would sit twice each year in each state to hear the most controversial cases—British debt cases, important federal criminal cases, and cases founded upon diversity of citizenship and alienage—except that jurisdiction over states as defendants was confined to the Supreme Court. Opposition by Anti-Federalists to the breadth of federal-court jurisdiction was diffused by leaving out all pending and most petty British debt cases, by stripping the Supreme Court of its constitutional power to overturn factual findings or damage awards made by juries, and by confining appeals from state courts to issues of federal law decided against federal interests.[21]

But the opposition was only temporarily diffused, as most of the officials of the new government well knew. In order to energize the new system, they had to walk a tightrope between action that exercised the government's power to assert national interests but that might activate or heighten divisiveness, and inaction or nonthreatening action to promote harmony but that might permanently diminish some important national power. When it became necessary to emphasize the government's power, none of the judges hesitated, for they were proponents of a system that they felt to be absolutely necessary for their own and the nation's welfare. Moreover, their support for the Constitution meant conscious support for the governmental policies of Washington and Hamilton. They firmly believed that the power of the government over revenue, civil order, prize, and trade had to be maintained; that aliens and out-of-state citizens, mostly creditors and entrepreneurs, were not to be discriminated against by localistic juries or anticommercial laws or rulings; and that the national dignity and integrity of the United States must be upheld, especially with regard to British creditors. In grand jury charges throughout the decade, the judges trumpeted the necessity, the power, and the goodness of the Federalist government. But in court, they often hesitated, and they acted firmly only when they thought it was called for, since they also understood how perilous the government's position was. Everything might collapse if too much domestic opposition were excited.[22]

## Blair the Cautious Virginia Federalist

John Blair had no debt problem, and his own social, economic, and political interests as a wealthy planter and merchant were congruent with those of the Federalist regime. Several Virginians who were in a socioeconomic position similar to Blair's, but who were in debt or were suspicious of the potential dominance of the national government over their large and relatively powerful commonwealth, opposed it from the beginning (though many of these, such as Patrick Henry, changed to a position of support during the 1790s). Many other Virginians in Blair's class, such as Edmund Pendleton, sooner or later moved from support into opposition as the national government exercised its great powers.[23] Several factors not only kept but strengthened Blair's allegiance to the government of Washington and Hamilton. Its economic policies remained congruent with his interests; for example, Hamilton's federal redemption of state-issued Revolutionary War securities at par would greatly enhance the value of his Virginia loan office certificates.[24] Blair spent much of the year away from Virginia and in association with other Federalists (particularly those on the Court, such as his friend James Wilson), and he was always by training and personality inclined to listen and defer to the strong members of his class. As judge he had continuous contacts with the federal government, and his travel throughout the United States was as the living symbol of its presence and power.

These traits and experiences kept his fires of devotion to the Federalist government and its policies burning strong. Like that of his fellow Virginians George Washington and John Marshall, Blair's support for the government grew as he witnessed what he thought to be the disintegration of popular allegiance and an increasing foreign danger to the fledgling republic during the mid-1790s. But, like the other judges, Blair came to feel the dangers of moving too precipitously in exerting national power, and they all began to exercise great caution in being bold about Federalism.

Initially, Blair and the other judges may not have fully realized the depths of the potential opposition to federal power, but an instance in the first year of the Court brought starkly home to them the perils that might be aroused by forthrightness, and the need to flex the federal muscle only in crucial situations. Robert Morris of Pennsylvania, merchant and financier, one of the wealthiest of Americans, and land speculator upon a spectacular scale—who as financial wizard of the United States during the Revolution had disfavored the interests of the southern states—had in North Carolina in 1783 suffered an adverse jury verdict for more than three times the face value of the debt he owed. Morris, furious at what he considered local prejudice, in 1787 begged the North Carolina Superior Court for an injunction to stay another judgment against him that he thought equally biased. The injunction had not been acted upon when the Constitution went into effect in North Carolina in June 1790. Without notice to the other side, he immediately asked the judges of the new federal Supreme Court to issue a writ of certiorari to the North Carolina court, commanding it to transfer the suit to the Circuit Court for North Carolina.

Blair joined Justices James Wilson and John Rutledge in approving the writ. The North Carolina judges, however, refused to accept a peremptory writ that would label them both biased and inferior to the federal court. The federal demand seemed to "justify all the fears of the Anti-Federalists about the creation of a consolidated national government" and about the elimination of the state courts. Moreover, these very North Carolina judges were Anti-Federalists who had just spearheaded an almost successful effort to have their state reject the Constitution. Their refusal plus the action of the North Carolina legislature in praising them created an uproar in Philadelphia. An anguished Blair wrote Wilson about "ideas which never before occurr'd" to him, and indeed it seems to have been the first time he had thought deeply about the extent to which the states were now subordinate to the federal government. He supposed issuance of the writ "hasty" and that "it would be more *convenient* to acknowledge our faults than to plunge deeper into it," since "[t]here appears to be no certain boundary, clearly & distinctly marked, between federal & State jurisdiction." The judges should not provoke unnecessary dissension, he concluded; the case was not very important. However, the fright and caution of the Court was emphasized when, in 1791, similar requests for certiorari to transfer important pending British debt cases from the state to the federal courts in Virginia and Georgia were quickly denied by his colleagues while on their circuits.[25]

The Supreme Court's first announced decision, in August 1791, appears to be a similar exercise of caution. *West v. Barnes* involved a constitutional challenge to the validity of Rhode Island's notorious 1786 law making its depreciated paper money legal tender at face value. Federal jurisdiction had been erected precisely to stanch such anticreditor practices. But Blair's opinion, like those of his colleagues delivered seriatim, refused to ignore the Judiciary Act's plain if ill-conceived requirement that writs of error (the only mode of appeal) be returned to the clerk of the Supreme Court within ten days of the rendering of the judgment complained of at circuit. That had not been done in *Barnes* and, as Barnes's counsel aptly noted, because distances were so great, strict adherence would effectively deny to most folks their right to appeal; the requirement was an apparent legislative oversight concerning what was a matter solely of form. The Court was probably worried about open disagreement between two branches of the new government at its beginning. Moreover, as was shown when the case was retried at circuit the next June, it had been hastily brought, so that it was a poor vehicle in which to make such a potentially upsetting ruling in a state that, like North Carolina, had been dubious of entering the union.[26]

## The Circuit-Riding Controversy

The judges also, at first, were cautious about making public their complaints to the president and to Congress about riding circuit, which was expensive, arduous, and dangerous, and took them for long periods away from their homes and their families. Complicated and brought to a boil by the permanent assignment of a feisty James

Iredell to the sprawling Southern Circuit—he thought the assignment arbitrary and discriminatory, and relentlessly pressed his colleagues for relief—discussion of circuit riding consumed much of their August 1790 meeting. Chief Justice John Jay argued that the practice was unconstitutional, looking solely to the structure of the judiciary as outlined in Articles I and III: the Constitution contemplated that lower courts would have their own judges; that the Supreme was to be a court of last resort only "& it is perhaps rather nice to distinguish between a court & the judges of that court"; and, tendentiously, that only the president and not the Congress (through creation of courts not staffed by their own judges) could nominate federal judges. Blair added the separation-of-powers argument, which, in his prior Virginia experience, had been decisive: the judges were not given greater salaries for their extra circuit court duties.[27]

Probably both because of the dangers of allegations of unconstitutional congressional action so early in the new government's history, and because they learned that Attorney General Edmund Randolph argued strongly against circuit riding in a report on the state of the judiciary he was soon to present to the House of Representatives upon its request, the judges did not communicate their sentiments to the other departments of government.

However, Congress did not act upon Randolph's suggestions that winter, to the chagrin of the judges. At a contentious February 1791 Supreme Court session, Blair demonstrated that at times he could be independent of the dominant leadership by siding with Iredell's demand for rotation of the judges among the circuits. When Jay, William Cushing, and Wilson adamantly refused to leave their circuits, Blair amiably helped Iredell out by swapping his Middle Circuit for the brutal Southern Circuit in the spring of 1791. The judges continued to make no official protest while reform of the judiciary was still before Congress; as if to underscore this decision, evidence of continuing Anti-Federalist opposition to the judiciary began to appear during 1791.[28]

By January 1792, however, it had become clear that "no radical reform of the Judiciary law will be made," and caution gave way to action. Iredell's brother-in-law Senator Samuel Johnston, on Iredell's behalf, engineered a law requiring rotation of the judges among the circuits. The judges openly ruled an act of Congress unconstitutional, in *Hayburn's Case*. And in August 1792 they openly petitioned Congress for an end to circuit riding, in language emphasizing practical difficulties, not constitutional ones. The draft this time was written by Iredell, not Jay. Congress responded only by reducing to one the number of justices required at circuit, and thus to one the number of circuits each had to ride per year. The justices petitioned Congress again in February 1794 to end circuit riding but to no avail. No termination of these duties came to the judges in the 1790s. Thomas Johnson certainly, and John Jay and John Rutledge probably, left the Court in large part over the difficulties of circuit riding; Iredell's death at age forty-nine in 1799 was likely hastened by them; and it is not unlikely that an ill and aging John Blair, who with uncharacteristic anger protested his consecutive assignments to circuit duties in the fall of 1794, the spring of 1795, and the fall of 1795, finally resigned in no small part due to them.[29]

### Blair Opposes Virginia Debtors on British Debts

Caution also initially accompanied the judges in their dealings with the potentially explosive British debt cases in Virginia. About 45 percent of the total debt was owed from the Old Dominion—about $6.5 million in 1790 terms—and its courts had been completely shut to British creditors since spring 1774. Many Virginians were adamant about not paying blood money to their erstwhile enemies. Virginia was by far the largest and most populous state, and it had barely voted for the Constitution to begin with.[30] Its continued membership in the imperiled Union was absolutely essential in the 1790s.

British creditors filed dozens of claims once the federal circuit court in Virginia was established, and they expected at last to obtain justice quickly. But Patrick Henry, John Marshall, and the other able lawyers for the debtors, who were determined to avoid payment if possible, raised complicated defenses and "employed every device at their disposal to drag out the proceedings." Probably in part to ensure both legitimacy and proper handling of Virginia law, the Court assigned John Blair to the Virginia circuit for three of its first four terms of court. This included the term when argument finally began on November 24, 1791, in *Jones v. Walker*, a case chosen by the attorneys because it raised all of the important issues. The courtroom was packed for the weeklong arguments. An attending creditor bitterly recounted that "all the declamatory talents of Patrick Henry were displayed to inflame Mens minds, prevent their Judgments & drive them to acts of Outrage." It was Henry's last great case, and his three-day peroration not only closed down the General Assembly for want of attendance but was remembered decades later by awed auditors. The court's records show that Blair was not present to enjoy Henry; he left the bench on November 23 and did not return until December 3 because he was financially interested in one of the issues in dispute. Justice Thomas Johnson of Maryland and District Judge Cyrus Griffin of Virginia, the other two men on the bench, found "two [of the] points of Law perfectly novel" and refused to decide, calling for a new argument at the next term. The creditors were outraged, both by the procrastination and because debtors theretofore resigned to paying up were now defiant; "[T]he courts of Justice in Virginia are still shut for the recovery of British debts," one of them fumed.[31]

After another postponement, the cautious approach of the circuit court bench ended, and all of the legal defenses Virginia debtors raised in *Walker* save one (the question Blair was interested in) were unanimously denied by Judges Jay, Iredell, and Griffin in December 1793. The single issue was appealed, but, to the grudging satisfaction of the British creditors, scores of debts in cases not involving that issue were finally brought to judgment in the two long terms the Virginia Circuit held in 1794. Blair patiently sat in both of them, since the issue in which he was interested could not be before him. Juries still frustrated creditors by deducting at least eight years' interest in every case as punishment for British wartime depredations. This was illegal under the treaty; Blair, in an equity case where there was no jury ordered full wartime interest on a British debt, but was helpless to overturn jury verdicts in the other cases. He had also joined a unanimous Supreme Court the previous February, in *Georgia v. Brailsford*, in holding that a Georgia wartime law sequestering British debts was ineffective to divest British creditors of title.[32]

Thus, after caution was replaced by action, Blair's legal position on the states' "British debts" impediments proved to be procreditor, courageously contrary to that of most Virginians and the same as those of all his Federalist Court colleagues except the North Carolinian Iredell. Given Johnson's equivocation on the Virginia Circuit in 1791, John Blair was the only southern justice who gave full support to the British creditors' position.

## Blair as Able Judicial Technician

*Georgia v. Brailsford* presented not only an important substantive question involving British debts but also two technical and difficult issues of equity law on which the Court issued opinions in August 1792 and February 1793. In these rulings Blair demonstrated that his nine years on Virginia's highest equity court had made him an able judicial technician in that sometimes arcane field.

Brailsford, a British subject, had sued Spalding, a Georgian, on a 1774 debt in the Georgia federal circuit court. Spalding's chief defense had been Georgia's wartime act sequestering to the state all debts Georgians owed to British subjects, and barring recovery on them by any but the state. The state of Georgia, afraid of collusion between Brailsford and Spalding, had asked to be impleaded in order to protect its rights, but Iredell, riding circuit, had denied the request on grounds that the Judiciary Act gave the Supreme Court exclusive federal jurisdiction over suits involving states. He had then found that the bar on recovery was repealed by the Peace Treaty, and had given judgment for Brailsford on the merits.[33]

Georgia filed a bill in equity in the Supreme Court, asking for an injunction to restrain in his hands any moneys collected by the marshal upon execution of the lower court judgment, and demanding payment of the debt to it. In August 1792, Blair, understanding that one purpose of equity was to correct defects in the common-law process, among which was the inability of Georgia to have been heard in the lower court, forcefully argued for issuance of the requested injunction in order to protect whatever rights Georgia might have pending a hearing on the merits. Since Johnson and Cushing found such protection unnecessary, the chief justice's vote with them would have produced a tie denying the injunction, but Jay said that his mind had been changed during the argument, likely by the clarity of Blair's exposition, and completed the 4–2 vote to issue the injunction.[34]

The tougher equitable question was its availability: litigants who had an adequate remedy at law could not obtain equitable relief. Three members of the now five-member Court (with Johnson's resignation), upon argument the next February, thought that Georgia had an adequate remedy at law. Blair alone argued that the Court, sitting in equity, had to expand the equitable action in the nature of interpleader to take care of the situation because Brailsford, an alien, might decamp with the proceeds of his judgment before any proper legal process from Georgia's common-law action reached him. It seems that Blair again was persuasive in part, since the majority, speaking through Jay, continued its injunction in force.[35] Of all the justices, Blair alone seemed comfortable with the expansive powers of an equity court, and fully knowledgeable about equitable jurisprudence.

## Blair Upholds the Power of the Confederation

Blair made two important circuit court rulings. One of these was *Penhallow v. Doane*, in which he ingeniously and resoundingly upheld the power and authority of the national government. Hastening from Massachusetts the week before Congress was to ban commerce with Great Britain in 1775, Elisha Doane's ship *The Lusanna* had taken on British registry and, with possible Loyalist Shearjashub Bourne in charge, had traded at London and Gibraltar before sailing for Halifax, Nova Scotia, with a cargo of British war materiel. When captured by John Penhallow's privateer *McClary* out of Portsmouth, New Hampshire, Bourne claimed that he was a Patriot but had been caught abroad and had had to register falsely and to take on war materiel to get home again. Two New Hampshire state prize court juries were dubious and, taking British registry and war materiel at face value, awarded prize to Penhallow in 1778 (despite an able defense by John Adams in his last case).[36]

New Hampshire law did not allow American citizens an appeal to Congress in prize cases. The Articles of Confederation gave Congress plenary appellate power in prize, and a 1775 act provided for appeals in such cases; the Articles were not ratified, however, till 1781. Doane, "one of the richest men in New England," appealed, claiming local prejudice. Congress thereafter established a prize court, which in 1783 accepted jurisdiction over the case, reversed the decree, and awarded the ship to Doane's estate. This was typical of the Confederation court: "In practically every such case decided on appeal [in which American merchants trying to do business had had to resort "to ruses" and "to give complicated and implausible explanations . . . to protect their property," and were disbelieved by state prize juries], the [federal] judges restored the captured property." Now New Hampshire appealed to Congress, and a committee report by Thomas Jefferson agreed with New Hampshire, and Penhallow, that before 1781 Congress had had no power to require appeals from a state's prize court unless the state agreed. However, Congress took no action, either to reverse its court or to enforce the decree.[37]

After 1789 the case was brought by Doane's estate into federal court, seeking enforcement. Blair heard it on circuit in New Hampshire in the fall of 1793 and upheld the 1783 Confederation court award. He deftly obviated the retroactivity issue raised by Jefferson by finding prize jurisdiction to be an inherent aspect of the power to wage war that the colonies had given Congress from the beginning, deducing that this made competent both appellate power and Confederation court. He then refused to contemplate an attack on that court's finding that it had jurisdiction. This ringing affirmation of national power won both admiration from Federalists, and, when the case finally reached the Supreme Court in 1795, a chorus of echoes from the other judges endorsing Blair's rationale. Moreover, Blair's calm and straightforward but narrow legal ground for national supremacy produced no Anti-Federalist outcry, while the additional angry, tendentious argument that Justice William Paterson advanced in *Penhallow*—that the states had never been sovereign and thus New Hampshire had to yield to a sovereign Congress—not only provoked the opposition but also forced his Federalist colleagues to upset and disavowal.[38] It was one of John Blair's finest hours as a supporter both of the Federalist government and of the commercial ethos of "ruses" and profit.

## Blair, Judicial Review, and Natural Law Jurisprudence

The other important circuit ruling occurred in Pennsylvania in April 1792. Not only had Congress failed to terminate circuit riding in the winter of 1792, it had saddled the justices, as circuit court judges, with the wearisome duty of hearing and assessing the viability of pension claims by Revolutionary War veterans. Anger and frustration led them to cast off their caution about revealing disagreements with Congress over the meaning of the Constitution, and they probably agreed upon this bold path during the February 1792 Supreme Court session. On April 12 Blair, Wilson, and District

Judge Richard Peters refused to hear the pension claim of veteran William Hayburn, holding unconstitutional the 1792 Invalid Pension Act. This first such judicial declaration about a national statute sent shock waves through Philadelphia, provoking precisely the kind of divisive commentary from Anti-Federalists that Federalists had feared. Word soon arrived that Jay and Cushing had taken a similar stand on the New York Circuit. Later Iredell, on circuit in North Carolina, and Johnson, on circuit in South Carolina, added their voices to make the decision a unanimous one among all six sitting Supreme Court justices.[39]

Blair's opinion was entirely consistent with the opinions he had joined as a Virginia judge in 1788 and 1789, demonstrating concern with preservation of the independence of the judicial branch, and refusing to accept burdensome uncompensated duties. The Invalid Pension Act required the circuit judges to certify to the secretary of war their findings and opinion, which might then be revised by that official before submission to Congress for possible further revision. Jay and Cushing had not waited for a claimant, but, when court opened on April 5, announced their wholly advisory opinion that the doctrine of separation of powers forbade judges' opinions from being subject to revisal by members of the other branches of government. Wilson and Blair waited until Hayburn and other claimants appeared, then announced their opinion based upon the same principles but stating plainly that "[s]uch revision and control" by the other branches is "radically inconsistent with the independence of that judicial power . . . so strictly observed by the constitution of the United States." Consistent with their opinion that the act was void, Wilson and Blair refused to hear the claimants. Jay, Cushing, and Iredell chose to hear pension claims as "commissioners."[40]

Federalist anger focused on the presumed "infallibility" of the judges and on their refusal to do what Congress ordered them to do rather than on their belief that judicial review was unconstitutional; that is, upon judicial supremacy, not judicial review. Federalist congressional leader Fisher Ames thought the decision "indiscreet and erroneous," likely to "embolden the states and their courts to make many claims of power." No one seemed to think that it was improper for the judges to exercise judicial review. The repute of *Marbury v. Madison* as the first act of judicial review by the Supreme Court has been engendered by several factors. Some originated in the

1790s: the lack of directness and lack of cohesion of the justices (who issued differing opinions in different circuits), Federalist phobias against promoting dangerous division by continuing to talk about the matter, and much sentiment that judicial review was uncontroversial: many were well aware that several *state* statutes had already been ruled unconstitutional by the justices on circuit.[41] But modern positivist biases have been the chief obstacle: positivists as authoritarians accept judicial lawmaking only when entombed in formal opinions in litigated cases;[42] and positivists focus legalistically and hierarchically upon the titles of courts, not (as did the natural-law sentiment of the 1790s) upon the moral authority of the justices who sat in them.

Iredell had promised to change his view "if we can be convinced this opinion is a wrong one." The attorney general, Edmund Randolph, moved the Supreme Court in August 1792 to issue a writ of mandamus, commanding the Pennsylvania circuit court to hear Hayburn's claim. Randolph appeared on behalf of no client, but as the legal representative of the United States, claiming that the Judiciary Act's authorization that the attorney general "prosecute all suits in the Supreme Court in which the United States shall be concerned" had granted him the same power as the English attorney general, who regularly made such appearances. Chief Justice Jay challenged him as to whether he could thus act without authorization from the president. Other questions were asked, but apparently no justice challenged his ex parte appearance. "The question the Supreme Court took upon itself was apparently narrow: could the Attorney General speak on his own, or must the President be the one speaking through his authorized cabinet representative?" Blair joined Iredell and Johnson in voting to allow Randolph to appear ex parte, but the motion failed upon an even division, Jay, Cushing, and Wilson voting to require presidential authorization.[43]

Given the similar action Blair had joined in Virginia a few years earlier—issuing an opinion ex parte, as it were, and having it spread on the record—he did not share modern positivist notions that require lawyers to have clients when they appear before courts, and courts to issue opinions only in such litigated instances. Further, neither Blair nor the other judges thought it odd when, in 1782, Chief Justice Pendleton asked members of the bar to give their opinions on judicial review in the *Caton* case, or when, in 1793, Chief Justice Jay invited any member of the bar to speak on behalf of the absent state in *Chisholm v. Georgia*.[44] Blair and the other southern judges shared the traditional notion that the attorney general of a government was its general legal representative and could appear ex parte before the bar in the public interest; the other justices demanded only presidential authorization and did not disapprove such ex parte appearances. These actions and ideas appear strange to positivists today but excited no comment then.

Positivists believe that law is commands, that these commands are positively made by authoritative sources (either by legislative bodies in statutes and regulations, or by judicial bodies in opinions), and that the law wholly consists in these commands. Natural lawyers, on the other hand, believed that the law was only what "the community" accepted as the law and that it accreted over a course of years by acceptance of legal opinions of legislatures and of those trained in the law: judges, treatise writers, and members of the bar. *Any* legal opinion was only *evidence* of the law, not "the law." Members of the bar had a professional responsibility, as well as a civic one, to give their best opinion as to what the law was. Authority was moral and consensual, not legalistic and peremptory. Thus, the opinion of a judge was *more* authoritative, but all professional opinions deserved respect and were to be judged primarily by their wisdom, not by the status of their holders—which is why the old reports are replete with the arguments the lawyers made; why opinions of the judges were often delivered seriatim; why so many of the old cases have little or no judicial opinion; why the opinions of that time give treatise writers respect equal to that of prior judicial decisions; why reporting *in haec verba* was unusual and not demanded in the 1790s; and why we call what judges say "opinions" rather than "rulings." It is also why Blair's actions summarized in the previous paragraph were not strange to the natural-law-trained lawyers and judges of the 1790s.[45]

Ultimately, the action of Wilson and Blair in refusing to sit as "commissioners" was completely vindicated. In February 1794 William Bradford, the new attorney general, filed in the Supreme Court a debt claim on behalf of the United States against Yale Todd, a Connecticut pensioner whose claim had been approved by Iredell as "commissioner" in 1792. The Court held for the United States, invalidating all the actions of the judges as "commissioners."[46]

## Chisholm and National Power

The controversy over *Hayburn* died down, and indeed *Hayburn* lessened fears among Anti-Federalists about the power of both the Court and the national government. But the Court's decision one year later, in *Chisholm*, brought all those fears back to the fore and tended to consolidate the emerging Jeffersonian opposition to the centralizing, commercially-oriented Federalist policies. That decision generated the largest uproar yet, alienating constituencies theretofore doubtful or even Federalist.

Chisholm's decedent, a South Carolinian, had sold supplies to the state of Georgia during the Revolution worth nine thousand pounds, and had never been paid.[47] Chisholm sued Georgia in the Supreme Court, and the state refused to appear, claiming immunity from suit as a sovereign. The Constitution contained express language giving to federal courts jurisdiction over suits "between a State and citizens of another State," which had provoked many Anti-Federalist objections during the ratification debates, but most Federalists, including Alexander Hamilton and John Marshall, had taken the position that Anti-Federalist fears were groundless. The Judiciary Act of 1789 contained a provision vesting such jurisdiction exclusively in the Supreme Court, but the Anti-Federalist fears seemed calmed.

In February 1793, after several postponements, the Court held, 4–1, with Iredell dissenting and Johnson just resigned, that the clauses meant what they said, and found that Chisholm's suit against Georgia was properly brought before it, even though Georgia refused to consent. Justice Wilson and Chief Justice Jay gave long and elaborate opinions—the one lyric, the other angry—from which one could conclude that they believed that states were or could be made entirely subordinate to the federal government, the greatest fear of the Anti-Federalists.[48]

Blair's opinion, in contrast, was simple, straightforward, and confined to the situation at hand. Carefully and clearly resting himself upon the plain words of the Constitution, "the only fountain from which I shall draw," he found meaningless its word order (from which others had implied that the only jurisdiction given was when a state was a plaintiff): "[a] dispute between A. and B. is surely a dispute between B. and A." The Constitution's other grants of jurisdiction over

"Controversies between two or more States" and between "a State and foreign States" were conclusive that it contemplated states' being made defendants in federal court without their consent. When a state adopted the Constitution, he concluded, "she has, in that respect [being 'amenable to the judicial power of the United States'], given up her right of sovereignty." The most important interest Blair had was to preserve the government and to keep its powers intact, and that "requir[ed] the submission of individual states to the judicial authority of the United States." Obedience to the new government, even in delicate situations like the one before him, was paramount. It seemed necessary to him, as Europe was becoming embroiled in general war, as foreign states cast covetous eyes toward United States territory, as rural dissidents maintained opposition to the government, and as Jefferson emerged as a viable leader of the opposition, to speak "clearly and decidedly" in favor of its dignity and capability. As was true in the British debt instance, Blair was the only southerner on the Court to take the Federalist position.[49]

The uproar was so strong and widespread that Congress devised, and the states passed, the Eleventh Amendment, withdrawing jurisdiction from the federal judiciary in diversity and alienage suits in which a state was an unconsented-to defendant.[50] This has remained, in the country's history, the only instance in which the constitutional grant of judicial power was directly diminished through amendment. However, during Washington's second term the nation's foreign and domestic troubles grew, so despite increased attacks on Federalist judges, they continued to exercise their authority to support and uphold the federal government where it was prudent to do so.

## The Neutrality Crisis and Domestic Insurrection

As 1793 progressed, the war in Europe heated up. The numerous French partisans within the United States demanded that aid be provided to the new republican government of the only country that had given the colonies significant help during the Revolution, and the Francophile secretary of state Jefferson and the domestic opposition gained strength. British partisans, mostly merchants and their allies (among whom was the Anglophile treasury secretary Hamilton), pointed to our cultural ties with and economic dependency upon Great Britain, and warned of the dangers of democratic excess. Jefferson and Hamilton agreed, however, that the weakness and vulnerability of the United States made involvement on either side unadvisable. The president declared the United States neutral, "friendly and impartial."[51]

The activist new French ambassador, Citizen Edmond Genet, by claim of right under the 1778 treaty, outfitted French privateers in American ports (crewing them with enthusiastic American volunteers), and had their prizes condemned by members of his staff sitting, on American territory, as French prize courts. The British minister was convulsed with protest at this disregard of neutrality. "All members of the cabinet . . . agreed that the fitting out of privateers, the recruitment of American crews, and the operation of the consular [prize] courts were improper." Washington asked the Supreme Court for assurance by way of an advisory opinion.

At their August 1793 term the justices unanimously rejected the president's request to answer the questions, citing separation-of-powers concerns and their reluctance to address questions extrajudicially, "our being Judges of a Court in the last Resort." The judges' response is surprising. Like the ex parte appearance of Randolph, the giving of advisory opinions was usual in the natural-law atmosphere of English tradition, and we have seen that, in *Hayburn*, none of the justices thought the practice unconstitutional. Blair had given them, and Jay gave so much advice to the president and Hamilton that he could almost have been considered a member of the cabinet; he was soon to become special ambassador to England to negotiate a new treaty.[52]

It was thus not advisory opinions in general that were rejected but *this particular* advisory opinion. It would have been characteristic of Blair to join his colleagues in following the lead of Jay, who (with Hamilton) believed that only a strong president acting alone, not in conjunction with any other branch, could provide adequate leadership in the crisis of foreign affairs then threatening the nation. They also wished a public rebuke for Jefferson, who desired that the Court and Congress join the president in leadership in foreign affairs, and who was becoming the focal point of domestic opposition. Wilson and Jay had already given well-publicized grand jury charges opposing Genet's activities, and legal challenges to the French prize awards were in the federal district courts and could find their way up to the Supreme Court, so there were judicial avenues for the judges to render their opinions.[53]

To the utter dismay of the Washington administration, four of the five federal district courts that considered challenges to the French prize courts declared that, according to the law of nations, questions of prize were exclusively for the courts of the captor nation and that neutral nations had no jurisdiction in such matters. The Supreme Court in February 1794 finally got to hear an appeal in one of them, and in *Glass v. Sloop Betsy*, the judges unanimously asserted, without giving any legal rationale, that the federal district courts *did* have jurisdiction, and that prize courts of another nation could not be erected in the United States. Thus, United States courts now had jurisdiction to hear these cases and a legal way to refuse to give preclusive effect to any award of a French prize court on American soil. The learned district judges surely knew the law of nations. Just as surely Blair and his colleagues, when they got the chance to act judicially, made an overtly political decision: to support the president's policy of neutrality and to oppose Genet no matter what the law of nations said. The politically cagey caution of summer 1793 was followed by direct political action in winter 1794.

For Blair and the other judges, troubles only mounted. Many poor and middling farmers and wage workers found Federalist national policy to favor merchants and the seaboard elites and to be inconsistent with their more democratic view of the goals and meaning of the Revolution. Resistance coalesced along the western frontier around Hamilton's excise tax on whiskey, which discriminated against underrepresented small farmers and small distillers, and, on the specieless frontier, ate directly into workers' wages and the local medium of exchange. It erupted into open armed protest in western Pennsylvania (the only frontier locale where officials actually tried to enforce the tax) in the summer and fall of 1794, with ensuing disturbances in central Pennsylvania, western Maryland and Virginia, and Kentucky. President Washington personally led a thirteen-thousand-strong army westward to crush the protest. Part of this show of force included the arrest, often for treason, of twenty or so mostly bedraggled protesters. Some were of middling wealth, such as John Hamilton, sheriff of Washington County; Thomas Sedgewick, a magistrate; and the Reverend John Corbley. Over local protest they were herded eastward in November to jail in Philadelphia, where they remained, accused of treason and awaiting indictment by a grand jury, when the Court met in February 1795.[54]

Blair was clearly alarmed by this event, and his two surviving grand jury charges, from the fall 1794 circuit in Delaware and the spring 1795 circuit in Georgia, demonstrate that he saw it as the gravest of threats among many then pressing on the government. Both directly contradicted the grievances raised by the westerners, asserting the responsiveness and representativeness of the government, the mildness of the tax, and the necessity that the burdens of majority rule be accepted by all. Both saw the government as weak militarily and as threatened with extinction by the revolt because of its occurrence during the delicate international situation. Despite the arrests and the apparent crushing of the revolt, the tone of the later charge is more desperate and alarming than that of the earlier, indicating that Blair, like other Federalists, saw the real threat as coming from the Jeffersonian opposition: "[H]ow dangerous it is to indulge too freely discontent with respect to the measures of government." He was worried about designing individuals who "fret the minds of the ignorant," turning them into "the deluded multitude."[55]

Blair's actions in the Supreme Court in February 1795 reflected these fears and prejudices. Corbley and others moved for the erection of a special circuit court, to be held in western Pennsylvania close to their witnesses. Hamilton, brought from prison on a habeas corpus writ, moved the Court for discharge because he had been jailed for treason without a hearing or, alternatively, for release on reasonable bail pending indictment. After holding these motions for several days, the Court unanimously denied the motion for a special circuit court in the West, on insubstantial if not specious grounds, and granted Hamilton bail in the enormous sum of $4,000 personally and $2,000 each for two sureties. The grand jury failed to indict Corbley, Hamilton, and Sedgewick for treason, and prosecution of Corbley on a "true bill" for misdemeanor was dropped. Only two persons were convicted of treason for the revolt, both of whom were poor, one of whom at least was simpleminded; both were pardoned.[56]

## *A Federalist to the End*

### Retirement

Having suffered from illness frequently while on the Court, John Blair was forced to leave the bench on circuit in South Carolina and to cancel the ensuing North Carolina circuit court in the spring of 1795. He described the malady as "a rattling, distracting noise" in his head, "nothing but an overbearing noise in [his] head which distracts [his] attention." The problem persisted, causing him to miss the Court's August 1795 session and the fall circuits, and on October 25 he tendered his resignation to the president.[57]

He lived for five more years, and, though he was ill at times, no further mention of any rattling in his head has come to light. Though distraught by the deaths of his only son in October 1791 and his wife a year later, Blair engaged in many pursuits happily and remained a sturdy supporter of the Federalist regime to the end. In the fall of 1796 the Jeffersonians were sure that he would become the Federalist candidate for the United States Senate, and in the spring of 1797 he appeared as foreman of the federal circuit court grand jury in Richmond that presented Jeffersonian Congressman Samuel Cabell for the "evil" contained in a circular letter to his constituents; Cabell had therein castigated Federalist policies and the election of John Adams. The presentment raised a great furor, not least of which was popular astonishment at Blair's participation. In the summer of 1799 he suffered a stroke, and he died on August 31, 1800.[58]

## A "Safe and Conscientious" Judge

As a judge, John Blair was, in historian Earl Gregg Swem's apt phrasing, "safe and conscientious." Neither innovative, complicated, nor deep, nor an erudite legal scholar, Blair dealt with the immediate problem, went only as far as he had to, ruffled few feathers, and may not have thought through the finer legal or political points, as he showed in his confusion over the Robert Morris certiorari instance. But Blair was "safe and conscientious" in that he was knowledgeable in the law, as he demonstrated in *Brailsford*, and in that he held firm to his duty, hewed to his Federalist principles, and spoke clearly and directly, if quietly, to the points at hand, as in *Chisholm*. A New Hampshire Federalist, who had probably attended and admired his handling of *Penhallow*, remembered him as "far superior to Cushing—a man of firmness, strict integrity, and of great candour." And he was "safe and conscientious" in that he was sufficiently independent not to be thought pliable. The Jeffersonian attorney general of Massachusetts was "much pleased with Judge Blair," praising Blair's "independence" when, on circuit, he openly if respectfully differed on a point of law from the Federalist-dominated Massachusetts high court, stating "that he could give no opinion but his own."[59]

More important, Blair was "safe and conscientious" in a way modern scholars of the judicial role do not customarily note. Both the New Hampshire and Massachusetts observers just quoted liked the political as well as the legal thrust of Blair's judicial opinions. The political dimension was then as now an inherent part of judging, but then it was recognized and expected. The most important value in Blair's great opinions, in *Penhallow* and *Chisholm*, was that they were clear and forthright legal affirmations of the power and federal superiority of the national government, a government greatly suspect to many Americans, a weak government under seige from foreign powers, a new and experimental government liable to momentary dissolution. John Blair proved time and again that he could be counted upon to support the Federalist position, which he saw as the national, the constitutional position.

Blair's other quality of greatness is also evident in his opinions in *Penhallow* and *Chisholm*, when contrasted with the strident tones and tendentious Federalism exhibited in the same cases by Justice Paterson, in the one, and Chief Justice Jay, in the other. The expansive and hard-edged nationalist metier adopted by his northern peers evoked much antipathy from both Antifederalists and southerners, but Blair, whose opinions were the opposite of those of most of his geographic compatriots, provoked only calm disagreement about the legalities of the problem, not hot political opposition.[60] Blair was "safe and conscientious" because he wrote calmly and maturely, clearly emphasizing national power through deliberate and bounded legal argument without being politically threatening or provocative.

He exhibited this quality in all his dealings. A British creditor who traveled the southern federal circuit in the 1790s, monitoring his many suits, was critical to the point of contempt of many of the justices for their delay and lack of courage, but he gave Blair respect.[61] And astonishment, not harsh words, formed the height of critique from Virginians of his 1797 federal grand jury foremanship. In an age of increasingly vituperative, politically charged personal attacks, Blair's Federalist partisanship stands out as calm, persuasive, and productive of ongoing dialogue and continuing relations rather than as disruptive and divisive. The proper criterion against which to judge the Supreme Court's opinions in the perilous 1790s is their political effectiveness in persuasively upholding the power, authority, and respect of the shaky new national government while exciting no dismembering dissent; and the proper gauges of its members are their courage and consistency in supporting the new Constitution and its constituted government. On both of these measures, the amiable, safe, conscientious Virginian John Blair ranks at the top.

Indeed, Blair was a "safe and conscientious" supporter of his class. The Revolutionary alliance between the merchants of the North and the planters of the South, embodied in the developmental and planter interests of the first president, was still fluid and viable in the 1790s, though it was breaking down and would not remain so for long. (Most supporters of the mercantile interest were still natural lawyers, like Blair, but the tendency would be for them to adopt the emerging positivist theory of law.) Blair, who also personified both sorts of interest, apparently (like most contemporaries) without seeing their incompatibility, emphasized solidarity with the developmental and mercantile interests of the Jay/Hamilton Federalists in his opinions, consistently upholding the might and, with regard to punishment of the whiskey rebels, the economic schemes of their new national government. Thanks to the qualities and circumstances just mentioned, his divergence from the planting interest also did not bring him criticism.

Eulogizers recalled Blair's mildness, gravity, and piety, his own absence of fanaticism, and the lack of any assault upon him by an enemy. St. George Tucker, one of the leading Virginia lawyers of the next generation, remembered him as quiet, dull, and gentlemanly.[62] Though not a strong thinker as a jurist, John Blair did have an ability to get to the heart of the matter, was an able and competent judge, and was, first and foremost, sturdily devoted to his own interests and to the cause of mercantile and planter republican independence, as later embodied in the Federalist Party.

## NOTES

1. [Earl Gregg Swem], Book Review, *William and Mary Quarterly (1st Ser.)*, 22:142 (1913).

2. "Resignation of the Judges," March 11, 1789, in David John Mays, ed., *The Letters and Papers of Edmund Pendleton 1734–1803* (2 vols., 1967) (cited hereafter as *Pendleton Papers*), 2:554 (opinion of the Virginia Court of Appeals,

written by Edmund Pendleton, joined by John Blair), dealt with at more length in text accompanying note 16.

3. See generally A. G. Roeber, *Faithful Lawyers and Republican Magistrates: Creators of Virginia Legal Culture, 1680–1810* (1981), esp. pp. 112–36; Joseph A. Ernst, "The Political Economy of the Chesapeake Colonies, 1760–1775: A Study in Comparative History," in Ronald Hoffman et al., eds., *The Economy of Early America: The Revolutionary Period, 1763–1790* (1988), pp. 196–243; Marc Egnal & Joseph A. Ernst, "An Economic Interpretation of the American Revolution," *W&MQ(3d)*, 35:401–28 (1972); Frederick Thornton Miller, "Juries and Judges vs. the Law: Virginia from the Revolution to the Confrontation Between John Marshall and Spencer Roane" (Ph.D. dissertation, University of Alabama, 1986), pp. 1–14.

4. Fred L. Israel, "John Blair, Jr.," in Leon Friedman et al., eds., *The Justices of the United States Supreme Court, 1789–1969: Their Lives and Major Opinions* (4 vols., 1969), 1:109; Allen Johnson et al., eds., *Dictionary of American Biography* (10 vols., 1927–1938) (cited hereafter as *DAB*), *s.v.* James Blair, 1:335–37, *s.v.* John Blair (1687–1771), 1:337, & *s.v.* John Blair (1732–1800), 1:337–38 (all written by Earl Gregg Swem); Daphne Gentry & Brent Tarter, "The Blair Family of Colonial Williamsburg," *Virginia Magazine of Genealogy*, 32:107, 108 (1994); Edmund Morgan, *American Slavery American Freedom: The Ordeal of Colonial Virginia* (1975), pp. 348–62; Deposition of John Blair in lawsuit of Margaret Eustace vs. Seth John Cuthbert, Dec. 29, 1787, in Blair Family Papers, Earl Gregg Swem Library, ViW; Roeber, *Faithful Lawyers* 132 (confuses John Blair junior for his father as member of Williamsburg city court in 1750s). Blair's plantations suffered terribly from British depredations during the Revolution, and many of his slaves escaped. John Blair to his sister [Mary Blair Braxton Burwell], Aug. 15, 1783, in Blair, Banister, Braxton, Horner, & Whiting Papers, ViWC.

5. *DAB*, *s.v.* John Blair (1732–1800); Maeva Marcus et al., eds., *The Documentary History of the Supreme Court of the United States, 1789–1800* (5 vols. to date, 1985–) (cited hereafter as *Documentary History*), 1:54–59; Robert Bolling, *Memoir of the Bolling Family* (1868), pp. 33–38; Gentry & Tarter, "Blair Family," pp. 109 & n.26, 111; *The* [Richmond] *Virginia Argus*, Feb. 29, 1804; E. Alfred Jones, *American Members of the Inns of Court* (1924), p. 21.

6. Roeber, *Faithful Lawyers,* 121 (source of the first quote); Charles T. Cullen, *St. George Tucker and Law in Virginia, 1772–1804* (1987) (reprinted Ph.D. dissertation, University of Virginia, 1971), pp. 25, 56, 62–63; Frank L. Dewey, *Thomas Jefferson LAWYER* (1986), pp. 1–8; *The* [Richmond] *Virginia Arqus*, Feb. 29, 1804 (source of the second quote); Israel, "Blair," 109.

7. William & Mary college records, John Blair, Jr., Folder, Faculty/Alumni Collection, Earl Gregg Swem Library, ViW; *DAB*, *s.v.* John Blair (1732–1800), p. 338; Israel, "Blair," 109–10; Earl Gregg Swem, "Williamsburg—The Old Colo-

nial Capital," *W&MQ(lst)*, 16:307 (1907); Joseph A. Ernst, "The Robinson Scandal Redivivus: Money, Debts, and Politics in Revolutionary Virginia," *Virginia Magazine of History and Biography*, 77:146–73 (1969); *Journals of the House of Burgesses, 1766–1769*, p. 158 (I owe thanks to Brent Tarter for the references to the journals in this and the succeeding note); Dewey, *Jefferson*, 44, 53; Earl Gregg Swem, "Williamsburg Lodge of Masons," *W&MQ(lst)*, 1:9–10 (1892).

8. Virginius Dabney, *Virginia: The New Dominion* (1971), pp. 112–14; *Journals of the House of Burgesses, 1766–69*, pp. 214–15; Israel, "Blair," p. 110 (source of the first quote); J. Elliot Drinard, "John Blair, Jr., 1732–1800," in *Proceedings of the Thirty-Eighth Meeting of the Virginia State Bar Association* (1927), pp. 437–39 (Blair's council proclamation quoted on p. 438); John E. Selby, *The Revolution in Virginia, 1775–1783* (1988), pp. 48–49.

9. Thad W. Tate, "The Coming of the Revolution in Virginia: Britain's Challenge to Virginia's Ruling Class," *W&MQ(3d)*, 19:336–37 (1962); Selby, *Revolution*, 76–77, 95–104, 106–21 (indeed, Selby's careful review of the primary sources found no Blair contributions to a single major or minor political decision in these momentous times). Edmund Randolph, writing much later, named Blair as one of the persons whom the public esteemed to be important in the 1776 Convention. Edmund Randolph, *A Political History of Virginia* (H. Shaffer, ed., 1970), p. 51.

10. Selby, *Revolution*, 119–20, 147–48, 156–57; Cullen, *St. George Tucker*, 28–31; Charles F. Hobson et al., eds., *The Papers of John Marshall* (7 vols. to date, 1974–) (cited hereafter as *Marshall Papers*), 5:xxviii–xxx; William T. Hutchinson et al., eds., *The Papers of James Madison* (23 vols. to date, 1962–) (cited hereafter as *Madison Papers*), 1:237 n.l. Whether Blair ever actually sat as admiralty judge is unclear. See Selby, *Revolution*, 148. He was appointed to the Continental Congress in 1781, but he never sat. See *Madison Papers* 3:161 & n.2.

11. Israel, "Blair," p. 110; Joseph Jones to James Madison, Nov. 24, 1780, *Madison Papers* 2:298; David John Mays, *Edmund Pendleton, 1721–1803: A Biography* (2 vols., 1952); Robert B. Kirtland, *George Wythe: Lawyer, Revolutionary, Judge* (1986) (reprinted Ph.D. dissertation, Harvard University, [197?]); Thomas Jefferson to James Madison, March 15, 1789, Julian P. Boyd et al., eds., *The Papers of Thomas Jefferson* (25 vols. to date, 1950–) (cited hereafter as *Jefferson Papers*), 14:659; Joseph Jones to James Madison, June 24, 1789, *Documentary History* 1:626; George Washington to James Madison, undated (before September 24, 1789), ibid. 1:665; George Washington to Edmund Randolph, November 30, 1789, ibid., 1:680.

12. "Pendleton's Account of the 'Case of the Prisoners' *(Commonwealth v. Caton)*," Va. Ct. App., November 1782, *Pendleton Papers* 2:416; *Commonwealth v. Posey,* 8 Va. (4 Call) 109 (Va. Ct. App. 1787); "Remonstrance of the Judges," Va. Ct. App., May 12, 1788, *Pendleton Papers* 2:504; "Resignation of

the Judges," Va. Ct. App., March 11, 1789, ibid., 2:553. Call's fourth volume of Virginia reports, which covers the 1780s, was not published until 1827 and for most of the cases reported (for that period) gives only the facts, the arguments of counsel, and the decree or judgment entered, but no opinions of the judges, which were, by that time, probably lost. It contains notorious errors, also, which is why I have chosen to use David Mays's treatment of *Caton* and his version of the last two opinions, both written by Edmund Pendleton.

13. Kirtland, *George Wythe,* 252–62; *Commonwealth v. Posey,* 8 Va. (4 Call) 109, 122 (Va. Ct. App. 1787); William R. Casto, *The Supreme Court in the Early Republic: The Chief Justiceships of John Jay and Oliver Ellsworth* (1995), p. 3 ("When the Court was created, virtually all American attorneys were natural lawyers who believed that judges did not and should not resort to considerations of policy in adjudicating cases. They believed that law was a comprehensive and systematic body of principles based upon divine wisdom and the perfection of human reason."). To Blair, as to many of his Virginia contemporaries, "the people" were those white males of sufficient property and standing to represent the community as a whole.

14. *Commonwealth v. Caton,* 8 Va. (4 Call) 5, 8 (Va. Ct. App. 1782) (source for Wythe's words); "Pendleton's Account of the 'Case of the Prisoners'," *Pendleton Papers* 2:426 (source for Blair's words); Mays, *Pendleton* 2:187–200; William Michael Treanor, "*The Case of the Prisoners* and the Origins of Judicial Review," *University of Pennsylvania Law Review*, 143:529–37 (1994).

15. Roeber, *Faithful Magistrates,* 153–208, 216–17, 220, esp. 172–73, 176, 189, 195–200; Cullen, *St. George Tucker,* 31–35, 71–82; Mays, *Pendleton* 2:151–52, 273–75; Emory G. Evans, "Private Indebtedness and the Revolution in Virginia, 1776 to 1796," *W&MQ(3d)*, 28:349–71, esp. 361–63 (1971); Peter J. Coleman, *Debtors and Creditors in America: Insolvency, Imprisonment for Debt, and Bankruptcy, 1607–1900* (1974), pp. 115, 200–201; Norman K. Risjord, *Chesapeake Politics, 1781–1800* (1978), pp. 160–66, 174–79; John Marshall to Charles Simms, June 16, 1784, *Marshall Papers* 1:124; "Remonstrance of the Judges," *Pendleton Papers* 2:507–8. The county courts reopened in 1778 only after British creditors were disabled from suing in them. Selby, *Revolution,* 148, 155–56.

16. "Resignation of the Judges," *Pendleton Papers* 2:553, 554. In Rhode Island in 1786, judges favoring judicial review had been summoned to appear before the legislature, and four of the five were replaced. Treanor, "Origins," p. 558.

The Court of Appeals established in 1789 was the first functioning modern appellate court—composed entirely of lawyers, having members not serving in any other branch of government, without trial jurisdiction, and not sharing its judges with any other court. See Wilfred J. Ritz, *Rewriting the History of the Judiciary Act of 1789: Exposing Myths, Challenging Premises, and Using New Evidence* (1990), pp. 27–46, esp. 43–44.

17. "Pendleton's Account of the 'Case of the Prisoners,'" *Pendleton Papers* 2:422 (Pendleton worried about how far a reviewing court might go "without exercising the power of legislation"); "Remonstrance of the Judges," ibid. 2:508 (the judges were "within the line of their duty, declaring what the law is, and not making a new law"); H. Jefferson Powell, "The Political Grammar of Early Constitutional Law," *North Carolina Law Review*, 71:996–97, 1006–8 (1993) (discussing the contemporary difference between judicial "judgment" and political "will"); Treanor, "Origins," pp. 538–40, 559–63 (judicial review uncontroversial in Virginia). See also William R. Casto, "James Iredell and the Origins of Judicial Review," *Connecticut Law Review*, 27:329–63 (1995).

18. Charlotte Balfour to [Eliza Whiting], November 10, 1789, in Blair, Banister, Braxton, Horner & Whiting Papers, ViWC; George Washington to John Blair, September 30, 1789, Blair to Washington, October 13, 1789, both in *Documentary History* 1:58. The phrase "National Security Court" in the subtitle is from Casto, *Supreme Court,* 71 et passim.

19. Israel, "Blair," pp. 110–11; James Monroe to Thomas Jefferson, July 12, 1788, *Jefferson Papers* 13:352; William Pierce, "Character Sketches of Delegates to the Federal Convention," in Max Farrand, ed., *The Records of the Federal Convention of 1787* (rev. ed., 4 vols., 1966 [orig. pub. 1911, 1937]), 3:95.

Pierce also described Blair as "one of the most respectable Men in Virginia, both on account of his Family as well as fortune." Only seven other Constitutional Convention delegates were noted by Pierce for their wealth, and only Charles Cotesworth Pinckney of South Carolina was also given the high accolade of being great in both family and fortune.

20. Support for this and the succeeding three paragraphs may be found in Wythe Holt, "'To Establish Justice': Politics, the Judiciary Act of 1789, and the Invention of the Federal Courts, 1989 *Duke Law Journal*, 1421–1531, and Casto, *Supreme Court,* 4–53. For the importance of prize and prize jurisdiction, see William R. Casto, "The Origins of Federal Admiralty Jurisdiction in an Age of Privateers, Smugglers, and Pirates," *American Journal of Legal History*, 37:117–57 (1993). For the origin of diversity jurisdiction, see Wythe Holt & James R. Perry, "Writs and Rights, 'clashings and animosities': The First Confrontation between Federal and State Jurisdictions," *Law and History Review*, 7:89–120 (1989). For Shays's Rebellion, see David P. Szatmary, *Shays' Rebellion: The Making of an Agrarian Insurrection* (1980).

21. Also important in diffusing opposition was the Bill of Rights, which was developed in Congress concomitantly with the Judiciary Act. See Ritz, *Judiciary Act,* 19–21; Holt, "'To Establish Justice,'" pp. 1513–15.

22. The best history of the Court in this period is Stewart Jay, "Most Humble Servants: The Advisory Role of Early Federal Judges" (unpublished manuscript, May 1995, in my possession), which emphasizes the intensely political role of the judges and gives in detail the fluid and confusing constellation of political tensions

and pressures constituting what I have here called the "tightrope" they had to walk. (Jay's manuscript was published in 1997 by Yale University Press.) See also William R. Casto, "Oliver Ellsworth: 'I have sought the felicity and glory of your Administration,'" in this volume; Wythe Holt, "'The Federal Courts Have Enemies in All Who Fear Their Influence on State Objects': The Failure to Abolish Supreme Court Circuit-Riding in the Judiciary Acts of 1792 and 1793," *Buffalo Law Review*, 36:306–8 (1987); Ralph Lerner, "The Supreme Court as Republican Schoolmaster," 1967 *Supreme Court Review*, pp. 127–80.

23. Pendleton's move can be precisely dated to the announcement that states could be sued in federal court, in *Chisholm v. Georgia*, in 1793. See Edmund Pendleton to Nathaniel Pendleton, August 10, 1793, *Documentary History* 5:232 (the opinions of Jay and Wilson are "very reprehensible as tending to prove the Fedral to be a consolodated Government for all America, & to Anihilate those of the States—a Principle, which, if established, would make that Constitution as great a curse as I have hitherto thought it a blessing").

24. For Blair's investment, see the story in note 31 below. This connection is part of my own debt to Forrest McDonald. See McDonald, *We the People: The Economic Origins of the Constitution* (1958), pp. 38–92, esp. 74, 90.

25. Holt & Perry, "Writs and Rights" (first quote is from p. 103; explanation of the contemporary meaning of certiorari on pp. 102–3); John Blair to James Wilson, February 2, 1791, *Documentary History* 2:126–29 (quotes are from pp. 128 and 129); John Sitgreaves to James Iredell, August 2, 1791, ibid. 2:196; *Jones v. Syme, Waterman v. Syme* (C.C.D.Va. 1791) (Wilson, J.), Order Book [for the Circuit Court for the District of Virginia], 1790–95, Federal Court Records, Vi; Richard Hanson to William Jones, May 14 & 30, 1791, Box 6, Treasury 79, PRO; *Stead v. Powell* (C.C.D.Ga. 1791) (Iredell, J.), Minute Book [for the Circuit Court for the District of Georgia], 1790–93, RG 21, National Archives Records Administration, East Point, Georgia.

The regular process under the Judiciary Act of 1789 for taking a case from a state court into federal court was "removal" under section 12, but, in another shrewd concession to Anti-Federalists, the right of removal had been limited to defendants. British creditors would have been plaintiffs in the state court debt cases lying on the books for so many years, so this provision in effect made nonretroactive the jurisdiction the Constitution and the peace treaty gave to federal courts over British debts. Holt & Perry, "Writs and Rights," p. 100; Holt, "'To Establish Justice,'" pp. 1487–88. The extraordinary writ of certiorari, then, should also have been unavailable to transfer pre-1789 cases.

26. *West v. Barnes, Federal Gazette and Philadelphia Advertiser*, August 11 & 12, 1791 (U.S., August 3, 1791); *Barnes v. West* (C.C.D.R.I. 1791), Final Record Book, 1790–94, RG 21, NARA, Waltham, Massachusetts; ibid. (C.C.D.R.I. 1792)(retrial of same case); *Providence Gazette and Country Journal*, June 16, 1792 (giving disposition upon retrial); James Iredell to George Wash-

ington, February 23, 1792, *Documentary History* 2:239–41 (describing *West* and the troubles it did not solve; requesting legislative relief). There does not seem to have been a decision on the constitutionality of the tender law, which expired in October 1789; but, at the same June 1792 term, in *Champion & Dickason v. Casey* (C.C.D.R.I. 1792), Final Record Book, John Jay, Justice William Cushing, and the district judge unanimously held unconstitutional a three-year stay on repayment of a debt granted specifically by the legislature to Casey, on ground that it "impair[ed] the Obligation of the Contract in Question," seemingly as volatile an issue as that of the tender law. [Boston] *Columbian Centinel*, June 20, 1792. Congress corrected the problem underlying *West v. Barnes* in the Process and Compensation Act of May 8, 1792, by permitting circuit court clerks to "issue writs of error . . . returnable to the Supreme Court." See *Documentary History* 4:180, 185 (section 9), 195 (section 1).

27. A much more detailed history of the circuit-riding controversy discussed in this and the next three paragraphs, plus citations to all the statutes mentioned, may be found in Holt, "'The Federal Courts Have Enemies.'" See John Blair to John Jay, August [5], 1790, *Documentary History* 2:83 (source of the quote; contains Blair's summary of the Court's August 1790 discussion, and Blair's additional suggestion); Justices of the Supreme Court to George Washington, ca. September 13, 1790, ibid., 2:89–91 (draft written by Jay and containing Jay's arguments, circulated to the other justices, but never sent).

Of course, it was also dangerous to travel to Philadelphia for the semiannual sessions of the Supreme Court. On his way in the summer of 1794 Blair's carriage "got overset six miles the other side of Dumfries" and he "rec.d a slight cut on the forehead & bruised his head just above the temple. Y.e headach followed for a short time, & a small degree of stupor lasted somewhat longer." Mary [Blair Braxton Burwell] Prescott to [Eliza Whiting,] August 24, 1794, in Blair, Banister, Braxton, Horner, & Whiting Papers, ViWC. The whale-proportioned Samuel Chase nearly drowned, and had to be hauled out of the freezing waters of the Susquehanna by three men, when he broke through "Ice that had been tried and would bear a Waggon and horses" before sunrise on his way to Court in the winter of 1800. Samuel Chase to Hannah Chase, February 4, 1800, *Documentary History* 1:888–89.

28. Wythe Holt, "'Federal Courts as the Asylum to Federal Interests': Randolph's Report, the Benson Amendment, and the 'Original Understanding' of the Federal Judiciary," *Buff. L. Rev.*, 36:341–72 (1987); James Iredell to John Jay, William Cushing, & James Wilson, February 11, 1791, *Documentary History* 2:132; John Blair to James Iredell, July 25, 1791, ibid., 2:196; John Jay to James Iredell, March 16, 1791, ibid., 2:154 (notes Blair's consenting to take the Southern Circuit); "Letter From an Anonymous Correspondent," [Boston] *Independent Chronicle*, March 3, 1791, ibid., 5:20–21 (criticizing state-defendant jurisdiction); James Sullivan, "Observations upon the Government of the United

States of America" (July 7, 1791), ibid., 5:21–32 (same); "A Citizen," [Philadelphia] *Dunlap's American Daily Advertiser*, December 20, 1791 (datelined November 19, 1791), ibid., 4:565–66 (criticizing federal criminal jurisdiction and the possibility of a jury trial for a Pittsburgh defendant being held at Philadelphia).

29. Roger Sherman to Simeon Baldwin, January 2, 1792, *Documentary History* 4:574 (source of quote); William Richardson Davie to James Iredell, May 25, 1792, ibid., 2:278–79 ("I congratulate you on the interposition of Congress in your behalf against the tyranny and injustice of your brothers of the bench,"); Justices of the Supreme Court to the Congress of the United States, August 9, 1792, ibid., 2:289–90; Justices of the Supreme Court to the Congress of the United States, February 18, 1794, ibid., 2:443–44; John Blair to James Iredell, September 14, 1795, ibid., 3:68 ("I am utterly at a loss to conceive why that course of duty [fall 1795 circuits] should have been assigned to either of us, when both of us had taken a tour in the spring, . . . besides [my] having had the Middle Circuit in the fall [of 1794].").

30. See Holt, "'To Establish Justice,'" pp. 1432–35 & nn.33, 36, & 41, 1438, 1443–44 & n.78, 1448–49, 1461, 1469–70 & n.179, 1476–77, 1487–88 & nn.233 & 234. When the Virginia courts were shut, total colonial indebtedness to Great Britain exceeded five million pounds; about two-thirds came from below the Mason-Dixon Line, and Virginia alone accounted for more than two million pounds. Emory G. Evans, "Planter Indebtedness and the Coming of the Revolution in Virginia," *W&MQ(3d)*, 19:511 (1962). A dollar was worth about three-tenths of a pound in 1790.

31. *Marshall Papers* 5:259–94 (first quote is from p. 262); William Wirt, *Sketches of the Life and Character of Patrick Henry* (9th ed., 1845), pp. 329–86; Alex[ande]r McCaul to James Ritchie, February 1, 1792, vol. 14, Foreign Office 4, PRO (source of next two quotes); Richard Hanson to William Jones, January 29, 1792, Class 30, T79, PRO ("Mr. Blair . . . thought himself interested in the payments into the Loan Office and refused to sit as Judge"); John Blair to William Cushing, June 12, 1795, *Documentary History* 1:757 (if *Ware v. Hylton* "should be brought on in August, I ought to remind you, that I have all along declined sitting in that cause"); Henry Glassford to William Molleson, February 1, 1792, James Ritchie to William Molleson, February 1, 1792 (source of last quote), both in vol. 14, F04, PRO.

Blair *was* interested in the suit. One of the "impediments" charged by the plaintiff was the 1779 Virginia law that allowed debtors to British creditors to discharge their debts by payment, in depreciated Virginia currency, into the state's Loan Office. In 1779–1781 Blair had made seventeen payments into the Loan Office, totaling nearly seven thousand pounds Virginia paper currency, to cancel debts of about 850 pounds sterling. RG48 (Register of Loan Certificates, 1777–1801), Vi. (I am indebted to Brent Tarter for this information.) Virginians excused Blair's nonattendance on grounds of his son's death, see, e.g., [Secretary of State] Thomas Jefferson to [British Minister] George Hammond, May 29, 1792, *Jefferson Papers* 23:584, but the very sickly Jimmy Blair died on October 25, 1791, see Gentry & Tarter, "Blair Family," p. 109, while Blair did not leave court until a month later.

In vivid contrast to Blair, James Wilson apparently gave no thought to recusing himself in *Chisholm v. Georgia* even though he was a named plaintiff in *Hollingsworth v. Virginia*. Since the latter suit was also brought under the Supreme Court's original jurisdiction over state-defendant litigation, the decision in *Chisholm* "was determinative of the Court's jurisdiction" in *Hollingsworth*. Casto, *Supreme Court* 195.

32. *Warre v. Daniel L. Hylton & Co.* (C.C.D.Va. 1793), Order Book, 1790–95, Federal Court Records, Vi; Richard Hanson to John Tyndall Warre, June 23, 1794, Class 30, T79, PRO ("had but two Judgments, one . . . without allowing any interest, the other . . . with Interest from 7.th July 1782"); John Hamilton to Lord Grenville, November 29, 1794 ("several Judgements obtained for British debts, but with the Deduction of Eight years Interest, this proceeds from the Verdict given by the Jury to which the Judges do not give their assent") and Andrew Ronald to John Hamilton, December 17, 1793 ("the Juries, notwithstanding the decision of the Court [William Paterson and Cyrus Griffin] that the Plaintiffs were intitled to full and unceasing interest, made it a uniform rule, to deduct 8 years interest"), both in vol. 6, F05, PRO; *Guls v. Murchie* (C.C.D.Va. 1794), Order Book, 1790–95, Federal Court Records, Vi (Blair orders interest from May 7, 1776); *Georgia v. Brailsford,* 3 U.S. (3 Dallas) 1, 4–5 (1794) (unanimous jury instructions given by Jay, C.J.); *Ware v. Hylton,* 3 U.S. (3 Dallas) 199 (1796). It was commonly held that the war had lasted from April 1775 to April 1783.

Blair, sitting upon what was to be his last circuit court in Georgia in the spring of 1795, had once again to recuse himself from all British debt cases because Georgia had a law like the one in Virginia still on appeal. John Hamilton to Lord Grenville, June 20, 1795, Class 11, F05, PRO.

33. James Iredell to George Washington, February 23, 1792, *Documentary History* 2:241 (explains his actions on circuit); Julius Goebel, *History of the Supreme Court of the United States: Antecedents and Beginnings to 1801* (1971), pp. 742–47.

34. 2 U.S. (2 Dallas) 402–9, esp. 406–7 (opinion of Blair), 408–9 (opinion of Jay)(1793). Commenting upon the decision, Edmund Randolph (the losing counsel) was quite critical of three members of the majority, and of the Court's lack of familiarity with equity. He complained that Justice James Wilson "knows not an iota of equity," that Chief Justice Jay, whose approach to the law "had no method, no legal principle, no system of reasoning," was "aim[ing] at the cultivation of Southern popularity," and that the members of the Court in general

would "take a score of years to settle . . . a regular course of Chancery." Randolph also criticized Iredell, who had denied Georgia access below but voted with Blair in the Supreme Court, but leveled no charges at Blair. Edmund Randolph to James Madison, August 12, 1792, *Madison Papers* 14:348–49.

35. 2 U.S. (2 Dallas) 417–18 (opinion of Blair), 418–19 (opinion of Jay). The writ *ne exeat* forbade a person from leaving the jurisdiction, and, as Attorney General Edmund Randolph had explained to Congress in his report on the state of the federal judiciary in December 1790, judicial power to issue such was necessary if a "proper plan" was to "be devised" to fill out the details of federal equity jurisdiction. Section 14 of the Judiciary Act of 1789 had authorized the federal courts to issue "all other Writs not specially provided for by Statute," but *ne exeat* had nowhere been mentioned. Thus it was doubtful in February 1793 whether such a writ could be issued. Spurred perhaps by Blair's concerns in *Brailsford*, Congress in section 5 of the Judiciary Act of March 2, 1793, authorized single justices of the Supreme Court to issue writs *ne exeat*. See *Documentary History* 4:162 n.7 (Randolph's *Report* of December 31, 1790), 71 (section 14 of the Judiciary Act of 1789), 205 (section 5 of the Judiciary Act of 1793), 202 n.8 & accompanying text (explanation of *ne exeat*).

36. The facts in this and the succeeding two paragraphs have been taken from L. Kinvin Wroth et al., eds., *The Legal Papers of John Adams* (2 vols., 1965) (cited hereafter as *Adams Papers*), 2:352–95; Henry Bourguignon, *The First Federal Court: The Federal Appellate Prize Court of the American Revolution, 1775–1787* (1977), pp. 242–52, 307–18.

37. *Adams Papers* 2:355 (source of first quote); Bourguignon, *First Court,* 242 (source of second quote).

38. *Penhallow v. Doane,* 3 U.S. (3 Dallas) 109–13 (1795) (Blair's opinion on circuit, embedded in his Supreme Court opinion); ibid., 108–9, 113–16 (Blair's Supreme Court opinion); ibid., 80–91 (opinion of Paterson, J., agreeing with Blair and arguing in addition that the states were never individually sovereign); ibid., 91–108, 116–20 (opinions of Iredell, J., and Cushing, J., agreeing with Blair but disagreeing vehemently with Paterson's additional argument).

Interestingly, Blair, whose vote was needed to make a majority of the six-person Court (reduced to four in this instance with Jay in England, negotiating a fresh treaty, and Wilson recused because he had represented Doane before the Confederation court: *Documentary History* 1:231 n.160 & 1:236 n.175), did not mention the difficulty of his having already heard and decided the case once, even though, when the judges were contemplating a strong protest about their circuit-riding duties in 1790, he had written that it was "liable to objection, that men who have decided a cause in one court, should determine it again in an appellative capacity." John Blair to John Jay, August [5], 1790, ibid., 2:84.

39. *Hayburn's Case,* 2 U.S. (2 Dallas) 409, 410–14n (1792) (note containing the opinions of Jay, Cushing, and the district judge of New York; Wilson, Blair,

and Peters; and Iredell and the district judge of North Carolina, issued as letters dated respectively April 5, April 18, and June 8, 1792); Opinion of Justice Johnson and District Judge Bee, October 26, 1792, Minute Book [for the Circuit Court for the District of South Carolina], RG 21, NARA, East Point, Georgia (Johnson did not ride circuit in the spring of 1792); Maeva Marcus & Robert Teir, "*Hayburn's Case:* A Misinterpretation of Precedent," 1988 *Wisconsin Law Review*, 527–46; Charles Warren, *The Supreme Court in United States History* (2 vols., rev. ed., 1926), 1:69–82 (notes holding of unconstitutionality; details the gleeful responses of Anti-Federalists to *Hayburn*); Edmund Randolph to George Washington, April 5, 1792, George Washington Papers, Library of Congress (Wilson in chance meeting with Randolph declared that he and Blair both doubted the law's constitutionality); James Madison to Henry Lee, April 15, 1792, *Madison Papers* 14:288 (the Pennsylvania federal judges had pronounced the law "unconstitutional and void"). The district judge of Vermont later joined Jay and Cushing to repeat (verbatim) the declaration they had previously made in New York. See Opinion of John Jay, William Cushing, and Nathaniel Chipman, June 18, 1792, filed with 1803 case files of Vermont Circuit Court, RG 21, NARA, Waltham, Massachusetts.

40. 2 U.S. (2 Dallas) at 411n; James Iredell to Hannah Iredell, September 30, 1792, *Documentary History* 2:301 ("I have reconciled myself to the propriety of doing the Invalid-business out of Court. *Judge Wilson altogether declines* it."). The records of the claims of the invalids indicate that very few were heard from the Middle Circuit courts attended by Blair in the spring of 1792, and all of those are without date and so are consistent with their having been handled by Cushing when he rode the Middle Circuit in fall 1792. See *American State Papers: Claims* (38 vols., 1854), 1:56–68, 107–22 (complete record of claims filed before the circuit judges acting as commissioners in 1792; none are certified by Blair or Wilson; claims from Virginia and Maryland circuits are without date).

41. Warren, *Supreme Court* 73–76; Fisher Ames to Thomas Dwight, April 25, 1792, in Seth Ames et al., eds., *Works of Fisher Ames* (2 vols., 1983), 2:942; Warren, *Supreme Court* 64–68; Holt, "'The Federal Courts Have Enemies,'" p. 323 nn. 88–89 & accompanying text.

42. Of course, in *Marbury* only one side argued the cause.

43. 2 U.S. (2 Dallas) 414 n; Edmund Randolph to James Madison, August 12, 1792, *Madison Papers* 12:258; [Philadelphia] *Federal Gazette*, August 18, 1792; Marcus & Tier, "*Hayburn's Case*," 534–40 (quote is from p. 538). After the tie vote, Randolph argued for mandamus on behalf of Hayburn, who was present. The judges, not wanting to embarrass their Federalist administration further with another holding of unconstitutionality, took the case under advisement until February, giving Congress another chance to act. Congress repealed the 1792 act and gave the abusive duties to the district judges.

44. Mays, *Pendleton* 2:193–94; George Morgan to Alexander McKee, February [20], 1793, *Documentary History* 5:222 ("No counsel appearing on behalf of the State, the Bench expressed a desire to the Gentlemen of the Bar, that of any of them held the negative of the question, they would speak; and that the Bench would be glad to hear them upon it. None offering, the Chief Justice, after a proper pause, expressed a wish and offer of whatever time should be required by any gentleman to prepare himself, but this was also declined."). Interestingly, Edmund Randolph appeared in all three cases, in *Caton* as attorney general of Virginia, and in *Chisholm* as private counsel for Chisholm.

45. On the concept of natural law as described in this paragraph, see Michael Lobban, *The Common Law and English Jurisprudence* 1760–1850 (1991); A. W. B. Simpson, "The Common Law and Legal Theory," in Simpson, ed., *Oxford Essays in Jurisprudence* (2d ser., 1973), pp. 77–99; Wythe Holt, "Positivism Overcome: Natural Law in the 1790s" (unpublished paper, 1994, in my possession).

Natural lawyers of the 1790s had been reared in an openly classed society, and most viewed "the community" which accorded authority to legal opinion from a class standpoint. Positivists today usually deny class but hedge against lower-class participation in government through their authoritarianism.

46. Marcus & Teir, "*Hayburn's Case*," 540–41; Susan Low Bloch & Maeva Marcus, "John Marshall's Selective Use of History in *Marbury v. Madison*," 1986 *Wisc. L. Rev.*, 306–10, 316 & n.56; W. J. Ritz, "United States v. Yale Todd (U.S. 1794)," *Washington & Lee Law Review*, 15:220–31 (1958).

47. The case is thoroughly treated in *Documentary History* 5:127–273. See also Holt, "'To Establish Justice,'" pp. 1464 nn.161–62, 1466 n.170, 1486 n.228, & 1495–96 n.258. The opinions are in 2 U.S. (2 Dallas) 427–79 (1793).

48. 2 U.S. (2 Dallas) 453–66 (opinion of Wilson), 469–79 (opinion of Jay).

49. 2 U.S. (2 Dallas) 450–53 (1793)(Blair's opinion); [Philadelphia] *Dunlap's Daily American Advertiser*, February 18, 1793, *Documentary History* 5:219 (reporting what each judge had said: "On the whole he [Blair] was clearly and decidedly in favour of the" jurisdiction); Shearjashub Bourne to Robert Treat Paine, February 19, 1793 ibid., 5:220 ("the Chief Justice, J.s Cushing, Wilson & Blair clearly and decidedly in favour of it").

50. *Documentary History* 5:597–638; Casto, *Supreme Court,* 197–212.

51. The neutrality crisis is covered ably in Casto, *Supreme Court,* 72–80; the quote near the end of the next paragraph is from p. 77. My understanding of the Court's rejection of the president's request has been greatly informed by Jay, "Most Humble Servants," especially pp. 170–93.

52. John Jay, James Wilson, John Blair, James Iredell & William Paterson to George Washington, August 8, 1793, in Henry Johnston, ed., *Correspondence and Public Papers of John Jay* (4 vols., 1891), 3:488; Stewart Jay, "Servants of Kings and Lords: The Advisory Role of Early English Judges," *Am. J. Leg. Hist.*, 38:117–96 (1994). For John Jay's quasi-cabinet status and his advisory opinions,

see Jay, "Most Humble Servants," pp. 69–92, 114; Casto, *Supreme Court,* 72–75. Casto also details advisory opinions by many of the other justices.

53. For the preference of Jay and Hamilton for executive power, especially in foreign affairs, see Jay, "Most Humble Servants," pp. 60–61, 72, 175–76; for the preferences of Jefferson and the collision of personality and principle between Jefferson and Hamilton, see ibid., 58–64, 66, 173, 176–77; for the institution of suits over the French prizes, see ibid., 133–38; and for grand jury charges of Jay to the Virginia Circuit on May 22, and of Wilson to the Pennsylvania Circuit on June 22, both of which spoke to many of the questions Jefferson would put to the judges in late July, see ibid., 131, 147–49.

54. See generally Dorothy E. Fennell, "From Rebelliousness to Insurrection: A Social History of the Whiskey Rebellion, 1765–1802" (Ph.D. dissertation, University of Pittsburgh, 1981); Thomas P. Slaughter, *The Whiskey Rebellion: Frontier Epilogue to the American Revolution* (1986); Richard A. Ifft, "Treason in the Early Republic: The Federal Courts, Popular Protest, and Federalism During the Whiskey Rebellion," in Steven R. Boyd, ed., *The Whiskey Rebellion: Past and Present Perspectives* (1985), pp. 165–82; Appendices A & B, ibid., pp. 191–201 (list of persons charged by federal courts in Whiskey Rebellion, nature of charges, and disposition of charges).

55. John Blair, Grand Jury Charge, October 27, 1794 (C.C.D.Del.), *Documentary History* 2:485–90; John Blair, Grand Jury Charge, April 27, 1795 (C.C.D.Ga.), ibid., 3:31–37 (quotes are from pp. 32, 34).

56. *United States v. Hamilton,* 3 U.S. (3 Dallas) 17–18 (1795); *Documentary History* 1:233–35, 238; Fennell, "Insurrection," pp. 58–59, 93, 143, 149–51, 161, 278–90; Boyd, *Whiskey Rebellion*, Appendices A & B.

57. Thomas Jefferson to Philip Mazzei, April 5, 1790, *Jefferson Papers* 16:307 (diary entry of December 3, 1789: "Called on Mr. Blair in Wmsburg. He was very sick."); *Documentary History* 1:183 n.56 (Blair too ill to attend February 1791 term of Court); John Blair to William Cushing, June 12, 1795, ibid., 1:756–57 (source of first quote); John Blair to James Iredell, October 10, 1795, ibid., 1:820 (source of second quote); ibid., 1:244 n.191 (Blair too ill to attend August 1795 term of Court); John Blair to George Washington, October 25, 1795, ibid., 1:59.

58. John Blair to [Mary Blair Braxton Burwell Prescott], January 15, 1796, January 27, 1796, August 15, 1796, all in Blair, Banister, Braxton, Horner & Whiting Papers, ViWC (mentions cold and colic, but no rattling in the head); Thomas Jefferson to Philip Mazzei, January 7, 1792, *Jefferson Papers* 23:29; "An Address by Henry T. Wickham, Esq., of Virginia" (pamphlet, 1913), p. 29, Faculty/Alumni Collection, Earl Gregg Swem Library, ViW; *The* [Richmond] *Virginia Argus*, February 29, 1804; Gentry & Tarter, "Blair Family," p. 108; Henry Tazewell to James Madison, October 3, 1796, *Madison Papers* 16:407; Grand Jury Presentment, May 22, 1797 (C.C.D.Va.), *Documentary History* 3:180;

Henry Tazewell to [John Page?], June 3, 1797, ibid., 3:189; Peregrine Fitzhugh to Thomas Jefferson, June 20, 1797, ibid., 3:201; John Blair to [Mary Blair Braxton Burwell Prescott], July 5, 1799, in Blair, Banister, Braxton, Horner & Whiting Papers; *DAB*, *s.v.* John Blair (1732–1800), 1:338.

59. [Swem,] Book Review; William Plumer to Jeremiah Smith, February 19, 1796, *Documentary History* 1:838; James Sullivan to William Bingham, October 20, 1793, ibid., 3:428.

60. See Edmund Pendleton to Nathaniel Pendleton, February 3, 1794, *Documentary History* 5:250 (compare "the Ch.f Justice & Judge Wilson plainly found theirs on a favorite wish to Anihilate the State Governments" with "[t]he other Judges [in *Chisholm*, i.e., Blair] appear to adhere too litterally to General words, which will indeed bear the meaning, but having an Application without, ought not to be extended to so important a case, in which, if meant to be comprehended, a mode of proceeding would surely have been pointed out").

61. Compare John Hamilton to Lord Grenville, April 4, 1793, File 2, F05, PRO (criticizing Justice Johnson's "evasional maneuver" of postponing the North Carolina Circuit because of indisposition) with Hamilton to Grenville, June 20, 1795, File 11, F05, PRO (no criticism of Blair's refusing to hear cases in which he was interested).

62. *The* [Richmond] *Virginia Argus*, February 29, 1804; "Wickham Address," pp. 5–6, 29.

*Chapter 7*

# James Iredell
## *Revolutionist, Constitutionalist, Jurist*

*Willis P. Whichard*

George Washington was ambitious for the federal judiciary of the infant American republic. Its "first arrangement," he told Edmund Randolph, was "essential to the happiness of [the] country, and to the stability of its political system."[1] Consequently, he sought "the first characters of the Union" for his initial judicial appointments.[2]

Within two days of enactment of the Judiciary Act of 1789, President Washington appointed, and the Senate promptly confirmed, six justices for the original United States Supreme Court. As the president had wished, all brought distinguished biographies to the new nation's highest bench. Washington's search was not over, however; five days after confirmation Robert Hanson Harrison, a prominent Maryland judge and Washington's comrade-in-arms in the Revolution, declined the appointment. He had been designated chancellor of Maryland, and he preferred that position. Further, his health was fragile, the circuit travel requirements were unsatisfactory, and Supreme Court service would interfere with his private affairs.[3]

The vacuum thus created was momentary, for the president soon named another "first character," James Iredell of North Carolina. Thirty-eight years old when appointed, Iredell remains one of the youngest persons ever to ascend the high bench.[4]

There is no evidence of a prior relationship between the president and his youthful appointee. While Washington knew Iredell's brother-in-law, Samuel Johnston, then a United States senator from North Carolina, he rested the selection on the new justice's reputation "for abilities, legal knowledge and respectability of character." That North Carolina was "of some importance in the Union" and had "given *No* character to a federal office" was also a factor.[5]

Iredell's origins made him an improbable candidate for this august station, and his presence there reflected the relative egalitarianism of the American experiment. The rigid class structure of his native England likely would have precluded the attainment of similar status by this grandson of an unremarkable clergyman and son of a failed merchant. Family poverty had impelled his voyage to America in 1768 at the age of seventeen. Health problems had forced his father's premature retirement from the mercantile business, and his mother's uncle secured for the youth the post of comptroller of customs in the northeastern North Carolina village of Edenton.[6]

Fortunately, the position left time for other pursuits—among them, the courtship and marriage of Hannah Johnston, sister of Samuel Johnston, Iredell's law teacher and probably Edenton's most respected and influential citizen.[7] Iredell also courted learning during these years, patronizing Johnston's library with its books on many subjects.[8]

While Iredell's studies were eclectic, the law clearly had priority. Roscoe Pound lists Iredell among early American leaders who implanted in the colonies a legal tradition in which the English Inns of Court had trained them.[9] No evidence supports this thesis. Iredell's formal legal education appears to have commenced in Edenton under Samuel Johnston's tutelage. He pursued the study intensely, berating himself when he strayed from contemplating Lyttleton's *Tenures* into losing at billiards.[10]

Once licensed, Iredell entered a much maligned vocation. It was "dangerous to virtue," his wealthy planter uncle told him, and included people properly called "pettifoggers" who were "very pickpockets [whose] company and example carry contagion along with them."[11] The craft had internal critics as well. Archibald Maclaine, Iredell's professional contemporary, blamed a perverse public for encouraging the "profligate character[s] at the bar" while "uniformly [opposing] every man of abilities and virtue."[12]

Iredell's law practice involved other hardships, more severe than adverse public opinion. It required extensive travel, and travel conditions were harsh, weather often inclement, and accommodations poor.[13] The nomadic, often solitary existence produced desolation, and Iredell occasionally acknowledged outright homesickness.[14] Considerable overhead was a further by-product, and indifferent courts often produced inadequate revenues.[15]

Still, Iredell clearly enjoyed his work. He reported himself always "greatly refreshed" after doing business.[16] His economic complaints notwithstanding, he was successful, ultimately acquiring more business than he could well handle[17] and the reputation of a superior lawyer—second, if to anyone in his region, only to his mentor, Samuel Johnston.[18]

The confiscation of Tory estates in North Carolina following the Revolution spawned the most significant case in which Iredell participated as counsel, one that marked a confluence of his private and public personas. Iredell was an avid supporter of the American cause in the Revolution; and as attorney general under the new state government, he prosecuted treason and disloyalty cases (discussed below). The excesses of the Revolution's aftermath appalled him, however, particularly the confiscation acts and practices. He decried both the injury to individuals and the violations of the peace treaty with Britain. The laws, he said, sacrificed "every principle of decency and justice," and "no consideration under heaven" would induce him to participate in their execution.[19] Accordingly, he often represented Tory clients who were attempting to retain or regain their property;[20] as a consequence, he was, he said, "looked upon by the patrons of violence with a hateful eye."[21]

A 1785 North Carolina statute sought to protect purchasers of expropriated estates and their heirs and assigns "from expensive and vexatious lawsuits" brought by "the obnoxious and disqualified persons" specified in the confiscation acts and those claiming through them. Titleholders under lawfully conducted confiscation sales were deemed "not liable to answer" such suits; courts were to dismiss the actions upon the defendants' presentation of motions or affidavits accompanied by deeds from confiscation commissioners showing prima facie title in the defendants. Seeking unmistakable clarity, the General Assembly provided that the act applied notwithstanding "any law, usage or custom to the contrary."[22]

The 1776 North Carolina constitution established the right to trial by jury in all controversies respecting property. This provision, it emphatically declared, "ought to remain sacred and inviolable [and] . . .

never . . . be violated on any pretense whatever."[23] The palpable contrariety between this directive and the act for quieting confiscated titles virtually assured a clash between the legislative and judicial branches of the fledgling state government. It came when Elizabeth Cornell Bayard sought to recover from Spyers Singleton, the purchaser at a confiscation sale, property her father, a British subject and Loyalist, had deeded to her.[24]

Iredell's precise role in this momentous case is unclear. There is evidence that Iredell and other leading attorneys received retainers from Singleton, ostensibly to represent him but in reality apparently to silence them.[25] However, the official report of the case lists Iredell, with Samuel Johnston and William R. Davie, as counsel for Bayard.[26] It is clear that Iredell was an early and cogent advocate of judicial review of legislative acts, the formidable issue at stake; the theory that his appearance may have been as a "friend of the court," taking Bayard's side of this question,[27] is thus plausible.

Four years before *Bayard*, Iredell defined a republic as a form of government in which "the law is superior to any or all the individuals, and the constitution superior even to the legislature, *and of which the judges are the guardians and protectors*."[28] While *Bayard* was pending, he forcefully amplified this analysis in a pseudonymous letter addressed "TO THE PUBLIC" from "AN ELECTOR." The problem, Iredell posited, was how to impose restrictions on the legislature to guard against the abuse of unlimited power. The constitution undoubtedly limited and defined legislative power. It was the fundamental law that the legislature could not repeal and from which it derived all its power. Any act inconsistent with the constitution thus was void and could not be obeyed without disobeying the superior law. The judicial power, Iredell concluded, had authority to determine whether a legislative act was warranted by the constitution; this resulted inevitably from the constitution and the judicial office, the judges being servants of the whole people, not just of the Assembly.[29]

The court, composed of the state's three superior court judges, essentially adopted Iredell's position. In one of the early American cases on the power of judicial review, it held that the confiscation act, being inconsistent with the constitution, had no effect.[30] Iredell had said such a law was "void, and cannot be obeyed."[31]

In *Bayard*'s wake, Richard Dobbs Spaight, a delegate to the Philadelphia Constitutional Convention and a champion of legislative supremacy, continued to challenge the review concept. Iredell responded, persisting in defending it as not only proper but inevitable.[32] Scholars have considered Iredell's analysis superior even to Alexander Hamilton's in the *Federalist Papers*, viewing it as the clearest, most straightforward, and integral exposition of the subject in the literature.[33]

A comparison of John Marshall's language in *Marbury v. Madison*[34] with Iredell's discourses strongly suggests that Marshall was familiar with, and drew upon, Iredell's musings on the subject. On constitutions as borders of legislative power, Marshall said in *Marbury*: "The powers of the legislature are defined and limited; and that those limits may not be mistaken, or forgotten, the constitution is written."[35] Iredell had written similarly, though more cryptically: "[T]he power of the Assembly is limited and defined by the Constitution."[36] On constitutions as fundamental law, voiding all repugnant edicts, Marshall declared in *Marbury*: "[W]ritten constitutions . . . [form] the fundamental and paramount law . . . , and, consequently, . . . an act . . . repugnant to the constitution is void."[37] Earlier, Iredell had affirmed: "[T]he Constitution is . . . the *fundamental* law, and unalterable by the legislature. . . . For that reason, an act of Assembly, inconsistent with the constitution, is *void*."[38] On courts as the final arbiters of constitutionality, Marshall scribed in *Marbury*: "It is emphatically the province and duty of the judicial department to say what the law is. . . . [T]he court must determine which of these conflicting rules [constitution or statute] governs the case. This is of the very essence of judicial duty."[39] Iredell had antedated him, saying: "The judges . . . must take care . . . that every act of Assembly they presume to enforce is warranted by the constitution. . . . This is not a usurped or a discretionary power, but one inevitably resulting from the constitution of their office."[40]

Iredell's pre–Supreme Court public service sorts readily into three categories: he served his state and community in a variety of capacities, he was the leading essayist in his region for the American cause in the Revolution, and he was the bellwether for the Federalist forces in the North Carolina effort to ratify the federal Constitution.

## *State Service*

Following adoption of the North Carolina constitution of 1776, Iredell served on a commission to consider statutes formerly in force and to recommend to the next General Assembly for adoption those "consistent with the genius of a free people." The assembly adopted most of the commission's proposals.[41] Iredell also drafted North Carolina's first court bill and served as one of the state's first three judges. He resigned to resume his law practice, however, after completing only one circuit.[42]

His absence from public service was brief, for the following year, 1779, Iredell became the state's second attorney general. In that capacity, he traveled twice annually the same circuit he had as a jurist. The office functioned as a single, statewide district attorney now would, prosecuting criminal offenders in the superior courts. As noted, punishing significant political dissent was then deemed important to the internal security of the newly independent state, and much of Iredell's work involved prosecuting treason and disloyalty cases.[43]

Iredell repeatedly declined importunings toward legislative service, pleading irreconcilable conflicts with his law practice. He actively followed events in the state assembly, however, and counseled legislators who shared his governmental goals, particularly for the judicial system. He was directly involved in many legislative matters in the 1780s, and legislative enactments of the period reflect his surreptitious activities.[44]

In 1787 the North Carolina General Assembly appointed Iredell the sole commissioner to revise and compile the legislative acts of the late province and the state. The compilation, still known as "Iredell's Revisal," was completed in 1791, after Iredell had assumed his Supreme Court duties.[45] The assembly also elected him to the Council of State, an advisory body to the governor, in 1788 and 1789; he was its president in 1788.[46]

While Iredell was interested and enmeshed in public affairs generally, education was a particular concern for him. He served as an original trustee of the University of North Carolina, the nation's first operative public university. The university charter provided that a trustee's removal from the state created a vacancy; Iredell thus resigned when he moved to New York upon his appointment to the United States Supreme Court. He maintained an interest in the institution, however, and continued to promote it outside the state.[47] His pedagogic commitment was not restricted to higher education; he served as a trustee of lower-school academies in the North Carolina towns of Edenton and Hillsborough as well, actively recruiting faculty for the Hillsborough facility.[48]

The foregoing inventory would fully satisfy the average yen for public achievement. It represents the less significant aspects of Iredell's pre-Court career, however. He is remembered primarily not for these contributions but for his efforts in behalf of the American cause in the Revolution and the adoption of the federal Constitution.

## *Revolutionist*

Early in Iredell's American stay, his uncle cautioned him that, being a king's officer, he should not "meddle with politics." Iredell rejected the counsel, becoming "the letter writer of the war . . . [with] no equal amongst his contemporaries."[49]

The friction between Britain and the colonies was already extensive when Iredell assumed the comptroller's post at Edenton, and well before adoption of the Declaration of Independence, his friends were predicting a break with England if the extant trend continued.[50] Iredell nevertheless came to the Revolutionary cause reluctantly. As late as June 1776, in his essay on the causes of the Revolution, he wrote that in spite of great provocations, a continuing connection to Great Britain remained preferable to independence. He concluded, however, that he would assent to independence if necessary to America's safety.[51]

For some time previous, Iredell had written letters that furthered the American cause. The first responded to the royal governor's rejection of court laws allowing the provincial courts to attach property of defaulting debtors residing in England. Acting under royal directives, the governor then unilaterally established courts like the harsh prerogative tribunals of earlier English history. Writing pseudonymously as "A Planter," Iredell began to etch his political essays across the pages of history, attacking the clandestine rules of the new courts as "inconsistent with the very idea of civil liberty."[52]

A second major polemic assailed the concept of parliamentary sovereignty over America. If Parliament had absolute dominion, Iredell posited, the colonists had no liberty. Such a state was "the very definition of slavery," and the crown would be "fatally deceived" if it thought the colonies would "patiently bear" these hardships. Americans were not, he concluded, "conquered subjects."[53]

Iredell's next literary offering, "The Principles of an American Whig," bears unmistakable traces of consanguinity with the American Declaration of Independence. It declaims that "mankind were intended to be happy"; that government is the means of securing freedom and happiness; and that when a government deviates from this end, it is no longer entitled to allegiance. Like the Declaration, though in less detail, "Principles" recites perceived British abuses against the colonies, including the Stamp Act and other duties and taxation.[54]

Though apparently precursive of Jefferson's more illustrious Declaration, "Principles" did not decree Iredell's irrevocable commitment to the American cause. More or less contemporaneously with its composition, and for reasons admittedly pecuniary, he seriously contemplated a return to England. Patriotic considerations ultimately impelled his decision to stay. He was, he said, "impatient to be attached to [his] friends in the noblest of all causes, a struggle for freedom." While maintaining hope for reconciliation, his primary attachment was to America, and he would so opt if forced to choose.[55]

In his next—apparently widely circulated[56]—essay, Iredell chronicled the events since the Stamp Act that had brought the empire to the verge of decomposition. The only American crime, he wrote, was "*an ardent love of liberty,*" while entirely different principles motivated the enemy. Only slaves, he said, would have submitted to the British indignities. The revenue measures exposed the colonies to ruin and had to be rejected as inconsistent with liberty.

Iredell then drew upon his juridical expertise as he selected from the Coercive Acts for special criticism the bill for the "Impartial Administration of Justice." He found its provisions for trials in England at the court of king's bench particularly inconsistent with liberty. Trials by juries in the colonies were crucial, he posited, to secure both witnesses and fact finders who knew their character.[57]

As the new nation focused on the war to establish its freedom, Iredell became a clearinghouse for correspondents on the progress of the struggle.[58] He continued to expound justifications for the cleavage, however, postulating that it emanated from the king's adoption of measures free men could not support. Submitting to such, he said, would have made Americans "the most despicable slaves on earth."[59]

Iredell was among the first to take an oath of allegiance to the new state of North Carolina. As a judge of the state's courts, he charged grand juries with avowals of his patriotism, containing strong expressions of devotion to America. His instruction, the Edenton grand jury resolved, was "drawn from unalienable rights, and from real necessity, and grounded on incontestable facts."

Iredell presided over numerous trials of Tories, which produced frequent declamations suffused with suasions toward patriotism. He criticized the Carlisle Commission, through which England sought a reconciliation with its former subjects, signing his letter "A Man Who Despises Your Pardons."[60]

Peace—to Iredell "a most glorious affair"—did not end his public service to the American Revolution and its aftermath. He submitted resolutions to the citizens of Edenton calling for fulfillment of the terms of the peace, support of public credit, and redemption of public debts. And he drafted instructions from the citizens of Edenton to their state legislators designed to promote national unity, particularly endorsing Washington's appeal on the eve of victory not to lose the peace.[61]

Personal consequences, too, endured. Iredell's wealthy, childless uncle, who had advised him against meddling with politics, rejected his attempts to explicate his pro-American conduct and disinherited him for adhering to his convictions in the caldron of imperial disintegration.[62]

## *Constitutionalist*

Having won both peace and independence, the former English subjects confronted the necessity of establishing a government for the new nation. Their initial effort, the Articles of Confederation, proved an inadequate instrument for effective governance.[63] Delegates from the states thus assembled in Philadelphia in 1787, ostensibly to revise the Articles but, in fact, ultimately, to form a new constitution.

Iredell was not a member of the North Carolina contingent to the federal Constitutional Convention. He had declined an appointment to Congress in 1779 because of his "cursed poverty," and he apparently remained too poor to undertake a venture of this nature.[64] He nevertheless exerted influence in Philadelphia through correspondence with North Carolina's delegates. One wrote that he would "trouble [Iredell] frequently . . . and expect [his] opinion without reserve."[65] Others also corresponded with him, and their dispatches unfold the progress of the convention.[66]

Even before the convention's recommendations were known, the plan for a national government became an issue in North Carolina politics. Because the next Assembly would confront the measures the convention submitted, the 1787 legislative elections aroused considerable interest. Iredell became a participant inadvertently when friends nominated him without his knowledge or assent. He had written earlier that he had become so unpopular with the people, probably because of his support for refugees who had left the country during the Revolution, that he did not think he would be chosen. His assessment proved accurate, for he lost the election to another Federalist candidate.[67]

Although neither a delegate to the convention that proposed the Constitution nor to the state assembly that called a convention to ratify it, Iredell rendered perhaps the most outstanding of his many patriotic services in the ratification effort. He appears to have inaugurated the first public movement in North Carolina in favor of the Constitution. He drafted the preamble and resolutions for citizens who convened at Edenton to instruct their legislators to call a ratification convention and to urge approval of the document. He penned an address delivered by the foreman of the Edenton Grand Jury extolling the Constitution and urging the appointment of a convention for its early consideration.[68]

Indeed, Iredell's pen was seldom idle in these days of birthing the new government. The Antifederalists focused their ire on the absence from the proffered document of a bill of rights. Even Thomas Jefferson joined this lament. It was not Jefferson, however, but his fellow Virginian George Mason who next impelled Iredell to his inkstand. Mason had refused to sign the proposed instrument and had published eleven objections to it in a widely circulated document. Antifederalists rallied around his first sentence—"There is no Declaration of Rights"—as they decried the pace at which the Federalists were "hustling" ratification.[69]

Iredell assumed the task of answering Mason, responding to each of his demurrers and concluding with a resonant plea for the proposed government. His "Answers" preceded the majority of the *Federalist Papers*, and it thus attracted considerable attention. The author became favorably known in all Federalist sections.[70]

As Iredell penned his "Answers" to Mason, North Carolina was moving toward a ratification convention. Iredell was elected a delegate from Edenton. In thanking his supporters, he affirmed his deeply held conviction that "the security of everything dear to us depends on our adoption of the proposed constitution."[71] His sentiments were not universally shared, however; battle lines were being drawn, as Thomas Person, a leading Antifederalist delegate, denounced George Washington as "a damned rascal, and traitor to his country, for putting his hand to such an infamous paper as the new Constitution."[72]

Iredell continued his literary efforts as the convention approached, joining with William R. Davie in preparing a "collection on the subject of the Federal Government." He communicated with other Federalist leaders regarding the ratification effort in other states. He joined them in sharing information on the debates in other states as well as philosophical writings on the subject.[73]

On July 21, 1788, the debate focalized at the ratification convention in Hillsborough, North Carolina. Iredell served on a select committee to prepare and propose rules and regulations for governing the convention; many of the committee's recommendations, all but one of which were approved, were his work. He also served on the committee on privileges and elections, which recommended voiding the election of delegates from one county.[74]

Iredell's principal contribution, though, was as floor leader for the Federalist forces. Fully conversant with arguments presented throughout the country for and against the Constitution, he was prepared to answer any objections that might be offered. To him, "this [was] a very awful moment." "On a right decision of this question," he said, "may possibly depend the peace and happiness of our country for ages."[75] Thus motivated, he vigorously defended the proposed document, clause by clause, over a period of thirteen days of Antifederalist assaults. The effort failed; Iredell's eloquent words, as one Antifederalist delegate stated, went "in at one ear, and out at the other."[76]

From a personal standpoint, Iredell gained friends and benefited greatly from his role in the convention. A new North Carolina county was soon named for him,[77] and warm encomiums reflected the national recognition he had acquired from his dialectical prowess at Hillsborough.[78]

Iredell barely paused to savor this acclaim. The Antifederalists, while making an important point and deserving some credit for the ultimate adoption of the Bill of Rights, had placed North Carolina in a maligned, precarious, and impotent position. It was now a foreign or independent state, precluded from participation in the first presidential election, the devising of the constitutional amendments the convention had demanded, and the making of the nation's formative laws.[79] If this status continued, the state would, one Federalist leader feared, "become a by-word among the nations."[80]

These and other concerns prompted Iredell to continue the ratification effort. He again applied his considerable talents as a political essayist to the cause of the new government, noting the dangers inherent in his state's status as independent not only of other nations but of other states as well. The path chosen would, he said, "lead[] to misery and ruin, if we continue to pursue it." One convention, though, could repair the mischief of another. "[T]his fatal disunion," he concluded, should "last a very short time longer."[81]

This essay was not Iredell's only contribution to the literature of the post-Hillsborough ratification effort. He and William R. Davie had hired a reporter to record the convention debates, and they published them at their own expense. The publication was widely circulated and aided in the Federalist election victories of 1789.[82]

Iredell declined to be a candidate for the next General Assembly, the federal convention called to consider amendments, or the second ratification convention.[83] He continued to devote time, energy, and money to the ratification endeavor, however, joining other Federalists in circulating petitions requesting a second convention to consider the Constitution. Two months before North Carolina finally ratified, he was still sending materials favoring ratification for use in "the backcountry . . . in a manner in which . . . they will have the desired effect."[84]

In November 1789 a second North Carolina convention ratified the Constitution by a larger margin than that by which the first had defeated it.[85] Several factors influenced the reversal, not least among them the educational efforts of leaders such as Iredell and Davie.[86] In the immediate afterglow of the Federalist triumph, Iredell was widely recognized as at least among its principal architects;[87] later scholars would consider him "outstanding in debate,"[88] "the acknowledged leader for ratification,"[89] and the "ablest defender of the Constitution."[90]

## *Jurist*

The profound grasp of constitutional questions Iredell displayed in promoting ratification was the most significant reason for his Supreme Court appointment. The selection surprised both the recipient and his friends. Pierce Butler of South Carolina had hoped Iredell would join him in the United States Senate. Hugh Williamson had thought his friend might accept a federal judgeship in another state if North Carolina failed to ratify. Upon ratification, Archibald Maclaine had posed the possibility of Iredell's being the federal district judge for North Carolina. Iredell himself had thought he would fill that position, though he disavowed any exertions toward that end.[91]

Iredell's expeditious, unanimous confirmation[92] commenced a near-decade of intimate relationships with—and stalwart support for—George Washington, John Adams, and their administrations. Judicial service did not end his career as an essayist. When an excise tax on whiskey produced perhaps the new government's foremost domestic opposition and difficulties, Iredell reverted to his old form in defending the tax.[93] When the administration suppressed an insurrection against the tax, Iredell's friends viewed it as his personal triumph.[94] His ratification-era utterances contained the philosophical roots of this animated support for administration policies and the measures used to enforce them. A union was necessary to the safety and prosperity of the states, Iredell reflected; and the Union could not be preserved without reposing great confidence in those entrusted with its government.[95]

Iredell's intimacy with the presidents and their administrations was characteristic of jurists in the late eighteenth century. Federal judges, including Supreme Court justices on circuit, were seen as representatives or extensions of the Federalist administrations. It was largely through their contact with the judges sitting on the circuit courts that the American people became acquainted with the new institution of the federal judiciary, and it was mainly through the charges these judges made to grand juries that the principles of the new Constitution and the government it established became known to the public. While the partisan nature of the charges is discordant with modern concepts of judicial propriety, it was patriotic in motivation and consonant with the perceived needs of the time.[96]

Iredell was a consummate activist in this regard. As a jurist he was, as he had been in the ratification period, a bellman for the Union. Popular sentiment was not prerequisite to his praise from the bench for the government's measures. He rushed to defend even the Alien and Sedition Acts, despite mounting resentment to them in his home state and elsewhere.[97] His charges featured general prods toward patriotic appreciation for the extant government.[98] "Notwithstanding all the efforts made to vilify and undermine the government," he once instructed, "it has uniformly [risen] in the esteem and confidence of the people."[99]

Iredell's passionate commitment to the Union did not preclude a dual-sovereignty motif, however. The Union, he instructed, contained two sovereignties, and the federal Constitution did not interfere with the internal regulations of a state in matters solely of state concern. "Each of these governments," he urged, "deserves our equal confidence and respect."[100]

This dual- or residual-sovereignty theme was a font of Iredell's most significant Supreme Court opinion, his dissent in *Chisholm v. Georgia.*[101] The issue was whether the Supreme Court had jurisdiction to hear and determine a suit by a citizen of one state against another state. The question was important not only because of lingering concerns as to whether the states had relinquished all their sovereignties[102] but because the states feared that if the citizen-plaintiff prevailed, they could be subject to a deluge of actions in the Supreme Court by refugee Loyalists for debts forfeited by acts of attainder and similar legislation. The potential liability on the part of the states was considerable.[103]

Some leaders—notably George Mason and Richard Henry Lee, both of Virginia—had conveyed alarm over this prospect in the preratification period. Others of great stature, however—including Alexander Hamilton, James Madison, and John Marshall—had effectively countered these charges and concerns. The majority opinions holding Georgia subject to the suit thus shocked the country.[104]

These opinions took the view that sovereignty in America pertained not to princes but to the people collectively. Sovereignty was not incompatible with compulsory suability because princes had been liable to such suits. Since the individual sovereign or citizen might be sued by another individual, logically an aggregation of individual sovereigns organized into a state might also be. The states were clearly subjected to the Supreme Court's jurisdiction at the suit of other states; therefore, such suability involved no violation of sovereignty.

The only reason perhaps preventing a sovereign prince and the United States from being sued in their own courts—the fact that the executive power necessary to enforce the Court's judgment was held by the prince or the government—was inapplicable when a state was sued in the courts of the United States. Even if states had once had sovereign immunity, the Constitution—by its declared objectives of justice, interstate harmony, and protection for individual human rights—had divested them of it. Its express language and its failure to exclude suits by individuals against states attested the same results, as did the practical necessities involved in enforcing both the powers the Constitution gave the federal government and the restrictions it imposed on the states.[105]

Iredell alone dissented from these views. He summarized his reasoning as follows:

> -*1st.* That the Constitution, so far as it respects the judicial authority, can only be carried into effect by acts of the legislature appointing Courts and prescribing their methods of proceeding. *2nd.* That *Congress* has provided no new law in regard to this case, but expressly referred us to the old. *3d.* That there are no principles of the old law, to which we must have recourse, that in any manner authorize the present suit, either by precedent or by analogy.

The consequence, he concluded, "clearly is that the suit . . . cannot be maintained."[106]

Iredell's position was consistent with his answers to Mason's objections to the Constitution,[107] his ratification convention arguments,[108] and his prior charges to Grand Juries.[109] It also accorded with the perspective of other Federalist thinkers of the period—notably Hamilton, Madison, and Marshall.[110] Most important, it reflected contemporary public opinion. As John Marshall wrote years later: "The alarm [over the majority opinion] was general."[111] This ensured the swift introduction and passage of the Eleventh Amendment, which constitutionalized the result Iredell would have reached and protected the states from such suits in the future.[112]

Scholars and jurists have continued to debate who was "right" in *Chisholm*—the justices in the majority or Iredell—as well as the correct rationale underlying Iredell's position.[113] The questions are of academic interest only, however. The significant practical reality is that the Eleventh Amendment incorporated the outcome Iredell alone would have imposed, as well as his concept of divided or residual sovereignty,[114]into the Constitution, where they remain almost two centuries later.

It appears that the early Supreme Court justices did not always reduce their opinions or the totality of their opinions to writing.[115] Iredell's written and reported opinions other than *Chisholm*, to the extent that they merit summary treatment, do so at least as much for his commentary in dicta as for the significance of their holdings.

In *Penhallow v. Doane's Administrators*,[116] the Court resolved an important issue of state versus national sovereignty adversely to the contentions of the states, upholding the jurisdiction of the federal courts to decide prize cases. Iredell's opinion reflected a strongly nationalistic interpretation, as he reverted on occasion to his form as a Revolutionary-period essayist, stating:

> When acts were passed by the Parliament of Great Britain which were thought unconstitutional and unjust, and when every hope of redress by separate applications appeared desperate, then was conceived the noble idea, which laid the foundation of the present independence and happiness of this country, (though independence was not then in contemplation) of forming a common council to consult for the common welfare of the whole, so far as an opposition to the measures of Great Britain was concerned.[117]

Congress, Iredell concluded, was the appropriate body to exercise the external national sovereignty. "I think *all prize causes* whatsoever ought to belong to the national sovereignty," he wrote: "They are to be determined by the law of nations. A prize court is, in effect, a court of all the nations in the world, because all persons, in every part of the world, are concluded by its sentences in cases clearly coming within its jurisdiction."[118]

*Penhallow* marked "[a] notable beginning . . . in the assertion by judicial construction of national sovereignty in the federal government."[119] His dissent in *Chisholm* notwithstanding, it is not surprising that Iredell, who had championed independence and union, joined in spawning this "notable beginning."

In *Talbot v. Jansen*,[120] Iredell discoursed on the right of national expatriation. Legislative bodies could impose restraints on the right in the public safety or interest, he declared, but should so limit individual freedom only for the most compelling of reasons.[121] "[A] Legislature," he said, "must be weak to the extreme verge of folly to wish to retain any man as a citizen whose heart and affections are fixed on a foreign country in preference to his own."[122]

In *Hylton v. United States*,[123] Iredell joined his colleagues in holding that a tax on the use of carriages was not a direct tax required by the Constitution to be apportioned. In his view, the Constitution contemplated no taxes as direct save those that could be apportioned; this one clearly could not be, so the decision was self-evident.[124] The case is important because it was the first in which the Supreme Court passed upon the constitutionality of an act of Congress and because of its significance in the history of the federal government's capacity to raise revenue effectively.[125] Further, explicit declaration here of an act's constitutionality implicitly proclaimed the Court's equal empowerment to pronounce acts unconstitutional. "[T]he signpost was up."[126]

*Ware v. Hylton*[127] has similar import as the first case in which the Court declared a state law unconstitutional (as superseded by the federal Treaty of 1783).[128] Iredell, having sat on the case on circuit, recused. He nevertheless filed an extended discussion on the treaty power,[129] again on occasion reverting to his style as a Revolutionary-period essayist, saying of the treaty: "It insured, so far as peace could insure them, the freest forms of government, and the greatest share of individual liberty, of which perhaps the world has seen any example."[130]

Finally, and most notably, the case of *Calder v. Bull*[131] is less known for its resolution of whether the ex post facto clause applied to civil cases than for the Chase-Iredell debate, in dicta, on whether natural law is a valid reference point for judicial review of legislative acts. Justice Chase, drawing on the Preamble to the Constitution and "certain vital principles in our free Republican governments," posited that it was. It was "against all reason and justice," he said, to treat legislative powers otherwise.[132] Iredell, contrastingly, thought the framers had defined the limits of legislative power with precision. A passion for certitude prompted this view. "The ideas of natural justice are regulated by no fixed standard," Iredell observed, and courts and legislatures thus could have divergent opinions on whether a measure was "inconsistent with the abstract principles of natural justice."[133]

The Chase-Iredell debate has reverberated through two centuries of American constitutional law—"a running battle that never has simmered down completely." Iredell's view is generally considered to have prevailed for nearly a century, but Chase's to have ultimately triumphed under such rubrics as "substantive due process."[134]

Thus, as the Supreme Court in its early years "set a pattern of constitutional adjudication that was to endure,"[135] James Iredell was a vigorous and vocal participant in its deliberations and decisions. In *Penhallow* he avowed an approach to opinion writing that characterized all his work. "I will endeavor to state my own principles on the subject with so much clearness," he wrote, "that whether my opinion be right or wrong, it may at least be understood what the opinion really is."[136] This passion for clarity produced opinions that aided one scholar in concluding that among the early justices, Iredell and Paterson "seem the most impressive." Iredell "receives favorable marks," he writes, "for his attention to history in *Chisholm* and for his opposition to limitless judicial nullification in *Calder*."[137] Another scholar concludes that Iredell and Wilson "possessed the finest legal minds on the high court during this period."[138] To have participated in setting a pattern of constitutional adjudication that was to endure, and to be considered one of the most impressive of the early justices and one of the eighteenth-century Court's finest legal minds, is clearly a worthy legacy.

Supreme Court service meant that Iredell would spend most of his last decade "lead[ing] the life of a postboy," traveling as much as nineteen hundred miles in covering a single federal circuit.[139] Under the Judiciary Act of 1789, the federal circuit courts heard appeals in some instances from the district courts but mainly functioned as the primary federal trial courts for certain categories of cases. Two (later, one) of the six Supreme Court justices, together with the district court judge resident in the state or district where the court sat, composed the circuit court. Each justice thus traveled through one of the three circuits twice annually.[140]

The fact that Congress had established courts without judges created problems, especially the conflict of interest when one or two of the justices sitting in the Supreme Court had sat on the circuit court.[141] Considerations of economy, quality control, politics, and uniformity of federal law supported the arrangement, however. In particular, the high judges were to act as "republican schoolmasters," carrying the law to citizens in their own states and fashioning support for the new national government in the process.[142]

The judges chafed under the plan, however, and were in the vanguard of reform efforts. Iredell, being the most severely affected because assigned to the harshest circuit, the Southern, led the endeavor. He described his duties as "very severe & expensive," and Chief Justice Jay acknowledged that Iredell's "share of the task [was] more than in due proportion."[143]

Iredell first proposed internally that the circuits be rotated among the justices or that any permanent assignment of circuit duty at least be accomplished by lot. He alone voted against permanent assignments, however; and the Court's vote favoring them surprised him. With permanent assignments based on the home states of the justices, the most difficult and arduous of the circuits would be his recurrent fate. He thus continued to protest, lamenting that no judge could "conscientiously undertake to ride the Southern Circuit constantly and perform the other parts of his duty." If his colleagues persisted in construing the Judiciary Act as they had, he threatened, he would be forced to seek congressional action.[144]

When neither internal nor legislated change was forthcoming, a rather desperate Iredell suggested that the judges each agree to surrender $500 per year of their salary if circuit riding were terminated. All ultimately agreed, yet there is no evidence that the proposal was presented to Congress. Iredell obtained a modicum of relief when Congress enacted a bill providing for rotation of the circuit assignments. No justice, without his consent, would have to ride the same circuit twice consecutively unless the public service and the vote of four justices required it.[145]

The justices now united in their desire to eliminate circuit riding altogether. The goal proved elusive, however; and a near-century would pass before Supreme Court justices ceased to be regular riders of the circuits. They were, in Iredell's words, "doomed . . . to be wretched Drudges."[146]

In addition to their standard fare of suits at common law and in chancery, criminal prosecutions, and admiralty causes, for a time the justices had the duty of determining the merits of claims under the Invalid Pensions Act, which provided government financial assistance to veterans injured in the Revolutionary War and to their widows and orphans.[147] All justices save one demurred to these new duties,[148] and Justices Blair and Wilson and District Judge Peters altogether refused to perform them.[149]

Iredell responded to the act by writing what was, in effect, an advisory opinion on the separation of powers.[150] Philosophical objections notwithstanding, however, he ultimately rationalized that he could perform the task as a commissioner on an individual rather than a judicial basis.[151] The work was onerous. "The Invalid business has scarcely allowed me one moment's time," he once wrote, "and now I am engaged in it by candlelight, though to go at three in the morning."[152]

The invalid-claims function enhanced the rigors of the already arduous circuit life. The familial effects were harsh, as the jurists spent months at a stretch on their treks.[153] "Many a sigh directs me towards Carolina," Iredell wrote during one of his many prolonged absences from home.[154]

There were other grievances too. Stages ran irregularly, "broke down," or were missed by the barest of time periods.[155] Horses replaced them and at times became lame.[156] Roads were "execrable," making travel by stage or horse severe.[157] Adverse weather conditions produced inconvenience, peril, and criticism for unavoidable defaults in scheduled court appearances.[158] Accommodations were meager but costly.[159] Sporadic criminal activity affected the roving jurists,[160] and at times personal possessions were simply lost.[161] Accidents were common,[162] disease was a near neighbor,[163] and fatigue was a constant companion.[164] The entire lifestyle was, as Judge Nathaniel Pendleton said of traveling the Southern Circuit, "more than the strength of any man can bear."[165]

Amenities did abound. There were pleasant days and delights to Iredell's travel as he witnessed and chronicled the early development of his country.[166] There was the utmost in civility, cordiality, and generosity as he wended his way through the cities, towns, and countryside of an evolving nation.[167] There were pleasant traveling companions,[168] dinners,[169] teas,[170] dances,[171] and theater.[172] There were testimonials and encomiums in plenitude.[173] Foremost, there was felicitous interaction with contemporary eminences,[174] including the great lawyers of the time.[175]

Still, the justices were not just whining about the hardships. They were real; they were severe; over time, they could be devouring. A prolonged and arduous session at Philadelphia followed by an immensity of business at Richmond took a special toll on Iredell during the spring circuit of 1799. After a brief respite at Edenton, he commenced his return to Philadelphia for the Supreme Court's August term. From Richmond, on July 31, he returned home, physically unable to complete the journey. When the Court convened, the huge oaken chair provided for the sixth of its original justices was again vacant. Its tenant for the first near-decade of the Court's history remained too ill to attend. He would not occupy the seat again.[176]

On October 20, 1799, "[o]ld Time, that greatest and longest-established Spinner of all,"[177] ceased to weave for Iredell. While death came at age forty-eight before he had fully bloomed, he left an epistolary legacy considered "invaluable for an understanding of social and political affairs in the later eighteenth century."[178] His letters while on the Supreme Court "illuminate the contemporary scene."[179] "Without Iredell, the chronicler," editors of *The Documentary History of the Supreme Court of the United States* acknowledge, "these volumes would not be possible."[180]

Further, despite the untimeliness of his demise, his ardent Revolutionary-period essays, his articulate defense of judicial review and the Constitution, and his abiding commitment to the residual sovereignty of the states were firmly chiseled into the fabric of the American experiment. As a consequence, when the cold pen of history records the ablest of the American founders, it spares ink unwisely if James Iredell is not among them.

## NOTES

1. George Washington to Edmund Randolph, September 27, 1789, in Jared Sparks, ed., *The Writings of George Washington* (Boston: Russell, Shattuck, and Williams, 1836), 10:34.
2. George Washington to James Madison, August 10 (?), 1789, in ibid., 26.

3. Richard B. Bernstein and Kym S. Rice, *Are We To Be a Nation? The Making of the Constitution* (Cambridge: Harvard University Press, 1987), 260. See also Douglas S. Freeman, *George Washington: A Biography* (New York: Charles Scribner's Sons, 1954), 6:253, 253 n.95; Charles G. Haines, *The Role of the Supreme Court in American Government and Politics* (Berkeley: University of California Press, 1944), 1:121; Julius J. Marke, *Vignettes of Legal History* (South Hackensack, N.J.: Fred B. Rothman & Co., 1965), 53; Charles Warren, *The Supreme Court in United States History* (Boston: Little, Brown and Co., 1922), 1:42–43. Harrison died on April 2, 1790, just before the Court held its first session; his tenure thus would have been transient in any event. Freeman, *George Washington: A Biography*, 6:253 n.95.

4. Hugh T. Lefler in Virginius Dabney, ed., *The Patriots: The American Revolution Generation of Genius* (New York: Atheneum, 1975), 140.

5. Donald Jackson and Dorothy Twohig, eds., *The Diaries of George Washington* (Charlottesville: University Press of Virginia, 1979), 6:28–29; see also William S. Baker, *Washington After the Revolution MDCCLXXXIV–MDCCXCIX* (Philadelphia: J.B. Lippincott Co., 1898), 171.

6. Don Higginbotham, ed., *The Papers of James Iredell*, 2 vols. (Raleigh: Div. of Archives and History, N.C. Dept. of Cultural Resources, 1976), 1:xxxvii (ed. essay), 12 (Henry E. McCulloh to Francis Iredell, March 3, 1768).

7. Ibid., 1:xlix, li (ed. essay); Iredell to Hannah Johnston, ca. April 1, 1772, ibid., 94 (proposing marriage); Iredell to Samuel Johnston, April 7, 1772, ibid., 96 (requesting permission to marry Hannah).

8. Ibid., 1:xlv–xlvi (ed. essay); Archibald Henderson, *North Carolina: The Old North State and the New* (Chicago: Lewis Publishing Co., 1941), 1:567–68, 624.

9. Roscoe Pound, *The Formative Era of American Law* (Boston: Little, Brown and Co., 1938), 81, 127 n.1.

10. Higginbotham, *Papers of Iredell*, 1:li (ed. essay), 172 (Iredell's diary entry, August 22, 1790).

11. Griffith J. McRee, *Life and Correspondence of James Iredell*, 2 vols. (New York: D. Appleton and Co., 1857 (I), 1858 (II)), 1:92–93 (Thomas Iredell to Iredell, August 19, 1771).

12. Archibald Maclaine to Iredell, August 29, 1787, Iredell Papers, Duke University, Durham, N.C. (Duke).

13. Travel conditions: Christopher C. Crittenden, "Overland Travel and Transportation in North Carolina, 1763–1789," *North Carolina Historical Review* 8 (1931): 239 (passim); Higginbotham, *Papers of Iredell*, 2:3, 147 (Iredell to Hannah Iredell, January 14, 1778; May 13, 1780); McRee, *Life of Iredell*, 2:111 (Iredell to Hannah Iredell, October 15, 1784). Accommodations: Higginbotham, *Papers of Iredell*, 1:452, 2:7, 39, 364 (Iredell to Hannah Iredell, May 2, 1777; March 12, 1778; July 2, 1778; December 2, 1782).

14. Higginbotham, 1:445, 2:90 (Iredell to Hannah Iredell, April 28, 1777; June 14, 1779); Iredell to Nelly Blair (Hannah's niece), October 22, 1785, Charles E. Johnson Collection, N.C. Div. of Archives and History, Raleigh (NCAH).

15. Higginbotham, *Papers of Iredell*, 1:106 (Iredell to Francis Iredell, Sr., July 20, 1772), 2:90, 158, 196 (Iredell to Hannah Iredell, June 14, 1779; May 24, 1780; November 26, 1780); Iredell to Hannah Iredell, October 17, 1786, NCAH.

16. Higginbotham, *Papers of Iredell*, 1:193 (Iredell's diary entry, December 9, 1772).

17. Ibid., 2:194, 415 (Iredell to Hannah Iredell, November 18, 1780; June 2, 1783), 424 (Iredell to Arthur Iredell, July 30, 1783), 470 (Iredell to Thomas Iredell, ca. November 1783); McRee, *Life of Iredell*, 2:101 (Iredell to Thomas Iredell, May 28, 1784).

18. Higginbotham, *Papers of Iredell*, 1:449 (ed. note); see also William H. Hoyt, ed., *The Papers of Archibald D. Murphey* (Raleigh, N.C.: E. M. Uzzell & Co., 1914), 1:205 (letter refers to Iredell as among principal lawyers in North Carolina at that time); John C. Waldrup, "James Iredell and the Practice of Law in Revolutionary Era North Carolina" (Ann Arbor, Mich.: University Microfilms, 1985), 150, 383 of unpublished Ph. D. dissertation, University of North Carolina at Chapel Hill.

19. McRee, *Life of Iredell*, 2:51 (Iredell to Hannah Iredell, May 21, 1783), 133 (Iredell to William Hooper, January 29, 1786), 134 (Iredell to James Hogg, January 29, 1786).

20. Higginbotham, *Papers of Iredell*, 1:lxxxv–lxxxvi (ed. essay); see ibid., 2:74–79 (Iredell's petition on behalf of Henry Eustace McCulloh); ibid., 372–74, 380–82, 383–85 (McCulloh to Iredell, February 5, 1783; March 17, 1783; March 28, 1783); McCulloh to Iredell, February 20, 1784, and August 1 (?), 1790, Duke; Higginbotham, *Papers of Iredell*, 2:395–96, 467–69 (Iredell to McCulloh: ca. May 1, 1783; November 28, 1783); McRee, *Life of Iredell*, 2:103–4, 116–17 (Iredell to McCulloh, June 15, 1784; January 6, 1785); ibid., 252 (Nathaniel Dukinfield to Iredell, February 4, 1789); Higginbotham, *Papers of Iredell*, 2:203–4, 204 (ed. note) (petition of Margaret Pearson).

21. McRee, *Life of Iredell*, 2:93 (Iredell to Pierce Butler, March 14, 1784).

22. Walter Clark, *The State Records of North Carolina*, 26 vols. (Goldsboro, N.C.: Nash Bros., 1905), 24:730–31 (1785 N.C. Session Laws); James Iredell, *Laws of the State of North Carolina* (Edenton, N.C.: Hodge & Wills, 1791), 553–54 (same).

23. Clark, *State Records*, 23:977, 984 (1776 N.C. Const. §§ XIV ["The Declaration of Rights"], XLIV).

24. *Bayard v. Singleton*, 1 N.C. 5 (1787).

25. McRee, *Life of Iredell*, 2:119–20 (Archibald Maclaine to Iredell, March 7, 1785) (reference to Singleton's having "silenced" Iredell and others); ibid., 489

(Iredell memorandum that he had "received a retaining fee in the case on behalf of the purchasers under the act").

26. 1 N.C. at 10.

27. See Quinton Holton, "History of the Case of *Bayard v. Singleton*" (unpublished master's thesis, University of North Carolina, Chapel Hill, 1948), 125–26, 126–27 n.29; Waldrup, "Iredell and the Practice of Law in Revolutionary Era North Carolina," 261–69.

28. Higginbotham, *Papers of Iredell*, 2:449 (Iredell's "Instructions to Chowan County Representatives") (emphasis added).

29. McRee, *Life of Iredell*, 2:145–49.

30. 1 N.C. at 6–7.

31. McRee, *Life of Iredell*, 2:148.

32. Ibid., 2:169–70 (Richard Dobbs Spaight to Iredell, August 12, 1787), 172–76 (Iredell to Spaight, August 26, 1787).

33. See, e.g., John H. Dougherty, *Power of Federal Judiciary Over Legislation* (New York: G. P. Putnam's Sons, 1912), 32; Charles G. Haines, *The American Doctrine of Judicial Supremacy* (New York: Macmillan Co., 1914), 54. For a recent general treatment, see William R. Casto, "James Iredell and the American Origins of Judicial Review," *Connecticut Law Review* 27 (1995): 329. As to Hamilton's thought, see *The Federalist*, Nos. 78, 80, 81 (J. Cooke ed., 1961), 528, 535, 541 (Alexander Hamilton).

34. See *Marbury v. Madison*, 5 U.S. (1 Cranch) 137, 175–79 (1803).

35. Ibid. at 176.

36. McRee, *Life of Iredell*, 2:146 ("TO THE PUBLIC").

37. 5 U.S. (1 Cranch) at 176.

38. McRee, *Life of Iredell*, 2:148 ("TO THE PUBLIC").

39. 5 U.S. (1 Cranch) at 177.

40. McRee, *Life of Iredell*, 2:148 ("TO THE PUBLIC").

41. Clark, *State Records*, 23:987; Higginbotham, *Papers of Iredell*, 1:lxxviii (ed. essay).

42. Clark, *State Records*, 11:825, 13:341, 24:iii; Higginbotham, *Papers of Iredell*, 1:lxxviii (ed. essay), 2:32–34 (Iredell to Richard Caswell, June 13, 1778).

43. John L. Cheney, Jr., ed., *North Carolina Government, 1585–1979: A Narrative and Statistical History* (Raleigh: N.C. Dept. of Secretary of State, 1981), 182, 195 nn. 47–49; Clark, *State Records*, 13:948; Higginbotham, *Papers of Iredell*, 1:lxxix (ed. essay); Waldrup, "Iredell and the Practice of Law in Revolutionary Era North Carolina," chapter 2 (passim).

44. Higginbotham, *Papers of Iredell*, 2:379 (Archibald Maclaine to Iredell, February 21, 1783); Iredell to H. E. McCulloh, June 15, 1784, NCAH; McRee, *Life of Iredell*, 2:144 (Archibald Maclaine to Iredell, August 3, 1786); Iredell to Electors of Edenton, August 15, 1788, NCAH; McRee, *Life of Iredell*, 2:249–50 (Iredell to William Cumming, January 6, 1789); Waldrup, "Iredell and the Prac-

tice of Law in Revolutionary Era North Carolina," 366 n.1 (examples of legislators reporting to Iredell and seeking his advice).

45. Clark, *State Records*, 20:573, 21:139, 24:888–89; McRee, *Life of Iredell*, 2:277 (ed. note); Iredell to speakers of N.C. Senate and House, October 16, 1789, NCAH.

46. Clark, *State Records*, 20:491, 500; 21:26, 37, 251, 611; 23:981–82 (1776 N.C. Const. § XVI); Cheney, *North Carolina Government, 1585–1979*, 165.

47. Clark, *State Records*, 25:22; McRee, *Life of Iredell*, 2:270, 357 (ed. notes); Kemp P. Battle, *History of the University of North Carolina*, 2 vols. (Raleigh, N.C.: Edwards & Broughton, 1907 (I), 1912 (II)), 1:821, 2:426; R. D. W. Connor, *A Documentary History of the University of North Carolina* (Chapel Hill: University of North Carolina Press, 1953), 1:23, 33 n.19, 34, 72–73, 158; Iredell to University trustees, November 16, 1790, NCAH; William Samuel Johnson to Iredell, August 5, 1795, Duke.

48. Clark, *State Records*, 24:454–55; file marked "James Iredell, Sr.—Miscellaneous Papers, Robert Smith Estate," NCAH; John Witherspoon to Iredell, January 8, 1787, and Iredell to Witherspoon, February 25, 1787, Cupola House Papers, Southern Historical Collection, University of North Carolina at Chapel Hill.

49. McRee, *Life of Iredell*, 1:74 (Thomas Iredell to Iredell, undated; David L. Swain to Griffith J. McRee, 1855).

50. Higginbotham, *Papers of Iredell*, 1:lv–lvi (ed. essay), 231 (William Hooper to Iredell, April 26, 1774), lxxv (quoting Joseph Hewes to Samuel Johnston, July 8, 1775, and February 11, 1776), 305 (Joseph Hewes to Iredell, May 23, 1775), 348 (Samuel Johnston to Iredell, April 5, 1776).

51. Ibid., 410–11 (Iredell's essay "Causes of the American Revolution").

52. Ibid., lix–lxi (ed. essay), 163–65 (Iredell's "Essay on the Court Law Controversy").

53. Ibid., 251–67 (Iredell's essay "To The Inhabitants of Great Britain").

54. Ibid., 328–38 (Iredell's essay "The Principles of an American Whig").

55. Ibid., lxxii (ed. essay), 354–55 (Iredell to Joseph Hewes, April 29, 1776).

56. McRee, *Life of Iredell*, 1:283 (ed. note).

57. Higginbotham, *Papers of Iredell*, 1:lxxiii (ed. essay), 370–411 (Iredell's essay "Causes of the American Revolution").

58. See, e.g., ibid., 412–13 (John Johnston to Iredell, July 4, 1776), 415–16 (Thomas Jones to Iredell, July 23, 1776).

59. Ibid., 427–43 (Iredell's essay "To his Majesty George The Third, King of Great Britain, & c.").

60. Helen B. Smith and Elizabeth V. Moore, "John Mare: A Composite Portrait," *North Carolina Historical Review* 44 (1967): 18, 34 (oath); Higginbotham, *Papers of Iredell*, 2:16–23 (charge), 15 (resolution of appreciation for charge); Samuel A. Ashe, *History of North Carolina* (Greensboro, N.C.: Charles L. Van Noppen, 1908), 1:591–92 (Tory trials; urging patriotism); Higginbotham,

*Papers of Iredell*, 2:45–48 (Iredell's essay "To the Commissioners of the King of Great Britain for restoring Peace, & c."), 48 (ed. note) (Carlisle Commission).

61. Higginbotham, *Papers of Iredell*, 2:393 (Iredell to Hannah Iredell, April ?, 1783), 430–32 (resolutions), 446–51 (instructions), 1:lxxxvii–lxxxix (ed. essay, Washington's letter).

62. Ibid., 2:438 (Arthur Iredell to Iredell, August 18, 1783), 458 (Arthur Iredell to Iredell, November 17, 1783), 469–72 (Iredell to Thomas Iredell, ca. November 1783); McRee, *Life of Iredell*, 2:101–3 (Iredell to Thomas Iredell, May 28, 1784), 134–37 (Iredell to Thomas Iredell, February 23, 1786).

63. See Alpheus T. Mason, *The States Rights Debate: Antifederalism and the Constitution* (Englewood Cliffs, N.J.: Prentice-Hall, 1964), 11, 27; James G. Exum, Jr., and Gary R. Govert, "North Carolina and the Federal Constitution: A Commitment to Liberty," in A. E. Howard, ed., *The Constitution in the Making: Perspectives of the Original Thirteen States* (Williamsburg: National Center for State Courts, 1993), 183, 187–88. For Iredell's perspective on the problems under the Articles, see his Charge to the Grand Jury for the District of Virginia, May 23, 1796, in McRee, *Life of Iredell*, 2:484.

64. McRee, *Life of Iredell*, 2:55–56 (Iredell to Rev. Arthur Iredell, July 30, 1783); Clinton L. Rossiter, *1787: The Grand Convention* (New York: W. W. Norton & Co., 1987), 127, 150; Gordon S. Wood, *The Radicalism of the American Revolution* (New York: Vintage Books, 1991), 287.

65. McRee, *Life of Iredell*, 2:161 (William R. Davie to Iredell, May 30, 1787).

66. E.g., ibid., 162, 168–70 (Richard Dobbs Spaight to Iredell, July 3, 1787, and August 12, 1787), 163, 167 (Hugh Williamson to Iredell, July 8, 1787, and July 22, 1787), 167–68 (William R. Davie to Iredell, August 6, 1787).

67. Ibid., 104–5 (Iredell to Archibald Neilson, June 15, 1784) (re: unpopularity), 170–71 (ed. note); Iredell to Whitmell Hill, probably May 1787, NCAH; Louise I. Trenholme, *The Ratification of the Federal Constitution in North Carolina* (New York: Columbia University Press, 1932), 100–102.

68. McRee, *Life of Iredell*, 2:180–81 (ed. note), 181–83 (Grand Jury Address).

69. Robert A. Rutland, *James Madison: The Founding Father* (New York: Macmillan Co., 1987), 21–27.

70. McRee, *Life of Iredell*, 2:186 (ed. note), 186–215 (text); Hugh T. Lefler, ed., *A Plea for Federal Union: North Carolina, 1788* (Charlottesville: University Press of Virginia, 1947), 12 (Answers "attracted national attention"). Fifty of the eighty-five *Federalist Papers* postdate Iredell's "Answers." Compare McRee, *Life of Iredell*, 2:186 ("Answers" dated January 8, 1788) with *The Federalist* (J. Cooke, ed., 1961).

71. McRee, *Life of Iredell*, 2:220 (Iredell to The Freemen of the Town of Edenton, undated).

72. Ibid., 224–25 (Thomas Iredell to Iredell, May 22, 1788).

73. Ibid., 223–24 (William R. Davie to Iredell, May 1, 1788), 225–26 (Archibald Maclaine to Iredell, June 4, 1788), 227–28 (Hugh Williamson to Iredell, July 7, 1788), 230 (William R. Davie to Iredell, July 9, 1788).

74. Jonathan Elliot, ed., *The Debates in the Several State Conventions on the Adoption of the Federal Constitution* (Philadelphia: J. B. Lippincott Co., 1907), 4:1–3.

75. Trenholme, *Ratification of Federal Constitution in North Carolina*, 147; Elliot, *Debates on Adoption of Federal Constitution*, 4:228.

76. Elliot, *Debates on Adoption of Federal Constitution*, 4:143.

77. McRee, *Life of Iredell*, 2:235 (ed. essay); Samuel Johnston to Iredell, November 20, 1788, NCAH; David L. Corbitt, *The Formation of North Carolina Counties, 1663–1943* (Raleigh: N.C. Div. of Archives and History, 1950), 127–29.

78. See McRee, *Life of Iredell*, 2:248 (Hugh Williamson to Iredell, January 5, 1789), 263–64 (Pierce Butler to Iredell, August 11, 1789), 265 (Hugh Williamson to Iredell, August 12, 1789), 267 (John Steele to Iredell, September 26, 1789).

79. Trenholme, *Ratification of Federal Constitution in North Carolina*, 226–32; William S. Powell, *North Carolina Through Four Centuries* (Chapel Hill: University of North Carolina Press, 1989), 229.

80. McRee, *Life of Iredell*, 2:238 (William Hooper to Iredell, September 2, 1788).

81. Lefler, *Plea for Federal Union*, 21–22, 35–38. While this essay is not identified beyond peradventure as Iredell's, Lefler was convinced, and the present author is convinced, that he was the author.

82. William S. Powell, *North Carolina: A History* (Chapel Hill: University of North Carolina Press, 1977), 91; Maeva Marcus et al., eds., *The Documentary History of the Supreme Court of the United States, 1789–1800* (New York: Columbia University Press, 1985), 1 (pt. 2): 649 n.1; John C. Cavanagh, *Decision at Fayetteville: The North Carolina Ratification Convention and General Assembly of 1789* (Raleigh: N.C. Div. of Archives and History, 1989), 11.

83. McRee, *Life of Iredell*, 2:236 (ed. note); Trenholme, *Ratification of Federal Constitution in North Carolina*, 197, 205, 215; Iredell to Hugh Williamson, January 22, 1789, NCAH. Iredell may actually have sought election to the second ratification convention and lost. See Archibald Maclaine to Iredell, September 15, 1789, Duke.

84. Trenholme, *Ratification of Federal Constitution in North Carolina*, 199; McRee, *Life of Iredell*, 2:266 (John Williams to Iredell, September 11, 1789).

85. Cavanagh, *Decision at Fayetteville*, 27; William Dawson to Iredell, November 22, 1789, Duke; William R. Davie to Iredell, November 22, 1789, Duke; Samuel Johnston to Iredell, November 23, 1789, Duke.

86. Albert R. Newsome, "North Carolina's Ratification of the Federal Constitution," *North Carolina Historical Review* 17 (1940): 287, 297.

87. McRee, *Life of Iredell*, 2:272 (William Dawson to Iredell, November 22, 1789; Samuel Johnston to Iredell, November 23, 1789), 273 (Charles Johnson to Iredell, November 23, 1789).

88. Trenholme, *Ratification of Federal Constitution in North Carolina*, 147.

89. Henry G. Connor, "James Iredell: Lawyer, Statesman, Judge. 1751–1799," *University of Pennsylvania Law Review* 60 (1912): 225, 236.

90. Trenholme, *Ratification of Federal Constitution in North Carolina*, 120.

91. Hampton L. Carson, *The History of the Supreme Court of the United States with Biographies of all the Chief and Associate Justices* (Philadelphia: P. W. Ziegler and Co., 1902; reprint, New York: Lenox Hill Publishers, 1971), 1:154–55; McRee, *Life of Iredell*, 2:264 (Pierce Butler to Iredell, August 11, 1789), 265 (Hugh Williamson to Iredell, August 12, 1789), 275 (Archibald Maclaine to Iredell, December 9, 1789); Iredell to Henry McCulloh, March 31, 1790, NCAH; Iredell to John Rutledge, April 9, 1790, Duke.

92. See Samuel Johnston to Iredell: February 11, 1790, NCAH; March 6, 1790, Duke.

93. McRee, *Life of Iredell*, 2:307–20 ("TO THE CITIZENS OF THE UNITED STATES" from "A CITIZEN OF PENNSYLVANIA").

94. Ibid., 431 (William R. Davie to Iredell, December 15, 1794).

95. Ibid., 320 ("TO THE CITIZENS . . ." letter).

96. Ibid., 431 (William R. Davie to Iredell, December 15, 1794, noting "conciliatory effect with respect to the government" of Justice Wilson's conduct while holding court), 435 (ed. essay).

97. Ibid., 551–70 (Charge to United States Grand Jury for the District of Pennsylvania, April 11, 1799); as to resentment, see Herbert S. Turner, *The Dreamer Archibald DeBow Murphey* (Verona, Va.: McClure Press, 1971), 53.

98. E.g., Charges to Grand Jury at Richmond, Virginia: May 23, 1796, Duke; May 22, 1797, McRee, *Life of Iredell*, 2:508–9.

99. McRee, *Life of Iredell*, 2:569 (Charge to United States Grand Jury for Pennsylvania, April 11, 1799).

100. Charges to United States Grand Juries: Trenton, April 2, 1793; Philadelphia, April 11, 1793; and Annapolis, May 7, 1793 (NCAH). The Annapolis charge is in McRee, *Life of Iredell*, 2:386, 387.

101. 2 U.S. (2 Dall.) 419 (1793).

102. Warren, *Supreme Court in U.S. History*, 1:92–93.

103. Julius Goebel, Jr., *History of the Supreme Court of the United States: Antecedents and Beginnings to 1801* (New York: Macmillan Co., 1971), 741–42; Kemp P. Yarborough, "*Chisholm v. Georgia*: A Study of the Minority Opinion" (Ann Arbor, Mich.: University Microfilms, 1991), 33 of unpublished Ph. D. dissertation, Columbia University, 1963.

104. Elliot, *Debates on Adoption of Federal Constitution*, 3:523–27, 533, 555–56; Warren, *Supreme Court in U.S. History*, 1:96; Yarborough, "*Chisholm*

*v. Georgia*: A Study," 17, 30–31, 52–58, 194–95; see also William A. Fletcher, "A Historical Interpretation of the Eleventh Amendment: A Narrow Construction of an Affirmative Grant of Jurisdiction Rather than a Prohibition Against Jurisdiction," *Stanford Law Review* 35 (1983): 1033, 1047–50.

105. See 2 U.S. (2 Dall.) at 450–79 (passim); Yarborough, "*Chisholm v. Georgia*: A Study," 178–79.

106. 2 U.S. (2 Dall.) at 449 (Iredell, J., dissenting).

107. McRee, *Life of Iredell*, 2:193; Yarborough, "*Chisholm v. Georgia*: A Study," 192–95.

108. Elliot, *Debates on Adoption of Federal Constitution*, 4:35; Yarborough, "*Chisholm v. Georgia*: A Study," 192, 232–33.

109. McRee, *Life of Iredell*, 2:348, 387; Yarborough, "*Chisholm v. Georgia*: A Study," 234–35, 235 n. 1.

110. *The Federalist* (J. Cooke ed., 1961), No. 9, at 55; No. 32, at 200; No. 81, at 548–49 (Alexander Hamilton); Elliot, *Debates on Adoption of Federal Constitution*, 3:533 (James Madison), 555–56 (John Marshall); see Samuel F. Miller, *Lectures on the Constitution of the United States* (New York: Banks & Bros., 1891), 380–82; Yarborough, "*Chisholm v. Georgia*: A Study," 233–34, 240–41, 318.

111. *Cohens v. Virginia*, 19 U.S. (6 Wheat.) 264, 406 (1821).

112. Robert Shnayerson, *The Illustrated History of the Supreme Court of the United States* (New York: Harry N. Abrams, 1986), 70; Francis N. Thorpe, *A Constitutional History of the American People, 1776–1850* (New York: Harper & Bros., 1898), 1:177; see also Jefferson B. Fordham, "Iredell's Dissent in *Chisholm v. Georgia*: Its Political Significance," *North Carolina Historical Review* 8 (1931): 155, 162–63; William D. Guthrie, "The Eleventh Article of Amendment to the Constitution of the United States," *Columbia Law Review* 8 (1908): 183, 185–86; Yarborough, "*Chisholm v. Georgia:* A Study," 180–87, 192–93.

113. See, e.g., John V. Orth, *The Judicial Power of the United States: The Eleventh Amendment in American History* (New York: Oxford University Press, 1987), 13–14, 22, 42, 69–70, 74–75, 137–38, 149, 159; John V. Orth, "The Truth About Justice Iredell's Dissent in *Chisholm v. Georgia* (1793)," *North Carolina Law Review* 73 (1994): 255 (passim). Professor Orth's thesis is that Iredell's dissent rested on the absence of a statutory remedy, not on the lack of constitutional power.

114. Leon Friedman and Fred L. Israel, *The Justices of the United States Supreme Court, 1789–1969: Their Lives and Major Opinions* (New York: Chelsea House, 1969), 1:131, 133.

115. See David P. Currie, *The Constitution in the Supreme Court: The First Hundred Years, 1789–1888* (Chicago: University of Chicago Press, 1985), 9 n.29. In *Calder v. Bull*, Iredell stated that he had "not had an opportunity to reduce

[his] opinion to writing." 3 U.S. (3 Dall.) 386, 398 (1798). The statement was made in an opinion that covered three pages of the official reports, so his meaning is unclear. It lends support to the notion that opinions were not always reduced to writing, however.

116. 3 U.S. (3 Dall.) 54 (1795).

117. Ibid., 90.

118. Ibid., 91.

119. Haines, *Role of the Supreme Court*, 1:141.

120. 3 U.S. (3 Dall.) 133 (1795).

121. Ibid., 161–64.

122. Ibid., 163.

123. 3 U.S. (3 Dall.) 171 (1796).

124. Ibid., 181–83.

125. Goebel, *U.S. Supreme Court: Antecedents and Beginnings*, 778; Leonard W. Levy, *Original Intent and the Framers' Constitution* (New York: Macmillan Co., 1988), 59; Warren, *Supreme Court in U.S. History*, 1:146–47.

126. Friedman and Israel, *The Justices of the U.S. Supreme Court*, 1:192.

127. 3 U.S. (3 Dall.) 199 (1796).

128. Currie, *Constitution in the Supreme Court, 1789–1888*, 4, 39, 41.

129. 3 U.S. (3 Dall.) at 256–80.

130. Ibid., 270.

131. 3 U.S. (3 Dall.) 386 (1798).

132. Ibid., 387–89.

133. Ibid., 399.

134. Currie, *Constitution in the Supreme Court, 1789–1888*, 47–48; Jethro K. Lieberman, *The Enduring Constitution: A Bicentennial Perspective* (St. Paul, Minn.: West Publishing Co., 1987), 263.

135. Currie, *Constitution in the Supreme Court, 1789–1888*, 58.

136. 3 U.S. (3 Dall.) at 92.

137. Currie, *Constitution in the Supreme Court, 1789–1888*, 57–58.

138. William S. Powell, ed., *Dictionary of North Carolina Biography* (Chapel Hill: University of North Carolina Press, 1988), 3:254 (entry by Don Higginbotham).

139. McRee, *Life of Iredell*, 2:306 (Arthur Iredell to Iredell, February 1, 1791).

140. See Wythe Holt, "'The Federal Courts Have Enemies in All Who Fear Their Influence on State Objects': The Failure to Abolish Supreme Court Circuit-Riding in the Judiciary Acts of 1792 and 1793," *Buffalo Law Review* 36 (1987): 301, 305–6.

141. See Charles Warren, "New Light on the History of the Federal Judiciary Act of 1789," *Harvard Law Review* 37 (1923): 49, 95.

142. See Holt, "Failure to Abolish Circuit-Riding," 307–8; Wythe Holt, "'To

Establish Justice': Politics, The Judiciary Act of 1789, and the Invention of the Federal Courts," *Duke Law Journal* (1989): 1421, 1488–89, 1489 n.235; Maeva Marcus and Emily F. Van Tassell, "Judges and Legislators in the New Federal System, 1789–1800," in Robert A. Katzmann, ed., *Judges and Legislators: Toward Institutional Comity* (Washington, D.C.: Brookings Institution, 1988), 31, 32.

143. Iredell to Thomas Iredell (uncle), July 6, 1791, NCAH; John Jay to Iredell, March 16, 1791, NCAH.

144. Holt, "Failure to Abolish Circuit-Riding," 311–12; Marcus et al., *Documentary History of U.S. Supreme Court*, 2:132, 135 (Iredell to John Jay, William Cushing, James Wilson, February 11, 1791) (same letter in McRee, *Life of Iredell*, 2:322–25).

145. Holt, "Failure to Abolish Circuit-Riding," 328–29; Marcus et al., *Documentary History of U.S. Supreme Court*, 2:235–37 (ed. essay), 247 (Iredell to Thomas Johnson, March 15, 1792), 248 n.6, 249 (John Jay to Iredell, March 19, 1792).

146. Marcus et al., *Documentary History of U.S. Supreme Court*, 2:235 (ed. essay), 245 (James Wilson to Thomas Johnson, March 13, 1792); McRee, *Life of Iredell*, 2:465 (Iredell to Hannah Iredell, March 31, 1796). The Judiciary Act of 1801, which temporarily eliminated circuit riding, came too late to benefit Iredell, who died in 1799. That act was repealed in 1802, and almost another ninety years would pass before circuit riding by the justices was again eliminated. Marcus et al., *Documentary History of U.S. Supreme Court*, 2:341 n.19, 444 n.4.

147. There are numerous accounts of the Invalid Pensions Act. See, e.g., Goebel, *U.S. Supreme Court: Antecedents and Beginnings*, 560–65; Marcus et al., *Documentary History of U.S. Supreme Court*, 2:235–36 (ed. essay); McRee, *Life of Iredell*, 2:357–58.

148. Goebel, *U.S. Supreme Court: Antecedents and Beginnings*, 560–61.

149. McRee, *Life of Iredell*, 2:361 (Iredell to Hannah Iredell, September 30, 1792); *Hayburn's Case*, 2 U.S. (2 Dall.) 409, 411–12 (1792) (reporting the April 18, 1792, Pennsylvania Circuit opinion of Justices Wilson and Blair, and District Judge Peters).

150. *See* Maeva Marcus and Robert Tier, "*Hayburn's Case:* A Misinterpretation of Precedent," *Wisconsin Law Review* (1988): 527, 533–34.

151. McRee, *Life of Iredell*, 1:361 (Iredell to Hannah Iredell, September 30, 1792); Iredell's "Reasons for acting as a Commissioner on the Invalid Act," October 1792, NCAH; Marcus and Van Tassell, "Judges and Legislators," 39–40.

152. McRee, *Life of Iredell*, 2:362 (Iredell to Hannah Iredell, September 30, 1792).

153. See, e.g., McRee, *Life of Iredell*, 2:440 (Iredell to Hannah Iredell, February 26, 1795); Robert J. Wagman, *The Supreme Court: A Citizen's Guide* (New York: Pharos Books, 1993), 41 (Iredell away from home eleven months in first year on Supreme Court).

154. Iredell to Helen Blair Tredwell (Hannah's niece), May 27, 1795, NCAH.

155. Iredell to Hannah Iredell, January 31, 1795, Duke; January 21, 1795, July 29, 1796, and January 23, 1797, NCAH.

156. Iredell to Hannah Iredell, October 27, 1791, and April 7, 1794, NCAH.

157. McRee, *Life of Iredell*, 2:385 (Iredell to Hannah Iredell, May 5, 1793).

158. E.g., Iredell to Hannah Iredell, October 2, 1791, and April 10, 1798, NCAH; Iredell to Annie Iredell, August 5, 1795, NCAH; Marcus et al., *Documentary History of U.S. Supreme Court*, 3:257 (City Gazette, Augusta, Georgia, May 5, 1798), 280–81 (John Young Noel to William Paterson, July 20, 1798).

159. E.g., Iredell to Hannah Iredell, September 19, 1791, and October 2, 1791, NCAH.

160. Iredell to Hannah Iredell, November 11, 1791, NCAH.

161. Marcus et al., *Documentary History of U.S. Supreme Court*, 2:295–97 (Iredell to Hannah Iredell, September 23, 1792).

162. McRee, *Life of Iredell*, 2:346–47 (Iredell to Hannah Iredell, April 26, 1792); Iredell to Hannah Iredell, January 23, 1795, and February 3, 1796, NCAH.

163. Goebel, *U.S. Supreme Court: Antecedents and Beginnings*, 553; McRee, *Life of Iredell*, 2:400–401 (Dr. Duffield to Iredell, September 5, 1793; Pierce Butler to Iredell, September 9, 1793).

164. E.g., McRee, *Life of Iredell*, 2:371 (Iredell to Hannah Iredell, October 21, 1792), 394 (Iredell to Hannah Iredell, May 20, 1793), 477 (Iredell to Hannah Iredell, July 29, 1796).

165. Marcus et al., *Documentary History of U.S. Supreme Court*, 2:249 (Nathaniel Pendleton to Iredell, March 19, 1792).

166. E.g., McRee, *Life of Iredell*, 2:296 (Iredell to Hannah Iredell, September 14, 1790); Iredell to Hannah Iredell, May 7, 1795, NCAH; January 29, 1797, Duke.

167. E.g., McRee, *Life of Iredell*, 2:288 n. (hard money at his disposal); John Hay to Iredell, November 1, 1790, Duke (free lodging); Iredell to Hannah Iredell, May 28, 1790, NCAH (Justice Rutledge's kindness); Iredell to Hannah Iredell, May 31, 1790, Duke (Judge Pendleton's wife's "civilities").

168. E.g., McRee, *Life of Iredell*, 2:288 (Iredell to Hannah Iredell, May 10, 1790); Iredell to Hannah Iredell, February 3, 1796, NCAH.

169. E.g., McRee, *Life of Iredell*, 2:373 (Iredell to Hannah Iredell, November 5, 1792) (dinner with Governor John Hancock of Massachusetts).

170. E.g., Iredell to Hannah Iredell, September 25, 1792, NCAH; April 15, 1795, Duke (teas with Mrs. John Jay).

171. E.g., McRee, *Life of Iredell*, 2:300 (Iredell to Hannah Iredell, October 30, 1790); Iredell to Hannah Iredell, October 13, 1792, NCAH.

172. E.g., McRee, *Life of Iredell*, 2:439 (Iredell to Hannah Iredell, February

5, 1795), 456 (Iredell to Hannah Iredell, November 27, 1795), 494 (Iredell to Hannah Iredell, February 24, 1797).

173. E.g., Marcus et al., *Documentary History of U.S. Supreme Court*, 2:480–81 (John Gabriel Guignard to Iredell, August 22, 1794); Resolution of the Grand Jury at Raleigh, [N.C.,] June 4, 1798 (Circuit Court, June Term 1798), NCAH.

174. E.g., McRee, *Life of Iredell* 2:297 (Iredell to Hannah Iredell, September 15, 1790) (Thomas Mifflin of Pennsylvania), 363 (Iredell to Hannah Iredell, October 7, 1792) (Elbridge Gerry of Massachusetts); Iredell to Hannah Iredell, May 9, 1791, NCAH (Charles Carroll of Maryland); May 5, 1793, NCAH (Luther Martin of Maryland).

175. E.g., Patrick Henry—see McRee, *Life of Iredell*, 2:394 (Iredell to Hannah Iredell, May 27, 1793); John Marshall—see Albert J. Beveridge, *The Life of John Marshall* (Boston: Houghton Mifflin, 1916), 2:188; Irwin S. Rhodes, *The Papers of John Marshall: A Descriptive Calendar* (Norman: University of Oklahoma Press, 1969), 1:480–81.

176. See Frank Nash, "An Eighteenth Century Circuit Rider" (Proceedings of the Twentieth and Twenty-First Annual Sessions of the State Literary and Historical Association of North Carolina, Publications of the North Carolina Historical Commission, Bulletin No. 28, Edwards & Broughton, Raleigh, N.C., 1922), 69–70.

177. Charles Dickens, *Hard Times* (New York: Oxford University Press, 1989 ed.), 95.

178. William K. Boyd, *History of North Carolina: The Federal Period, 1783–1860* (Spartanburg, S.C.: Reprint Co., 1973) (original ed., 1919), 2:385.

179. Henderson, *North Carolina*, 1:418.

180. Marcus et al., *Documentary History of U.S. Supreme Court* 2:4.

## Chapter 8

# William Paterson
## *Small States' Nationalist*

*Daniel A. Degnan, S.J.*

Appointed by George Washington in 1793 as a justice of the Supreme Court of the United States,[1] William Paterson was in the unique position given to a Founder. At the Constitutional Convention of 1787, he had helped to frame the Constitution under which he exercised judicial office.[2] In the first Senate, he had been one of the principal authors of the Judiciary Act of 1789, which constructed the federal judicial system. Indeed, the first nine sections of the act, which included the composition of the Supreme Court and the establishment of the district and circuit courts, were in Paterson's handwriting.[3] Thus, Paterson was a Founding Father both of the nation and of the federal judiciary.

Consequently, this study of Paterson's work as a justice of the Supreme Court has an unusual aspect. Paterson's influence on the Court through his work in the convention and his structuring of the federal judiciary were more important to the nation and to the Supreme Court itself than even his substantial contributions as a justice. This essay, accordingly, has two parts: the convention and the Judiciary Act, and Paterson's work on the Court.

First, however, a brief look at his roots in New Jersey helps to explain much about William Paterson. He was born in Antrim, Ireland, in 1745. In 1747, his Scotch-Irish parents came to America. His father

An earlier version of this essay appeared as "Justice William Paterson—Founder," 16 *Seton Hall Law Review* 313–38 (1986). Permission to reprint the essay is appreciated.

opened a general store in Princeton, across from Nassau Hall of the College of New Jersey. Paterson was fourteen when he entered the college in 1759. He studied the classics and moral philosophy, read Pope and Dryden, was strongly religious, and saw no conflict between religion and the rationalism of John Locke and Thomas Hobbes. He was anxious to advance himself and to become a gentleman.[4]

Paterson was rather short, slight, not handsome, and he waited fourteen years after college to marry. He was a leader, however, and he helped found the Cliosophic Society, a social and debating club, at Princeton.[5] After graduation, he read law in Princeton under Richard Stockton.[6] He finally left Princeton, with misgivings, for a country practice in Raritan. There, besides being a surrogate, he seems to have spent a great deal of time handling his father's financial problems.[7]

Paterson thought that both private and public life rested on moral virtue, and virtue in turn rested on discipline. The enemy of virtue was luxury, and Paterson saw luxury in the British monarchy. As a good Calvinist, Paterson saw the people as also prone to luxury.[8] He thought, however, that morals and republican government together would help to keep the citizens virtuous. Even so, to Paterson, government depended upon a natural aristocracy of virtuous leaders who would seek the public interest.[9]

Paterson was a blend of the moralistic and the practical, an ambitious and perhaps a somewhat insecure person in his early years. These personal paradoxes were evident during the Constitutional Convention. A consistent nationalist, Paterson introduced the New Jersey, or Paterson, plan for amending the Articles of Confederation; he opposed Madison's Virginia plan, which became the eventual basis of the Constitution.[10] After achieving equality for the small states, Paterson left the convention on July 23, when half of the work was still to be done.[11] These contradictions seem to fit William Pierce's description of Paterson at the convention:

> [O]ne of those Men whose powers break in upon you, and create astonishment. He is a Man of great modesty, with looks that bespeak talents of no great extent,—but he is a Classic, a lawyer, and an Orator;—and of a disposition so favorable to his advancement that everyone seemed ready to exalt him with their praises.[12]

In spite of these paradoxes, Paterson had a set of consistent principles and great opportunities. Property and political stability were sacred to him.[13] As a lawyer, Paterson sued debtors, and as attorney general during the Revolution, he pursued Tories and fought for political and financial stability in New Jersey.[14] Paterson joined his friends and mentors from Princeton in a rebellion against a monarchy that he saw as luxury-ridden and contemptuous of republican principles.[15]

Paterson represented the middle-class, Presbyterian New Jersey of the colonial era. He served as secretary to both New Jersey's Provincial Congress and its constitutional convention before being named attorney general.[16] In 1787, he was chosen as one of New Jersey's delegates to the federal Constitutional Convention in Philadelphia.[17] The convention, in the words of his biographer John E. O'Connor, was his finest hour.[18]

## *The Constitutional Convention*

It was as a politician, lawyer, and strategist that William Paterson distinguished himself at the Constitutional Convention. Madison of Virginia and Wilson of Pennsylvania were to be the principal architects of the new government, not only because of ability and political principle but because the interests of their states coincided with the creation of a strong national government and with proportionate representation by population in both branches of the legislature. Madison, Wilson, and Gouverneur Morris were determined to institute a national or consolidated government that would give the states a distinctly subordinate role, the opposite of government under the Articles of Confederation.[19]

William Paterson, representing New Jersey, led the coalition of small states that stopped the large-state juggernaut and brought about the Great Compromise.[20] The compromise provided for proportional representation in the House of Representatives, but equal representation in the Senate.[21] It ensured also that the new government would be a federal one having a significant role for the states. Indeed, Paterson was later to describe the federal system as "sovereignties moving within a sovereignty."[22] To political thinkers like Paterson, the Great Compromise was necessary to prevent the demise of small states' rights and autonomy in the new government.

Nowhere was this more evident than in Paterson's home state. New Jersey, having no major ports, had to import and export through New

York and Philadelphia, both of which laid duties on New Jersey's commerce. Paterson's home state was, in Madison's words, "likened to a cask tapped at both ends."[23] New Jersey, like Connecticut, Maryland, and Delaware, was a relatively small state. Along with those states and New York, it had no claims to western territory. If the new government were to be based on representation according to population, Paterson and others believed, New Jersey could anticipate that the large states such as Virginia, Pennsylvania, Massachusetts, and others would subordinate New Jersey's interests to theirs and would perhaps even destroy the smaller states.[24] By contrast, for the large states with significant populations or the prospect of new western lands, proportional representation in the national government posed little apparent threat to their interests.[25] In addition, Madison, Wilson, and some of the others from the large states had backgrounds of national and even international experience, while Paterson had served New Jersey during the Revolution as its attorney general.[26]

We must analyze Paterson's role in the course of the convention in order to understand and appraise it. In the first two weeks, from May 30 to June 13, the delegates met as a committee of the whole while Randolph, Madison, Wilson, and others formulated the Virginia plan. The plan, largely drafted by Madison, presented the idea of a national government consisting of three branches with broad national powers. Of these branches, the lawmaking body was a two-house legislature to be chosen according to proportional representation. The plan envisioned a new form of government rather than an amendment to the Articles of Confederation.[27]

While the different resolutions of the Virginia plan were being adopted, Paterson remained silent.[28] On June 9, however, Paterson rose to object to the proposal for proportional representation. In his carefully prepared speech, Paterson argued that the body was moving beyond its mandate from the states, which was to amend the Articles of Confederation.[29] More important, Paterson stated that the small states could never agree to the dominance by the large states embodied in the Virginia plan.[30] Madison's notes recorded the speech and the peroration:

> He alluded to the hint thrown out heretofore by Mr. Wilson of the necessity to which the large States might be reduced of confederating among themselves, by a refusal of the others to concur. Let them unite if they

please, but let them remember that they have no authority to compel the others to unite. New Jersey will never confederate on the plan before the Committee. She would be swallowed up. He had rather submit to a monarch, to a despot, than to such a fate. He would not only oppose the plan here but on his return home do everything in his power to defeat it there.[31]

Wilson replied that the large states could not agree to representation not based upon population, in which a minority could rule the majority.[32] The Committee of the Whole voted on June 11 to accept the principle of representation in both houses according to population, but the convention resolved to take the matter up again.[33]

On June 13, a Wednesday, the Committee of the Whole decided to report the Virginia plan to the convention.[34] Paterson's intervention on June 9, however, had initiated a great debate between the large states and the small. The next move by Paterson was the introduction of an alternative to the Virginia plan—the New Jersey, or Paterson, plan.[35] After obtaining a recess to complete its preparation, and with backing by New Jersey, Connecticut, Delaware, and Luther Martin of Maryland, Paterson presented the plan on June 15.[36] Essentially, Paterson's plan expanded the powers of the Confederation.[37] After several days of debate on the two plans, capped by a speech from Madison, the Virginia plan was approved on June 19 by the Committee of the Whole by a vote of seven to three.[38] Madison, Wilson, and others had eloquently presented the Virginia plan, while the New Jersey plan had been thrown together hastily.[39] The small state delegates were united only in their demand for equality.[40]

Nevertheless, the New Jersey plan and Paterson's earlier intervention of June 9 had dramatically highlighted the cause of the small states for equality. From June 21 to June 26, the convention took up each detail of the Virginia plan as submitted by the Committee of the Whole.[41] On June 27, the debate over representation was renewed by Luther Martin of Maryland in a long, rambling speech.[42] On June 28, Dayton of New Jersey and Lansing of New York moved for equality among the states in the lower branch.[43] Their motion was lost, with Connecticut, New York, New Jersey, and Delaware on the losing side, and Maryland divided.[44] Representation in the Senate was considered next, with Ellsworth of Connecticut moving for equality and expressing doubt that any state north of Pennsylvania, except Massachusetts, would consent to anything other than equal representation.[45] A tie vote ensued on July 2, and a special committee was elected to report a compromise.[46]

Paterson, who had remained silent during this debate, was elected to the committee.[47] The composition of the committee meant that the convention favored a compromise with the smaller states. Madison and Wilson were not elected; large state delegates who were willing to compromise were chosen instead.[48] The result, reported on July 5, was the Great Compromise: representation by population in the House and equal representation in the Senate.[49]

After a long debate on other parts of the compromise—the number of representatives in the House, the counting of slaves, and the power over money bills[50]—the convention adopted the full compromise on July 16.[51] Connecticut, New Jersey, Delaware, Maryland, and North Carolina voted yes (New York was absent); Pennsylvania, Virginia, South Carolina, and Georgia voted no; Massachusetts was divided.[52] Randolph of Virginia then asked for an adjournment to enable the large states to evaluate their position, and he suggested that the small states might also consider a method of conciliation.[53] At this point, Paterson, not one to let the victory slip away, intervened. He would be happy to second Randolph's motion for an adjournment for the purpose of consulting with his constituents, he said, because the small states would never yield their demand for equality in the Senate.[54] Randolph replied that he had never intended more than a day's adjournment.[55] The next day, July 17, after inconclusive discussion among large-state delegates, the compromise was left intact, much to Madison's distress.[56]

On this same day, Paterson wrote to his wife, "I expect to be with you on or about the first of next month and hope that I shall not be under the necessity of returning."[57] Paterson seems to have had pressing business at home; he was uncomfortable in Philadelphia and avoided the social life the convention called for;[58] and he had, as always, one foot in New Jersey. Perhaps he decided to leave only a few days later, on July 23, because he realized that the work of the convention would take some weeks more. Nevertheless, he returned on September 17 to sign the proposed constitution.[59]

Despite persistent impressions to the contrary, which are attributable in part to Madison's notes of July 7, it seems clear that Paterson supported the Great Compromise.[60] Above all, he was satisfied with the work of the convention. In the letter of July 17 to his wife, Paterson also wrote, "The business is difficult and unavoidably takes up much time, but I think we shall eventually agree upon and adopt a system that will give strength and harmony to the Union and render us a great and happy people."[61] For Paterson at that time, the principles had been settled upon to his satisfaction, and only the detail remained. In an August 23 letter to Oliver Ellsworth, he stated:

> What are the Convention about? When will they rise? will they agree upon a System energetick and effectual, or will they break up without doing any Thing to the Purpose? . . . I hope you will not have as much Altercation upon the Detail, as there was in getting the Principles of the System. . . . I wish you much Speed, and that you may be full of good Works, the first mainly for my own Sake, for I dread going down again to Philadelphia. . . .[62]

Paterson's departure once the small states were protected symbolized his role at the convention.[63] The success of the convention depended upon an accommodation with the small states, which Madison, Wilson, and Morris were unwilling to make. That the debate was held, that it was conducted on legal and political principles (whatever the issues of property and power concerning the western lands), and that it was able to continue instead of leading to the dissolution of the convention can be attributed in large part to Paterson, who was able to stand up to the ablest men of the convention, such as Madison, Wilson, and Gouverneur Morris.[64]

The focus of Paterson's efforts, in turn, is directly traceable to New Jersey's place in the nascent attempts to establish the bases of American political philosophy. As a small state, New Jersey needed a strong national government to protect its interests. Paterson's intimacy with New Jersey as a student, lawyer, and public official made him acutely aware of this need. This intimacy ensured that New Jersey and other small states would have a cogent and formidable voice speaking for them at the convention.

Well educated and thoughtful as he was, however, Paterson was more the skilled common-law and chancery practitioner than the scholar or political philosopher. Yet in his own political and moral philosophy, he was a strong advocate of stability and authority, with these convictions often directed to securing the rights of property. Paterson also stressed the people's compact, a principle apparently derived from John Locke, and a theory of sovereignty that bore echoes of Thomas Hobbes and may have owed much to William Blackstone.[65] In his later arguments supporting the Constitution and in his work on the Supreme Court, Paterson was an outspoken Federalist, or nationalist. No fundamental change in Paterson's views seems to have been necessary, only the kind of development shared by most of the Founders. He was, from his experience, a true Federalist, seeking national, sovereign power while retaining an important role for the states, which would remain "sovereign" in the exercise of their own nonnational powers.

One also senses about Paterson a certain underlying modesty and rectitude about his duties. On July 17, when he saw that the compromise would hold, his contribution to the convention was sufficient; it was time to return home to his family and his law practice. What Paterson had done was to furnish the strong but moderate opposition that the great plan of Madison required. If the Constitution were to be proposed and adopted, it was not only essential that the small states be protected; it was also critical that the convention itself be a means for argument, debate, and compromise. Paterson's first argument on June 9 raised the question of representation. Then the New Jersey plan created the vehicle for the great debate. It is significant that Paterson was elected to the Committee of Compromise, and that Madison, Wilson, and Gouverneur Morris were not. One can only speculate about what might have happened to the convention if the small states had not been represented by a skillful, determined, and courageous advocate who was, at base, in agreement with Madison, Washington, and the other nationalists.

## *The Judiciary Act of 1789*

New Jersey was the third state to ratify the Constitution.[66] By August 1788, the required nine states had done so.[67] On November 25, 1788, William Paterson was chosen by a joint session of the legislature to be one of New Jersey's two senators.[68] He took his seat in the Senate on March 19, 1789, in New York City. On April 7, the Senate appointed a committee "to 'bring in a bill for organizing the judiciary of the United States.'"[69] Paterson was appointed to this committee, which produced the Judiciary Act of 1789.[70]

The first nine sections of the Judiciary Act of 1789 were in William Paterson's handwriting.[71] Almost identical to the printed version, the handwritten draft discovered by Charles Warren[72] led to a reappraisal of Paterson's contribution to this "great law."[73] Oliver Ellsworth chaired the committee and is considered to have been the leading draftsman, but Paterson played a considerable role.[74]

While the House was considering the constitutional amendments that became the Bill of Rights, the Senate was undertaking to establish the federal courts. The select committee numbered ten (half of the Senate), among whom Ellsworth, Paterson, and Caleb Strong were the leading lawyers.[75] In addition, Ellsworth and Paterson were the principal drafters.[76] Paterson, from his practice of law in New Jersey, had the most extensive experience in both the common law and the equity or chancery jurisdiction for which New Jersey was noted.[77]

In the first nine sections, written by Paterson and enacted into law, the bill stated: "Be it enacted by the Senate and representatives of the United States of America in Congress assembled, That the Supreme Court of the United States shall consist of a chief justice and five associate justices, any four of whom shall be a quorum. . . ."[78] The next paragraph provided as follows: "And be it further enacted by the authority aforesaid, That the United States shall be, and they hereby are divided into eleven districts. . . ."[79]

The provision for United States district and circuit courts, in Paterson's hand, was of primary importance. The new federal government had fashioned "its own judicial machinery for enforcing its claims and safeguarding its agents against the obstructions and prejudices of local authorities."[80] Important matters such as financing the government, commerce among the states, and foreign trade would be facilitated by the federal courts.[81]

The division of the country into districts recognized the interests of the states. Each federal district had a district court and was made coextensive with the geographic boundaries of a state, helping to ease the apprehension, as Goebel puts it, that the federal courts would obliterate those of the states.[82] Second, except for admiralty, the jurisdiction of the district courts was narrowly limited,[83] and the original jurisdiction of the circuit courts, while broader, was carefully defined.[84]

The famous section 25 provided for review by the Supreme Court, through writs of error, of the judgments of the highest courts of the states in law or equity when federal questions were involved.[85] It was Paterson who had introduced the supremacy clause during the convention as part of the New Jersey plan.[86] Section 25, "perhaps the boldest" section of the Judiciary Act, was an essential implementation of this clause.[87] As Laurence Tribe puts it, the Judiciary Act gave the Supreme Court the power "to review federal question decisions of state courts."[88] The Supreme Court later concluded that the Constitution gave it the power to accept such review.[89] In addition, section 34 of the act provided that state laws would furnish the rules of decision in common-law trials in the courts of the United States.[90]

Paterson, with his unusual combination of nationalism and concern for the states, must have been a force on the committee for both national power and the integrity of the states. Because he was the most widely experienced lawyer on the panel, the more technical aspects of the bill must also have owed much to him. It is unnecessary to detract from Ellsworth's leadership in order to recognize this. Paterson's drafting of the first nine sections seems a good sign of the importance of his contribution to the Judiciary Act.

In short, the Judiciary Act of 1789 established the system of federal courts, and Oliver Ellsworth and William Paterson were its principal authors. Of the act itself, Frankfurter and Landis have written:

> The Act has three claims to greatness. It devised a judicial organization which, with all its imperfections, served the country substantially unchanged for nearly a century. Through supervision over state courts conferred upon the Supreme Court by its famous Section Twenty-five, the Act created one of the most important nationalizing influences in the formative period of the Republic. But the transcendent achievement of the First Judiciary Act is the establishment for this country of the tradition of a system of inferior federal courts.[91]

## *Paterson's Work on the Supreme Court*

In 1790, when Governor Livingston died, William Paterson was chosen by the legislature to be New Jersey's second governor.[92] Then, in 1793, George Washington appointed Paterson to the Supreme Court of the United States.[93] Paterson was to serve on the Court until his death in 1806,[94] but there was also other evidence of his position and influence in the new nation. In 1795, Washington, who had presided at the Constitutional Convention, offered Paterson the office of secretary of state, but he declined.[95] Before Oliver Ellsworth was appointed chief justice in 1796, published reports indicated that the promotion of Justice Paterson was imminent.[96] In 1800, Paterson was the candidate of the Senate for the chief justiceship, but the senators yielded to Adams's determination to appoint John Marshall.[97]

In the early days of the Supreme Court, nearly every case established precedent. As in the convention, therefore, the way to follow Paterson's work is chronologically, and Paterson's Supreme Court opinions will be discussed in the order in which they were written. Paterson also presided in the circuit courts, most notably at two trials for treason arising from the Whiskey Rebellion[98] and at two trials for violation of the alien and sedition laws.[99] It suffices to say that in the treason cases, Paterson carefully delineated the elements of proof of treason,[100] and in the sedition trials, Paterson took a severe, Federalist position.[101]

The importance of Paterson's work on the Supreme Court paralleled the importance of the early Court in preparing the way for the great cases of the Marshall era. From a reading of the early opinions and from the assessments of historians of the early Court, this work appears to have been an indispensable prelude.[102] William Paterson's opinions show that he was both a skillful lawyer on the bench and an articulate exponent of national power, including the power of judicial review. In fact, Paterson's charge to the jury in *Vanhorne's Lessee v. Dorrance*[103] served as one of the most important justifications of judicial review in the initial years. Nevertheless, to the reader today, there is a somewhat unformed quality to these cases, not only because the opinions of the justices were delivered separately, or seriatim, but also because the great cases would take time to develop. On the Supreme Court, Paterson, who had been the right age for leadership in the Revolutionary War and the Constitutional Convention, would help to prepare the way for younger men like John Marshall, Joseph Story, and others.

When William Paterson joined the Supreme Court in the February Term of 1794, the federal judiciary had begun to win some measure of public confidence.[104] Paterson's first full opinion appears in *Penhallow v. Doane's Administrators*,[105] the most important of three cases decided in the February Term of 1795.[106] In 1777, Congress formed a standing committee of five members to hear appeals from the state admiralty courts in cases of capture.[107] That same year, the brig *M'Clary* captured the brig *Susanna*, and the owners of the *M'Clary*, Penhallow and others, successfully brought a libel in the New Hampshire courts to have the *Susanna* declared a lawful prize.[108] The New Hampshire Superior Court affirmed the judgment.[109] In 1778, the *Susanna*'s owners, Doane and others, appealed to Congress, and in 1779, the standing committee determined that it had jurisdiction to decide the controversy.[110] In 1780, however, Congress directed that "all appeals in cases of capture, now depending before Congress, or the Commissioners of Appeals" be adjudicated by the newly created "Court of Appeals in cases of capture" established by the Articles of Confederation.[111] That court in 1783 reversed the decrees of the New Hampshire court and declared in favor of the *Susanna*'s owners.[112] In 1794, a United States circuit court decree enforced that judgment.[113] The owners of the *M'Clary* appealed on the ground that the New Hampshire courts had exclusive jurisdiction of the case.[114]

Paterson narrated the facts of the case,[115] and he then delivered the first and longest of the opinions affirming the decree of the circuit court.[116] He stated that the issue was one of the jurisdiction of the Commissioners of Appeal and the Court of Appeals, and that the issue turned upon the competency of Congress to authorize these tribunals.[117] He held that Congress possessed such authority:

> Congress was the general, supreme, and controuling council of the nation, the centre of union, the centre of force, and the sun of the political system. To determine what their powers were, we must enquire what powers they exercised. Congress raised armies, [and] fitted out a navy. . . . These high acts of sovereignty were submitted to, acquiesced in, and approved of, by the people of America. . . . In every government, whether it consists of many states, or of a few, or whether it be of a federal or consolidated nature, there must be a supreme power or will. . . . The truth is, that the States, individually, were not known nor recognized as sovereign, by foreign nations, nor are they now; the States collectively, under Congress, as the connecting point, or head, were acknowledged by foreign powers as sovereign, particularly in that acceptation of the term, which is applicable to all great national concerns. . . .[118]

Paterson also stated: "Besides, every body must be amenable to the authority under which he acts."[119] The captain of the *M'Clary* had been commissioned as a privateer by Congress.[120] Therefore, "[the captain] must ultimately be responsible to Congress, or their constituted authority.[121]

The other justices expressed a narrower view of the powers of the Continental Congress, though agreeing that the states had given to Congress external sovereignty sufficient for the present case.[122] Justice Blair noted the argument that New Hampshire could revoke the authority it had given to Congress and said that a satisfactory answer was made to this: if the state had the right, it was never exercised.[123]

An overriding issue in the early federal courts was their power to review state acts and, especially, acts of Congress.[124] Paterson had introduced the supremacy clause of the Constitution during the convention as part of the New Jersey plan.[125] In addition, Oliver Ellsworth and William Paterson had coauthored in the Senate the Judiciary Act of 1789.[126] Section 25 of that act gave to the federal judiciary not only the power to pass upon state legislation but also the power to reverse or affirm a decision of a state court passing upon the validity of an act of Congress.[127] In the April Term of 1795, Justice Paterson, sitting in the Pennsylvania District of the United States Circuit Court, met the issue judicially for the first time.[128] The *Vanhorne's Lessee* case involved conflicting claims of title to Pennsylvania land in the possession of the defendant.[129] The plaintiff based his claim on a chain of title from the proprietors of the colony; the defendant based his on the claim of settlers from Connecticut, whose title rested on a "quieting and confirming act" passed by the Pennsylvania legislature.[130] The act declared title to the land to be in the settlers and recited that those who had title to the land who will be "deprived thereof by the operation of this act" should be compensated in equivalent lands.[131]

Paterson's charge to the jury is reported.[132] The principal question he considered was the constitutionality of the quieting and confirming act.[133] Eight years before *Marbury v. Madison*,[134] Paterson delivered the following charge:

> What is a Constitution? It is the form of government, delineated by the mighty hand of the people, in which certain first principles of fundamental laws are established. The Constitution is certain and fixed; it contains the permanent will of the people, and is the supreme law of the land; it is paramount to the Power of the Legislature, and can be revoked or altered only by the authority that made it. . . . What are Legislatures? Creatures of the Constitution; they owe their existence to the Constitution; they derive their

> powers from the Constitution; It is their commission; and, therefore, all their acts must be conformable to it, or else they will be void. The Constitution is the work or will of the People themselves, in their original, sovereign, and unlimited capacity. Law is the work or will of the Legislature in their derivative and subordinate capacity. The one is the work of the Creator, and the other of the Creature. The Constitution fixes limits to the exercise of legislative authority, and prescribes the orbit within which it must move. In short, gentlemen, the Constitution is the sun of the political system, around which all Legislative, Executive and Judicial bodies must revolve. Whatever may be the case in other countries, yet in this there can be no doubt, that every act of the Legislature, repugnant to the Constitution, is absolutely void.[135]

Paterson concluded that the confirming act was void because it gave compensation for the lands taken in the form of other lands, when "[n]o just compensation can be made except in money."[136] Therefore, the act was a deprivation of "one of the natural, inherent, and unalienable rights of man"—"the right of acquiring and possessing property"—which by the Constitution of Pennsylvania "was made a fundamental law."[137] Having stated that the act was unconstitutional, Paterson went on to say that even if it were valid, the settlers had failed to comply with several of its requirements.[138] Because the act was now repealed, however, it was too late for them to establish title.[139]

It seems sufficient that this opinion or instruction stand on its own merits. In fact, there is little evidence of its impact on the country, although works on constitutional law note it as an early statement of the doctrine of judicial review.[140]

In the August 1795 Term, the Supreme Court heard two cases.[141] A long opinion by Paterson appears in *Talbot v. Jansen*.[142] The chief question raised there, although unnecessary to the eventual resolution of the case,[143] was whether a citizen of Virginia, one Ballard, had been expatriated.[144] Ballard had been commissioned as a privateer by the French and had captured a Dutch brig.[145] If he had remained a United States citizen, his commission was invalid and the capture illegal.[146]

The justices agreed that in any event, the initial outfitting of the brig in Charleston was done in violation of federal law, and hence the subsequent capture was tainted with illegality.[147] Paterson and Iredell, however, also discussed the question of expatriation and concluded that Ballard had not lost his United States citizenship.[148] One section of Paterson's opinion is noteworthy for the picture of the federal system that it presents. In rejecting the proposition that the Virginia law on expatriation could operate on United States citizenship, Paterson said:

> The sovereignties are different; the allegiance is different. . . . We have sovereignties moving within sovereignty. Of course there is complexity and difficulty in the system, which requires a penetrating eye fully to explore, and steady and masterly hands to keep in unison and order. A slight collision may disturb the harmony of the parts, and endanger the machinery of the whole.[149]

In the February Term of 1796, the important cases of *Hylton v. United States*[150] and *Ware v. Hylton*[151] were decided. The first is famous as holding that a tax on the use of carriages was not a direct tax.[152] It was also the first instance in which the Supreme Court passed upon the constitutionality of a federal law.[153] Paterson's opinion in *Hylton* was the second in series; Justice Chase had been appointed recently, and as junior member, he gave the first opinion.[154] Chase stated that the issue was whether "'[a]n act to lay duties upon carriages, for the conveyance of persons,' is unconstitutional and void. . . ."[155] The taxpayer's argument was that the tax was a direct tax, and was therefore void because it was not apportioned among the states as the Constitution required.[156] The three justices rendering opinions, Chase, Paterson, and Iredell, agreed that the tax was not direct.[157] Chase added that because it was not direct, it was unnecessary to determine "whether this court, constitutionally possesses the power to declare an act of Congress void."[158] Neither Paterson nor Iredell expressed any such doubt. At the beginning of Paterson's opinion, he stated: "If it be a direct tax, it is unconstitutional, because it has been laid pursuant to the rule of uniformity, and not to the rule of apportionment."[159]

The justices agreed that since the carriage tax would not admit of apportionment, it must be an indirect rather than a direct tax.[160] In the words of Iredell, "[I]t is evident that the Constitution contemplated none as direct but such *as could be apportioned.*"[161] Paterson, however, analyzed the nature of the tax itself:

> All taxes on expences or consumption are indirect taxes. A tax on carriages is of this kind, and of course is not a direct tax. Indirect taxes are circuitous modes of reaching the revenue of individuals, who generally live according

> to their income. In many cases of this nature the individual may be said to tax himself. I shall close the discourse with reading a passage or two from Smith's *Wealth of Nations*.[162]

Paterson then quoted Adam Smith's proposition that the state, finding it impossible to tax people directly in proportion to their revenue, does it indirectly by taxing their expenses through a levy upon the consumable commodities for which they pay out their income.[163]

In *Ware*, the second landmark case decided during the February 1796 Term, the Court declared the supremacy of the treaty power over state law and held that a clause in the treaty of 1783 providing for recovery of debts owed British creditors nullified a Virginia law that had confiscated those debts.[164] Of the four opinions, Justice Iredell's furnished the most extended discussion of the nature of the treaty power.[165] Paterson's opinion was devoted principally to the meaning of the treaty itself, ending on the note that commercial contracts should be inviolable even in wartime.[166] Paterson also stated that "[t]he construction of a treaty made . . . for the restoration and enforcement of pre-existing contracts, ought to be liberal and benign."[167]

Justice Paterson's next significant opinion appeared in *Calder v. Bull*,[168] a 1798 decision. The Connecticut legislature had passed a law setting aside a decree of the probate court, which had invalidated a will.[169] The law also granted a new trial.[170] On appeal from the new trial, which upheld the will, the Connecticut law was attacked as ex post facto.[171] The Supreme Court of Errors of Connecticut rejected this argument and affirmed the second decree.[172]

The United States Supreme Court affirmed the decision of the Connecticut court.[173] The justices agreed that only penal and criminal statutes could be ex post facto laws and that the constitutional prohibition does not extend to retroactive civil laws.[174] Chase's opinion was again the first and seems to be the most frequently cited.[175] Paterson stated that his decision was made despite "an ardent desire to have extended the provision . . . to retrospective laws in general," since such laws do not accord with "the fundamental principles of the social compact."[176] Nevertheless, he was convinced that ex post facto provisions were limited to criminal laws.[177]

*Calder* was the first case to review state legislation on a writ of error to a state court. *Ware*, which had declared a state law invalid as in conflict with the treaty power, and *Fletcher v. Peck*,[178] which was to be the first decision in which the Supreme Court held a state law violative of a provision of the federal Constitution,[179] came before the Court from federal circuit courts.[180] The *Calder* Court, in reviewing the decision of the Supreme Court of Errors of Connecticut, tacitly expressed not only the rule of *Fletcher* but also the power to review state court decisions,[181] which would be promulgated by Story in *Martin v. Hunter's Lessee*[182] and Marshall in *Cohens v. Virginia*.[183]

Paterson's contribution to this important question was not limited to his participation in *Calder*, however. The power to review state court decisions on federal questions was conferred on the Supreme Court by the twenty-fifth section of the Judiciary Act of 1789, which Ellsworth and Paterson had coauthored.[184] It was the validity of this section that was challenged and upheld in *Martin v. Hunter's Lessee* and *Cohens v. Virginia*.

There were no opinions by Paterson among the three Supreme Court decisions rendered in 1799. In 1800, Paterson gave opinions in *Cooper v. Telfair*[185] and *Bas v. Tingy*.[186] In *Cooper*, it was contended that an act of the Georgia legislature that had confiscated Cooper's estate for treason was an unconstitutional exercise of the judicial power by the legislature and also constituted a denial of the right to a trial by jury.[187] The justices found nothing in the Georgia Constitution prohibiting the act, and Paterson added:

> [W]herever the legislative power of a government is undefined it includes the judicial and executive attributes. . . . [T]he power of confiscation and banishment . . . is a power, that grows out of the very nature of the social compact, which must reside somewhere, and which is so inherent in the legislature, that it cannot be divested, or transferred, without an express provision of the constitution.[188]

In *Bas*, Congress had provided that if a ship should be recaptured from "the enemy" after being in the captor's hands for more than ninety-six hours, one-half instead of one-eighth salvage would be earned.[189] An American ship had been recaptured from the French under these conditions, but its owners claimed that France was not an "enemy" because war had not been declared.[190] The justices, including Paterson, agreed in separate opinions that the limited hostilities authorized by Congress against France qualified her as an enemy and that therefore a "limited" war was being conducted at sea.[191]

John Marshall joined the Supreme Court as chief justice in the August Term, 1801.[192] His practice of writing the opinions for the Court necessarily relegated Paterson and the other justices to a relatively obscure role.[193] On one important occasion, however, Paterson wrote the opinion for the Court, Marshall having disqualified himself. The case was *Stuart v. Laird*,[194] decided less than a week after *Marbury* in 1803. In 1802, Congress repealed the Federalists' Judiciary Act of 1801,[195] which had created sixteen new circuit court judgeships and had also relieved the Supreme Court justices of their circuit-riding duties.[196] The repealer by the Republican Congress, the Judiciary Act of 1802, was passed over the opposition's claim that Congress had no power to destroy the judgeships it had created.[197] *Stuart* decided this question.

At issue was the transfer of a case from the Fourth Circuit to the Fifth, made pursuant to the Act of 1802, which had abolished the Fourth Circuit court.[198] The appellant contended that the transfer in question could not take place because the act was unconstitutional.[199] Congress had no constitutional power to destroy the circuit courts, it was argued, if it thereby deprived a judge of his office, because the Constitution placed the federal judges beyond the reach of the legislative and executive powers.[200] The appellant also claimed that the act had unconstitutionally assigned Supreme Court justices to circuit court duty because the Constitution vested only appellate jurisdiction in the Supreme Court.[201]

Paterson wrote a very brief opinion. He dealt first with the argument raised against the transfer, and stated merely that "Congress have [sic] constitutional authority to establish from time to time such inferior tribunals as they may think proper; and to transfer a cause from one such tribunal to another."[202] The present case, he held, was nothing more than such a transfer.[203] This short rejection or avoidance of the argument raised by the Federalists not only established Congress's power in this field but disposed of an especially dangerous threat to the Court's power.[204] The Republicans were in no mood to submit to an attempt to void the act.[205]

Paterson's answer to the second argument—that the justices could not ride circuit—established an important principle of constitutional construction. He stated:

> To this objection, which is of recent date, it is sufficient to observe, that practice and acquiescence under it for a period of several years, commenc-

> ing with the organization of the judicial system, affords an irresistible answer, and has indeed fixed the construction. It is a contemporary interpretation of the most forcible nature. This practical exposition is too strong and obstinate to be shaken or controlled. Of course, the question is at rest, and ought not now to be disturbed.[206]

When Marshall disqualified himself in a few other cases, the other justices delivered opinions in series.[207] Paterson's opinions appear in these, but none of them are of special importance. Paterson voted with Marshall in *Marbury*, and he concurred in the other opinions by Marshall with one exception.[208] His relationship with Marshall appears to have been a cordial one during the period they served together. Paterson's last opinion was delivered in *Randolph v. Ware*,[209] the last case reported for the February Term, 1806. His was the longest and most detailed of the separate opinions, which dealt with a breach of a promise to insure.[210]

## *Conclusion*

The title page of Cranch's report for the February Term of 1807 lists a new justice, Brockholst Livingston, appointed "in the place of the honourable WILLIAM PATERSON, deceased."[211] Paterson had become ill during the summer recess.[212] He died on September 9, 1806.[213]

William Paterson's thirteen years on the Supreme Court capped, in a quiet way, the great work and themes of his political life. There was, first, the new system of national power, with the states operating as "sovereignties within a sovereignty." Paterson consistently supported an extensive national power. Although the states retained the inherent powers of government, they remained subject to federal law. Thus, the doctrines of judicial review of state laws and of acts of Congress were necessary elements of national sovereignty and constitutional government. Behind Paterson's constitutional theories of power and sovereignty was a constant awareness of the principle upon which the Revolution had been fought and the Constitution established: the compact or consent of the people. The Constitution was the supreme law of the land not because it said so but because the people had created it. "What is a Constitution?" Paterson asked the jury in *Vanhorne's Lessee*.[214] "It is the form of government, delineated by the mighty hand of the people, in which certain first principles of fundamental laws are established."[215]

Paterson's devotion to law, property, authority, and stability and his Federalist view of the judicial role were tempered, one thinks on reading his opinions, by his experience at constitution making in New Jersey and in the Constitutional Convention of 1787. The Constitution, he continued in *Vanhorne's Lessee*, "is the work or will of the People themselves, in their original, sovereign, and unlimited capacity. . . . In short, gentlemen, the Constitution is the sun of the political system, around which all Legislative, Executive and Judicial bodies must revolve."[216] Thus, for William Paterson, no branch of government, including the judicial, was master of the Constitution.[217] The Constitution belonged to the people in their sovereign capacity.

## NOTES

1. J. O'Connor, *William Paterson: Lawyer and Statesman, 1745–1806* 224 (1979).
2. See M. Farrand, *The Framing of the Constitution of the United States* 84–86, 200 (1913); C. Rossiter, *1787: The Grand Convention* 175–76 (1966); C. Warren, *The Making of the Constitution* 220–32 (1937).
3. 1 J. Goebel, Jr., *History of the Supreme Court of the United States: Antecedents and Beginnings to 1801* 457–508 (1971).
4. See J. O'Connor, supra note 1, at 7–19; C. Rossiter, supra note 2, at 99.
5. J. O'Connor, supra note 1, at 28.
6. Id. at 32.
7. Id. at 33–34.
8. Id. at 59–61.
9. Id. at 18–19, 48–55.
10. M. Farrand, supra note 2, at 84–85.
11. See C. Warren, supra note 2, at 719.
12. J. O'Connor, supra note 1, at 134.
13. Id. at 47–49.
14. Id. at 50, 100.
15. Id. at 45–55.
16. Id. at 71, 77, 84.
17. Id. at 133–34.
18. Id. at 131. See generally J. Pomfret, *Colonial New Jersey* 218–46 (1973) (explaining social and political atmosphere in New Jersey prior to the Revolution).

19. See generally C. Rossiter, supra note 2, at 159–81; C. Warren, supra note 2, at 134–200.

20. See C. Rossiter, supra note 2, at 175–79; C. Warren, supra note 2, at 199, 220–31.

21. C. Rossiter, supra note 2, at 186. See generally C. Warren, supra note 2, at 267–312.

22. *Talbot v. Jansen*, 3 U.S. (3 Dall.) 133, 154 (1795) (opinion of Paterson, J.).

23. I. Brant, *James Madison: Father of the Constitution 1787–1800* 65 (1950).

24. See J. O'Connor, supra note 1, at 135–36; see also I. Brant, supra note 23, at 65 (noting problem of trade for New Jersey and Connecticut).

25. I. Brant, supra note 23, at 61.

26. See C. Rossiter, supra note 2, at 99, 101–9, 117–26.

27. C. Warren, supra note 2, at 146–219; see C. Rossiter, supra note 2, at 171–73.

28. J. O'Connor, supra note 1, at 138.

29. Id.

30. C. Warren, supra note 1, at 138.

31. 1 *The Records of the Federal Convention of 1787* 179–80 (M. Farrand ed. 1911) [hereafter cited as 1 *Records*] (Madison's notes); see also id. at 185–91 (Paterson's notes of his speech).

32. Id. at 183; C. Warren, supra note 2, at 200.

33. 1 *Records*, supra note 31, at 192–94. See generally C. Warren, supra note 2, at 207–12.

34. 1 *Records*, supra note 31, at 238–39.

35. M. Farrand, supra note 2, at 84–85.

36. Id.

37. See 1 *Records*, supra note 31, at 242–45.

38. C. Warren, supra note 2, at 231–32.

39. See generally 1 *Records*, supra note 31, at 248–322.

40. C. Rossiter, supra note 2, at 176.

41. Id. at 182–84; C. Warren, supra note 2, at 236–45. See generally 1 *Records*, supra note 31, at 334–435.

42. C. Warren, supra note 2, at 245–47.

43. Id. at 249.

44. 1 *Records*, supra note 31, at 468.

45. C. Warren, supra note 2, at 255; see 1 *Records*, supra note 31, at 468–69.

46. M. Farrand, supra note 2, at 96–98.

47. J. O'Connor, supra note 1, at 153.

48. 1 *Records*, supra note 31, at 516; C. Rossiter, supra note 2, at 187; C. Warren, supra note 2, at 264.

49. M. Farrand, supra note 2, at 99; 1 *Records*, supra note 31, at 526.

50. See generally C. Warren, supra note 2, at 274–308.

51. Id.

52. 2 *The Records of the Federal Convention of 1787* 15 (M. Farrand ed. 1911) [hereafter cited as 2 *Records*].

53. Id. at 17–18.

54. J. O'Connor, supra note 1, at 156–58.

55. Id. at 158; C. Rossiter, supra note 2, at 194–95.

56. See C. Rossiter, supra note 2, at 192–94; C. Warren, supra note 2, at 313.

57. 4 *The Records of the Federal Convention of 1787* 70 (M. Farrand rev. ed. 1937) [hereafter cited as 4 *Records*]; see J. O'Connor, supra note 1, at 160.

58. See J. O'Connor, supra note 1, at 160–61.

59. C. Warren, supra note 2, at 719. Once the small states like New Jersey had won equality, they were strong supporters of national power. See C. Rossiter, supra note 2, at 196; see also C. Warren, supra note 2, at 310 n.1 (quoting Letter from James Madison to Martin Van Buren, (May 13, 1828).

60. Madison's notes have Paterson as saying, in debate with Madison and Gouverneur Morris on July 7, "For himself he should vote [against] the Report, because it yields too much." 1 *Records*, supra note 31, at 551. King's notes also report Paterson as saying, "I think I shall vote [against] the Report." Id. at 554. In any event, Paterson's words appear in the context to be a debating tactic.

Paterson's July 16 tactics on adjournment are cited by Warren and seem to have influenced Rossiter, who quotes the entire exchange. See C. Rossiter, supra note 2, at 194–95; C. Warren, supra note 2, at 311–12; see also supra notes 53–55 and accompanying text. O'Connor, however, correctly reads this as maneuvers by Randolph to upset the compromise and by Paterson to protect it. See J. O'Connor, supra note 1, at 156–58.

61. J. O'Connor, supra note 1, at 160; 4 *Records*, supra note 57, at 70.

62. 4 *Records*, supra 57, at 73; see J. O'Connor, supra note 1, at 161.

63. Clinton Rossiter, appraising each of the Framers, calls Paterson "the stubborn and successful advocate of state equality, whose departure in late July may have robbed him of a much higher ranking." C. Rossiter, supra note 2, at 250. Paterson, Rossiter says, "set some sort of record for stubborn courage." Id. at 205.

64. Rossiter notes that the Constitution and its federal structure were at stake in the battle between "prideful Virginia and tenacious New Jersey." Id.

65. See L. Rosenberg, *The Political Thought of William Paterson* 43–50, 180 (1967). Rosenberg emphasizes the influence of Locke. Id.; see also 12 W. Holdsworth, *A History of English Law* 712 (1938) (noting Blackstone's influence in the American colonies).

66. C. Warren, supra note 2, at 768.

67. J. O'Connor, supra note 1, at 167–68.

68. Id. at 168.

69. Id. at 168.

70. Id.

71. Id. at 170.

72. See Warren, "New Light on the History of the Federal Judiciary Act of 1789," 37 *Harv. L. Rev.* 49, 50–51, 60 (1923); see also 1 J. Goebel, Jr., supra note 3, at 463–65. Goebel believes that the manuscript discovered by Warren must be distinguished from an undiscovered "final version" from which the bill was then reprinted. Id. at 465. Goebel's comparison of the actual draft and the printed bill does show a few small differences. See id. at 465–66 n.28. For a reproduction of the first page of Paterson's handwritten draft, see id. at 464.

73. See F. Frankfurter & J. Landis, *The Business of the Supreme Court* 4 (1927).

74. 1 J. Goebel, Jr., supra note 3, at 459; J. O'Connor, supra note 1, at 169–71; 1 C. Warren, *The Supreme Court in United States History* 8–9 (1922).

75. 1 J. Goebel, Jr., supra note 3, at 458–59.

76. Warren, supra note 72, at 50.

77. 1 J. Goebel, Jr., supra note 3, at 459.

78. Id. at 469.

79. Id.; see also id. at 464 (Paterson's handwritten manuscript).

80. F. Frankfurter & J. Landis, supra note 73, at 10.

81. Id. at 7–11. For a summary and appraisal of the act, see P. Bator, P. Mishkin, D. Shapiro, & H. Wechsler, *Hart and Wechsler's The Federal Courts and the Federal System* 32–36 (2d ed. 1973).

82. See 1 J. Goebel, Jr., supra note 3, at 471.

83. See Judiciary Act of 1789, ch. 20, sec. 9, 1 Stat. 73, 76–77.

84. See id. sec. 11, 1 Stat. at 78–79. See generally F. Frankfurter & J. Landis, supra note 73, at 12.

85. Judiciary Act of 1789, ch. 20, sec. 25, 1 Stat. 73, 85–86 (current version at 28 U.S.C. sec. 1257 (1982)).

86. M. Farrand, supra note 2, at 85.

87. 1 J. Goebel, Jr., supra note 3, at 480–81; 1 C. Warren, supra note 74, at 10–11.

88. L. Tribe, *American Constitutional Law*, sec. 3-4, at 27 (1978); see G. Gunther, *Constitutional Law* 29 (11th ed. 1985).

89. *Martin v. Hunter's Lessee*, 14 U.S. (1 Wheat.) 304, 342 (1816).

90. Judiciary Act of 1789, ch. 20, sec. 34, 1 Stat. 73, 92. Section 34 was not in the bill as drafted. It was, however, introduced in the Senate debate. Its original version was in Ellsworth's hand, as Charles Warren discovered. 1 J. Goebel, Jr., supra note 3, at 502 & n.149.

91. F. Frankfurter & J. Landis, supra note 73, at 4.

92. J. O'Connor, supra note 1, at xii, 185.

93. Id. at 223. As governor and chancellor of New Jersey, Paterson undertook

a complete compilation and revision of New Jersey statutory law; he completed the work while on the Supreme Court. See id. at 202–22.

94. See id. at 278.

95. Id. at 238.

96. 1 C. Warren, supra note 74, at 140.

97. J. O'Connor, supra note 1, at 260.

98. *United States v. Vigol*, 2 U.S. (2 Dall.) 346 (Paterson, Circuit Justice 1795); *United States v. Mitchell*, 2 U.S. (2 Dall.) 348 (Paterson, Circuit Justice 1795).

99. 1 J. Goebel, Jr., supra note 3, at 638–39; 1 C. Warren, supra note 74, at 164–65; see F. Wharton, *State Trials of the United States During the Administrations of Washington and Adams* 333–44, 684–87 (Philadelphia 1849). See generally Sedition Act, ch. 74, 1 Stat. 596 (1798) (repealed 1801); Alien Enemies Act, ch. 66, 1 Stat. 577 (1798) (repealed 1801).

100. See *United States v. Vigol*, 2 U.S. (2 Dall.) 346, 346–47 (Paterson, Circuit Justice 1795); *United States v. Mitchell*, 2 U.S. (2 Dall.) 348, 355–56 (Paterson, Circuit Justice 1795). See generally L. Baldwin, *Whiskey Rebels* 262–64 (1939); Hurst, "Treason in the United States," 58 *Harv. L. Rev.* 226 (1944).

101. See 1 J. Goebel, Jr., supra note 3, at 637–39; F. Wharton, supra note 99, at 334–42, 684–87.

102. See 1 J. Goebel, Jr., supra note 3, at 722–93; 1 C. Warren, supra note 74, at 31, 65–84, 91–168. But see G. Haskins & H. Johnson, *History of the Supreme Court of the United States: Foundations of Power: John Marshall, 1801–15* 7, 13–14 (1981). Haskins and Johnson term the early Court "[a] relatively feeble institution," ascribing its real beginning to Marshall. Id. Nonetheless, they also state that "[b]y this date [1801], the Supreme Court had already upheld and extended Federalist principles of nationalization and centralization; and under Marshall's leadership it would continue much further in that direction." Id. at 147.

103. 2 U.S. (2 Dall.) 304 (Paterson, Circuit Justice 1795).

104. 1 C. Warren, supra note 74, at 65. Confidence in the federal bench had eroded as a result of *Chisholm v. Georgia*, 2 U.S. (2 Dall.) 419 (1793). That case upheld the right of a citizen of South Carolina to sue the state of Georgia. Id. at 479 (opinion of Jay, C.J.). The *Chisholm* rule was promptly repealed by a constitutional amendment. See U.S. Const. amend. XI. See generally 1 C. Warren, supra note 74, at 91–99.

105. 3 U.S. (3 Dall.) 54 (1795).

106. The Court also decided *United States v. Lawrence*, 3 U.S. (3 Dall.) 42 (1795), and *Bingham v. Cabbot*, 3 U.S. (3 Dall.) 19 (1795), during that Term.

107. *Penhallow*, 3 U.S. (3 Dall.) at 60.

108. Id. at 60–61.

109. Id. at 61.

110. Id.

111. Id. at 62.
112. Id.
113. Id. at 64.
114. Id.
115. See id. at 54–66.
116. See id. at 79–89 (opinion of Paterson, J.).
117. Id. at 79–80 (opinion of Paterson, J.).
118. Id. at 80–81 (opinion of Paterson, J.).
119. Id. at 81 (opinion of Paterson, J.).
120. Id.
121. Id. Goebel comments that "Paterson, who knew very well what the actual political conditions had been, was evidently transported by his own rhetoric." 1 J. Goebel, Jr., supra note 3, at 768.
122. See, e.g., *Penhallow*, 3 U.S. (3 Dall.) at 94–95 (opinion of Iredell, J.).
123. Id. at 112–13 (opinion of Blair, J.). Paterson's view of sovereignty played a role in the case of *United States v. Curtiss-Wright Export Corp.*, 299 U.S. 304 (1936). Justice Sutherland's opinion drew upon Paterson's *Penhallow* opinion for the doctrine that in the foreign relations field, the federal government possesses inherent rather than enumerated powers. Id. at 316–17, 319. The argument made was that a congressional resolution authorizing the president to declare an arms embargo constituted an unconstitutional delegation of legislative power. Id. at 314. Sutherland answered by stating that the proposition that the government can exercise only such express and implied powers as are granted to it applies only to internal affairs. Id. at 315–16. But see 1 J. Goebel, Jr., supra note 3, at 768 & n.29 (Supreme Court's argument in *Curtiss-Wright* was "historically indefensible").
124. See 1 J. Goebel, Jr., supra note 3, at 589–92; 2 G. Haskins & H. Johnson, supra note 102, at 186–91. According to Goebel, this power was not questioned in the earliest years. See 1 J. Goebel, Jr., supra note 3, at 590.
125. J. O'Connor, supra note 1, at 146; see supra notes 28–40 and accompanying text.
126. See supra notes 71–74 and accompanying text.
127. See supra notes 85–89 and accompanying text.
128. See *Vanhorne's Lessee v. Dorrance*, 2 U.S. (2 Dall.) 304 (Paterson, Circuit Justice 1795).
129. Id. at 304–5.
130. Id. at 304–7.
131. Id. at 313. For the earlier history of the dispute, see 1 J. Goebel, Jr., supra note 3, at 188–94. See also L. Rosenberg, supra note 65, at 165–66, 181. One author described the controversy as "[a] few wealthy Philadelphia land speculators with paper titles in their pockets . . . arrayed against several thousand small farmers who had brought schools, churches, and settlements to the upper Susquehanna." Boyd, "William Paterson, Forerunner of John Marshall," in *The Lives of*

*Eighteen from Princeton* 16 (W. Thorp ed. 1946). The dispute had been dragging on for twenty-five years and was extremely bitter. Id.

132. See *Vanhorne's Lessee*, 2 U.S. (2 Dall.) at 307–20.

133. See id. at 307–16.

134. 5 U.S. (1 Cranch) 137 (1803).

135. *Vanhorne's Lessee*, 2 U.S. (2 Dall.) at 308.

136. Id. at 315; see id. at 316.

137. Id. at 310.

138. Id. at 317–18.

139. Id. at 319–20.

140. E.g., 1 J. Goebel, Jr., supra note 3, at 590; 1 C. Warren, supra note 74, at 69. Boyd says that the landowners who filled the courtroom printed Paterson's charge in pamphlet form and distributed it throughout the nation. Boyd, supra note 131, at 17. Goebel confirms this. 1 J. Goebel, Jr., supra note 3, at 590 & n.177.

141. *Talbot v. Jansen*, 3 U.S. (3 Dall.) 133 (1795); *United States v. Peters*, 3 U.S. (3 Dall.) 121 (1795).

142. 3 U.S. (3 Dall.) 133 (1795).

143. Id. at 169 (opinion of Rutledge, C.J.).

144. Id. at 152–53 (opinion of Paterson, J.).

145. Id. at 133–34.

146. See id.

147. Id. at 154–55 (opinion of Paterson, J.).

148. Id. at 152–54 (opinion of Paterson, J.); see id. at 161–65 (opinion of Iredell, J.). Justice Iredell discussed the expatriation of the plaintiff, William Talbot. Id.

149. Id. at 154 (opinion of Paterson, J.).

150. 3 U.S. (3 Dall.) 171 (1796) [hereafter cited as *Hylton*].

151. 3 U.S. (3 Dall.) 199 (1796) [hereafter cited as *Ware*].

152. *Hylton*, 3 U.S. (3 Dall.) at 1809 (opinion of Paterson, J.).

153. 1 C. Warren, supra note 74, at 147.

154. *Hylton*, 3 U.S. (3 Dall.) at 172–75 (opinion of Chase, J.).

155. Id. at 172 (opinion of Chase, J.).

156. Id. at 172–73 (opinion of Chase, J.).

157. Id. at 175 (opinion of Chase, J.); id. at 180 (opinion of Paterson, J.); id. at 183 (opinion of Iredell, J.).

158. Id. at 175 (opinion of Chase, J.).

159. Id. at 176 (opinion of Paterson, J.).

160. Id. at 181 (opinion of Iredell, J.).

161. Id.

162. Id. at 180 (opinion of Paterson, J.).

163. Id. at 180–81 (opinion of Paterson, J.). "Paterson had been present at the

Federal Convention when the rule of apportionment of taxes as well as representation was decided. He was thus qualified to speak with some assurance about the intentions of that body." 1 J. Goebel, Jr., supra note 3, at 781. In his opinion in *Hylton*, Paterson also said: "It is not necessary to determine, whether a tax on the product of land be a direct or indirect tax. Perhaps, the immediate product of land, in its original and crude state, ought to be considered as the land itself. . . . Land independently of its produce, is of no value." *Hylton*, 3 U.S. (3 Dall.) at 176–77 (opinion of Paterson, J.).

Justice Fuller's opinion in the income tax case, *Pollock v. Farmers' Loan & Trust Co.*, 157 U.S. 429, aff'd on reh'g, 158 U.S. 601 (1895), quoted this, and Fuller appears to have relied heavily upon Paterson's notion that land and its product are identical in order to justify his holding that a tax on the income from land is a direct tax on the land itself. Id. at 581, 583. Fuller stated: "This law taxes the income received from land and the growth or produce of the land. Justice Paterson observed in *Hylton's* case 'land, independently of its produce, is on no value;' and certainly had no thought that direct taxes were confined to unproductive land." Id. at 581 (quoting *Hylton*, 3 U.S. (3 Dall.) at 177 (opinion of Paterson, J.)). The dissenting opinion in *Pollock*, however, pointed out that Paterson had also stated that he "never entertained a doubt that the principal . . . objects that the framers of the Constitution contemplated as falling within the rule of apportionment were a capitation tax and a tax on land." Id. at 644 (Harlan, J., dissenting) (quoting *Hylton*, 3 U.S. (3 Dall.) at 177 (opinion of Paterson, J.)).

164. *Ware*, 3 U.S. (3 Dall.) at 244–45 (opinion of Chase, J.).

165. Id. at 271–79 (opinion of Iredell, J.).

166. Id. at 255 (opinion of Paterson, J.).

167. Id. at 256 (opinion of Paterson, J.).

168. 3 U.S. (3 Dall.) 386 (1798).

169. Id. at 386 (opinion of Chase, J.).

170. Id.

171. Id. at 386–87 (opinion of Chase, J.).

172. Id. at 386–87 (opinion of Chase, J.)

173. Id. at 401.

174. See id. at 390–91 (opinion of Chase, J.); id. at 397 (opinion of Paterson, J.); id. at 399 (opinion of Iredell, J.).

175. See, e.g., 1 J. Goebel, Jr., supra note 3, at 704–5.

176. Id. at 397 (opinion of Paterson, J.).

177. Id.

178. 10 U.S. (6 Cranch) 87 (1810).

179. See id. at 139.

180. See id. at 87; *Ware*, 3 U.S. (3 Dall.) at 199.

181. *Calder*, 3 U.S. (3 Dall.) at 399 (opinion of Iredell, J.).

182. 14 U.S. (1 Wheat.) 304 (1816).

183. 19 U.S. (6 Wheat.) 264 (1821).

184. See supra notes 85–89 and accompanying text. Paterson's coauthorship of the Judiciary Act has had more effect than all of his decisions. Warren quotes John C. Calhoun as stating that without the Judiciary Act of 1789, the entire course of the federal government would have been altered. 1 C. Warren, supra note 74, at 18.

185. 4 U.S. (4 Dall.) 14 (1800).

186. 4 U.S. (4 Dall.) 37 (1800).

187. See *Cooper*, 4 U.S. (4 Dall.) at 16–17.

188. Id. at 19 (opinion of Paterson, J.).

189. *Bas*, 4 U.S. (4 Dall.) at 37; see act of Mar. 2, 1799, ch. 24, sec. 7, 1 Stat. 709, 716 (repealed 1800).

190. *Bas*, 4 U.S. (4 Dall.) at 38.

191. Id. at 43 (opinion of Chase, J.); see id. at 45–46 (opinion of Paterson, J.).

192. See *Talbot v. Seeman*, 5 U.S. (1 Cranch) 1 (1801).

193. 2 G. Haskins & H. Johnson, supra note 102, at 105, 382–86.

194. 5 U.S. (1 Cranch) 299 (1803). Marshall had decided the case below. Id. at 308.

195. 2 G. Haskins & H. Johnson, supra note 102, at 163–68.

196. See id. at 122–33.

197. Id. at 163–68. The argument of the Federalists resulted in the famous debate in Congress over the power of the Supreme Court to review acts of Congress. 1 C. Warren, supra note 74, at 215–22.

198. *Stuart*, 5 U.S. (1 Cranch) at 302–3.

199. Id. at 303.

200. Id. at 304.

201. Id. at 305.

202. Id. at 309.

203. Id.

204. See 2 G. Haskins & H. Johnson, supra note 102, at 217, 650; 1 C. Warren, supra note 74, at 269–73.

205. See 1 C. Warren, supra note 74, at 269–73.

206. *Stuart*, 5 U.S. (1 Cranch) at 309.

207. See 2 G. Haskins & H. Johnson, supra note 102, at 382–86.

208. *Simms v. Slacum*, 7 U.S. (3 Cranch) 300, 309–11 (1806) (Paterson, J., dissenting).

209. 7 U.S. (3 Cranch) 503 (1806).

210. See id. at 510–13 (opinion of Paterson, J.).

211. 8 U.S. (4 Cranch) xiii (1807).

212. J. O'Connor, supra note 1, at 278.

213. Id. at xiii.

214. *Van Horne's Lessee*, 2 U.S. (2 Dall.) at 308.

215. Id.

216. Id.

217. See 2 G. Haskins & H. Johnson, supra note 102, at 650. *Marbury v. Madison* and *Stuart v. Laird* "presaged the development of a full-scale concept of rule of law and a deep-seated respect for the primacy of legislative power as well as for the concept of separation of powers." Id.

## Chapter 9

# The Verdict on Samuel Chase and His "Apologist"

*Stephen B. Presser*

Was the appointment of Samuel Chase to the United States Supreme Court "one of the most regrettable nominations in the Court's history,"[1] or did his jurisprudence make an important and positive contribution to the development of the young republic? Until recently, virtually every historian of the early Court dismissed Chase as the "bad boy" of the Ellsworth Court[2]—a rabid partisan, a bully, an American Jeffreys, or worse. He was, of course, the only United States Supreme Court justice ever to be impeached, and though the impeachment did not result in his removal from office by the Senate because the required two-thirds majority could not be cobbled together, a majority of senators did vote to convict him on some of the charges. At least one prominent reviewer of Chase's record, Raoul Berger, has flatly declared that the Senate should have thrown him off the bench.[3]

One can often make a lot of money in the stock market by doing what everyone else is not, and, similarly, young academics seek often to make splashes by writing revisionist works. So it has been with me and Samuel Chase. No one, I figured, when I *was* young, and when I began writing the legal history of the Third Circuit,[4] for which Chase served one important term as circuit justice, could have been as bad as Chase was then made out to be. Moreover, there had been times in our history when he appeared to be highly regarded,[5] and I thought that this made him a ripe candidate for a revisionist work. I finally published the book-length work in 1991, *The Original Misunder-*

*standing: The English, The Americans, and the Dialectic of Federalist Jurisprudence*, and, as befits a revisionist effort, it garnered a variety of interesting responses.

I thought I would use this forum, then, not only to describe the work of Chase but to examine and reply to the critics of my book in the hope that such an effort might further contribute to the ongoing assessment of the early republic's Supreme Court and its most controversial judicial figure. In what follows I will begin by setting forth Samuel Chase's relevant biographical facts, and I will go on to present the assertions I made evaluating his career, reviewers' responses to those assertions, and what all of this suggests with regard to conclusions to be drawn about constitutional jurisprudence on the pre-Marshall Court, about the character and value of Samuel Chase, about the perils of working the intersection of law and history, and about future avenues that scholars might profitably pursue.

## *The Facts*

Samuel Chase of Maryland (b.1741–d.1811; associate justice of the United States Supreme Court, 1796–1811) signed the Declaration of Independence, served in the Revolutionary War Congress, and served as a judge on the Maryland bench as well as the federal judiciary.[6] His political and judicial career was constantly the subject of criticism and controversy, flowing from two undeniable facts. First, he had a personally rough manner, he denounced in no uncertain terms those who disagreed with him, he was not given gladly to suffering fools, and his hair-trigger temper could be easily ignited by those who sought to discredit or embarrass him. Second, there was admittedly much with which his critics had to work. There was at least the appearance (if not the reality) of impropriety in his financial dealings, at least early in his career. He appears to have profited from his state legislative service through his participation in the issuance of paper money in Maryland, and from his congressional service by speculating in the flour futures market at a time when he may have known that Congress was going to make significant wartime orders for bread.[7] His political associations, say his critics,[8] turned more on personal advantage than philosophical conviction, with the best evidence being perhaps that he was a strong and vocal opponent of the federal Constitution, but, once the document had been approved, he quickly sought appointment to the new federal government.

It was not uncommon for the leading men of late-eighteenth-century America to profit from their public service, to, as it were, do well by doing good—even John Marshall was not above engaging in this art[9]—but Chase appears to have gone a bit beyond the norm.[10] Nevertheless, if we are about the business of judging his jurisprudential contribution and not simply of seeking to single him out for censure because of his business dealings, it is what he did as a Supreme Court justice that will determine in what regard we ought ultimately to hold him. There is much in his judicial record that shows proof of at least his brilliance, if not his true eminence.[11]

For example, in his maiden Supreme Court opinion in *Ware v. Hylton* (1796),[12] the longest of the four seriatim opinions delivered by the justices in the case, Chase engaged in an exhaustive study of civilian treatises on the law of nations to solve an exceptionally politically sensitive constitutional problem. A Virginia statute passed in 1777 had directed that debts due to British creditors could be obliterated by paying them into the loan office in Virginia (in grossly depreciated Virginia currency), but this conflicted with a provision in the Treaty of Paris. That pact, which ended the Revolutionary War, and which was signed in 1783, provided that no legal impediments would be permitted to defeat the claims of British creditors against American debtors, and that those debts were payable in sterling. In *Ware* a British creditor, relying on the treaty and the supremacy clause of the United States Constitution, sought to collect a debt allegedly discharged by the Virginia statute of 1777. The Virginia debtor's position, that the Virginia statute was a valid exercise in state sovereignty that the federal treaty could not override, was argued before the Supreme Court by none other than John Marshall. Marshall's argument was rejected by Chase and his fellows, however.

In his *Ware* opinion, which reflected not only exhaustive study of the relevant treatises but also the theory of popular sovereignty, Chase held that the plain meaning of the treaty and the supremacy clause governed, and that even though Virginia possessed the power to nullify the debt in 1777, the treaty in 1783 had reinstated it. Chase noted that the effect of his decision was to make the debtor liable to paying twice (since he had already paid into the Virginia loan office and was now liable to pay a second time, to the British creditor), but that the debtor had a claim for just compensation under the Constitution. Chase's opinion was a "tour de force"[13] that not only rested on the law of nations, the construction of treaties, and the nature of popular sovereignty but also drew heavily on the concept of "justice" itself. His opinion also has been taken by commentators to have performed the valuable service of settling the question of whether the supremacy clause would be construed by the courts as meaning what it said, or whether exceptions would be carved out to meet the political demands of powerful states.[14]

In his most widely quoted Supreme Court opinion, that in *Calder v. Bull* (1798),[15] Chase explored what might be regarded as the natural-law basis for the federal Constitution.[16] In that case he explained that there were some supraconstitutional principles that circumscribed any legislature, whether or not such principles had been explicitly spelled out in the written fundamental law. Chase gave only two examples in his opinion—making a person judge and party in his or her own case, and taking A's property and giving it to B without any compensation to A—but his work has been taken to have established the doctrine now referred to as "substantive due process," the reading into the Fifth or Fourteenth Amendment's "due process" clause guarantees of particular rights or liberties not expressly found elsewhere in the Constitution, rights or liberties generally drawn from some sort of conception of natural-law theory.[17]

This sort of approach to constitutional law, recently favored by many advocates of "liberal" constitutional theory, has always been opposed in our history by judicial conservatives, who have maintained that "strict construction" or "original intent" is more of a certain guide to appropriate constitutional interpretation. Curiously, however, Chase is also one of the founders of the "strict constructionist" approach. While Chase may have been revealing a belief in natural law in *Calder v. Bull*, he apparently thought that the natural-law basis for constitutional jurisprudence was a very limited one. Many, if not all of his Federalist fellows believed that the natural-law basis of the federal government was broad enough to include the jurisdiction to punish crimes that had not yet been prohibited by federal statute, but in one of his most notable opinions while riding circuit, that in *United States v. Worrall* (1798),[18] Chase became the only late-eighteenth-century federal judge to reject this theory of the "federal common law of crimes." The argument of the champions of the federal common law of crimes was that any government had a sort of natural right to self-defense, and thus the federal government could punish crimes such as bribery or seditious libel even before Congress prohibited such particular conduct by means of a specific statute. Chase apparently believed that these matters of the criminal law were more policy choices than they were immutable principles and, consequently, that for the federal courts to punish crimes without statutes would create too much uncertainty and injustice in the law. His view on this point was eventually upheld by the Supreme Court, in the early nineteenth century.

Riding on circuit, Chase also relied in his opinions on the principle of judicial review to declare unconstitutional acts of Congress void, the principle later famously brought to national attention in Marshall's opinion in *Marbury v. Madison* (1803). The most important such instance was in the *Callender* trial of 1800, discussed below, a federal prosecution for seditious libel when the defendants' lawyers sought to get the jury to reject the Federalist statute as unconstitutional. Chase carefully borrowed arguments from Hamilton's *Federalist* 78 to demonstrate that only the judges—and not the jury—could declare a law void because it went beyond constitutional limits. Marshall was reported to have been in the audience during Chase's pronouncement on judicial review in *Callender*, and to have adopted some of Chase's language for use in *Marbury*.

Once he joined the Federalist bench, Chase made pronouncements that clearly indicated that he had become a political as well as a judicial conservative. He found himself impeached by the Jeffersonians as a result of his presiding over several criminal trials and proceedings in which he sought to implement the Adams administration's attempts to silence what it believed to be destructive and dangerous attacks on the government by rebels and mendacious critics. These trials occurred in Pennsylvania and Virginia when Chase rode circuit in 1800. Most important, perhaps, in Pennsylvania he presided over the second trial of John Fries, a leader in the "Fries Rebellion" or "Hot Water War," an uprising over federal taxes in eastern Pennsylvania. Before the trial began, Chase distributed a written opinion to counsel and jury in which he stated that he would not permit citation or discussion of English constructive treason cases. Chase's objective was to forestall the defense from using English abuses to discredit the federal prosecutors' attempt to construe American treason law to include armed resistance to federal tax officials. Their defense strategy foreclosed, Fries's counsel stormed off the case, claiming Chase deprived their client of his rights to argue law to the jury. This became the first of the impeachment charges brought against Chase. Chase's defense was that the law was the law, it was the judge's job to say what the law was, and no defendant had the right to try to mislead the jury on the law.

The two other most notable 1800 circuit cases involved alleged violations of the Federalists' seditious libel statute passed in 1798. In the Pennsylvania Circuit trial of Thomas Cooper, Chase, when the defendant raised truth as a defense, applied English civil libel rules and required the defendant to prove truth "beyond a marrow." Since Cooper's assertions—that the United States had a standing army, that President Adams paid too high a rate of interest during peacetime, and that President Adams improperly interfered in a judicial proceeding involving a murder suspect[19]—could have been construed as matters of opinion that might have gone either way, putting a severe burden of proving truth on Cooper probably ensured his conviction. On the other hand, at least some of Cooper's charges were demonstrably false,[20] and, under the terms of the statute at least, his conviction was probably not a miscarriage of justice. For this reason, although Cooper's case has provided fodder for Chase's critics, it was not made a part of the impeachment proceedings against him.

This was not the case for the other notable seditious libel prosecution over which Chase presided, the 1800 trial of James Thomson Callender in Virginia. Callender, who was perhaps charitably described as a "little reptile," and who was once ejected from the Virginia legislature for being covered with lice and filth, had written an over-the-top book critical of President Adams, the mildest comment of which was probably that Adams was "a hoary-headed incendiary."[21] According to most accounts, Chase was handed Callender's book by his friend Luther Martin (who was to be his principal defense lawyer at the impeachment) when he began the trek by stage to Virginia, he was enraged by what he read, and when he got to Virginia he manipulated the grand jury to secure Callender's indictment. This story is probably apocryphal, at least insofar as it suggests Chase demanded that no Jeffersonian sympathizers be allowed on the grand jury,[22] but it was Chase's conduct at the trial itself, of which we have a clear record, that was to provide some of the most serious impeachment charges against him.

Callender had been indicted on nineteen counts of violation of the seditious libel statute. His lawyers, three aggressive Jeffersonians, after having failed to convince Chase to postpone the trial for a year to allow them to gather more evidence (Chase said that they had failed to demonstrate a need for delay, although he apparently offered a postponement of one month, which they declined) chose to defend Callender by arguing the truth of only one of the charges, and, as indicated above, by trying to get the jury to throw out the federal statute as unconstitutional. In hindsight, it seems clear that they were far more interested in scoring political points off Chase than they were in defending their hapless client.[23] Most probably sensing what was going on, Chase was condescending in his treatment of the three, whom he referred to as "young gentlemen," refused their only offer of evidence on the probably correct ground that it was of dubious relevance and prejudicial,[24] and, as also indicated earlier, refused to allow them to make the constitutionality argument to the jury, on the grounds that constitutionality, as a matter of law, was for the judge, not the jury. Callender's lawyers, as had Fries's lawyers before them (one wonders whether they were imitating the latter's tactics) stormed off the case. Callender, as Fries had been, was convicted.

At Chase's trial on the impeachment charges, John Randolph, the fiery manager for the prosecution, sought to portray Chase's conduct in the Callender trial as that of a zealous partisan hell-bent on Callender's conviction. Although John Marshall waffled somewhat when he was a witness in defense of Chase's trial conduct, Chase and his lawyers did a fair job of demonstrating that his rulings were in accordance with an orthodox understanding of the law of evidence and the Constitution, and that while he was guilty of being irritated by counsel and what he believed to be their inappropriate arguments, he had violated no law, and thus committed no impeachable offense.

In other moves that undoubtedly sparked the interest of those who sought to remove him from the bench, Chase had unsuccessfully sought to convince Marshall that the Jeffersonians' elimination of the position of circuit judges (the famous "midnight judges," appointed pursuant to the 1801 Judiciary Act passed in the waning hours of the Adams administration)[25] should be ruled unconstitutional and reversed. The final event that triggered his impeachment, however, happened during the early years of Jefferson's administration, when, having failed to get Marshall and his other colleagues to act, Chase delivered a charge to a Baltimore grand jury blasting the Jeffersonians at the federal and state levels for undermining judicial independence. Chase warned that such conduct would destroy the basis of the rule of law on which constitutional government rested, and violated as well basic political principles that insisted that law be undergirded with morality, and morality with religion. Chase's grand jury charge borrowed heavily from the philosophy of Edmund Burke, with whom Chase had spent a fortnight on a trip to England in 1784, and warned that unthinkingly democratic Jeffersonian advocates of the "rights of man" were plunging the country in the direction of mobocracy.

This was too much for Jefferson and his Republican colleagues in Congress, who had assumed control of the national legislature following the defeat of Adams and the Federalists in 1800. Following on the heels of John Marshall's reminder in *Marbury* that the legislature would be subject to judicial review, the Baltimore grand jury charge apparently convinced Jefferson that Chase (and some of his Federalist allies) were set on using the judiciary to frustrate the efforts of the new Jeffersonian majorities in Congress and the states. Jefferson apparently gave his consent to the attempted removal of Chase, and urged his congressional lieutenants to act. Within a few months, and following the removal by impeachment of the mentally incompetent United States District Court judge John Pickering, impeachment articles were filed in the House against Chase. The best lawyers among the Adams Federalists immediately enlisted in Chase's defense, agreeing to work for no fees because of their belief that Jefferson and the congressional Republicans were attempting to destroy the independence of the judiciary. At Chase's trial before the Senate in 1805, he and his defenders argued that the impeachment charges were little more than politically motivated calumny. The strategy was successful, as some of the more moderate Republicans joined the remaining Federalists in preventing a two-thirds majority necessary to remove Chase. At Chase's trial before the Senate, John Marshall played a rather disappointing role, refusing to do much in Chase's defense and even suggesting, contrary to his reputation as a great defender of judicial review, that perhaps Congress ought to be the only arbiter of the constitutionality of its own acts.[26]

The failure of the Senate to remove Chase is usually pointed to by historians as a victory for judicial independence, and as having established the precedent that a judge could not be removed merely for stating political views from the bench. More correctly, however, the proceeding ought to be seen as establishing the principle that it was dangerous for a judge, such as Chase, to articulate political philosophy, particularly one at odds with the prevailing democratic ethos of the Jeffersonians.

There were some apparent inconsistencies in Chase's jurisprudence and politics, but they were more apparent than real. He opposed the federal Constitution before its ratification, but he became the staunchest of Federalist defenders of the Adams administration against its critics. He was the only Federalist justice to reject the federal common law of crimes, but, as indicated earlier, he believed that there were certain supraconstitutional principles that restrained any and all governments. On at least one occasion he expressed reservations about the power of the Supreme Court to reject legislative acts on the grounds that they conflicted with the federal Constitution, but on other occasions, most notably Callender's trial before a hostile Virginia audience, he made clear that the Court was the only body that could declare that a law was unconstitutional. He had originally been a professed champion of the people, particularly against the aristocratic proprietary interest in Maryland, but he ended his career opposed to the party of Madison and Jefferson, and as a judge who carefully circumscribed the operation of the petit jury, arguably the most important popular institution in the legal system.

Many of these inconsistencies evaporate when Chase's actions are put in context. He appears to have believed that the moment for active popular sovereignty was the time of the American Revolution, but that once the American people had established a federal Constitution, their duties were to obey the rules of the government they had established, to refrain from resisting its laws, and to take directions from their constitutionally selected judges. Throughout his life Chase was a firm supporter of the notion that judges had limited discretion, circumscribed by the written word of statute or constitution. Nevertheless, he believed that there were certain things no government could do and still call itself "Republican." For example, even if the Constitution was silent on the point, Chase indicated in *Calder*, no government could make an act criminal and then proceed to punish those who committed the act before the legislation was passed. Similarly, as he again stated in *Calder*, no government could transfer the property of one citizen to another, whether or not any written constitutional directives prohibited such a transfer. Chase apparently believed that it was the duty of the judge to enforce such unwritten rules when necessary.

Still, because his study of law had convinced him that the common-law rules embraced by the thirteen new states were different in each state, and because the federal government had never explicitly adopted any state's common law, Chase rejected the notion of a federal common law of crimes. For a judge to declare a particular act a federal common-law crime, to Chase, looked like a legislative act that prohibited something lawful when done. Thus, for the same reason he rejected ex post facto criminal legislation in *Calder*—inherent uncertainty—Chase rejected the federal common law of crimes.

This notion of the certainty and predictability of the law is also what led him to try to restrict the discretion of his juries. It was an American legal maxim that the jury was to be the "judge of law and fact," and while Chase appeared to accept this notion, he gave it limited application. Many of the Federalists' foes in Virginia and Pennsylvania believed that the jury's ability to render a general verdict (a verdict of "guilty" or "not guilty" without explaining the basis of the finding) meant that they could decide for themselves whether the law they were asked to apply was just. To them, this meant that the jury could refuse to enforce a law—for example the Federalists' seditious libel legislation of 1798—because they believed it to be unconstitutional. Chase would have none of that. He informed his juries that they were duty-bound to follow the law as *he* saw it, he issued instructions on the law (in one case even before the evidence was heard) that his jurors were *not* to sway from, and he made clear that the only body capable of passing on the constitutionality of legislation was the court, not the jury. For Chase, then, the traditional American (and English radical) ability of the jury to find "law" meant only the ability to apply the law the judge gave them to the facts of the case. They could find the "law of the case," in other words, but not reject the legal rules dictated to them by the judge. To do anything more, Chase believed, would be for the individual jurors to substitute their will for the will of the American people expressed in legislation or constitution. That, for Chase, would be to betray nothing less than the American ideal of popular sovereignty itself. Because Chase feared the possibility of arbitrary and prejudicial behavior on the part of the jury above all, he was also zealous in restricting arguments of counsel to the clearly relevant, and was probably the most sophisticated expositor of the rules of evidence on the early federal bench. For this he earned the enmity even of politically friendly lawyers in some of his circuit sittings.

All of the early federal judges could have been described as "Republican schoolmasters" because of the manner in which they used their grand jury charges to instruct in the finer points of the new federal government, but Chase pushed this practice to the limits, and beyond, triggering his impeachment by the Jeffersonians after he blasted some of their actions in his famous Baltimore grand jury charge of 1803. In that charge Chase laid out the fundamental maxims of his politics and jurisprudence as they had finally matured, including the notions that property would be insecure in a regime where the unpropertied could vote (a view he shared with most of the Federalists) and that the legislature had no power to abolish courts once they were established. To elaborate on the latter point, Chase believed that the courts were supposed to be the guardians of the security of person and property and that any trifling with them could well lead to "mobocracy"—the worst of all governments. Finally, Chase made clear in his grand jury charges that he subscribed to the fundamental Federalist set of beliefs that while popular sovereignty might be the American creed, that sovereignty itself was subject to the rules of the Almighty. Thus, Chase believed (as did George Washington, for example) that there could be no law without morality and no morality without religion. It was accordingly the job of the people and their government to promote morality and religion, and to live and legislate pursuant to the directives of these twin pillars of good government.

## *Themes from The Original Misunderstanding*

In *The Original Misunderstanding* I tried to limn Chase's judicial philosophy, one that I thought corresponded roughly with the "Court" philosophy of seventeenth- and eighteenth-century English Tories, and contrast it with a Jeffersonian "Country" variant, which owed much to the thought of British theorists Harrington, Sidney, Trenchard and Gordon, and others. I tried to draw a parallel between the battles in late-eighteenth-century England (involving what might be described as a rerun of "Court" and "Country" philosophies, played out in English courts over the issues of jury prerogatives, especially in seditious libel cases) and what happened in America during the so-called Federalist "reign of terror" when Jeffersonian editors were prosecuted under the Federalist Alien and Sedition Law of 1798. Essentially, I suggested that judicial events in both England and America could best be understood as a reaction to the challenge posed by radical ideas, especially those flowing from the contemporary French Revolution. I tried to build on the work of many American historians who had dealt with concepts of "republicanism" and "liberalism" in the early republic, to mix in the reaction to the French Revolution, and then to present Chase as an apostle of conservative "Republican" theory who confronted what appeared to be a Francophilic Jeffersonian "liberalism," which he sought to crush in his courtroom.

I tried to present Chase's conservatism as something that had grown over time, that had led him to reject the democratic excesses of his youth and to move from the camp that opposed the federal Constitution as too tightly constricting the sovereignty of the states (because of their belief in democratic prerogatives) to join the forces of Federalism in the Washington and Adams administrations. I tried to show that Chase changed his mind about what the nation needed, partly as a result of a visit to England in 1783–1784 and partly as a result of developments in the young republic, particularly the Whiskey Rebellion and the Fries Rebellion—which seemed to Chase and other Federalists to come too close to what was happening in France to be tolerated. I also tried to show, however, that there were some consistent strains in Chase's judicial philosophy over the years, principally his regard for the rule of law itself, and what I took to be a firm Christian basis for his jurisprudence. I suggested that his foes, principally Thomas Jefferson, evinced much less of a regard for the rule of law and for the notion that religion and morality undergirded the law.

At about the same time that I began the series of articles that were incorporated in *The Original Misunderstanding*, two biographies of Chase appeared.[27] I thought that the time might be ripe for rescuing Chase from the opprobrium he had been under for most of the twentieth century, an opprobrium that I thought had something to do with the current American academy's preference for liberal democratic politics (which regards Jefferson as its avatar)[28] and its antipathy to Jefferson's critics, such as Hamilton and the High Federalists. I thought that Chase was also something less of a trimmer than was John Marshall, particularly on the issues of judicial review and the independence of the federal judiciary, and I thought that it was time that Chase received some credit for the courage he demonstrated in sticking to his principles.

By the late eighties, when I was trying to put the manuscript into book form, events in Europe and America suggested that the turn to the left in national and European politics was coming to something of an end, and I thought that closer scrutiny of an old conservative approach might have resonance for today. This seems to have been realized by at least one prominent formerly left-leaning American historian,[29] and it is true as well that, at long last, the Supreme Court might be poised to reexamine some of what has usually been characterized as the "liberal" decisions of the Warren and Burger Courts, particularly those regarding race and religion. Can the study of Chase's trials and tribulations help in the working out of a jurisprudence for the twenty-first century?

Or is this question even appropriate? This sort of teleological approach flies in the face of much that some (perhaps most) current American historians hold dear. Conceivably practicing history for its own sake, they look with jaundiced mien on those whose study of history follows the directive of Santayana. For example, David Thomas Konig, a distinguished colonial legal historian, writing a few pungent paragraphs in a key professional journal for American historians, the *American Historical Review*, stated that *The Original Misunderstanding* "must be read with great caution and an awareness of its intended 'relevance for the present.'"[30]

Konig, all but dismissing the book as "idiosyncratic," suggested that I drew "broadly, indiscriminately and reductionistically on numerous elements of eighteenth century thought."[31] I suppose I was a reductionist, as must be anyone who tries to capture the unmanageable sprawl of reality in the pages of a book, although I thought I worked with more discrimination than Konig apparently was willing to allow. Indeed, Konig's review is a rather dangerous exercise in reductionism itself. Konig found "dubious" what he called my assertion that "Americans understood no distinction between the law of nations and . . . a federal common law," while all I was doing was stating what is increasingly becoming the orthodox understanding that for early Americans (at least those of whom were Federalist judges) there was a federal common law that incorporated the law of nations.[32] Perhaps this is a sign that some of the more orthodox historians have found it difficult to keep track of what the lawyers have been doing with the jurisprudence of the early republic.

We are now beginning to understand that in the early republic most members of the legal profession were natural lawyers,[33] but positivism continues to reign supreme at elite law schools and the upper reaches of our profession. Even among people who would otherwise describe themselves as conservatives, it is troubling, perhaps even horrifying, to suggest that law ought to be coupled with morality. Knud Haakonssen, an intellectual historian writing in the *William and Mary Quarterly*, appeared sympathetic to the notion that my aim in writing on Chase was "to deliver a moral lesson from history," or, as he put it, that "America has to rekindle the right telos for the republic, a civic humanistic communitarianism for which the judiciary can be the guardian."[34]

Still, while Haakonssen conceded that a review of Chase's work might add to the ongoing philosophical and political debate over whether there is something to be learned from our constitutional history, and, in particular, whether there was "a historically given essence of the American Constitution that a historicist method of unraveling the dialectics of history can discern," he thought I hadn't captured it, nor did he think that my presentation had provided a "sustained argument for the moral, legal, and political values" I wanted to further. Moreover, Haakonssen, protested my "uncritical acceptance" of the dichotomy drawn by J. G. A. Pocock between republicanism and liberalism, because "the debate between Lockean liberalism vs. Neo-republicanism is . . . a false alarm."[35]

Haakonssen, reflecting his own notable research in the natural-law roots of American jurisprudence,[36] argued that what American constitutional historians ought to address was *not* the battle between liberals and republicans but the manner in which republicanism was intertwined with natural-law arguments drawn not only from Locke but also from the civilians.

Haakonssen's point about the importance of natural-law theories is well taken. The domination of legal positivism in this country may be facing an uncertain future, examination of the past is vital in finding a substitute, and our natural-law tradition is clearly a good framework within which to search. I thought I understood and communicated this, but perhaps the temptation to dabble in the then-trendy "republicanism" rhetoric obscured the contribution I sought to make.

I have had only limited success in getting my fellow legal and constitutional historians enthused about the value of studying Chase. Neil Duxbury, a prolific younger legal historian who teaches at the University of Manchester, writing in the legal history fraternity's senior professional journal, the *American Journal of Legal History*, provided some great advertising copy blurbs: "well researched," "highly engaging," "wonderful job of putting Chase's ideas and attitudes in their historical context," a "delightfully ambitious book," "impressive and provocative." But even Duxbury thought that the book was a "too flattering portrait of Chase," and "too much of an apology."[37] Alas, it is difficult to concoct precisely the right amount of flattery or apology.

The dean of practicing American judicial biographers, R. Kent Newmyer,[38] in his review of *The Original Misunderstanding* for the *Review of American History*, declared that "by establishing the doctrinal compatibility of Chase and [United States District Court judge Richard] Peters, who was recognized as a judge of fairness and probity, Presser makes a good case for Chase's being within the mainstream of Federalist jurisprudence—indeed being a courageous and uncompromising guardian of that conservative legal tradition."[39] Upon reading this, I rejoiced, since that's all I had set out to do in the book. Nevertheless, Newmyer wondered why there wasn't more in the book about the Supreme Court as a whole, and stated that, in particular, I probably erred by failing to see the Callender trial and other developments as more about a contest between the federal courts and "entrenched legal localism"[40] than about competing distinct legal ideologies.

Newmyer's magisterial work on Joseph Story did have a lot about the Supreme Court, and if his comprehensiveness is the measure of a successful effort at book writing in legal history, my effort clearly falls short. On the other hand, so do the books of most of the rest of us. The localism versus central authority point is tougher to deal with. That's been a staple of writing about the Federalists and Antifederalists for years, but does it make sense when applied to the judiciary? The question still becomes, localism or centralism to accomplish what? Why is local control better? What values are thereby promoted or discouraged? I thought that by focusing on questions involving judge, jury, and the nature of law, I might better address the important ideological questions that lay behind the centralism and localism questions.

Newmyer, to my surprise, suggested that what I had done fit nicely with Yale law professor Bruce Ackerman's ongoing review of constitutional law as a "community of discourse." One couldn't ask for more than to be linked with one of the law school faculties' leading luminaries. Moreover, it appeared that Newmyer accepted what he called my "main point," that "in the unfragmented intellectual universe of the 1790's, politics, morality and law were interconnected if not indistinguishable."

While Newmyer rejected parts of my characterization of John Marshall as presenting a new synthesis of the views of the Adams Federalists and the Jeffersonians, he apparently agreed enough to end his review with the observation that "the secular pragmatic, instrumental American jurisprudence Marshall helped create for the new nation finally left Chase and his friends in the historical dust."[41] Since my task was explicitly to rescue Chase from the "dustbin" of history, I was a little miffed by Newmyer's choice of metaphor, and, further, I'm coming to believe that Chase's brand of jurisprudence never vanished after all (and was even employed by Newmyer's man Story).[42] Still, Newmyer had gotten enough of what I had to say, he was more than fair in calling the book "short, densely argued [and] provocative," and, basking in the kind comments of one of my role models, I was somewhat fortified for the stinging rebukes that were still to come.

The most painful was from *Seriatim*'s own Sandra F. VanBurkleo, who teaches history at Wayne State University, writing in the *Law and History Review*, which is now the official journal of the American Society for Legal History. She declared that *The Original Misunderstanding* was "a maddening book."[43] VanBurkleo's principal point seems to have been that, as a monograph, the book should have contained more elaboration than was included in the previous articles on which it was based. "[T]he book disappoints," she declared, suggesting it was "mystifying" that the argument wasn't "carried to fresh ground."[44] I did think that I had said a few things I hadn't in the previous articles, but whence cometh the rule that once you move to hard covers (where you can reach an audience greater than you can with law reviews or specialized historical journals), you must plow "fresh ground"?

While VanBurkleo adopted the familiar pose of the reviewer who wants very much to have something nice to say, who has great respect for the author, and who wants to be helpful ("To avoid misunderstanding, let me say that I would greatly prefer to applaud this project, and not just because we all work hard on our books and hope for better than I've been able to give"),[45] we seem to have again the problem that my book is not how she would have done it. She was gracious enough to pinpoint exactly what I could do to conform with her Platonic form of a work in legal history: "One [presumably, she] hopes that he will write another, less idiosyncratic account of the motivations and fate of Chase the Antifederalist-cum-Federalist jurist, situate himself firmly within relevant literatures, and, as they say in Reno, let the chips (read 'policy implications') fall where they may."[46]

One [I] suspects that it is this "policy implications" problem that really disturbs VanBurkleo, and I think she could speak for many members of her generation of legal historians. Still, her other points need some rebuttal before we reach this question. VanBurkleo bemoaned its "idiosyncratic approach"—neither a comprehensive history of the courts at the time nor a full judicial biography, nor a treatise on all aspects of early constitutional law. The writing of history, or any other form of scholarship, it seems to me, benefits from divergent approaches (isn't that the theoretical justification of "diversity" as an academic goal, after all?), and if we seek to remove idiosyncrasy we'll be the poorer for it. Who wants a bunch of conformists respouting each generation's conventional wisdom? Isn't the power of some of the greatest recent works in American legal history the strong individual voices of their respective authors? (One thinks here of Morton Horwitz's Bancroft Prize–winning *Transformation of American Law, 1776–1860* [1977].)[47]

But I digress. VanBurkleo's objection to my idiosyncrasy is firmly grounded in two other problems. First, she argued that in my work on Chase, I had failed to situate myself "firmly within the relevant literatures." Apparently unaware that others, such as Kent Newmyer, had concluded exactly the opposite on this point,[48] VanBurkleo declared that the dichotomous approach I had employed was wrong, and that I would have done better to use the same Kent Newmyer's approach of a "matrix or set of ideological choices." Instead of trying to situate

Chase within a bipolar construct of liberals and republicans, I should have examined him as a proponent of "liberal republicanism."[49] I should have done more with the earlier studies, she suggests, that led to the recent monographs by Isaac Kramnick, Joyce Appleby, and Gordon Wood.[50] These, she asserts, do a much better job of fleshing out the nuances of philosophy and ideology in the early republic.

In sum, VanBurkleo declares, it would have been better to "fully exploit the crisis of the 1790's to explain Chase's seeming conversion to Federalism as well as ongoing resistance to federal judicial overreach on the criminal law question."[51] Since this was precisely what I thought I had done, should I have been satisfied with the implication that I had at least "partially exploited?" Isn't that enough for one work?

It must be said, however, that VanBurkleo does draw some real blood with her point that recent scholarship on the Antifederalists and the Jeffersonians does suggest that the former were more religious than the Federalists, and that the latter could be as much free-marketeers as the Federalists. Thus, my claim that Chase's religiosity could be regarded as typical of the Federalists,[52] and my suggestion that John Marshall moved beyond the Jeffersonians to embrace the free market needed further amplification. Nevertheless, and again invoking Newmyer, *he* appeared to have found enough to suggest that Chase *was* a representative (if extreme) spokesman for the Federalist position, and while VanBurkleo doubts that Chase has "utility as a window into juridical federalism,"[53] isn't it significant, as Newmyer thought, that Chase's views *do* seem to correspond with those of other Federalists, particularly Richard Peters (who, after all, acknowledged that in Fries's case Chase had stated his views on the law better than Peters could have done himself)?[54]

VanBurkleo asks, unconvinced by the arguments that moved Newmyer, "What if Chase was indeed a loon (as critics kept insisting) and a pseudo-Federalist bully to boot?"[55] But it was a common tactic in the late eighteenth century to label your opponents as lunatics,[56] and a loon could not have written *Calder v. Bull*, *Ware v. Hylton*, the opinions in the *Fries*, *Cooper*, and *Callender* cases or the Baltimore grand jury charge, all of which are sophisticated treatments of constitutional law and theory. Perhaps VanBurkleo is correct that Chase was "a loose cannon," but I think she too quickly reaches the conclusion that he was "(occasionally) no friend of liberty."[57]

What Chase and his Federalist fellows understood, if they understood anything, was that for liberty to flourish there must be security for person and property, and that with American rights had to come American responsibilities.[58] From the hindsight provided by two hundred years, it looks to us as if the Federalists were excessive in trying to implement these policies, but that doesn't mean they were not the correct ones for *their* time[59] (or, even, with some modifications, for ours). It is the necessary linkage between rights and responsibilities, for example, that fuels the surprising (to members of the chattering classes) effort to pass the Flag Protection Amendment, which has so far garnered the support of forty-nine state legislatures, more than two-thirds of the United States House of Representatives, and sixty-three votes in the United States Senate, as well as (by some polls) 80 percent of the American people. The Flag Amendment, like the views of the Federalists, strikes most American academics as insufficiently protective of American freedoms (the Flag Amendment is habitually denounced by those who ought to know better as the first attempt in two hundred years to amend the Bill of Rights), when it is really a simple statement of the need for a baseline of civility, decency, and reciprocal responsibility so that liberty may flourish.[60]

VanBurkleo believes that Chase "bullied jurymen into ferreting out libels so that he might prosecute them," and that he "repeatedly trashed political and legal processes."[61] But if I am an apologist for Chase, surely this is an uncritical acceptance of the calumny of the Jeffersonians. The historical record (even that which I reviewed) simply does not support such blanket assertions. Granted there are those who would disagree (such as Raoul Berger),[62] but a study of the impeachment defense that Chase mounted makes clear that he had persuasive legal arguments to support each of the actions he took, as well as the concurrence of respected judges such as Peters of Pennsylvania and Griffin of Virginia.[63] Further, at least some of the impeachment evidence adduced against him comes from sources whose credibility is doubtful,[64] and much of the information to support the charge that Chase zealously ferreted out potential defendants in seditious libel cases appears to be based on press accounts published by Jeffersonian republican editors, hardly an objective source.[65]

Is it too much to suggest that, in the final analysis, VanBurkleo's own policy preferences may have colored her evaluation of what I had to say about Chase (and the Federalists generally)? Dismissing Chase, and a fellow Federalist who held similar views, Associate Justice William Paterson, who cautioned grand jurors that occasionally the people might do better to "mind [their] own business" and defer to their elected representatives, VanBurkleo asks why we should "give pride of place to a party harboring the likes" of the two of them.[66] VanBurkleo then quotes Linda Kerber to indicate that Americans need "Locke, not Machiavelli," and goes on to ask whether it isn't true that "every variety of revolutionary republicanism and civic humanism, by virtue of the privileging either of property rights or patriarchy and the establishment of a single subjectively constructed but functionally 'objective' and universalized political truth, perpetuated racism, sexism, anti-Semitism, and so on, and would do so again if revived wholesale. . . ."[67]

The implication appears to be that unless a historian is willing to accept the current ideology of politically correct feminism, and probably willing to "trash" two thousand years of Western civilization and the attempt to fashion an objective "rule of law" besides, the policy "chips" will not be falling in the place from which VanBurkleo would like to gather them. Alas, I'm afraid I'm doomed to continue to madden and disappoint her.[68]

The most ambitious of the reviewers of my book, and the last I'll consider here, was Stewart Jay, a law professor at the University of Washington, best known in legal history circles for two fine pieces on the federal common law.[69] Jay did me and Chase the honor of actually writing a thirty-page law review essay on the book.[70] While Jay had some nice words to say about the part of *The Original Misunderstanding* that dealt with the federal common law of crimes (chapter 6, in which Chase plays only a cameo role), noting in particular that he and I agreed on most issues relating to that limited topic, Jay dissented vigorously from my interpretation of Chase. Unlike VanBurkleo, who to her credit took the ideology of the late eighteenth century seriously, Jay argued that the best way to understand late-eighteenth-century Federalists and Chase in particular was as men concerned with furthering their own careers and seeking their own financial advantages.

Essentially Jay made what is best characterized as a neo-Beardian argument that the "aim of Federalist Constitutionalism was the stabilizing of credit through enforcement of major debts";[71] that the proponents of the Constitution were hypocritical in their claims that the

Constitution was based on popular sovereignty;[72] that there was "a lack of an original understanding about the nature of the Constitution"; and that the pre-Marshall justices can best be viewed as "adherents of commercial prosperity and [believers] that the national government should play a significant part in its accomplishment."[73] For Jay, Chase and his fellows were crass commercialists bent on feathering their own nests, and thus he rejected my view of them as sincerely seeking to articulate a civic republican philosophy based on popular sovereignty. Instead of their being altruistic civic republicans, Jay, as may be true of VanBurkleo as well, finds the Federalists to have been simply authoritarian and intolerant.[74]

Jay marshaled an impressive amount of data to support his claims, and demonstrated a thorough familiarity with the biographical literature on Chase and many of the other late-eighteenth-century Federalists. A point-by-point response or refutation to the arguments made by Jay, which by rights he deserves, is, alas, not possible here, in an essay ostensibly devoted to fleshing out an understanding of Chase, particularly for those encountering him for the first time. Still, some issues can be raised and suggested for resolution by others' efforts.

What then of Jay's suggestion that Chase (and his fellow Federalists) were motivated only by "pursuit of lucre," selfish financial concerns, or a desire for power? In particular, is it correct, as Jay states, that Alexander Hamilton, who blasted Chase's dabbling in flour futures,[75] had a better grasp on the essential Chase than I did?[76] What *did* Hamilton think of Chase, and particularly of Chase's efforts to battle the Jeffersonians? Perhaps Hamilton altered his enmity to Chase because Hamilton was solicited, along with other leading Federalists, to serve on Chase's defense team at the impeachment trial, although Burr apparently killed him before he could reply.

If Chase was motivated solely by his own personal interest, as Jay suggests, is it likely that he would have put his personal political fortunes frequently in jeopardy by being as outspoken as he was? Indeed, Jay, because of his thoroughness, unearths some behavior of Chase's—for example, seeking to clamp down on pro-French demonstrators in Maryland, and thus losing one of his Maryland judiciary positions, when some Francophilic Maryland legislators sought to punish him—that does suggest that principle rather than advantage motivated Chase.[77]

I suppose that Jay could conclude that Chase's Baltimore grand jury charge (in which he criticized the Jeffersonian legislature of Maryland and the Jeffersonians in Congress) was simply an attempt to stir the citizenry to turn out the Jeffersonians and return Chase's Federalist fellows back to power, but since Chase had little personally to gain (he was already ensconced on the Supreme Court at the time), it is far more likely that he was again acting from principle not personal advantage. Isn't it even possible that Chase knew that the Baltimore grand jury charge and his machinations with Marshall to get his fellow justices to condemn the Jeffersonian Judiciary Act of 1802 were activities that might risk impeachment, and he welcomed the opportunity to fight for what he believed in rather than simply acted only for short-term advantage? Jay is gracious enough to suggest that "Samuel Chase may have been braver than his Chief Justice [Marshall] in combating enemies, but Marshall derives his fame from picking the fights he could win."[78] But is "winning" what historians, or those evaluating historical actors, ought most to admire? Is it better to defend principle at great personal cost, or is it better to lay low and strike when you know you're not in danger?

Curiously, Jay defends John Adams against my charge that Adams acted cynically and politically in pardoning Fries, after Fries's second conviction, over which Chase presided,[79] and thinks that Adams acted out of dispassionate concern with treason law because the Fries imbroglio cost Adams heavily with the Hamilton wing of his party—which defected and, in effect, made it all but certain that Jefferson would triumph in the election of 1800.[80] I suspect that Adams simply made a bad political calculation, but, in any event, isn't it significant and doesn't it say something positive about Chase, that, unlike Hamilton, Chase remained loyal to Adams and even (admittedly raising other problems) actively campaigned for his reelection?[81] Is it likely that Adams was the only person of principle among the Federalists, or is it more likely that the Federalists were like other human beings, sometimes principled, sometimes not?

Reading Jay, I did wonder whether Chase really was a sort of Rorschach blot that different legal historians could read as they chose, or whether we legal historians were really as much spinners of the facts as contemporary politicians. For example, knowing that Chase (no stranger to the knife and fork) did have personal habits that led him to suffer from the gout, Jay declares that Chase's 1803 grand jury charge (of which I make so much) "is the bitter lament of a man whose declining health promised a brief future of gout-ridden discomfort spent observing his enemies implement a form of government he despised, but for which he was in no small part responsible."[82] But Chase lived on eight years more to 1811, and following a financial windfall after his impeachment, when his 1783–1784 efforts in recovering English monies due on Maryland debts came to fruition, Chase appears to have been quite happy with his lot in life. If contemporary accounts are reliable, he even was philosophical about his cherished and beautiful daughter's marrying a Jeffersonian.[83]

No doubt the world looked bleaker to Chase in 1803, but many other Federalists also were convinced that things had taken a dire turn for the worse in 1800,[84] and, for my money, it was not personal idiosyncrasy (of a kind from which Chase and I both suffer) or bitterness or self-loathing that led Chase to make the statements in the Baltimore grand jury charge but, rather, sincere political beliefs. But even if Chase's (and Adams's, and even Hamilton's) political beliefs were sincere, just what *were* those beliefs? Jay joins Kitty Preyer (and Kent Newmyer) in suggesting that, with regard to Chase's confrontations with Virginians at the Callender trial, what was at stake were not questions about the nature of the Constitution, or the rule of law, or the abstract nature of the roles of judge and jury but, rather, the Virginians' hostility to "a sustained defense of federalist centralizing."[85]

And yet, when one considers that Chase encountered similar issues in Pennsylvania, and that when Randolph, making the case for Chase's removal from office at the impeachment trial in the Senate, criticized his conduct from a point of view about theories of the role of the judge and jury and the nature of the rule of law,[86] it is very difficult to believe that only localism versus centralism was at stake. Indeed, even Jay, who is very hostile to interpretations based on ideological development or consistent ideology of actors,[87] appears to concede that there *was* a "dominant Republican Constitutional theory" in Virginia under "Federalist assault."[88] Further research on the judiciary in the late eighteenth century, I think, ought to address whether the "dominant Republican Constitutional theories" were about localism versus centralism, "practical politics," or, as I suspect, sincere differences over how American practice ought to emulate or differ from the British model. Other questions include whether hierarchy and aristocracy were inescapable components of any regime committed to the rule of law,[89] and whether juries ought to be free to disregard the law in the service of conscience, or whether popular sovereignty is best served by holding juries to the directions of judges. As anyone who has been following contemporary trials can tell you, none of these issues has yet been resolved, and there is still much history has to offer in putting them in perspective.

## *Conclusion*

Perhaps Samuel Chase is, when all is said and done, just too strange to hang much grand theory on.[90] On the other hand, if he didn't exist, the Jeffersonians might have had to invent him, or find his attributes in somebody else—perhaps Paterson, or even Peters (who was, after all, initially a target of impeachment along with Chase).[91] Personality is always of interest, but the issues transcend particular persons. Although in America the tendency is to try to undermine principle by demonizing the proponents of those principles with which you disagree,[92] I think it obscures more than it clarifies to boil all disputes down to personal turf wars. *I* am convinced, at any rate, that the appointment of Chase (admittedly one that cost the Federalists dearly) was not a horrible mistake, as so many historians now believe. He articulated well the beliefs of his fellow Federalist jurists, and he boldly stood up for those beliefs. His jurisprudence, I hope we will one day understand, made a positive contribution then, and still has much to recommend it now. After all, John Marshall, someone who learned from others' mishaps, appears to have read Chase's struggles with the Jeffersonians as meaning that he should seek to have the judiciary portrayed as somehow different from and above "politics," the better to maintain the notion that there are "objective" answers to constitutional questions. In our own time, when this view remains under sustained attack and, in particular, as conservatives search for a reasoned constitutional philosophy emphasizing responsibilities over rights, what I believe to be the honestly held Burkean beliefs of Chase and his fellows such as Peters, Ellsworth, Paterson, Wilson, and later Story, might be due for an impressive resurgence. In the flush of youthful enthusiasm I once thought that there was a chance that when future scholars began to view Chase as more than a rabid partisan, he might be placed in the judicial pantheon, very possibly at the level of Marshall himself. I now think that if it ever happens I won't live to see it.

Still, as I reach the point where I'm happy to leave archival research and the refutation of factual hypotheses to younger scholars, I begin to wonder whether it makes any sense to try to reach ultimate judgments about the worth of historical characters. The generation of legal historians to which I belong was given to emulating the lawyers they studied. Lawyers try to win cases by piling on enough evidence to convict or acquit, and hoping to persuade a jury. A trial has a resolution, and, the way our court system works, there are definable winners and losers and an authoritative right and wrong answer to legal questions, at least with regard to particular litigants. But, if I've learned anything from my critics, the study of history may not actually resolve anything other than the folly of naively believing that there are simple, eternally valid reductionist explanations for historical events. Biographers in particular seem to strive to write the "definitive" work on a particular person, but perhaps the effort is misplaced.

I have no wish to step into the New Criticism's trap of believing that every reader remakes the text, but I do think that we ought to regard all of what we do in legal history as leaving room for future enhancements of understanding. Jefferson Powell may have a point when he views our constitutional struggles as about the articulation of a "political grammar" to sustain debate, the same point Kent Newmyer appeared to be making (if I understood him correctly) by suggesting that Bruce Ackerman and I were engaged in an ongoing conversation about fashioning a morally based principled alternative to hereditary aristocracy and monarchy.[93] In this endeavor, often the best (and perhaps the only) thing we'll be able to do is raise questions that will need to be pursued by others.

I now believe that Samuel Chase was neither completely a saint nor completely a demon but the same uneasy combination of the two, as are most of the rest of us. In *The Original Misunderstanding* I had more kind things to say about Chase and fewer bouquets to toss in the direction of Jefferson and Marshall, who represented for me less worthy proponents of the ideals of constitutional government than I thought Chase did. On the other hand, as at least one of my reviewers, Duxbury, understood, I had no intention of obliterating these two titans of American history but merely sought to redress the balance by rescuing Chase from utter obloquy.[94] I wanted to save Chase from being perceived as only a loon; I wanted to transform him into a tool to be used in unpacking Federalist judicial theories, or as a window onto an interesting period in our history. There is some evidence that's beginning to happen.[95]

I didn't expect to settle the issues regarding Chase or the Federalists, and since the battle between the ideals of the Federalists and Republicans are still motivating factors that divide Americans politically in the present, I don't expect to see them resolved anytime soon. Indeed, perhaps it is the tension between divergent approaches to the good polity that provides the dynamic to American life, and if the tension is ever resolved, the genius of our politics will evaporate. Maybe Jefferson, in his inaugural address, was saying this when he proclaimed that "we are all Republicans, we are all Federalists."[96] If Jefferson was correct, then the task of future legal historians ought to be to help explain to us just what it meant (and still means) to be a Federalist or a Republican, or a Republican or a Democrat—or all at once. As VanBurkleo and Jay noticed, Samuel Chase, at one time or another, was all of the above, and studying Samuel Chase, I think, can only help in understanding who we are and who we might become.

## NOTES

1. William R. Casto, *The Supreme Court in the Early Republic: The Chief Justiceships of John Jay and Oliver Ellsworth* 97 (1995) (hereafter, Casto).

2. Herbert A. Johnson, "Editor's Preface" to Casto, at xii, n.1.

3. I would have included Berger's cogent comments in criticism of my book in this piece but for the fact that our dialogue on Samuel Chase has already been published in three pieces in the Brigham Young University Law Review. See Raoul Berger, *Justice Samuel Chase v. Thomas Jefferson: A Response to Stephen Presser*, 1990 B.Y.U.L.Rev. 873; Stephen B. Presser, *Et tu, Raoul? or "The Original Misunderstanding" Misunderstood,* 1991 B.Y.U.L.Rev. 1475; Raoul Berger, *The Transfiguration of Samuel Chase: A Rebuttal*, 1992 B.Y.U.L.Rev. 559. Those seeking elaboration of Berger's views on Chase, and my reply to Berger are directed there.

4. Stephen B. Presser, *Studies in the History of the United States Courts of the Third Circuit* (1983).

5. Following the failure of the Senate to remove Chase from office, among biographers in the nineteenth and early twentieth centuries Chase appears to have

been uniformly highly regarded. See, e.g., the sources cited in Stephen B. Presser, *The Original Misunderstanding: The English, the Americans, and the Dialectic of Federalist Jurisprudence* 195 nn.17–19 (1991) (hereafter, *Original Misunderstanding*), and see especially L. Carroll Judson, *The Sages and Heroes of the American Revolution* (1851), reprinted in *Multimedia U.S. History: The Story of a Nation* (CD-ROM, 1993, Bureau of Electronic Publishing, Inc.) (hereafter, Judson), where all stops are pulled out in praising Chase, who is described as, inter alia, "bold, fearless, undisguised, independent in mind, language and action but honest, patriotic, and pure in his motives," "an ornament to the judiciary, an honor to his country, the faithful friend of human rights and equal justice." Judson concludes, "He possessed a noble and benevolent disposition—was a friend to the poor and needy, to education and to everything that enhanced the happiness of those around him and the human family."

6. The "facts" in this section are taken in part from my article on Chase in Kermit L. Hall, ed., *The Oxford Companion to the Supreme Court of the United States* 137–139 (1992) (hereafter, Hall).

7. See generally for the flour futures episode, James Haw, Francis F. Beirne, Rosamond R. Beirne, and R. Samuel Jett, *Stormy Patriot: The Life of Samuel Chase* 105–108, 118–119 (1980) (hereafter, *Stormy Patriot*). While the evidence that Chase abused his congressional position was flimsy at best, ibid., his speculative activity resulted in denouncement by Alexander Hamilton himself, writing, as he was later to do in the *Federalist*, as "Publius." 1 *The Papers of Alexander Hamilton* 580 (H. Syrett, ed., 1961).

8. See, e.g., Stewart Jay, *The Rehabilitation of Samuel Chase*, 41 Buff. L. Rev. 273 (1993) (hereafter, Jay, *Rehabilitation*).

9. For Marshall's misdeeds in this regard, see Mary Kay Tachau, *Federal Courts in the Early Republic* 186–189 (1978), and Richard Brisbin, *John Marshall on History, Virtue, and Legality,* in Thomas Shevory, ed., *John Marshall's Achievement: Law, Politics, and Constitutional Interpretations* 101 (1989) (Marshall "took advantage of the greatness of the nation to enrich himself and at the same time improve his community"). See also *Stormy Patriot*, at 104 ("Many prominent merchants of the day, such as Philadelphia's Robert Morris, closely intertwined business and politics with no thought of wrongdoing. Some contemporaries found such dealings improper, but Chase did not"). See also for James Wilson's peccadilloes in this regard, Casto, at 60–61, 195.

10. Jay, *Rehabilitation*, at 291.

11. Casto, who still thinks that Chase's appointment was a mistake, concedes his "obvious brilliance." Casto, at 97.

12. *Ware v. Hylton*, 3 U.S. (3 Dall.) 199 (1796).

13. Julius Goebel, Jr. 1 *History of the Supreme Court of the United States: Antecedents and Beginnings to 1801* 751 (1971) (hereafter, Goebel).

14. See generally Casto, at 98–101, 187, 252; Charles F. Hobson, *Ware v.*

*Hylton,* in Hall, at 910–911. Julius Goebel observed, "For what the Justices (Paterson, Wilson, and Cushing) who concurred in Chase's conclusion had to offer, they might as well have let his opinion stand as that of the court." Goebel, at 753.

15. *Calder v. Bull*, 3 U.S. (3 Dall.) 386 (1798).

16. For further development of this idea, see Stephen B. Presser, *Should a Supreme Court Justice Apply Natural Law? Lessons from the Earliest Federal Judges*, 5 Benchmark 103 (1994), and R. Randall Kelso, *The Natural Law Tradition on the Modern Supreme Court: Not Burke, but the Enlightenment Tradition Represented by Locke, Madison, and Marshall*, 26 St. Mary's L.J. 1051 (1995).

17. For Robert Bork's condemnation of Chase as the father of substantive due process, see Robert H. Bork, *The Tempting of America: The Political Seduction of the Law* 19–20 (1990). For my refutation of Bork's view of Chase, see my Benchmark article cited in note 16.

18. *United States v. Worrall*, 28 Fed.Cas. 774 (C.C.Pa. 1798) (No. 16,766).

19. On this last matter, involving the infamous case of "Jonathan Robbins," see the superb article by Ruth Wedgewood, *The Revolutionary Martyrdom of Jonathan Robbins*, 100 Yale L.J. 229 (1990) (hereafter, Wedgewood).

20. The charge involving the alleged interference in the murder case appears to have been complete fabrication. See in addition to Wedgewood, Dumas Malone, *The Public Life of Thomas Cooper, 1783–1839* 121 (rev. ed., 1961) ("[T]he action of Adams [in the Jonathan Robbins matter] seems to have been entirely justifiable, and Cooper's invective appears to have been a bit of sheer demagoguery, but his position was in full accord with that of the most distinguished Republicans").

21. See generally *Original Misunderstanding*, at 132–136, and sources there cited.

22. Chase's witnesses for his defense at the impeachment trial "destroyed" the credibility of those claiming that Chase had sought to influence jury selection in the *Callender* case. See *Stormy Patriot*, at 231. Remarkably, this smear on Chase's record has been accepted as true by virtually all modern historians.

23. 3 Albert Beveridge, *The Life of John Marshall* 191–192 (1919), and Norman Rosenberg, *Protecting the Best Men: An Interpretive History of the Law of Libel* 295–296 (1986). See also *Original Misunderstanding*, at 134, 232 n.13, and sources there cited.

24. *Original Misunderstanding*, at 133–136.

25. See generally Kathryn Turner, *The Midnight Judges*, 109 U.Pa.L.Rev. 494 (1961).

26. See generally *Original Misunderstanding*, at 162–164, and sources there cited.

27. See *Stormy Patriot*, and Jane Ellsmere, *Justice Samuel Chase* (1980).

28. Stephen B. Presser, *Recapturing the Constitution: Race, Religion, and*

*Abortion Reconsidered* 5–8 (1994) (hereafter, Presser, *Recapturing the Constitution*).

29. Eugene D. Genovese, *The Southern Tradition: The Achievement and Limitations of an American Conservatism* (1994).

30. David Thomas Konig, Book Review, 97 Am.Hist.Rev. 1590 (1992).

31. Ibid.

32. See generally *Original Misunderstanding*, at 67–99; Casto, at 129–147; and John D. Gordon III, *United States v. Joseph Ravara: "Presumptuous Evidence," "Too Many Lawyers," and a Federal Common Law Crime*, in Maeva Marcus, ed., *Origins of the Federal Judiciary: Essays on the Judiciary Act of 1789* 106 (1992). It is instructive that one of my critics, Stewart Jay, himself an expert on the federal common law, while he raises other objections to my portrait of Chase, agrees with what I had to say about the federal common law. See text following note 70.

33. See, e.g., Casto, at 2. See generally Scott Douglas Gerber, *To Secure These Rights: The Declaration of Independence and Constitutional Interpretation* (1995).

34. Knud Haakonssen, Book Review, 34 Wm. & Mary Q. (3d ser.) 186–187 (1993).

35. Ibid., at 188.

36. See, e.g., Knud Haakonssen, *From Natural Law to the Rights of Man: A European Perspective on American Debates*, in Michael J. Lacey and Knud Haakonssen, eds., *A Culture of Rights: The Bill of Rights in Philosophy, Politics and Law—1791 and 1991* 19 (1991); Knud Haakonssen, *Natural Jurisprudence in the Scottish Enlightenment: Summary of an Interpretation*, in Neil MacCormick and Zenon Bankowski, eds., *Enlightenment, Rights and Revolution: Essays in Legal and Social Philosophy* (1989), 36; and Knud Haakonssen, *Natural Law and Moral Realism: The Scottish Synthesis*, in M. A. Stewart, ed., *Studies in the Philosophy of the Scottish Enlightenment* 61 (1990).

37. Neil Duxbury, Book Review, 37 Am. J. Leg. Hist. 363 (1993) (hereafter, Duxbury).

38. A status earned by virtue of the magisterial R. Kent Newmyer, *Supreme Court Justice Joseph Story: Statesman of the Old Republic* (1985).

39. R. Kent Newmyer, *Dusting Off Samuel Chase: Fresh Thoughts on Early National Jurisprudence*, 20 Rev. Am. Hist. 487, 489 (1992) (hereafter, Newmyer, *Dusting Off*).

40. For this point, Newmyer cited Kathryn Preyer, *United States v. Callender: Judge and Jury in a Republican Society*, in Maeva Marcus, ed., *Origins of the Federal Judiciary: Essays on the Judiciary Act of 1789* 173, 185 (1992) (hereafter, Preyer).

41. Newmyer, *Dusting Off*, at 491.

42. For the extended elaboration of this assertion, see generally Presser, *Recapturing the Constitution.*

43. Sandra F. VanBurkleo, Book Review, 12 Law & Hist. Rev. 409 (1994) (hereafter, VanBurkleo).

44. Ibid., at 411.

45. Ibid., at 414.

46. Ibid.

47. Morton J. Horwitz, *The Transformation of American Law, 1776–1860* (1977). For an appraisal of Horwitz's book, see, e.g., Stephen Presser, *Revising the Conservative Tradition: Towards a New American Legal History*, 52 N.Y.U.L.Rev. 700 (1977).

48. Newmyer, *Dusting Off*, at 487 (Newmyer declared my use of the historiographical literature "excellent").

49. VanBurkleo, at 411.

50. Ibid.

51. Ibid., at 412.

52. I still suspect it was, at least among the Supreme Court justices. See, e.g., Casto's recent discussion of James Wilson's views on American common law and constitutional law, and how they were both grounded in divine natural law. Casto, at 131–132, 194–195.

53. VanBurkleo, at 413.

54. Letter from Richard Peters to Timothy Pickering (Jan. 24, 1804), 10 Peters Papers, Historical Society of Pennsylvania, 91.

55. VanBurkleo, at 413.

56. See, e.g., Casto, at 92, suggesting that charges about Chief Justice Rutledge's alleged insanity were political cover for attacking him based on his opposition to the Jay Treaty. See also seditious libel trial defendant Representative Matthew Lyon's publication of the suggestion that when the House and Senate heard John Adams quote Edmund Burke on the perfidy of the French, "We wondered that the answer of both Houses had not been an order to send him to a mad house." Stephen Presser and Jamil Zainaldin, *Cases and Materials on Law and Jurisprudence in American History* 201–202 (3d ed. 1995) (hereafter, Presser and Zainaldin, *Cases and Materials*).

57. VanBurkleo, at 413. Compare the more admiring view of Chase's commitment to liberty in Judson, and *Stormy Patriot.*

58. One of the best statements of this point of view is to be found in Samuel Chase's manuscript jury charge book, discussed in *Original Misunderstanding*, at 141–149.

59. There is an increasing sensitivity among historians for approaching the late eighteenth century on its own terms, without being blinded by our preconceptions. Especially valuable here is Casto.

60. See, e.g., Stephen B. Presser, *Testimony Before the United States House of Representatives Judiciary Committee Subcommittee on the Constitution in Support of H.J. Res. 79* (May 24, 1995).

61. VanBurkleo, at 414.

62. See note 3.

63. See generally Chase's Answer to the Articles of Impeachment, edited and reprinted in Presser and Zainaldin, *Cases and Materials,* at 232.

64. See note 22.

65. Their objectivity also can be gauged by their uniform distortion of the Jonathan Robbins matter. See notes 19–20.

66. VanBurkleo, at 414.

67. Ibid.

68. For further maddening and disappointing reading, VanBurkleo might consult my recent *Recapturing the Constitution*, an attempt to build on some of the work in *Original Misunderstanding* so as to articulate an objective constitutional jurisprudence for the present.

69. Stewart Jay, *Origins of Federal Common Law: Part One,* 133 U.Pa.L.Rev. 1003 (1985); Stewart Jay, *Origins of Federal Common Law: Part Two*, 133 U.Pa.L.Rev. 1231 (1985).

70. Jay, *Rehabilitation.*

71. Ibid., at 305. See generally Charles Beard, *An Economic Interpretation of the Constitution of the United States* (1913) (which argues that those at the Philadelphia convention were motivated by personal financial concerns). But see Forrest McDonald, *We the People: The Economic Origins of the Constitution* (1958) (a powerful refutation of the Beard thesis).

72. Jay, *Rehabilitation*, at 305.

73. Ibid., at 306.

74. Ibid., at 303.

75. See note 7.

76. Jay, *Rehabilitation*, at 286–287.

77. Ibid., at 290–291.

78. Ibid., at 307.

79. *Original Misunderstanding*, at 112.

80. Jay, *Rehabilitation*, at 294–295.

81. *Stormy Patriot*, at 207–208.

82. Jay, *Rehabilitation*, at 302.

83. *Original Misunderstanding*, at 158, 241 n.34.

84. Ibid., at 15–17, 34–36.

85. Jay, *Rehabilitation*, at 299, citing Preyer, 173, 185.

86. See, e.g., the excerpt from the impeachment proceedings reprinted in Presser and Zainaldin, *Cases and Materials*, at 243–244.

87. Basing his comments in part on Wythe Holt's work suggesting that the

early judiciary's conduct can be explained by the "practical politics" of the moment, Wythe Holt, *"To Establish Justice": Politics, the Judiciary Act of 1789, and the Invention of the Federal Courts*, 1989 Duke L.J. 1421, Jay remarks that "Criticizing a Jefferson or a Chase for ideological inconsistency or alternatively, finding a coherent evolution in their thinking is an all too easy and ultimately uninteresting endeavor." Jay, *Rehabilitation*, at 304.

88. Jay, *Rehabilitation*, at 296.

89. Jay, as was true of VanBurkleo, apparently has some trouble differentiating between the hierarchy to be found in any system committed to organic civil responsibility (on the inevitability of some aristocratic character in any organized society, see Russell Kirk, *The Conservative Mind from Burke to Eliot* 95–96 [7th ed. 1986]) and authoritarianism and intolerance. Jay, *Rehabilitation*, at 303.

90. Raoul Berger agrees with VanBurkleo and Jay that Chase is too weird to support any inferences about proper judicial philosophy. See generally our dialogue referred to in note 3.

91. *Original Misunderstanding*, at 12.

92. Jay accuses Chase of this, with some merit, Jay, *Rehabilitation*, at 299, but I think Chase's critics were better at demonizing him than he was at demonizing them.

93. For Powell's views, see H. Jefferson Powell, *The Political Grammar of Early Constitutional Law*, 71 N.C.L.Rev. 949 (1993) (hereafter, Powell). See also Newmyer, *Dusting Off*, at 490.

94. Duxbury, at 362.

95. Some of the evidence can be found in Powell, as well as H. Jefferson Powell, *The Moral Tradition of American Constitutionalism: A Theological Interpretation* (1993). Casto's fine book on the Jay and Ellsworth Courts supports this proposition as well. Even though he claims that Chase's appointment was a mistake, he belies this claim by his fulsome discussion of Chase's many accomplishments and his intellectual leadership on the Ellsworth Court. See, e.g., Casto, at 100–108, 121–123, 144–47, 167–172, 225–236, 244–245.

96. Thomas Jefferson, *First Inaugural Address* (March 4, 1801), in Thomas Jefferson, *Writings* 492, 493 (Library of America edition, 1984).

*Chapter 10*

# Oliver Ellsworth

## *"I have sought the felicity and glory of your Administration"*

*William R. Casto*

In March 1797, President Washington retired from public office, and Oliver Ellsworth, the chief justice of the United States, bid the president a cordial farewell. In a private letter, Chief Justice Ellsworth noted that he had sought with "ardor . . . the felicity and glory of your Administration."[1] Undoubtedly, Ellsworth was referring in part to his service in the Senate from 1789 to 1796, but he penned these words at the end of his first year as chief justice. Surely no justice of today's Supreme Court would claim to have sought with ardor the felicity and glory of a particular president's administration. Chief Justice Ellsworth, however, probably did not distinguish in this regard between his legislative and judicial service. Certainly his letter contains not the slightest hint of such a distinction. As a senator and then as chief justice, he consciously sought to support the Federalist administrations of George Washington and John Adams.

This theme of support was an omnipresent facet of Ellsworth's chief justiceship. Just five days after being sworn into office, he wrote a detailed private advisory opinion on President Washington's legal obligation to comply with a request by the House of Representatives for confidential papers related to the Jay Treaty. Similarly, he had no qualms about advising cabinet-level officers on issues related to criminal and civil litigation impressed with a national interest. Moreover, Ellsworth—like his fellow Federalist justices—used grand jury charges to deliver lectures on politics and to provide public advisory opinions on pressing issues of the day. Finally, he assumed without objection a number of minor nonjudicial duties and spent the last year of his chief justiceship in Europe as a commissioner to negotiate an end to the undeclared quasi war with France.[2]

## *Ellsworth's Personal and Intellectual Background*

Ellsworth's long career of public service and support for the establishment began in Connecticut, where he was born in 1745 in the wake of the Great Awakening. As a consequence of the Great Awakening, Connecticut was riven by a struggle between conservative Old Lights, who essentially opposed change, and evangelical New Lights, who sought to reinvigorate Calvinism. Among other things, the New Lights emphasized the importance of receiving grace in an actual and personal regenerating experience with God. Ellsworth was the second son of a prosperous (but not wealthy) New Light farming family, and his parents intended that he should enter the ministry. Following this plan, he received his college preparatory education from Joseph Bellamy, the colony's leading New Light minister, and attended Yale College for two years. He then attended the College of New Jersey (Princeton) where he was graduated in 1766. After graduation he returned to Connecticut and spent a year under the tutelage of John Smalley, a respected New Light minister known for preparing graduates for the ministry. Ellsworth decided, however, against the ministry and after a brief stint as a teacher turned to the law. Although Ellsworth became a lawyer, his early religious studies—especially under Joseph Bellamy—imbued him with a thoroughgoing Calvinism that completely dominated his understanding of human society.[3]

Although Ellsworth became a lawyer rather than a minister, he was a deeply religious individual who cleaved to his parents' and teachers' strict Calvinism throughout his life. As a young man, he personally experienced God's grace and made a public profession of his regeneration. He never ceased being a serious student of religion, and in later years as the head of his family he presided over daily prayer meetings within the privacy of his home. Shortly after Ellsworth's retirement from the federal bench, a young Daniel Webster noted with obvious respect that Ellsworth was "as eminent for piety as for talents" and that his piety made him an "ornament" to the profession.[4]

Ellsworth was trained in the strict Calvinist tenets of the Westminster Confession of Faith—the same creed that Max Weber posited as the purest basis for the Protestant work ethic. He epitomized this work ethic, but his calling was more in public service than in commerce. Because the Westminster Confession attained a certain amount of gloss throughout the eighteenth century, the most reliable sources for the substance of Ellsworth's faith are found in two bookends to his adult life. At the end of his life stands *A Summary of Christian Doctrine and Practice*, written by Ellsworth and fellow members of the Connecticut Missionary Society. At the beginning of his life is the work of Joseph Bellamy, especially *The Wisdom of God in the Permission of Sin*.[5]

The Westminster Confession, Joseph Bellamy, and *A Summary of Christian Doctrine* all envisioned an all-powerful God and a thoroughgoing doctrine of predestination. At the same time, "men are totally depraved; and, in themselves, utterly helpless." Individuals cannot earn their salvation. They can only hope that God will unilaterally pardon their inherent sinfulness. Even those whom God elects for salvation are personally undeserving "because, the personal ill-desert of believers remains and [even] faith itself, which interests them in it, is the gift of God."[6]

This rigorous, unbending model of God's pervasive omnipotence combined with man's inherent depravity had obvious implications for the governance of human society. In 1790, Nathan Strong, who had been Ellsworth's minister when Ellsworth lived in Hartford, noted that "human nature must be taken by the civil governor as he finds it." Ten years later, Ellsworth reiterated this idea when he insisted in a conversation with a French philosopher that any comprehensive plan of government must take into account "*The Selfishness of Man.*" This concern about selfishness is little more than a restatement of the Calvinist doctrine that condemned humankind as inherently depraved. Even the phraseology is taken from the New Lights' Calvinism that defined sin exclusively in terms of selfishness.

Among other things, Ellsworth's Calvinist pessimism about human nature led him to distrust democracy and juries chosen by random ballot.[7] At the Constitutional Convention, he favored the election of senators by state legislatures because "more wisdom [would] issue from the Legislatures; than from an immediate election of the people." Similarly, he initially favored the idea that the Constitution should be approved by the state legislatures rather than by the people in conventions because "more was to be expected from the legislatures than from the people." This pervasive distrust of the general populace surfaced again while he was drafting the Judiciary Act of 1789. In private conversations he expressed a dislike for using random ballots to select juries because "a very ignorant Jury might be drawn by Ballot."[8]

At first glance, the doctrine of inherent depravity presents immense obstacles to good government. After all, rulers are themselves human beings. Calvinist theology, however, provided an escape from this cul de sac. Ellsworth's teacher at Princeton, his former pastor in Connecticut, and other Calvinist theologians took the position that righteous rulers were personally selected to their positions by God. This theology of divine appointment was embraced by Ellsworth in Senate debates. Therefore good government was possible, but good government came from God's intervention rather than from the good works of men.[9]

In theory, Ellsworth's firm belief in and strict compliance with this rigid, monolithic theology might have made him an unbending, true believer who could broke no compromise. In fact, however, he was a gifted politician who thoroughly understood the art and utility of compromise. Therefore unless he was quite a hypocrite, he must have been able to reconcile his active participation in shaping political compromises with his unbending personal beliefs. The theoretical basis for such a reconciliation is Joseph Bellamy's extended essay *God's Wisdom*, which was published in 1758 immediately before Ellsworth entered Bellamy's tutelage and which Bellamy undoubtedly incorporated into young Oliver's studies. *God's Wisdom* was a rigorously logical theodicy that remained ruthlessly true to Calvinist doctrine in explaining the existence of evil. Bellamy explained that the course of human events follows a perfectly predestined plan conceived by a perfect God to craft the best possible world. This plan, however, is "as absolutely incomprehensible by us as it is by children of four years old." As part of this plan God had decided that the permission of sin is the best method for instructing man in God's perfection and man's imperfection. Only individuals who thoroughly understand their sinfulness are fit to be saved by God. Thus Bellamy's basic message was optimistic. We should not be disheartened by the presence of evil in the world. To the contrary, sin is part of God's plan, and all will come right in the end.[10]

The skeptical optimism of *God's Wisdom* provides a wondrously flexible tool for comprehending life's travails. Inevitable tribulations are accepted on faith as part of God's unknowable plan. In the political arena, a politician who is, himself, saved may nevertheless deal freely with the unsaved and even participate in apparently sinful compromises with the confident faith that all is part of the plan. These implications are consistent with the history of Connecticut politics in the wake of the Great Awakening. Initially, the colony's New Lights were persecuted in the 1740s by the Standing Order, but the New Lights quickly became effective manipulators of the political system. They were careful to distinguish themselves from the radical separatists and Baptists and made it clear that they were Calvinists who intended to work within the existing religious and political order. By the end of the 1760s, they had effective political control of the colony and retained this control throughout Ellsworth's life.[11]

In 1762, the New Lights' growing political power was recognized when Ellsworth's teacher, Joseph Bellamy, was chosen to deliver the colony's annual election sermon. In his sermon, Bellamy advocated religious tolerance and expressly assured Anglicans that if fellow colonists "desire to declare for the Church of England, there is none to hinder them." Four years later, the Old Light Calvinists lost control of the government in the election following the Stamp Act crisis. As part of the political maneuvering, the New Lights struck a deal with the Anglicans in which William Samuel Johnson became the first Anglican elected to the upper house of the colony's legislature in return for Anglican support of New Light candidates. The Johnson deal and similar arrangements in other elections established a pragmatic approach to the allocation of political power within the colony. These were the rules of the game that Ellsworth learned as he climbed the ladder of political success in Connecticut's New Light–dominated Standing Order.[12]

## *Ellsworth's Early Political Career and Service in the Senate*

After terminating his postgraduate religious studies, Ellsworth read law and was admitted to the bar in 1771. His first few years of practice were a financial disaster, but his prospects improved when he married into one of Connecticut's most influential families. With this entree into the colony's power structure, Ellsworth was almost immediately elected to the General Assembly and became a justice of the peace. During the Revolutionary War, he progressed from obscure but important administrative assignments to becoming one of the state's most important young political leaders. By 1780, at age thirty-five, he was state's attorney for Hartford County and a member of the upper house of the state legislature and the Council of Safety. He also was a delegate to the Continental Congress.[13]

Ellsworth thrived in the Continental Congress and had no qualms about the moral ambiguities of power politics. In 1779, the minister of his church evidently complained to him about the Revolutionary War's impact upon the world's "moral State." Consistent with Calvinist theology, Ellsworth wrote from Philadelphia that he did not know "the design of Providence in this respect," but he conceded that "the powers at war have very little design about [the world's moral state] and terminate their views with wealth and empire, leaving religion pretty much out of the question." He then concluded with a mild rebuke to his doubting minister. Restating the central theme of *God's Wisdom*, Ellsworth noted, "[I]t is sufficient, dear Sir, that God governs the world, and that his purposes of Grace will be accomplished."[14]

After the war, Ellsworth was appointed to the Connecticut Superior Court, the state's highest judicial court, and served until 1789. During this service, he also represented Connecticut at the Constitutional Convention in Philadelphia and played a significant role in crafting the Constitution. In the convention's plenary sessions, he helped shape the Constitution on comparatively minor points like enlarging Congress's authority to define crimes and the election of senators by state legislatures rather than popular vote. More significantly, he was one of the five-person Committee of Detail that wrote the working draft of the document finally adopted by the convention.[15]

Ellsworth also played a significant role in brokering some of the convention's most important compromises. He was a leading proponent of the compromise on the importation of slaves and was similarly involved in resolving the dispute over whether states would be represented in Congress on an equal footing or proportionally by population. As a small-state delegate, he was dead set against proportional representation, but he was also a skilled politician who understood the value of compromise. He clearly participated in shaping the Grand Compromise that gave the big states control of the House but provided for equal state representation in the Senate. He was the delegate who formally moved the adoption of this compromise and subsequently was selected as the only small-state delegate on the Committee of Detail.[16]

In later years James Madison recollected that "from the day when every doubt of the right of the smaller states to an equal vote in the senate was quieted . . . Ellsworth became one of [the general government's] strongest pillars." In the subsequent ratification process, Ellsworth wrote an influential series of essays entitled *Letters of a Landholder*, and at least one knowledgeable observer commented that "'the Landholder' will do more service . . . than the elaborate works of Publius." At the Connecticut ratification convention, Ellsworth was the Constitution's leading advocate and among other things endorsed the concept of judicial review. He reassured the convention, "If the general legislature should . . . make a law which the Constitution does not authorize, it is void; and the judicial power, the national judges . . . will declare it to be void." After ratification, Ellsworth was Connecticut's unanimous choice to represent the state in the new federal senate.[17]

For seven years Ellsworth was the de facto leader of the Federalists in the Senate, and during that time he worked on more committees than any other senator. His best-known legislative work is the Judiciary Act of 1789, which he and his Calvinist friend William Paterson of New Jersey drafted. The Constitution created just the bare bones of a federal judicial system and left many significant issues to the discretion of Congress. In particular, Congress was to decide whether the new judicial system would consist of a single, relatively isolated national Supreme Court or whether there would also be a system of lower federal courts distributed throughout the nation.[18]

In crafting the Judiciary Act, Ellsworth had to bring to bear the full extent of his remarkable ability to broker pragmatic compromises. There was substantial practical and theoretical opposition to the creation of an extensive system of federal courts. At a theoretical level, many were concerned that the federal courts would supplant the state judiciaries. In addition, the Supreme Court's power to review state court decisions made conflicts between the Court and state courts inevitable. These theoretical objections were directly implicated by a huge number of pre-Revolutionary War contracts between American debtors and British creditors. In the Treaty of Paris, the United States had agreed that the British creditors "shall meet with no legal impediment to the recovery of the full value in sterling money of all bona fide debts heretofore contracted." Many states, however, had notoriously refused to enforce this treaty obligation and had in effect closed their courts to British creditors. When the first Congress was convened, many members—particularly southern members—were adamantly opposed to using the new federal courts to enforce this treaty obligation.[19]

Ellsworth's approach to this opposition was masterful. He insisted upon a complete system of federal trial courts distributed throughout the United States and supervised by the Supreme Court. At the same time he agreed to limit the federal courts' jurisdiction to comparatively narrow groups of cases in which the federal interest was clear and immediate. The federal trial courts were given plenary power over the enforcement of federal revenue statutes and federal criminal law. They were also given complete authority to resolve prize cases that so frequently involved foreign relations.[20]

Under Ellsworth's plan, litigation that demanded immediate, day-to-day attention was entrusted to a federal district court that would be staffed by a resident federal district judge in each state. In particular, these district courts were vested with jurisdiction over admiralty cases, which included prize cases, and the enforcement of federal revenue laws. Further, he created a system of federal circuit courts that were given appellate authority over the district courts and original or trial jurisdiction over criminal prosecutions and civil cases involving aliens or citizens of different states. The expectation was that these circuit courts would be the principal federal trial courts for civil and criminal litigation other than prize and revenue cases.[21]

The circuit courts, which were to be located in each state, were to be staffed by the local federal district judge and circuit-riding Supreme Court justices. The theory behind this innovative arrangement was that the circuit-riding justices would provide some uniformity of decision throughout the nation, lend weight and dignity to the federal trial courts, and obviate the need for appeals to the distant capital. In practice, these objectives were largely obtained, but the justices came to hate the rigorous and onerous travel required by circuit riding.[22]

The circuit courts' alienage jurisdiction obviously included British creditors' claims and therefore might have been quite controversial. But Ellsworth defused this potential problem by limiting alienage and diversity jurisdiction to cases involving more than $500. As a practical matter, this amount-in-controversy requirement barred the great majority of British claims from the federal trial courts because most of the claims were for lesser amounts. In other words, Ellsworth acquiesced in the ongoing violations of the Treaty of Paris in order to obtain an extensive system of federal trial courts with complete jurisdiction over the essential categories of prize cases, revenue cases, and criminal prosecutions.[23]

Ellsworth was equally pragmatic in limiting the Supreme Court's appellate jurisdiction over state courts' judgments. There was substantial opposition to the Court's power to review state courts' determinations of facts, but Ellsworth mooted this objection by stripping the Court of this power. Undoubtedly this compromise was made easier by the existence under his plan of federal trial courts to conduct fact-finding in litigation affecting the federal government's vital interests. In addition to eliminating the appellate review of facts, Ellsworth's plan limited the Court's power to review legal determinations. In cases appealed from the state courts, the Court could consider only specific issues governed by positive, written federal laws—specifically, "the constitution, treaties or laws of the United States or [a federal] commission."[24]

These and other compromises defused most of the congressional opposition to an extensive federal judicial system. Ellsworth's plan passed both houses of Congress by large majorities and even received a majority of southern votes in each house. As a result the judicial branch was launched with comparatively little controversy and a clear consensus of approval.[25]

## *Ellsworth's Appointment and Service as Chief Justice*

Ellsworth continued to serve ably in the Senate until 1796, when, as part of the Jay Treaty's fallout, he became chief justice of the United States. The Jay Treaty was a national political watershed that enabled the Jeffersonian Republicans to focus upon their disappointments with Federalist policy and to solidify their coalition of interests into a loose organization resembling an opposition political party. Before the treaty, the Republicans more or less deferred to George Washington's Federalist administration. The treaty, however, convinced the Republicans of the need for firm and open opposition.

In the early spring of 1794, an effective British maritime campaign against American commerce in the West Indies brought the two countries to the brink of war. While the Congress was enacting legislation to prepare for war, a small group of influential senators, including Oliver Ellsworth, decided that war could be best averted by sending an envoy to England to adjust the countries' differences. Ellsworth went to President Washington as the group's representative and proposed the mission. The president agreed, and in the spring of 1794 Chief Justice Jay was despatched as special envoy to Great Britain. Jay returned in the next year with a treaty and almost immediately resigned his chief justiceship to become governor of New York. President Washington then offered the position to John Rutledge of South Carolina.[26]

Meanwhile the Jay Treaty was being considered by the Senate in secret executive session, where it met severe opposition from southern senators. Despite this opposition, the Federalists, led by Oliver Ellsworth, approved the treaty by a close vote of 20–10. When the terms of the treaty were published, the nation was furious. Britain had prevailed on virtually every issue in controversy. From the American point of view, the best that could be said was that the treaty avoided a war and established a diplomatic precedent that under certain circumstances Britain was willing to enter into a treaty with the United States. Many viewed the treaty as a national humiliation. Laborers demonstrated on the Fourth of July in Philadelphia, the nation's capital. They burned John Jay in effigy, and overpowered a force of cavalry called out to quell the "riot." Alexander Hamilton was stoned in New York. In the midst of these ignominious affronts to Federalist policy came a hubbub in Charleston, South Carolina. Mobs rioted for two days in opposition to the treaty, and on the third day at a public meeting John Rutledge vehemently attacked the treaty and Jay. Unfortunately for him, a detailed account of his intemperate speech was published in newspapers throughout the nation, and his appointment was doomed. Although he served briefly under a recess appointment as the second chief justice of the United States, the Senate rejected his nomination in December of 1795.[27]

Rutledge was, above all else, a gentleman whom Washington trusted. After Rutledge was rejected by the Senate, the president turned to another trusted personal acquaintance—Patrick Henry—but Henry declined. The president wrote that this inability to find a new chief justice was "embarrassing in the extreme," and perhaps in desperation he nominated William Cushing, who was the Court's senior associate justice. But Cushing also declined. Finally Washington turned to Oliver Ellsworth as his fourth choice.[28]

Ellsworth was nominated on March 3, 1796, and confirmed by the Senate the next day. Almost immediately he became embroiled in another facet of the general controversy over the Jay Treaty. As a practical matter, the treaty could not be implemented without money, and opponents seized upon the appropriations process in the House of Representatives as an opportunity to reconsider the treaty's merits. Ellsworth was keenly aware of these legislative maneuvers, and just a few days before he became chief justice he wrote his wife, "[T]here remains yet to be made one violent effort in the House of Representatives to destroy the Treaty." He believed, however, "that the effort will be unsuccessful and that the Treaty will be carried into effect, which the honor and interest of this Country very much requires."[29]

On March 7, 1796, the day before Ellsworth took his oath of office as chief justice, the House demanded that the president turn over all documents relevant to the treaty's negotiation. Today most justices would remain aloof from this kind of controversy between the executive and legislative branches, but Ellsworth apparently saw no reason for restraint. On March 13, five days after becoming chief justice, he wrote a detailed private advisory opinion on the House's authority to demand the documents.[30]

Ellsworth's opinion is found in a nine-page letter to Connecticut Senator Jonathan Trumbull and clearly was intended to be an advisory opinion. Senator Trumbull had discussed the treaty a few days earlier with President Washington, and after that discussion Trumbull asked Ellsworth for a legal analysis of the issues. Ellsworth's letter contains no chitchat and no customary closing enquiry about the well-being of Trumbull's family or mutual friends. Instead the letter is devoted exclusively to the legal questions presented by the House's demand for documents. Ellsworth predictably concluded that the House lacked authority either to reject the treaty or to demand the documents. Although the letter was addressed to Senator Trumbull, it wound up in President Washington's files docketed under the subject "treaty making power." Whether Ellsworth knew that his opinion would be passed on to the president is not known to a certainty, but as a shrewd and knowledgeable politician, he must have known or anticipated this event. In any case the letter obviously was intended by the chief justice as a detailed advisory opinion on a hotly debated constitutional controversy.[31]

Almost as soon as Ellsworth delivered his advisory opinion, he wrote his wife with "some pain" that he had to ride the Southern Circuit that spring and preside over the federal circuit courts in each southern state. A month later he convened the court in Savannah, Georgia, and delivered a grand jury charge that was published in at least twelve newspapers in eight states. Following the custom of the times, Ellsworth's charge was not so much an explanation of criminal law as it was a political essay extolling the federal government's virtue. In particular, he explained, "The national laws are the national ligatures and vehicles of life. Tho' they pervade a country, as diversified in habits, as it is vast in extent, yet they give to the whole, harmony of interest, and unity of design." This emphasis upon "harmony of interest, and unity of design" is a restatement of the Calvinist vision of a perfect society, and in the next sentence Ellsworth expressly affirmed that the federal government was part of God's plan. The national laws, he said, "are the means by which it pleases heaven to make of weak and discordant parts, one great people."[32]

While Ellsworth was penning this grand jury charge, he was undoubtedly concerned about the Jay Treaty's fate in the House of Representatives. In the charge, he applauded the wisdom of distributing legislative power to two "maturing and balancing bodies, instead of the subjection of it to momentary impulse, and the predominance of faction." In this regard, he probably considered the Senate to be "maturing and balancing" and the House to be subject to "momentary impulse, and . . . faction." Notwithstanding his concern about the treaty's fate, his private conviction was that the treaty would be funded, and on April 30 the House approved the required funds by a close vote of 51–48.[33]

This legislative victory confirmed Ellsworth's Calvinist understanding of government under the relatively new Constitution. Soon after learning about the Jay Treaty's victory in the House, he reiterated the basic principle of *God's Wisdom* to his son-in-law Ezekiel Williams. "Of politicks," he wrote Williams, "I will converse with you when I come, and am satisfied in the mean time that God governs the world, & will turn all the wrath & folly of men to good account." At about the same time, he reassured President Washington that "the publick mind, as well Southward as elsewhere, is pretty tranquil, and much more so than it would have been had our Country[, through a failure to fund the Treaty,] been dishonored and exposed by a violation of her faith."[34]

After defending the wisdom of the federal government in his charge to the Georgia grand jury, Ellsworth proceeded from Savannah to South Carolina, where he dealt with the important neutrality question of whether the Jay Treaty forbade the French to sell British prizes in American ports notwithstanding an ambiguous provision possibly to the contrary in the Treaty of Alliance with France. The British consul in Charleston initially asked the local federal district judge to rule on this issue, but the judge, who usually ruled against the British, seized upon a technicality and refused to decide the matter. As soon as Chief Justice Ellsworth arrived in town, the consul renewed his petition, and Ellsworth immediately heard the case and gave full effect to the Jay Treaty.[35]

Later that spring the chief justice held court in North Carolina and in *Hamilton v. Eaton* addressed a conflict between British creditors' treaty rights to recover debts and a North Carolina statute designed to impede those rights. Ellsworth had not participated in the Supreme Court's earlier decision of *Ware v. Hylton* that national treaties override state laws, so he used the North Carolina case to pronounce his views on the subject and to reaffirm the supremacy of federal law over state law. Among other things, he brushed aside the defendant debtor's argument that the Treaty of Paris was an improper taking of the defendant's private property. Ellsworth met this argument head-on and bluntly ruled, "It is justifiable and frequent, in the adjustments of national differences, to concede for the safety of the state, the rights of individuals."[36]

When the chief justice arrived in Philadelphia for the Supreme Court's August Term of 1796, he was presented with yet a third opportunity to decide a case in a manner that would support the national government. In the 1790s about 90 percent of the federal government's revenues came from the impost, and federal admiralty courts, which did not use juries, were used to enforce the impost. In *United States v. La Vengeance*, the Court was called upon to decide whether there was an entitlement to a jury trial in cases governed by laws like the impost statute. Although traditional principles of admiralty law clearly indicated that a jury should be used in these cases, Chief Justice Ellsworth delivered a majority opinion that ignored the traditional principles and denied a right to trial by jury. Years later Justice Samuel Chase recalled that the Court was motivated by "the great danger to the revenue if such cases should be left to the caprice of juries."[37]

Although President Washington finally decided that summer not to seek a third term of office, Ellsworth's faith in the federal government was not shaken. In the fall of 1796, he optimistically wrote a good friend and fellow Calvinist that "we may however yet hope that the gates of Hell will not prevail." This reference to the Book of Matthew 16:18 was used by Connecticut Calvinists to assure themselves and others that God was looking after their institutions. Ellsworth continued in this Calvinist strain by immediately "pray[ing] especially that good men everywhere may make their Election sure." Ellsworth was clearly writing about politics, but he could not have meant the word "Election" to refer specifically to the coming political elections because all "good men everywhere" were not running for election. Instead, he was referring to God's election of good men for salvation. In Ellsworth's mind, God's elect were supporters of the federal government, and they made their personal Election sure by voting properly in the November elections. When the Fifth Congress was convened in 1797, the Federalists had a majority in both houses. Moreover, John Adams, whom Ellsworth had fully supported, continued the Federalists' control of the presidency.[38]

Notwithstanding these Federalist electoral triumphs, 1797 was a bad year for Ellsworth. The Supreme Court was convened in early February, but Ellsworth could not attend because he was sick. He probably was suffering from gout and gravel. This extremely painful illness usually appears in middle age and is caused by either a hereditary metabolic disorder or excessive accumulations of lead in the body (among eighteenth-century English-speaking people, typically from drinking large quantities of port wine). The illness is not degenerative, but it afflicted him with sporadic bouts of intense pain until he died in 1807. By the middle of March he reported to his son-in-law that his health was "pretty well restoring," and he was ready to ride the Eastern Circuit.[39]

While Ellsworth was recovering from his illness, he and other Federalists were deeply disturbed by a worsening of relations with France and the impact of Franco-American relations upon domestic American politics. The previous year the French had unsuccessfully attempted to bring about the election of Thomas Jefferson to the presidency. After John Adams was elected, they refused to accredit a new American minister to France and increased their maritime depredations on American commerce. These affronts caused the Federalists to believe that war with France was likely. At the same time Jeffersonian Republicans seemed to support France.[40] The Republicans' domestic support for French misconduct outraged New England Federalists. In early April, Ellsworth's friend, Connecticut Senator Uriah Tracy, wrote, "I presume we shall see at the coming Session of Congress the humiliating spectacle of a considerable number of the members of the Government take side with France & justify all the depredations." Tracy continued, "[I]f we must suffer the French Nation to interfere with our politics—by reason of a Geographical division of Sentiment, perversely bent on humiliating their own government to a foreign one—why then, Sir, I hesitate not a moment in saying a separation of the Union is inevitable."[41]

On the same day that Senator Tracy was speculating about a "separation of the Union," Chief Justice Ellsworth delivered an embarrassing grand jury charge in New York. The combination of his painful kidney ailment and uncertainty about the impact of relations with France upon domestic politics caused him to rail against "the baleful influence of those elements of disorganization, & tenets of impiety." He warned the nation that there were "impassioned" and "impious" people who are "radically hostile to free government." Even worse, this "disaffection opens a door to foreign [i.e., French] influence, that 'destroying angel of republics.'" All in all, the charge verged upon disjointed hysteria.[42]

A writer in the New York *Argus* disliked the religious undertone of Ellsworth's charge and wrote, "I like neither his politics nor his religion." After reading the charge, Abigail Adams was so exasperated that she wrote her husband, "[D]id the good gentleman never write before? can it be genuine? I am Sorry it was ever published." Perhaps during this time Ellsworth—like his friend Senator Tracy—began to have serious doubts about the viability of the new federal government. Within three years the chief justice was privately stating "that there is in a government like ours a natural antipathy to system of every kind." These are strong words indeed for a man who idealized system and order.[43]

If Ellsworth was pessimistic as early as 1797 about the federal government's basic viability, his doubts were temporarily abated by a speech that President Adams delivered to a special session of Congress in the middle of May. To counter the French depredations, Adams chose the same strategy that Ellsworth had recommended to President Washington three years earlier during the war scare with Great Britain. Adams committed the nation to attempt an "amicable negotiation" with France and simultaneously urged Congress to enact "effectual measures of defense." This strategy received immediate widespread public approval, and by the end of May, Ellsworth was feeling "triumph[ant]" that the president's speech had strengthened the Federalists' "political faith."[44]

The winter of 1798 brought a recurrence of Ellsworth's painful illness. In January he was "considerably unwell." By February he was somewhat better but reported that his "want of health requires that my movements shall be gentle & cautious." The illness continued into March, and he determined to ride a reduced circuit comprising only the states of Vermont and New Hampshire. He asked his Calvinist friend Justice Cushing to take Massachusetts and Rhode Island and offered "to furnish a little money for [Cushing's] expenses." Ellsworth explained that he was offering money "as it may never be in my power to repay you in kind [i.e., by riding circuit for Cushing]." This ominous explanation indicates that as early as April 1798, Ellsworth was contemplating vacating his position by resignation or possibly death.[45]

There is no evidence that Ellsworth's illness recurred in the winter of 1799, and that year he was able to preside over the Supreme Court's February Term for the first and only time during his chief justiceship. With his health restored, he bent to the wheel of government and vigorously participated in attempts to resolve domestic and foreign policy issues arising from the ongoing dispute with France. Ellsworth had been pleased with President Adams's decision in 1797 to attempt an "amicable negotiation" of the two nations' differences, but the upshot of the negotiation was disastrous. When the American diplomatic mission arrived in Europe the next year, the French demanded bribes as a condition to opening formal negotiations, and the mission fell through. This failure, which became known as the XYZ Affair, exacerbated the rift in Franco-American relations. Relatively minor maritime skirmishing in the West Indies was escalated to a limited quasi war, and on the domestic front Congress enacted the Sedition Act to discourage criticism of the government. Ellsworth began 1799 by writing private and public advisory opinions calculated to establish the act's constitutionality. He finished the year on a diplomatic mission to Europe to negotiate an end to the war.[46]

When the Sedition Act was initially debated in Congress, the measure's opponents vehemently attacked the proposal as unconstitutional, and the Federalists responded that the act would be a proper use of the Constitution's "necessary and proper" clause to protect the federal government. In addition, the Federalists had a powerful argument based upon the federal courts' preexisting authority to try common-law crimes. This idea of common-law crimes was based upon a natural-law belief that certain activities were inherently criminal even in the absence of a statute formally declaring them to be criminal. These activities included conduct like counterfeiting, bribing a public officer, and obviously seditious libel. Because the existence of the common-law doctrine of seditious libel was not seriously controverted, the only issue was whether common-law crimes against federal interests should be tried in state courts or federal courts. The Federalists argued that common-law crimes against the federal government should be tried in federal court. Therefore the Sedition Act was constitutional because it was essentially a codification of a common-law authority that the federal courts already had.[47]

Because the logic of this constitutional argument was unassailable, the opponents of the Sedition Act had to attack the argument's underlying premise. The opposition could not deny the existence of common-law crimes without appearing foolish or ignorant, so they were forced to deny that the federal courts had authority to punish them. Presumably, they would have conceded that the state courts had such authority. The opposition's arguments, however, were unavailing, and Congress passed the Sedition Act in the summer of 1798.[48]

In the 1790s, cabinet responsibility for supervising the U.S. attorneys' criminal prosecutions in the various states was allocated to the secretary of state rather than the attorney general, and Secretary of State Timothy Pickering evidently had some concerns about the Sedition Act. In 1796, Pickering had noted in official correspondence that on "weighty points" of law he could consult Supreme Court justices, whom he called "our first law-characters," and the attorney general. Moreover, that same year Pickering actually sought Chief Justice Ellsworth's legal advice in coordinating ongoing litigation in the federal courts. Consistent with this prior practice, the secretary evidently sought the chief justice's advice on the Sedition Act's constitutionality. In any event, in a letter penned to Secretary Pickering in December 1798, Ellsworth opined that the act was constitutional. Like other Federalists, the chief justice believed that because the act was a codification—actually, an amelioration—of the federal courts' preexisting authority to punish common-law seditious libel, the act's constitutionality was not subject to serious dispute. Ellsworth evidently had no qualms about giving an advisory opinion on a statute that he might subsequently have to administer in a criminal trial.[49]

This remarkable advisory opinion did not end the chief justice's ex parte defense of the Sedition Act. In early 1799, the act's opponents unveiled a new argument. The linchpin of the constitutional argument in favor of the act's constitutionality was the federal courts' preexisting authority over common-law crimes. During a congressional reconsideration of the act in February of that year, Representative Wilson Cary Nicholas challenged the federal courts' pretension to common-law jurisdiction as a dangerous arrogation of federal authority. Because the common law was "a complete system" that regulated all human relations, the federal courts' jurisdiction must extend to all human conduct, and Congress's legislative authority must be equally comprehensive. In other words, Nicholas argued that the constitutional implication of the Federalists' position was to consolidate virtually all state authority into the federal government.[50]

Chief Justice Ellsworth almost immediately began writing another advisory opinion to counter this new argument, and in May he presented his comprehensive analysis of federal common-law crimes in a charge to a grand jury in South Carolina. The charge was published in at least eleven newspapers in eight states. Ellsworth used a traditional natural-law analysis to establish the fundamental validity of the doctrine of federal common-law crimes. Like Representative Nicholas and virtually all American lawyers, Ellsworth assumed that the common law—like the law of gravity—existed in nature independent of government. Representative Nicholas had argued that to recognize a federal common-law jurisdiction would give the federal courts complete power over all human affairs, but Ellsworth emphatically rejected this idea. Given the fact that the common law of crimes already existed in nature, the federal courts seemed to be the most appropriate forum for punishing crimes against the national government. Ellsworth advised the jury (and the nation) that the doctrine was limited to acts "manifestly subversive of the national government" and emphasized that he said "*manifestly* subversive, to exclude acts of doubtful tendency, and confine criminality to clearness and certainty."[51]

In addition to explaining the substantive limits of this unwritten criminal law, Ellsworth saw the grand jury process itself as a procedural limit to common-law prosecutions. He cautioned the grand jurors that an indictment must not "be founded on *suspicion*; and much less on prepossession" and reminded them that they were "a shield from oppression [and not] the *instruments* of it." He concluded by emphasizing that grand jurors should not investigate "the *opinions* of men, but their *actions*, and weigh them, not in the scales of *passion*, or of *party*, but in a *legal* balance—a balance that is undeceptive—which vibrates not with popular opinion; and which flatters not the pride of birth, or encroachments of power."[52]

At the same time that the chief justice was defending the Sedition Act and the doctrine of federal common-law crimes, he was participating directly in efforts to resolve the diplomatic impasse between the United States and France. The previous fall, France had intimated to William Vans Murray, the United States minister resident to The Hague, that a new diplomatic mission to France for the resolution of the nations' differences would be received favorably. President Adams kept this overture secret because his secretaries of state, war, and treasury were High Federalists. They deferred to Alexander Hamilton, abhorred Adams's moderation, and sought war with France. In February of 1799 Adams nominated Murray to be minister plenipotentiary to France without prior cabinet consultation. This surprise nomination was dead on arrival. As one High Federalist wrote when the proposal was made public, "Surprise, indignation, grief & disgust followed each other in quick succession in the breasts of the true friends of our country." A select committee was appointed by the Senate to consider the matter, but a private meeting between the senators and the president degenerated into a shouting match.[53]

Although Chief Justice Ellsworth was quite friendly with and respected by most of the High Federalists, he was not one himself. He had been a firm supporter of President Adams from the beginning. In addition Ellsworth was philosophically inclined to seek political compromises. He was in the capital when Murray's name was submitted to the Senate and undoubtedly was appalled by the explosive shouting match between the president and the Select Committee. After this disaster, he reportedly took it upon himself to speak privately with the president and managed to convince Adams to appoint three ministers instead of one. The basic idea was that the three would represent different interests and guarantee that peace would be negotiated on acceptable terms.[54]

The president decided to name Ellsworth and Patrick Henry as the two additional nominees, and Ellsworth was in no position to refuse. Patrick Henry, however, did refuse, and the president subsequently had a number of conversations with Ellsworth in which either Ellsworth or Adams mentioned Governor William Davie of North Carolina as a possible replacement. When Ellsworth rode the Southern Circuit that spring, he consulted with Davie and recommended his appointment. Following this recommendation, the president then formally nominated Davie.[55]

Ellsworth did not really want to go to France and feared that the voyage would bring him illness. Nevertheless, he told the president to "disregard any supposed pains or perils that might attend me from a voige at one season more than another." Finally, he and Davie set sail in early November and after a rough passage of twenty-four days made landfall in Portugal. Unfortunately, his journey to Paris was not even half way through. From Portugal they set sail for France, "but were 10 days in getting out of the harbour owing to contrary winds, and were afterward 25 days at sea in a succession of storms one of which lasted 8 days, and were after all obliged to put into a port in Spain about 900 [miles] from Paris." Then they traveled overland in the dead of winter. After a journey of nine weeks in which their carriages broke down and they wound up on horseback, they arrived in Paris in early March.[56]

During this arduous trip by sea and land, Ellsworth's painful kidney ailment recurred and continued throughout the negotiations with the French government. The personal catastrophe, however, did not keep him from playing a leading role in the negotiations, and after six months, a compromise was reached. The naval war in the West Indies was terminated, and the two countries formally agreed to suspend embarrassing Franco-American treaties dating from the Revolutionary War and the period of the Confederacy. These aspects of the compromise were all well and good, but Ellsworth and his fellow commissioners had been instructed to insist that the French government compensate the United States for almost $20 million in spoliations against American commerce. As his opinion in *Hamilton v. Eaton* indicates, Ellsworth was perfectly willing to override individual property rights to secure safety for the nation. To obtain peace, he agreed to drop this important claim.[57]

Ellsworth knew that the abandonment of the spoliation claims would outrage his High Federalist friends who were opposed even to the idea of negotiating with France, but he did not care. He had been a politician for nearly his entire adult life and was satisfied that "more could not be done without too great a sacrifice, and it was better to sign a convention than to do nothing." Moreover, his righteous self-confidence gave him the inner strength to accept the High Federalists' inevitable snide attacks with equanimity. "If," he wrote, "there must be any burning on the occasion, let them take me, who am so near dead already with the gravel & gout in my kidnies, that roasting would do me but little damage."[58]

## *Ellsworth's Resignation*

In addition to accepting full political responsibility for the treaty, Ellsworth did something quite uncharacteristic. He resigned his chief justiceship. The traditional explanation for this resignation is that "the ministerial journey to the continent broke his health," and undoubtedly his recurring sickness played a significant role in motivating his resignation. But his gravel and gout do not completely explain the matter.[59]

Gravel and gout are very painful afflictions, but they are not degenerative. Ellsworth had already endured at least three and a half years of this recurring pain without resigning. Nor did the illness seem to have much impact after his resignation. He continued to be mentally and physically active. For example, upon returning to Connecticut, he insisted on walking a little over a mile to church each week rather than riding a carriage. The winter after his return from Europe, he invited five young men to study with him as law clerks, and in 1804 he began a regular series of essays and notes on agricultural topics in the *Connecticut Courant*.[60]

More significantly, his 1801 resignation was by no means a retirement from public life. He retired from the national political arena but continued to play an active role in Connecticut public life until a few months before he died. In 1802, he was elected to the upper house of the state legislature and was reelected each year for the rest of his life. As the leading member of that body, he chaired and played an active role in the 1802 attempt to resolve the Baptist Petition movement. In 1805, he led the upper house's consideration of, and personally drafted, the resolutions rejecting two proposed amendments (one on the importation of slaves; the other on the federal courts' jurisdiction) to the United States Constitution. That same year he served on the three-person committee charged with remodeling the state's judiciary system.[61]

In addition to his legislative services, Ellsworth's position in the legislature automatically made him an appellate judge because in Connecticut the upper house also was the Supreme Court of Errors. Ellsworth was a dominant member of this tribunal's considerations and personally wrote many of its opinions. Although *Day's Reports* does not tell who wrote the opinions, surviving dockets assigning opinion-writing responsibility for the court's June terms of 1803 and 1804 indicate that only one member of the court wrote more opinions than Ellsworth.[62]

Although Ellsworth's illness clearly played a significant role in his resignation from the Supreme Court, his health was hardly broken. The illness, however, probably made him unusually susceptible to a growing suspicion that the federal government was no longer a milestone on the direct path to a graceful national order. In 1796, he had confidently pronounced that the federal government would give "harmony of interest, and unity of design" to the country. But by 1800 he was thinking "that there is in a government like ours a natural antipathy to system of every kind." If the federal government was not to play a direct positive role in God's plan, Ellsworth, who knew himself to be one of God's elect, would have found continued federal service to be galling and surely would have preferred devoting himself to his orderly and righteous state of Connecticut. At the same time, however, there was something inherently dishonorable about quitting. In early middle age, Ellsworth had described himself as a soldier in public service and affirmed that "when a soldier goes forth in publick service he must stay until he is discharged, and though the weather be stormy and his allowance small yet he must stand to his post." This unbending noblesse oblige may have caused Ellsworth to place inordinate emphasis upon his illness as the reason for not standing to his post. Certainly a good soldier in public service could not be criticized if a serious illness beyond his control forced his discharge.[63]

Shortly after Ellsworth resigned, John Adams's loss in the 1800 presidential election confirmed Ellsworth's Calvinist pessimism about the national government. On hearing of Jefferson's victory, Ellsworth compared the task of governing under the Constitution to the legend of Sisyphus. "So," he wrote, "the Antifeds are now to support their own administration and take a turn at rolling stones up hill." This legend would have been particularly appealing to a Calvinist like Ellsworth who believed generally in predestination and specifically that governments were part of God's plan. Sisyphus was a clever ruler who tricked and betrayed the gods and who, as an exemplary punishment, was doomed by the gods to his eternal task. Like Sisyphus, Jefferson was a clever ruler, and New England Calvinists believed that he had betrayed God. By suggesting that Jefferson was as certainly doomed as Sisyphus, Ellsworth was reaffirming that the federal government with Jefferson at the helm was part of God's plan.[64]

Notwithstanding this pessimism, the essential optimism of *God's Wisdom* prevailed as Ellsworth regained his health. Shortly after writing about "rolling stones up hill," he commented that

> Jefferson dare not run the ship aground, nor essentially deviate from that course which has hitherto rendered her voyage so prosperous. His party also must support the Government while he administers it, and if others are consistent & do the same, the Government may even be consolidated & acquire new confidence.

Later he confided to his son-in-law that "Mr. Jefferson's Presidency may be turned to good account if people will let their reason & not their passions, tell them how to manage."[65]

## *Concluding Thoughts*

Twentieth-century analyses of Chief Justice Ellsworth and his fellow justices tend to be slightly out of focus because our modern understanding of what Supreme Court justices do has been shaped by two hundred years of evolution in the judicial process. Today we view the Court as a unique political institution whose power is more or less limited to the resolution of specific judicial cases and controversies. Consistent with this understanding, most modern analyses of the Court place predominant—even inordinate—emphasis upon the justices' opinions in individual cases. This modern understanding, however, becomes anachronistic when it is transported to the late eighteenth century. The justices of the early Supreme Court simply did not view their positions the way modern justices do.

In his first grand jury charge, Chief Justice Jay had viewed separation of powers and judicial independence as a doctrine in evolution. He frankly admitted that "there continues to be great Diversity of opinions [about] how to constitute and balance [the] Executive legislative and judicial." In his mind, the nation was embarking upon a "Tryal," and the doctrine's contours would have to be worked out "by Practice." Chief Justice Jay's approach to separation of powers was pragmatic, and Chief Justice Ellsworth continued in that tradition.[66]

As a teenager, Ellsworth had been instructed that a good public official is a righteous ruler whose obligations and actions are ordained by God. Moreover, he understood that there was no room for discord or even disagreement in a righteous nation. While Ellsworth was studying with Joseph Bellamy, Bellamy had emphasized that in a righteous or perfect nation "there are no sects, no parties, no division." Likewise unrighteous nations are "all riot and confusion." This same monolithic understanding of society and government is implicit in *The Summary of Christian Doctrine and Practice* written some forty years later by Ellsworth's committee at the Connecticut Missionary Society. According to the *Summary*, "The design of all government is to make every one feel the relation in which he stands to the community, and to compel him to conduct as becomes that relation." Similarly, in his first grand jury charge Ellsworth affirmed that the federal government would give "harmony of interest, and unity of design" to the nation. In contrast to this ideal of a monolithic society, the concept of separation of powers is designed for a society in conflict—one in which there is disorder and confusion. Therefore Ellsworth must have been mentally predisposed to reject separation of powers.[67]

As chief justice, Ellsworth probably did not view himself as much a judge as a righteous ruler who happened to be serving as a judge. He wrote judicial opinions in support of the Washington and Adams administrations, but he was equally willing to support these two presidents in a nonjudicial capacity. He wrote private advisory opinions for the president and the secretary of state. He actively defended the Sedition Act. He even went to Europe as a diplomat. Therefore his letter assuring President Washington that he had "sought the felicity and glory of your Administration" is not surprising. All of his actions were part of a seamless web of support for good government.

## NOTES

1. Oliver Ellsworth to George Washington, Mar. 6, 1979, George Washington Papers, Library of Congress, Washington, D.C.

2. William R. Casto, *The Supreme Court in the Early Republic: The Chief Justiceships of John Jay and Oliver Ellsworth* (Columbia: University of South Carolina Press, 1995), 97–98, 115–17, 149–52, 174, & 118–19.

3. William G. Brown, *The Life of Oliver Ellsworth* (New York: Macmillan, 1905), 12–21. For the Great Awakening in Connecticut, see Richard L. Bushman, *From Puritan to Yankee: Character and the Social Order in Connecticut, 1690–1765* (Cambridge: Harvard University Press, 1967), ch. XII–XIV. As the century progressed, the New Light ministers who worked within Connecticut's Standing Order elaborated a theology known as New Divinity Calvinism. This New Divinity theology was heavily influenced by Jonathan Edwards but was

founded and led by Joseph Bellamy, who was young Oliver Ellsworth's teacher, and Samuel Hopkins. See Sydney E. Ahlstrom, *A Religious History of the American People* (New Haven: Yale University Press, 1972), ch. XXV; Joseph A. Conforti, *Samuel Hopkins and the New Divinity Movement* (Washington, D.C.: Christian University Press, 1981).

4. William R. Casto, "Oliver Ellsworth's Calvinism: A Biographical Essay on Religion and Political Psychology in the Early Republic," *Journal of Church and State* (1994), 36:508; Brown, *Oliver Ellsworth* 328; Daniel Webster to Thomas A. Merrill, Jan. 4, 1803, in *Papers of Daniel Webster, Legal Papers*, ed. A. Konefsky & A. King (Hanover, N.H.: University Press of New England, 1982), 1:19–20.

5. Missionary Society of Connecticut, *A Summary of Christian Doctrine and Practice: Designed Especially for the use of the People in the New Settlement of the United States of America* (Hartford, Conn.: Hudson & Goodwin, 1804) (Ellsworth's authorship explained in Casto, "Oliver Ellsworth's Calvinism," 511 n. 23); Joseph Bellamy, *The Works of Joseph Bellamy*, 2 vols., ed. Tryon Edwards (Boston: Doctrinal Tract and Book Society, 1853).

6. *Summary of Christian Doctrine*, ch. V, VIII, XIV; Joseph Bellamy, *True Religion Delineated* (1750), in Bellamy, *Works*, 1:1–361; *Westminster Confession of Faith* (1648), in Williston Walker, *The Creeds and Platforms of Congregationalism* (New York: Scribner, 1893), 367–402.

7. Nathan Strong, *A Sermon Delivered in the Presence of His Excellency Samuel Huntington, Esq. L.L.D. Governor, and the Honorable the General Assembly of the State of Connecticut* (Hartford, Conn.: Hudson and Goodwin, 1790) 14 (Evans No. 22913); Oliver Ellsworth Papers, Bancroft Transcript, New York Public Library, 63 (emphasis in original).

8. *Records of the Federal Convention of 1787*, ed. Max Farrand (New Haven: Yale University Press, reprint ed. 1966), 1:406, 2:91; William Laughton Smith to Edward Rutledge, August 9, 1789 (quoting Ellsworth), in *South Carolina Historical Magazine* 69 (1968), 23.

9. Strong, *Sermon*, 20; Samuel Finley, *The Curse of Meroz; the Danger of Neutrality, in the Cause of God, and our Country* (Philadelphia: James Cattin, 1757), 10 (Evans No. 7893); Casto, "Oliver Ellsworth's Calvinism," 513–14.

10. Joseph Bellamy, "The Wisdom of God in the Permission of Sin," in Bellamy, *Works*, 2:1–155.

11. Bushman, *From Puritan to Yankee*, ch. XV & XVI.

12. Joseph Bellamy, "An Election Sermon," in Bellamy, *Works*, 1:577–96; Bushman, *From Puritan to Yankee*, ch. XV; Bruce Steiner, "Anglican Officeholding in Pre-Revolutionary Connecticut: The Parameters of New England Community," *William and Mary Quarterly*, 3d ser. 31 (1974), 369, 381–87.

13. Ronald J. Lettieri, *Connecticut's Young Man of the Revolution: Oliver*

*Ellsworth* (Hartford, Conn.: American Revolution Bicentennial Commission of Connecticut, 1978), ch. II & III.

14. Oliver Ellsworth to Theodore Hinsdale, Jan. 26, 1779, in *Letters of Delegates to Congress, 1774–1789*, ed. Paul Smith (Washington, D.C.: Library of Congress, 1985), 11:518–19. For another letter expressing similar sentiments, see Oliver Ellsworth to Jonathan Trumbull, March 18, 1780, in ibid., 14:548–49.

15. Farrand, *Records of the Federal Convention*, 1:466, 2:97, 316.

16. Lettieri, *Connecticut's Young Man*, ch. V.

17. Ibid.; Farrand, *Records of the Federal Convention*, 4:88–89; *The Documentary History of the Ratification of the Constitution*, ed. Merrill Jensen (Madison: State Historical Society of Wisconsin, 1978), 3:553 (judicial review); Rufus King to Jeremiah Wadsworth, Dec. 23, 1787, in Jensen, *Documentary History*, 15:70–71.

18. Roy Swanstrom, *The United States Senate, 1787–1801*, (Washington, D.C.: Government Printing Office, 1985), 268–69 (Senate Doc. 99–19); Casto, *Supreme Court*, ch. II.

19. Wythe Holt, "'To Establish Justice': Politics, the Judiciary Act of 1789, and the Invention of the Federal Courts," *Duke Law Journal* (1989), 1989:1421–1531; Casto, *Supreme Court*, 8–9, 29–31.

20. Casto, *Supreme Court*, 31–33.

21. Ibid., 38–41, 44–46.

22. Ibid., 45, 55.

23. Ibid., 46–47.

24. Ibid., 33–38.

25. Ibid., 50–51.

26. Ibid., 87–90.

27. Jerald A. Combs, *The Jay Treaty* (Berkeley: University of California Press, 1970), 159–62; *Annals of Congress*, 4:862–63; Casto, *Supreme Court*, 90–94; Ronald Schultz, *The Republic of Labor: Philadelphia Artisans and the Politics of Class, 1720–1830* (New York: Oxford University Press, 1993), 137–39.

28. Casto, *Supreme Court*, 95; George Washington to Henry Lee, Jan. 11, 1796, in *Documentary History of the Supreme Court of the United States, 1789–1800*, ed. Maeva Marcus (New York: Columbia University Press, 1985), 1:829.

29. Combs, *Jay Treaty*, 171–87; Oliver Ellsworth to Abigail Ellsworth, Feb. 26, 1796, Oliver Ellsworth Homestead, Windsor, Connecticut.

30. Combs, *Jay Treaty*, 175–77; Oliver Ellsworth to Jonathan Trumbull, March 13, 1796, George Washington Papers, Library of Congress, Washington, D.C.

31. *Supreme Court Documentary History*, 3:88 n. 7; Oliver Ellsworth to Jonathan Trumbull, March 13, 1796, George Washington Papers, Library of Congress, Washington, D.C.

32. Oliver Ellsworth to Abigail Ellsworth, March 20, 1796, in *Supreme Court Documentary History*, 3:99–100; Oliver Ellsworth, "Charge to the Grand Jury of the Circuit Court for the District of South Carolina," April 25, 1796, in ibid., 3:119–20.

33. Ibid.; Oliver Ellsworth to Abigail Ellsworth, Feb. 26, 1796, Oliver Ellsworth Homestead, Windsor, Connecticut; *Annals of Congress* 5:1291.

34. Oliver Ellsworth to Ezekiel Williams, Jr., May 29, 1796, Williams Family Papers, Watkinson Library, Trinity College, Hartford, Connecticut; Oliver Ellsworth to George Washington, June 19, 1796, George Washington Papers, Library of Congress, Washington, District of Columbia.

35. See Casto, *Supreme Court*, 115–17; Alexander DeConde, *Entangling Alliance: Politics & Diplomacy under George Washington* (Durham: Duke University Press, 1958), 437–38.

36. *Hamilton v. Eaton*, 11 F. Cas. 336, 340 (C.C.D.N.C. 1796) (No. 5980); *Ware v. Hylton*, 3 U.S. (3 Dall.) 199 (1796); Casto, *Supreme Court*, 98–101.

37. *United States v. LaVengeance*, 3 U.S. (3 Dall.) 297 (1796); *United States v. The Schooner Betsy*, 8 U.S. (4 Cranch) 443, 446n. (1808) (Chase, J.); Casto, *Supreme Court*, 105–09.

38. Oliver Ellsworth to Caleb Strong, Oct. 25, 1796, Caleb Strong Papers, Forbes Library, Northampton, Massachusetts. The phrase "gates of Hell" is explained in Casto, "Oliver Ellsworth's Calvinism," 520 n. 74. For Ellsworth's support of John Adams, see Oliver Wolcott, Sr., to Oliver Wolcott, Jr., Dec. 12, 1796, Wolcott Papers, Connecticut Historical Society, Hartford.

39. Oliver Ellsworth to Ezekiel Williams, March 16, 1797, Conarroe Collection, Pennsylvania Historical Society, Philadelphia.

40. See DeConde, *Entangling Alliance*, ch. XIV; Alexander DeConde, *The Quasi-War: The Politics and Diplomacy of the Undeclared War with France, 1797–1801* (New York: Scribner's, 1966), ch. I.

41. Uriah Tracy to Samuel Dana, April 1, 1797, Pennsylvania Historical Society, Philadelphia.

42. Oliver Ellsworth, "Charge to the Grand Jury of the Circuit Court for the District of New York," April 1, 1797, in *Supreme Court Documentary History*, 3:158–60.

43. *Argus*, April 11, 1797; Abigail Adams to John Adams, April 17, 1797, in *Supreme Court Documentary History*, 3:161–62; Alexander Hamilton to James McHenry, Feb. 19, 1800 (quoting Ellsworth), in *The Papers of Alexander Hamilton*, ed. Harold Syrett (New York: Columbia University Press, 1976), 24:237–38.

44. James D. Richardson, ed., *Messages and Papers of the Presidents* (Washington, D.C., 1896), 1:233–39; George Cabot to Oliver Wolcott, Jr., May 31, 1797, in Henry Cabot Lodge, *Life and Letters of George Cabot* (Boston: Little, Brown, 1877), 139–140; Oliver Ellsworth to Oliver Wolcott, Jr., May 29, 1797, in *Supreme Court Documentary History*, 3:182.

45. Frederick Wolcott to Oliver Wolcott, Jr., Jan. 23, 1798, in *Supreme Court Documentary History*, 1:857; Oliver Ellsworth to William Cushing, Feb. 4, 1798, in ibid., 1:857; Abigail Adams to Hannah Cushing, March 9, 1798, in ibid., 1:859; Oliver Ellsworth to William Cushing, April 15, 1798, in ibid., 3:251.

46. DeConde, *Quasi-War*, ch. II–III.

47. See James Morton Smith, *Freedom's Fetters: The Alien and Sedition Laws and American Civil Liberties* (Ithaca: Cornell University Press, 1956), ch. VII–VIII.

48. See Casto, *Supreme Court*, 148–50 & 155–62.

49. Ibid., 116–17, 149; Timothy Pickering to Ambassador Rufus King, July 27, 1796, King Papers, Huntington Library, San Marino, California; Oliver Ellsworth to Timothy Pickering, Dec. 12, 1798, Pickering Papers, Massachusetts Historical Society, Boston, excerpted in Henry Flanders, *The Lives and Times of the Chief Justices of the Supreme Court of the United States* (New York: James Cockcroft, 1875), 2:193–94.

50. Casto, *Supreme Court* 149–50.

51. Oliver Ellsworth, "Charge to the Grand Jury of the Circuit Court for the District of South Carolina," May 7, 1799, in *Supreme Court Documentary History*, 3:357–59 (emphasis in original); Casto, *Supreme Court*, 149–52.

52. Oliver Ellsworth, "Charge to the Grand Jury of the Circuit Court for the District of South Carolina," May 7, 1799, in *Supreme Court Documentary History*, 3:357–59 (emphasis in original).

53. DeConde, *Quasi-War*, ch. V–VI; George Cabot to Rufus King, March 10, 1799, in *The Life and Correspondence of Rufus King*, ed. Charles R. King (New York: G.P. Putnam's Sons, Da Capo Press ed. 1971), 2:551–52.

54. DeConde, *Quasi-War*, 185.

55. Ibid., 185–87; Oliver Ellsworth to Timothy Pickering, March 21, 1799, William R. Davie Papers, North Carolina State Archives, Raleigh; John Adams to Timothy Pickering, May 8, 1799, in *The Works of John Adams*, ed. Charles F. Adams (Boston: Little, Brown, 1856), 8:641.

56. Oliver Ellsworth to John Adams, Sept. 26, 1799, Adams Manuscript Trust, Massachusetts Historical Society, Boston; Oliver Ellsworth to Abigail Ellsworth, Feb. 10, 1800, Oliver Ellsworth Papers, Connecticut Historical Society, Hartford.

57. See Peter P. Hill, *William Vans Murray Federalist Diplomat: The Shaping of Peace with France, 1797–1801*, (Syracuse: Syracuse University Press, 1971), ch. XIV–XV. For the *Hamilton* Case, see note 36 and accompanying text.

58. Oliver Ellsworth to Oliver Wolcott, Jr., Oct. 16, 1800, in George Gibbs, *Memoirs of the Administrations of Washington and John Adams* (New York: W. Van Norden, 1846), 2:434; Oliver Ellsworth to Elias Perkins, Oct. 10, 1800, New London Historical Society, New London, Connecticut.

59. *Supreme Court Documentary History*, 1:118; Michael Kraus, "Oliver

Ellsworth," in *The Justices of the United States Supreme Court, 1789–1969: Their Lives and Major Opinions*, ed. Leon Friedman and Fred L. Israel (New York: Bowker, 1969) 1:234; Lettieri, *Connecticut's Young Man*, 88; *Connecticut Courant*, Dec. 9, 1807, 3.

60. Brown, *Oliver Ellsworth*, 332–38.

61. 1 Day 1, 91, 189 (Conn. 1802–04); 2 Day 1, 227, 399 (Conn. 1805–07). For the Baptist Petition, see William McLoughlin, *New England Dissent, 1630–1833* (Cambridge: Harvard University Press, 1971), 2: ch. XLVII–L; Casto, "Oliver Ellsworth's Calvinism," 521–25. For the constitutional amendments, see *Connecticut Public Records*, 12:221–22; Connecticut Archives: Civil Offices, 2d ser., pp. 24–26 (manuscript resolutions in Ellsworth's hand and marginalia noting his leadership in the upper house) Connecticut State Library, Hartford. For the state judicial system, see *Connecticut Public Records*, 12:xl–xli.

62. Brown, *Oliver Ellsworth*, 331–33. Accord Anonymous Bench Notes, 1802–03, RG3, box 5, Connecticut State Library, Hartford. Supreme Court of Errors Docket, 1803 & 1804, Oliver Wolcott Jr. Papers, Connecticut Historical Society, Hartford.

63. See notes 32 & 43 and accompanying text; Oliver Ellsworth to David Ellsworth, March 24, 1780, in Brown, *Oliver Ellsworth*, 74.

64. Oliver Ellsworth to Rufus King, Jan. 21, 1801, Rufus King Papers, Huntington Library, San Marino, California; Casto, "Oliver Ellsworth's Calvinism," 509, 520–21.

65. Oliver Ellsworth to Rufus King, Jan. 24, 1801, Rufus King Papers, Huntington Library, San Marino, California; Oliver Ellsworth to Ezekiel Williams, March 20, 1801, Connecticut Historical Society, Hartford.

66. John Jay, "Charge to the Grand Jury of the Circuit Court for the District of New York," April 12, 1790, in *Supreme Court Documentary History*, 2:25–30.

67. Joseph Bellamy, "An Election Sermon," in Bellamy, *Works*, 1:583 & 586; *Summary of Christian Doctrine*, 54. Stephen B. Presser has capably demonstrated that Justice Chase had a similar monolithic view of human society. Stephen B. Presser, *The Original Misunderstanding* (Durham, N.C.: Carolina Academic Press, 1991).

# *Chapter 11*

# Heir Apparent
## *Bushrod Washington and Federal Justice in the Early Republic*

*James R. Stoner, Jr.*

Bushrod Washington (1762–1829) lived his life in close association with two great men, and to us two hundred years later he appears to have lived entirely in their shadows. They were, of course, his uncle George Washington, who, lacking a son of his own, seems early on to have fixed upon the son of his closest brother as his principal heir, and John Marshall, seven years Bushrod's senior, who was his fellow student of the law at William and Mary, fellow member of the Richmond bar in the 1790s, and chief justice of the United States for twenty-nine of Bushrod Washington's thirty-one years as a judge. Washington's modern obscurity is such as never to have earned him a book-length biography. Even his inclusion in this study of the Supreme Court before John Marshall is paradoxical, not only because he spent the bulk of his judicial career at Marshall's left hand but because he was appointed to the Court by President John Adams in 1798 only after Adams's first offer of an appointment was turned down, by Marshall himself.

Yet Bushrod Washington merits attention as very much his own man, significant not least for a modesty, noted even by his contemporaries, that was rather a virtue than a weakness. The tribute of Justice

The author wishes to express his gratitude to the National Endowment for the Humanities for a fellowship that made possible the preparation of this chapter.

Joseph Story, his companion on the bench for seventeen years, is particularly vivid:

> His mind was solid rather than brilliant; sagacious and searching, rather than quick or eager; slow, but not torpid; steady, but not unyielding; comprehensive, and at the same time cautious; patient in inquiry, forcible in conception, clear in reasoning. He was, by original temperament, mild, conciliating, and candid; and yet he was remarkable for an uncompromising firmness. Of him it may be truly said, that the fear of man never fell upon him; it never entered into his thoughts, much less was it seen in his actions. In him the love of justice was the ruling passion; it was the master-spring of all his conduct. He made it a matter of conscience to discharge every duty with scrupulous fidelity and scrupulous zeal. It mattered not, whether the duty were small or great, witnessed by the world, or performed in private, everywhere the same diligence, watchfulness, and pervading sense of justice were seen. There was about him a tenderness of giving offense, and yet a fearlessness of consequences, in his official character, which I scarcely know how to portray. It was a rare combination, which added much to the dignity of the bench, and made justice itself, even when most severe, soften into the moderation of mercy. It gained confidence, when it seemed least to seek it. It repressed arrogance, by overawing or confounding it.[1]

Story prefaces his character sketch thus: "Few men have left deeper traces, in their judicial career, of every thing, which a conscientious judge ought to propose for his ambition, or his virtue, or his glory."

I quote from Story's tribute at such length because it sets in sharp relief the character of a man who seemed never to have aimed at originality in his judicial thought, but whose character, thus sketched, nevertheless permeates his judicial opinions. Coming to the Court as the youngest man yet appointed to that body, dying in office with the longest tenure then achieved, sitting for most of his judicial career on the circuit that included Philadelphia, until recently the federal capital. All this conspired with his famous name and relation to make Bushrod Washington an important man in the early republic, a visible model of federal justice in its formative years, and a key figure for understanding the transition from the Jay and Ellsworth to the Marshall Court. He filled his role with a dedication to exact justice under law that made him, in the eyes of his contemporaries not necessarily a great statesman but a great judge—even if to modern eyes his mark has faded and so is thought not to have been made. That, again in

Story's words, "he indulged not the rash desire to fashion the law to his own views; but to follow out its precepts with a sincere good faith and a simplicity" testifies to the simultaneous suppression of self and assertion of law that typified this enigmatic and influential judge.

## *Preparation for "a Long judicial Life"*[2]

Bushrod Washington was born on June 5, 1762, at his family's estate, Bushfield, in Westmoreland County, Virginia.[3] First son of John Augustine Washington (the general's next younger brother) and Hannah Bushrod, bearing the names of two prominent Virginia families, young Bushrod was tutored at home and in the house of Richard Henry Lee. He entered The College of William and Mary in 1775, when he was only thirteen, and graduated in 1778, while his father served in various committees and conventions in Revolutionary Virginia. In the spring of 1780 he returned to William and Mary to attend George Wythe's lectures on the law, staying through the autumn; it was at this time that he was, with his fellow student John Marshall, elected a member of Phi Beta Kappa (he had been too young at the time of its founding in 1776). The following winter, now eighteen, he joined Colonel John Francis Mercer's cavalry, serving as a private of dragoons. He fought at Green Springs and witnessed Cornwallis's surrender to George Washington at Yorktown in 1781.

Apparently with some help from his illustrious uncle, Bushrod Washington removed to Philadelphia later that year to begin two years of legal study in the offices of James Wilson, signer of the Declaration of Independence and sometime member of Congress, who was soon to be a leading participant in the Federal Convention and an associate justice of the original Supreme Court. No records survive to detail what young Washington read in 1782 and 1783 or how Wilson may have guided him; surely he covered the classic English legal books, from Sir Edward Coke through Sir William Blackstone, and it would be strange if Wilson did not draw his attention to those many parts of the latter needing modification in America, a central theme of the "Lectures on Law" that Wilson delivered in Philadelphia less than a decade later.[4] (Letters do show George Washington's concern that his nephew keep to the straight and narrow while a student, as well as the latter's financial straits.)[5] In any event, between Wythe's lectures and Wilson's office, Bushrod Washington must have received the best legal education available in America at the time.

Returning to Virginia from Philadelphia, Washington began to practice law in his native Westmoreland County. In 1785 he married Julia Ann Blackburn, daughter of one of the general's aides de camp, to whom he remained devoted, though the marriage was childless. In 1786 he helped organize the Patriotic Society, an embryonic political party, which occasioned an interesting exchange of letters with his uncle, then at Mount Vernon in anxious retirement. Bushrod wrote the general asking his opinion of a society whose object was "to inquire into the state of public affairs, to consider in what the true happiness of the people consists . . . , to inquire into the conduct of those who represent us, and to give them our sentiments upon those laws, which ought to be or are already made[,] . . . [and] to instil principles of frugality into the minds of the people, both by precept and example." Writing in haste before a journey, George Washington voiced his disapproval:

> Generally speaking, I have seen as much evil as good result from such societies as you describe the constitution of yours to be. They are a kind of *imperium in imperio*, and as often clog as facilitate public measures. I am no friend to institutions, except in local matters, which are wholly or in a great measure confined to the county of the delegates. To me it appears much wiser and more politic to choose able and honest representatives, and leave them, in all national questions to determine from the evidence of reason, and the facts which shall be adduced, when internal and external information is given to them in a collective state.[6]

To this defense of the civic republican ideal, Bushrod Washington offers a spirited, if restrained, rejoinder. "The people are the best judges of their wants, their own interests, and can more sensibly feel those evils, which they wish to be corrected," and "they have a right to instruct their delegates," Bushrod wrote. The difficulty, he continued, is "that an appearance of corruption was discoverable in the mass of the people, or, what is as bad, a total insensibility to their public interest." To respect the people's right and at the same time to check their corruption, the Patriotic Society "of the most sensible and respectable gentlemen in this part of the country" undertook the task "of recommending to the people an attention to their own interests, and of furnishing them with the sentiments and opinions of a few, which they may either reject or adopt."[7] Here, in the process of formation, is the cast of mind that established the Federalist Party over the next decade, the recognition that democratic politics requires that the people be offered structured choices and the confidence that they can be persuaded to choose a common course with the "few."

In his politics, Bushrod Washington was from the first, as he was, if we can trust Joseph Story, to the last, "a good old-fashioned federalist" who "never lost his confidence in the political principles which he first embraced," though "he was always distinguished for moderation, in the days of their prosperity, and for fidelity to them in the days of their adversity."[8] As for the spirited letter, it caused the general to retreat a bit, pleading he had not understood that Bushrod was actually a member of the society of which he spoke, restricting his objection to the use of instructions concerning continental politics, on which local information was bound to be incomplete, and then demolishing one of the Patriotic Society's instructions that would allow the payment of taxes in staples rather than cash, a policy that had starved the army during the Revolution, he writes authoritatively. And he concludes with a question for his nephew: "How comes it to pass, that you never turned your eyes to the inefficacy of the federal government, so as to instruct your delegates to accede to the propositions of the commissioners at Annapolis, or to devise some other mode to give it that energy, which is necessary to support a national character?"

The sense of political engagement evident in Bushrod Washington's letters makes his election the following year to the Virginia House of Delegates seem a matter of course. That he and his friends heeded his uncle's advice on the federal question is confirmed by his election in 1788 to the Virginia convention called to ratify the Constitution. He sat with Madison and Marshall, attending regularly and voting in favor of ratification, but the record apparently attributes to him not a single speech.[9] Writing later that year to his uncle that he had found "from Experience (the best and only safe monitor) that the cares of a plantation and the attention due to a professional life, are altogether incompatible with each other,"[10] young Washington then left behind his family estate and his political career for Alexandria and full-time legal practice. Having only modest success in a city that was hardly thriving and having been rejected by his uncle, now president, for the position of United States attorney in Virginia for fear of the appearance of nepotism, he moved again, this time to Richmond, now the state capital, around 1790. Here, in the company of the best lawyers in the state, he was soon counted among the leading members of the bar, appearing often in the Court of Appeals, sometimes with, sometimes against his friend Marshall.

When, upon the death of James Wilson in 1798, President John Adams determined to make an appointment from either Pennsylvania or Virginia and found the three Pennsylvanians on his list indisposed, Marshall and Washington were the top Federalist lawyers in Virginia. While Marshall had, the previous year, serving as a presidential envoy to France, distinguished himself for resisting French pressure in the XYZ Affair and returned a hero, Washington had devoted himself to more sedentary pursuits, earning a reputation as a legal scholar, not least for his two volumes of *Reports of Cases Argued in the Court of Appeals of Virginia*, published in 1798, a pioneering effort in an age when there were no official court reporters or systematic written opinions. He had also continued the tradition, in which he had been raised, of training young lawyers in his office, his most famous student being Henry Clay.

In late August 1798, retired president George Washington summoned Bushrod Washington and John Marshall to Mount Vernon and over the course of several days in early September persuaded them both to sacrifice their lucrative legal practices in Richmond and stand for Congress in the elections that year. Marshall turned down Adams's offer of a seat on the Court in part to complete his (successful) campaign, but young Washington, whose ambition had turned from politics to the law, readily accepted Adams's commission, dropping out of the congressional race and leaving immediately to attend to circuit duties. When the Senate met in December, his appointment was readily confirmed, and the following February he took his seat on the supreme bench. For the rest of his life he was a judge, though he had never before presided in a court, and his conscientious nature made him devote himself to this calling before all else. To be sure, like his fellows on the bench, he continued to campaign for Federalist presidential candidates, although he outlived his party as an organized force. He served as executor of his uncle's will, as he had before handled his legal affairs, and after the death of his aunt in 1802 he inherited Mount Vernon, which became his permanent home and which he struggled to maintain. Responsible for George Washington's papers, he commissioned John Marshall to write an authorized biography and later Jared Sparks to produce an edition of the writings. He served as a vice president of the American Bible Society from its organization in 1816 until his death on November 26, 1829; he was president of the American Colonization Society from its inception on January 1, 1817, until his death. While these other activities kept him in association with the leading men of his day, they seem to have been at best distractions from his principal work: presiding twice a year at sessions of the federal circuit court (after 1802, for the Third Circuit, at Trenton, New Jersey, and Philadelphia, Pennsylvania) and sitting every winter at sessions of the United States Supreme Court.

## *Justice on a Court in Transition*

Bushrod Washington sat on the Supreme Court for two years before that body came under the sway of Chief Justice Marshall, and the meager record that survives of his activities there and then contains little to distinguish his jurisprudence from that of his fellows. Only three of his opinions on the supreme bench were published during that span, each in a case where the opinions of all the justices sitting appeared seriatim, and in each he votes with an apparently unanimous Court and writes self-assuredly, differing from the others only in nuance. If anything distinguishes Washington's opinions, it is his cautious determination to decide the case on the strictest grounds, eschewing an assertion of judicial power against the legislative. In the first case, *Fowler v. Lindsey* (1799), the parties to a property dispute concerning land that was claimed by both New York and Connecticut attempt to remove the case from the federal circuit court in Connecticut to the Supreme Court as a matter of original jurisdiction, on the ground that the real dispute is between the two states. The Court will have none of it, all three participating justices agreeing that the states were not, in this case, "either nominally, or substantially," the parties. Justice Washington's opinion here is the most thorough, treating the technical issue of certiorari and suggesting the process by which "an incorporeal right, as that of sovereignty and jurisdiction," might be settled: a bill of equity filed in the Supreme Court by one of the states against the other, with commissioners then appointed by the Court "to ascertain and report those boundaries."[11] In *The Eliza* (or *Bas v.*

*Tingy*), decided the following year, the proportion of salvage awarded for the recapture of an American vessel taken by a French privateer depends upon whether the term "enemy" in a 1799 statute was meant to include France, even though no declared state of war existed between the two countries. The Court decides it does, and so upholds the circuit court award of one-half rather than one-eighth salvage, with Washington submitting the most comprehensive opinion, including an able discussion of the definition of war to settle the matter of enmity and a probing search for the "legislative will" of Congress to establish that Congress meant to change the law.[12]

*Cooper v. Telfair* (1800) was the only one of the three cases involving a matter of constitutional law.[13] The case was brought in the federal circuit court for Georgia by an exiled Tory, now an inhabitant of Jamaica, contesting the confiscation of his property by the state during the Revolution, claiming a violation on the part of the state of its own constitution of 1777. In contrast to Justice Samuel Chase's more general discussion of constitutional matters, which notes that "there is no adjudication of the supreme court itself" as to whether "the supreme court can declare an act of congress to be unconstitutional, and therefore invalid," and which lays down that "the general principles contained in the [Georgia?] constitution [i.e., the separation of powers] are not to be regarded as rules to fetter and control; but as matter merely declaratory and directory," Justice Washington's reported opinion is succinct and restrained. Restricting his consideration to the question of whether the confiscation act comported with the Georgia constitution, since that act was passed before the federal Constitution was adopted with its prohibition of state as well as federal bills of attainder, Washington takes for granted the power of courts to review the constitutionality of legislation but establishes that "[t]he presumption, indeed, must always be in favor of the validity of laws, if the contrary is not clearly demonstrated." Here the Georgia constitution "does not expressly interdict the passing of an act of attainder and confiscation, by the authority of the legislature," so the remaining inquiry is whether by "necessary implication" of some "constitutional regulation" the act should fall. The most cogent argument he finds is the guarantee in that constitution of a jury trial "in the county where the crime was committed," but since Cooper's crime of taking up British arms was not committed in any Georgia county, that provision was not crossed by the confiscation. In other words, by reading constitutional protections strictly and construing the legislative power broadly, the presumption of validity wins out and the erstwhile Tory is denied the chance of using emergent American constitutional law, so to speak, against the Revolution itself. That Washington adhered throughout his career to the presumption of validity, which was to become so central to American constitutional law,[14] will become evident as we proceed.

If Washington's brief record on the supreme bench before Marshall shows him at once in harmony with his fellow justices and consistent with his subsequent opinions, what to make of his work on circuit is another matter. When, in the waning years of his life, he collaborated with Richard Peters, Jr., son of the federal judge with whom he sat on circuit for several decades in Philadelphia, to publish the meticulous notes he had kept of his circuit opinions, the text begins in 1803, shortly after the justices resumed circuit duty upon the repeal of the Judiciary Act of 1801.[15] His early years on variable circuits, sometimes in the deep South, sometimes in New York or New England, thus remain, apparently by his choice, undocumented, except in occasional newspaper accounts in an extraordinarily partisan press.[16] It seems from these that he was staunch in his support of prosecutions under the Alien and Sedition Acts, and if his actions were politically colored, he would be almost unique among Virginians, for even Marshall, as a Federalist congressional candidate in 1798, had opposed the acts, albeit on prudential rather than constitutional grounds.[17] Washington apparently presided at some stage of five sedition prosecutions: of Luther Baldwin and Brown Clark of New Jersey; of William Duane, editor of the Philadelphia *Aurora*; of Charles Holt, editor of the New London *Bee*; of William Durrell, editor of the Mount Pleasant (N.Y.) *Register*; and of Ann Greenleaf, publisher of the New York *Argus*. The first pair (indicted for drunken remarks) pleaded guilty and were fined; prosecution of the second was postponed, leading eventually to dismissal of the charge after Jefferson's election; Holt was fined and jailed for a few months; Durrell was fined and jailed and ordered to post bond, but President Adams quickly remitted all but the last part of the sentence; and Adams consented to drop prosecution of Mrs. Greenleaf for political considerations.[18] In short, though Washington participated in Sedition Act cases, the "chilling effect" of which ought not to be denied, and though his charges to the juries and to grand juries insisted upon the constitutionality of the act, his punishments were mild by comparison to the terms of the act, and in general his actions seemed to moderate rather than promote prosecutorial zeal.

The published record does not reveal what Bushrod Washington thought of the election of Jefferson to the presidency, though apparently he had thrown his support behind not Adams but Hamilton's candidate, Charles Cotesworth Pinckney.[19] One supposes that he viewed the presidential election with circumspection, but surely the appointment of his old friend to the chief justiceship must have given him great satisfaction. As the studies in this collection have demonstrated, John Marshall's innovation was not the assertion of the power of courts to set aside legislative acts as unconstitutional. This was widely presumed at the time of the Founding and admitted almost universally by the first generation of federal judges, whose youngest member Washington was. Marshall's achievement was to persuade the Court to speak through a single opinion in most cases, abandoning the practice of seriatim opinions and coupling the authority of judicial rationality with the authority conveyed by a single voice. He was to do for American federal jurisprudence what Sir William Murray, Lord Mansfield, had done for the common law in England a generation before. How Marshall persuaded justices in the habit of seriatim expression, at least in major cases, to suppress their differences is a matter of speculation, for the new policy was not publicly discussed. Thomas Jefferson, who saw the consequences of a single opinion in strengthening the authority of the Supreme Court, later denounced the practice in private correspondence.[20] In his first appointment to the Court, William Johnson in 1804, Jefferson chose a man who shared his opinion on this subject, though it is remarkable how often Johnson joined with Marshall in decision, even if he expressed himself independently. Johnson's much-quoted remark on the subject in a letter to Jefferson deserves repetition, for it offers a clue to the change:

> When I was on our State Bench, I was accustomed to delivering seriatim opinions in an Appellate Court, and was not a little surprised to find our Chief Justice in the Supreme Court delivering all the opinions. . . . But I remonstrated in vain; the answer was, he was willing to take the trouble, and it is a mark of respect to him. I soon, however, found the real cause. Cushing was incompetent, Chase could not be got to think or write, Paterson was a slow man and willingly declined the trouble, and the other

> two judges [Marshall and Washington] you know are commonly estimated as one judge.[21]

Whatever the justice or injustice Justice Johnson did to his other colleagues—Cushing was old, and Chase after all had troubles that might have made silence the prudent course—his mention of the close relation between Marshall and Washington is suggestive. In the friendship, personal, legal, and intellectual, of John Marshall and Bushrod Washington lay a key to the Supreme Court's newfound unity, perhaps in the modest deference of the younger to the senior and in the respect of the senior for the legal scholarship of his longtime associate at the bar.

To say that Bushrod Washington's contribution to the Marshall Court, or to the transition to the Marshall Court, lay in his silence, then, is not to indulge in postmodernist wordplay but to take note of the significant change in judicial practice that characterized the new era. In *Marbury v. Madison*, *Fletcher v. Peck*, *McCulloch v. Maryland*, and *Gibbons v. Ogden*, Washington silently joined the chief justice's opinion, and no one can know what influence he may have exerted on the product. The remarkable living arrangements of the Marshall Court, with the justices boarding together in a single house in the new capital, sharing meals and conversation, working with extraordinary speed and decision during their brief late winter term, without separate offices, not to mention separate clerks, suggest that Washington's contribution was substantial. What seems clear in the case of Justice Washington is that, for the remainder of his career, that is, from the time he was about forty until his death at age sixty-seven, his judicial thought on matters of concern to the Supreme Court must be seen in relation to Marshall, for that is how he seems to have seen it himself.

Two cases from their first years on the Court together offer a glimpse of such differences as are discoverable between Marshall and Washington. Both involve the interpretation of federal statutes, and in each Marshall writes an opinion of the Court that overturns a decision Washington himself made on the circuit level. In fact, both cases, which arose at circuit in April 1803, might be said to be holdovers from the Federalist era, since the statutes in question date from the 1790s. The first was the case of *Coxe v. Penington*, or later, *Pennington v. Coxe*, a test case devised to determine the tax due on sugar that had been refined but not sold as of the time the tax was repealed. At the circuit level, Washington had distinguished the refining of the sugar and the "sending out," holding the tax accrued at the first stage, to be collected at the second; he based his interpretation upon both the language of the statute in question and "the general system of duties and excises imposed upon other subjects," especially the tax on distilled spirits, which typically distinguished the "event . . . upon which the duty accrues" from the time of payment.[22] Reversing him the following year, in an opinion several times the length, Marshall concedes that "[t]he court has felt great difficulty on this point. It is one on which the most correct minds may form opposite opinions, without exciting surprise." His opposite conclusion depends in part on a different reading of the language of the act but also on a different assessment of what "general system" is to be invoked. "It has very properly been observed at the bar, that it was most apparently the object of the legislature through their whole system of imposts, duties and excises to tax expense and not industry," suggesting the tax accrues when the sugar is "sent out" and presumed sold, not when it is refined; as for the different modes of taxing distilled spirits and refined sugar, "[w]here the legislature distinguishes between different objects, and in imposing a duty on them evidences a will to charge them in different situations, it is not for the courts to beat down these distinctions on the allegation that they are capriciously made, and therefore to be disregarded." While Washington sought a distinction that would maintain a certain symmetry in the statutory scheme, Marshall by contrast looks to the "real effect of the law" and defers to mere legislative will.[23]

The other case, *United States v. Fisher*, was the more important of the two, both for the law itself and for understanding the differences between Washington and Marshall, since it involved a question of bankruptcy, the one issue on which the two judges were to differ dramatically later on. In question was whether a 1797 statute giving the United States priority in the collection of debts owed to it by an insolvent or bankrupt "revenue officer, or other person" should be read literally, to give the United States priority in any case where the bankrupt has a federal debt, or restrictively, so that federal priority attaches only to revenue officers and certain specified others. At circuit, Washington took the latter view: Since the title of the statute was "An Act to provide more effectually for the settlement of accounts between the

United States and receivers of public money," and since the other sections of the act concerned only such people, the "other person[s]" of section 5 of the act should be read to mean "other persons accountable for public money." He explained his principle of interpretation as follows:

> Where a law is plain and unambiguous, using either general or limited expressions, the legislature should be intended to mean what they have plainly expressed, and no room is left for construction. But, if from a view of the whole law taken together, or from other laws *in pari materia*, the evident intention is different from the import of the literal expressions used in some part of the law, the intention ought to prevail, for that in truth is the will of the law-makers. So, if the literal expressions would lead to absurd or unjust consequences, such a construction should be given to avoid such consequences, if, from the whole purview of the law, it can fairly be made. These rules are founded in law, and in plain honest good sense.

As he put the matter in his restatement on appeal, "These rules are not merely artificial; they are as clearly founded in plain good sense, as they are certainly warranted by the principles of common law."[24] That the consequences of a literal and hence expansive reading of the clause will be harmful, Washington has no doubt:

> As to public officers and agents, they are or may be known, and any person dealing with them does it at the peril of having his debt postponed to that of the United States—he acts with his eyes open. But if this preference be extended to all persons dealing with the government, there is no mode by which other citizens can be put on their guard against them, and consequently all confidence between man and man will be destroyed.[25]

Marshall begins the opinion reversing Washington with a conciliatory claim: "On the abstract principles which govern courts in construing legislative acts, no difference of opinion can exist. It is only in the application of those principles that the difference discovers itself." But to rely upon practical judgment in the law itself supposes a confidence in the capacity of the judge to distinguish the weight of different causes, and Marshall concedes as much by formulating the following principle:

> That the consequences are to be considered in expounding the laws, where the intent is doubtful, is a principle not to be controverted; but it is also true

> that it is a principle which must be applied with caution, and which has a degree of influence dependent on the nature of the case to which it is applied. Where rights are infringed, where fundamental principles are overthrown, where the general system of the laws is departed from, the legislative intent must be expressed with irresistible clearness to induce a court of justice to suppose a design to effect such objects. But where only a political regulation is made, which is inconvenient, if the intention of the legislature be expressed in terms which are sufficiently intelligible to leave no doubt in the mind when the words are taken in their ordinary sense, it would be going a great way to say that a constrained interpretation must be put upon them, to avoid an inconvenience which ought to have been contemplated in the legislature when the act was passed, and which, in their opinion, was probably overbalanced by the particular advantages it was calculated to produce.

That "only a political regulation" is at issue in the matter of federal priority Marshall makes clear in his opinion, though he does consider a constitutional objection to such a regulation, construing for the first time (a decade and a half before *McCulloch*) the necessary and proper clause: "Congress must possess the choice of means, and must be empowered to use any means which are in fact conducive to the exercise of a power granted by the constitution."[26]

Although the decision in the Supreme Court was, strictly speaking, unanimous, since Washington, following the custom of the Court, recused himself from review of his own circuit judgment, he took the extraordinary, perhaps unique, step of having the reporter publish a defense of his decision below, since "I owe it in some measure to myself, and to those who may be injured by the expense and delay to which they have been exposed, to show at least that the opinion was not hastily or inconsiderately given." Here he repeats and elaborates the argument from his as-yet-unpublished circuit opinion, even reiterating his fear that the Court's interpretation "would intend to destroy, more than any other act I can imagine, all confidence between man and man."[27] Seen in the light of *Pennington v. Coxe*, Washington again seems focused on the formal symmetry of the law, Marshall on legislative prerogative and judicial acquiescence, at least in matters of ordinary concern. Why the heat, to us today so apparently exaggerated, about the crisis of "confidence between man and man" should appear from the discussion that follows.

## *The Contract Clause at the Crux of Federal Jurisprudence*

For the remainder of his judicial career, the appellate cases that seemed most earnestly to engage the attention of Justice Washington and that led him to distinguish himself most clearly from the chief justice were those involving contracts, and so in constitutional law he wrote especially about the contract clause. Because this clause appears in the Constitution as a limit on the legislative authority of the states, it is important to make clear at the outset how a concern for the sanctity of contracts is consistent with the probing search for legislative will that characterizes even the earliest of Washington's judicial opinions. "All confidence between man and man," that is to say, society itself, is at risk when the rights of contract are obscured precisely if society itself is based upon a social contract, if the terms of social engagement are themselves a matter of human agreement. From this point of view, respect for the legislative will has a certain paramountcy, since that will establishes authoritatively the terms of social agreement, there being no other living source of law. At the same time, the legislative will might be governed by a written constitution, itself almost a social contract, as well as interpreted in the spirit of fair agreement and even limited by the need to reserve to individuals the liberty to make agreements or contracts to govern their own affairs and by the duty to see such contracts enforced. It is not that the theory of the social contract was the only account of social cohesion available to Bushrod Washington. It suffices to recall that he lent his name as a vice president to the American Bible Society, formed largely by laymen to supply Bibles for missionaries seeking to evangelize the western frontier, and he was himself, according to Story, "a Christian, full of religious sensibility, and religious humility."[28] But however he may have viewed religion as an underlying social bond, he seems to have thought it secondary in civil affairs, or to have interpreted faith in the light of contract or covenant rather than the reverse. Nor was he, like Story, to seek in common law an inherited source of authority or an emerging science, at least not immediately or ordinarily. Contract, rather, lay at the root of man's civil and legal affairs, with Christianity or common law offering nourishment rather than an anchor.

Washington's interest in contract law appears in the pages of the Supreme Court reporters, for he was often called upon to offer the opinion of the Court in cases involving contract or commercial law that lacked a constitutional dimension.[29] In the leading constitutional contract clause case of his era, *Trustees of Dartmouth College v. Woodward*, Washington was not content to leave expression of the case solely to the chief justice, though he apparently joined his opinion. In an opinion less prolix than the chief's and considerably less than his colleague Story's, Washington holds that the original royal grant to the college established "an obligation of the nature of a contract" on the part of the state toward the founder and the corporation. Then he explains how the statute impairs the obligation of the charter/contract: "all these powers, rights, and privileges [of a charitable corporation] flow from the property of the founder in the funds assigned for the support of the charity," and so cannot be unilaterally altered by the state.[30]

Another important example of his uncompromising voice on the Court for the adherence to contract comes in the case of *Green v. Biddle*, in which Washington on rehearing strengthens Story's decision invalidating a Kentucky law that allowed interim possessors of disputed land compensation for improvements they made before their titles were proven bad. This statute, Washington finds, impairs Kentucky's obligation under a 1789 compact with Virginia pledging to maintain land titles; indeed, he finds the rightful owners not only free from having to pay for the squatters' improvements but entitled to their profits. Whatever the sentimental case for those seeking compensation, Washington writes, "we hold ourselves answerable to God, our consciences, and our country, to decide this question according to the dictates of our best judgment, be the consequences of the decision what they may be."[31]

*Dartmouth College* and *Green v. Biddle* were, in their own way, isolated cases dealing with special circumstances, even if the former was to become an influential precedent. The bankruptcy cases, by contrast, unfold a drama, not least for the relation between Washington and Marshall. The story begins in the Third Circuit, with Washington's remarkable 1814 opinion in *Golden v. Prince*. Here the defendant sought to bar an action for the collection of a debt by claiming discharge under a Pennsylvania insolvency act. After entertaining and dismissing an attempt to use the Judiciary Act of 1789 to override the state insolvency law, Washington examines the latter's constitutionality and finds it doubly wanting. First, as applied in this case, where the debt was incurred before passage of the act that purports to discharge the debtor, the act is an unconstitutional impairment of contract because it would have altered the terms of a contract retrospectively. Second, even prospectively the act would fail, according to Washington, because the Constitution confers on Congress exclusive power over the issue of bankruptcy. He arrives at this opinion in part through a close reading of the text (it is implied, he thinks, by the stress on "uniform laws on the subject of Bankruptcies" in Article I, section 8, not to mention by being coupled with the naturalization power) but also by his insistence that there must be a way for Congress to establish the policy that there will be no bankruptcy in the United States, that is, no forced insolvency and subsequent discharge of debts. He writes in his opinion, "[W]e hold it to be our duty to embrace the first opportunity which presents itself, to express the unhesitating opinion which we entertain upon these great questions, and thus to pave the way for as early a decision of them, as possible, by the supreme national court."[32] Though this case was not to be appealed, Washington got his wish a few years later, when, during the busy spring when the judges decided *McCulloch v. Maryland* and *Dartmouth College*, the case of *Sturges v. Crowninshield* came before the Supreme Court.

Marshall wrote the only opinion in *Sturges*, apparently for a unanimous Court, but it is clear from the drift of the case and from what was revealed about it eight years later in *Ogden v. Saunders* that Washington had to be persuaded that his "unhesitating opinion" in *Golden v. Prince* would not become the law of the land, at least not in all respects. At issue in *Sturges* was a situation not unlike that before Judge Washington in 1814: The defendant in a suit to recover a debt pleaded his discharge under a state insolvency act (here, New York's) passed after the debt was established. Marshall reverses the order of the issues, beginning with the question of whether any state has the authority to pass a bankrupt law. The complication he discovers comes in discerning the difference between a bankruptcy law and an insolvency law; he acknowledges that the states have unquestioned authority to pass laws of the latter sort, while the Constitution gives Congress power to pass the former, but since the distinction between insolvency and bankruptcy is unclear, it is inadequate to serve as a bright line between two grants of exclusive authority. The way out is to hold the power over bankruptcy concurrent in the federal government and the states, so that Congress having chosen not to act on the subject of bankruptcy, power remains in the states to treat the matter in the first instance. The application of the law in question here, however, falls before the contract clause, since it seeks to operate retroactively upon a contract, that is, it operates to impair the obligation. Marshall is willing to concede the distinction between the obligation of a contract and the remedy the law affords; this allows for statutes of limitations, which are thus not said to impair the obligation of contracts. But here the insolvency law attempts to nullify the contract itself, not just tailor the remedy, and so fails the constitutional test.[33]

If Washington suppressed his doubts in *Sturges*, eight years later, in *Ogden v. Saunders*, he breaks with Marshall, driving him to a rare dissent in a constitutional case. (Actually, Marshall's famous "dissent" is technically a concurrence, for, although he is in the minority on the question of the constitutionality of state bankruptcy laws, Justice Johnson votes in the end to sustain the debt, on the ground that the New York insolvency law, though valid to relieve a debtor in New York, need not be recognized in federal court in Louisiana.) Though Marshall characteristically writes for the dissenters as a bloc, that is, for Justices Story and Duvall as well as himself, the majority opinions on the constitutional question are delivered seriatim, now, however, with the senior justice (Washington) first, rather than the junior justice, as in the 1790s. Washington's opinion is remarkable not only for its careful reasoning and modest expression—these are the hallmarks of his jurisprudence, after all—but for his admission that he continues in the opinion that the Constitution intended for Congress to have exclusive power to establish bankruptcy laws, "[b]ut it becomes me to believe, that this opinion was, and is, incorrect, since it stands condemned by the decision of a majority of this court, solemnly pronounced."[34]

Washington's argument in this case depends upon two distinctions: between a contract and its obligation, and between retrospective and prospective laws concerning contracts. The contract is, of course, the agreement, while the obligation, writes Washington citing Marshall in *Sturges*, is "the law which binds the parties to perform their agreement." This law is neither the moral law nor the "common law of nations," although these stand behind the law; it is the binding, positive "municipal law of the state" where the contract is made. The obligation of a contract is colored in many ways, by the laws of evidence, or laws of remedies, or statutes of limitations, and the like. This amalgam of municipal laws "forms, in my humble opinion, a part of the contract, and travels with it, wherever the parties to it may be found." What is crucial is that the laws operate only prospectively, for only in that way can they be considered incorporated into a contract without gross fiction. The constitutional ban on the impairment of contracts, then, is not a substantive limit on the legislative power of the states but a prohibition against the alteration of contracts already made. Washington reinforces this point with a close reading of the text of Article I, section 10: The prohibition against impairing the obligation of contracts is grouped by punctuation not with the legal tender clauses but with the prohibition against bills of attainder and ex post facto laws. And he concludes his opinion as he began it, with expression of doubt as to the correctness of his views, but then confident assertion: "But if I could rest my opinion in favor of the constitutionality of the law on which the question arises, on no other ground than this doubt so felt and acknowledged, that alone, would, in my estimation, be a satisfactory vindication of it. It is but a decent respect due to the wisdom, the integrity and the patriotism of the legislative body, by which any law is passed, to presume in favor of its validity, until its violation of the constitution is proved beyond all reasonable doubt."[35] That his adherence to the presumption in favor of state legislation gives Washington's jurisprudence a distinctive character can be seen by contrasting his opinion to Marshall's, for the latter insists that the Constitution's ban on laws impairing the obligation of contracts is not limited to retrospective legislation but has its origin in a duty to enforce the natural-law obligation of contracts and in the intention of the framers of the Constitution to stop the interference with the relative situation of creditors and debtors by state legislatures that was tending to "destroy all confidence between man and man."[36]

The coda to the debate over contracts comes in the case reported immediately after *Ogden v. Saunders* in Wheaton's Reports, namely *Mason v. Haile*, where Justice Washington delivers a rare, lone dissent to the opinion of the Court by Justice Smith Thompson.[37] The Court upholds the constitutionality of a peculiar insolvency arrangement in Rhode Island, whereby a debtor petitions the state legislature "for the benefit of the insolvent act of 1756," not otherwise in force, and the legislature, in granting the petition, releases the individual from his debts and, in this case, from prison. The Court finds the prison bond under which Haile was confined to have been "given subject to the ordinary and well-known practice in Rhode Island" of petitioning the legislature for discharge. Justice Washington, however, in an opinion delivered orally but not written, objects that the principle of prospectivity is violated here, since the contract involved in the prison bond had no provision for discharge, and the act of 1756 was not generally in force and so incorporated into the bond contract. Washington's singular leniency in giving the state legislatures room to experiment with the conditions of contracts translates, upon his strict distinction of prospectivity and retrospectivity, into singular harshness in the enforcement of contracts already made, even for debtors' imprisonment.

## *Enforcing the Law in Pennsylvania and Virginia*

Washington's usual reticence on the Supreme Court in the District of Columbia obscures, to the modern observer, what was called in a tribute at his death "the principal theatre of his judicial operations," the federal Circuit Court for the Third Circuit, especially as it sat in Philadelphia.[38] Here, in the city where he had served his legal apprenticeship and that was still capital of the United States when he was first appointed to the Supreme Court, Washington became a favorite of the bar during his nearly thirty years assigned to its circuit. If his Supreme Court opinions are modest, even diffident in tone, his circuit opinions, which usually take the form of charges to the jury (who seem always to act as he directs) bespeak the confident authority of one who sees himself as the embodied voice of federal law. Business varied in his time on the court, the early years dominated by marine insurance cases, later years giving rise to more general commercial cases and to patent cases, with procedural issues of evidence and jurisdiction always prominent.[39] Though it would be beyond the bounds of this essay to survey his circuit judgments in great detail, his portrait would be incomplete without some mention of his work as a federal trial judge.

High praise to Washington in this capacity came in a memoir on the Philadelphia bar by David Paul Brown, presumably an eyewitness:

> Perhaps the greatest *nisi prius* judge that the world has ever known, not excepting Chief-Justice Holt or Lord Mansfield, was the late Justice Washington. It is impossible to conceive of a better judicial manner, and, when

> to that is added great legal acquirement, great perspicuity and great-mindedness, exemplary self-possession and inflexible courage, all crowned by an honesty of purpose that was never questioned, he may be said, in the estimate of the bar and the entire country, to have stood among the judiciary, as *par excellence*.[40]

One finds little or nothing in the reports he assembled to contradict this assessment, and much to confirm it. In criminal cases, for example, one can recognize in his jury charges a scrupulous attempt to present the law with perfect clarity and fairness. In an 1804 case, Washington carefully explains to the jury that an indictment for perjury in bankruptcy proceedings cannot succeed after the bankruptcy law on which the prosecution was founded has been repealed; in 1805, he directs a verdict for acquittal against the charge of murder on the high seas, when the death in question occurred on land, and Congress had made no separate provision for such a circumstance; in 1814, he protects a man from a charge of treason by narrowly construing the intention of his alleged overt act.[41] His most spectacular case came in 1809 and involved the prosecution of a Pennsylvania militia officer for resisting a federal marshal at the direction of the state legislature and the governor. The case dated back to the Revolution and involved a Pennsylvania court prize award overturned by a special court of appeal established by Congress, the money, however, remaining in official hands in the state in defiance of the federal decree. Finally in 1803, process is renewed in the now-established federal district court, the state government resists, but finally the militia yields to the marshal and the money passes to federal hands and is properly awarded. An interested Philadelphia crowd was on hand for the trial of militia General Michael Bright, but Judge Washington merely adjourned the court until the following day in a larger courtroom and delivered a charge that vindicated the federal legal claim: "It is a truth not to be questioned that the power to declare the judgments of your courts void can never be safely lodged with a body who may enforce its decision by the physical force of the people. This power necessarily resides in the judicial tribunals, and can safely reside nowhere else." He then concluded:

> We enter not into the political discussions which have been so ably conducted on both sides, but we admonish you to discard from your minds all political considerations, all party feelings, and all federal or state preju-

> dices. The questions involved in this case are in the highest degree momentous, and demand a cool and dispassionate consideration. We rely upon your integrity and wisdom for a decision which you can reconcile to your consciences, and to the duties which you owe to God and to your country.[42]

The jury convicted the defendants on a special verdict, they were fined and imprisoned by the court, but they were "immediately pardoned by the president of the United States."[43]

If Washington was at his best in Philadelphia as the staunch defender of federal law without regard for popular sentiment, the less pleasant side of his unyielding support for positive rights and contempt for public opinion appeared when the issue of slavery arose, especially after the crisis of 1820. If the indices to his *Reports* are to be trusted, issues involving slavery came before his circuit court three times in almost thirty years. The first, in 1806, was a suit for his freedom by a servant of Pierce Butler, who established a house in Philadelphia during his time as a member of Congress from South Carolina but stayed on, only occasionally visiting his old plantation. The jury having ruled Butler a resident of the city, Judge Washington found him outside the exception for members of Congress or sojourners in the Pennsylvania emancipation statute of 1780, thus setting Ben Hopper free. The same term, Washington read a pair of federal statutes narrowly to defeat a prosecution for slave trading against an American ship that had transported two French ladies and their attendant slaves from St. Thomas to Havana in the Caribbean. A case some fifteen years later involves a similar statute and the transport of a slave who is later sold at the destination; Washington repeats the narrow reading but leaves the matter to the jury, and an acquittal follows, perhaps, the record hints, because the witness was unreliable.[44]

If there is nothing remarkable about these cases, Washington's personal involvement with the institution is more complex. As executor of General Washington's will, he was responsible for freeing his slaves upon his widow's death, and apparently did so, but to maintain Mount Vernon, he brought in new slaves of his own. In 1821, after four years as president of the Colonization Society, which had begun to make arrangements to establish a colony in Africa for free blacks, Washington's financial troubles at the plantation led him to sell about fifty slaves to two Louisiana dealers. The press found out and an angry exchange followed, with *Niles' Weekly Register* commenting,

"[T]here is something excessively revolting in the fact that a herd of them should be driven from Mount Vernon, sold by the nephew and principal heir of GEORGE WASHINGTON, as he would dispose of so many hogs or horned cattle; violating every tie that fastens on the human heart, and dissolving the connection of husband and wife, mother and child." Washington's lengthy reply is more revealing than he probably intended, both of his personal affairs and of the hardening of attitudes starting to take place on the slavery question. Admitting that humanity requires the attempt to keep families together, he insists on his efforts in this sale, families having been separated only when a few slave husbands owned by neighbors refused to be sold south, though he comments that it is "an extraordinary circumstance" that "so much sensibility should be felt" at the separation of slave families when emigration of whites to America routinely involves family separation. As to the necessity of the sale, he cites: his financial straits in maintaining the plantation; "the insubordination of my negroes, and their total disregard of all authority," a circumstance he blames on the steady stream of visitors to Mount Vernon, some of whom have presumed the slaves there to have belonged to the late general and thus to be owed their freedom, now or "at my death"; and the likelihood of "the escape of all the laboring men of any value, to the northern states, so soon as I should leave my home," several having "eloped without the pretense of a cause" the previous year. Seeing the whole controversy as designed to embarrass the Colonization Society, Bushrod Washington "take[s] the liberty, on my own behalf, and on that of my southern fellow citizens, to enter a solemn protest against the propriety of any person questioning our right, *legal or moral*, to dispose of property which is secured to us by sanctions equally valid with those by which we hold every other species of property."[45] Here is exact justice with a vengeance, excused, perhaps, by the judge's having overlooked the maxim against sitting in judgment of one's own cause.

## *Law and Liberty*

For the most part, then, Washington's contribution to the founding of the federal judiciary consisted in his steady enforcement of the written law and his fidelity to the sanctity of contracts. Story's observation of the marriage of mildness and firmness in his jurisprudence is apposite, for Washington was mild in deferring to statute and precedent as he understood them but firm in resisting the temptation to indulge either popular sentiment or noble rhetoric. He was a Federalist to the end in his support for the sanctity of property rights, but his emphasis on the importance of contract and his reluctance to build a jurisprudential system from the common law distinguished him not only from some of his colleagues on the bench in the 1790s but also from the judicial conservatives James Kent and Joseph Story who came to dominate legal scholarship in his later years. Friend to Marshall off the bench and on it, perhaps the key figure in establishing the deference of the associates to the chief, his work on the Court formed, in some respects, a bridge even beyond the Marshall Court to the Taney era, for his cautious opinion in *Ogden v. Saunders* anticipated the sort of delicate balancing of federal power, property rights, and state legislative authority that came to characterize the work of Marshall's successor—even as his staunch defense of slaveholders' rights anticipated that Court's darkest hour. Indeed, his influence might even stretch further because he was apparently an author of the doctrine that corporations ought to be considered citizens of the state in which they were incorporated for purposes of federal law, accepted by the Court in 1844 and used as the jurisdictional entry for much of the federal courts' business as the century progressed.[46]

In one of those odd but familiar instances in American constitutional law, Bushrod Washington is perhaps most commonly encountered by students today in a circuit case decided late in his career that later took on added importance thanks to developments he could hardly have anticipated. The case is *Corfield v. Coryell*, in which the issue is whether New Jersey can justifiably restrict fishing in its oyster beds to its citizens, and Washington, again anticipating the jurisprudence of the Taney Court, decides that it can. Citing dicta in *Gibbons v. Ogden* (the *Corfield* case apparently came to the circuit before the decision in *Gibbons*, but argument and decision were delayed until after), Washington insists that states reserve power to regulate their internal trade, not to mention "the right . . . to legislate, in such manner as in their wisdom may seem best, over the public property of the state"; and the Privileges and Immunities Clause of Article IV he confines, with "no hesitation," to "those privileges and immunities which are, in their nature, fundamental; which belong, of right, to the citizens of all free governments; and which have, at all times, been enjoyed by the citizens of the several states which compose this Union, from the time of their becoming free, independent, and sovereign."[47] Although the acknowledgment of extensive legislative authority in the states is characteristic of Washington throughout his career, the distinction between the fundamental and the incidental among rights, and the remarkable list of the former—including rights to protection, to the enjoyment of life, liberty, and property, to travel, to the writ of habeas corpus, to sue, to nondiscriminatory taxation, and to vote—seem more in the spirit of John Marshall or, for that matter, of James Wilson than of this usually cautious expounder of the letter of the law. Still, the passage from *Corfield v. Coryell*, known, of course, because of its quotation in *The Slaughter-House Cases* when a later Supreme Court begins the historic task of interpreting the Fourteenth Amendment, is in a sense a fitting tribute to this friend of Marshall's and heir of Washington's, for it articulates not only the justice of the law but its role as the source of liberty. In this Bushrod Washington professed sincerely to believe, and it would be churlish to deny his contribution to its achievement.

## NOTES

1. William W. Story, ed., *The Miscellaneous Writings of Joseph Story* (Boston: Charles C. Little and James Brown, 1852), 809; quoted in 3 Peters x–xi.

2. This phrase is from a tablet erected in his memory by the Philadelphia bar, the text of which is reproduced in 3 Peters xiii.

3. I have relied on the following sources for biographical information: Clare Cushman, ed., *The Supreme Court Justices: Illustrated Biographies, 1789–1993* (Washington, D.C.: CQ Press, 1993), 51–55; Albert P. Blaustein and Roy M. Mersky, "Bushrod Washington," in Leon Friedman & Fred L. Israel, eds., *The Justices of the United States Supreme Court, 1789–1969: Their Lives and Major Opinions* (New York: Chelsea House, 1969), 1: 243–257; Bushrod C. Washington, "The Late Mr. Justice Bushrod Washington," *Green Bag* 9 (1897): 329–335; Joseph Hopkinson, *Eulogium in Commemoration of the Hon. Bushrod Washington* (Philadelphia: T. S. Manning, 1830); and especially David Leslie Annis, "Mr. Bushrod Washington, Supreme Court Justice on the Marshall Court" (Ph.D. diss., Notre Dame University, 1974).

4. See Robert Green McCloskey, ed., *The Works of James Wilson* (Cambridge: Harvard University Press, 1967), I: 76ff.

5. Worthington Chauncey Ford, ed., *The Writings of George Washington* (New York: G. P. Putnam's Sons, 1891), 10: 133–35 (letter of 15 January 1783).

6. Ibid., 11: 69–71.

7. Ibid., 72, 71.

8. Story, *Miscellaneous Writings*, 811.

9. See Annis, "Mr. Bushrod Washington," 56.

10. Quoted in ibid., 57.

11. 3 Dallas 411; the quotations are all from Justice Washington's opinion, at 412–13.

12. 4 Dallas 37, at 42.

13. 4 Dallas 14; Chase's opinion is at 18–19, Washington's at 18.

14. See James Bradley Thayer, "The Origin and Scope of the American Doctrine of Constitutional Law," *Harvard Law Review* 7 (1893): 129–56. Justice Paterson's opinion in *Cooper v. Telfair* accords with Washington's presumption: "to authorize this court to pronounce any law void, it must be a clear and unequivocal breach of the constitution, not a doubtful and argumentative application." 4 Dallas at 19.

15. See *Reports of Cases Determined in the Circuit Court of the United States, for the Third Circuit, comprising the districts of Pennsylvania and New Jersey. Commencing at April Term, 1803*. Published from the Manuscripts of the Honourable Bushrod Washington. 4 vols. (Philadelphia: Philip H. Nicklin, 1826–29) (cited as Wash. C.C.). For a discussion of the changes in the practice of circuit riding, from the original three fixed circuits, to rotating annual assignments, to the establishment of separate circuit courts in the Judiciary Act of 1801, to the repeal of that act and the practice of fixed individual circuit assignments, see Charles Warren, *The Supreme Court in United States History* (rev. ed; Boston: Little, Brown, and Co., 1926), 1: 58ff., 85ff., 185ff., 204–9; also Maeva Marcus, ed., *The Documentary History of the Supreme Court of the United States, 1789–1800* (New York: Columbia University Press, 1990) 3: 469ff. (Appendix B).

16. See Marcus, ed., *The Documentary History of the Supreme Court of the United States, 1789–1800*, 398–401, for an example. Apparently no copies remain of his grand jury charges.

17. Annis, "Mr. Bushrod Washington," 88; William C. Stinchcombe and Charles T. Cullen, eds., *The Papers of John Marshall* (Chapel Hill: University of North Carolina Press, 1979), 3: 496ff.

18. See James Morton Smith, *Freedom's Fetters: The Alien and Sedition Laws and American Civil Liberties* (Ithaca: Cornell University Press, 1956), 271, 285ff., 379ff., 388ff., 415.

19. Annis, "Mr. Bushrod Washington," 97.

20. See his letters to Thomas Ritchie (December 25, 1820) and Justice William Johnson (October 27, 1822, and June 12, 1823), in Thomas Jefferson,

*Writings*, ed. Merrill D. Peterson (New York: Library of America, 1984), 1446–47, 1461–63, 1476–77.

21. Quoted in Annis, "Mr. Bushrod Washington," 116.

22. *Coxe v. Penington*, 1 Wash. C.C. 65 (1803), at 66.

23. *Pennington v. Coxe*, 2 Cranch 33 (1804), at 55, 61–62, 59, 54.

24. *United States v. Fisher*, 1 Wash. C.C. 4 (1803), at 7–8; *United States v. Fisher*, 2 Cranch 358 (1805), at 400.

25. 1 Wash. C.C. at 8.

26. *United States v. Fisher*, 2 Cranch at 389–90, 396.

27. Ibid., at 398, 402.

28. See Henry Otis Dwight, *The Centennial History of the American Bible Society* (New York: Macmillan Co., 1916); Story, *Miscellaneous Writings*, 810. See also Annis, "Mr. Bushrod Washington," 170–71.

29. See, e.g., *Eliason v. Henshaw*, 4 Wheaton 225 (1819); *Thornton v. Wynn*, 12 Wheaton 183 (1827); *Buckner v. Finley and Van Lear*, 2 Peters 586 (1829). The *Thornton* case is an especially elegant example of judicial reasoning in the common law of contract.

30. *Trustees of Dartmouth College v. Woodward*, 4 Wheaton 518 (1819), at 661.

31. *Green v. Biddle*, 8 Wheaton 1 (1821, 1823); Washington's opinion begins at 69, with the quotation from 93.

32. *Golden v. Prince*, 10 Fed. Cases 542 (No. 5,509) (C.C.D.Pa. 1814).

33. *Sturges v. Crowninshield*, 4 Wheaton 122 (1819).

34. *Ogden v. Saunders*, 12 Wheaton 213 (1827), at 264.

35. Ibid., at 259, 270.

36. Ibid., at 355.

37. 4 Wheaton 370; Washington's dissent begins at 379.

38. Hopkinson, *Eulogium in Commemoration of the Hon. Bushrod Washington*, 22.

39. See the indices to the four volumes of Washington's *Reports*, cited above.

40. Quoted in Bushrod C. Washington, "The Late Mr. Justice Bushrod Washington," 331.

41. *Anonymous*, 1 Wash. C.C. 84 (1804); *United States v. Magill*, 1 Wash. C.C. 463 (1806); *United States v. Pryor*, 3 Wash. C.C. 234 (1814).

42. *United States v. Bright*, 24 Fed. Cas. 1232 (No. 14,647; C.C.D.P. 1809), at 1237, 1238. For the story, see Bushrod C. Washington, "The Late Mr, Justice Bushrod Washington," 332–33; and Hopkinson, *Eulogium in Commemoration of the Hon. Bushrod Washington*, 22 ff.

43. The Pennsylvania militia figured as well in a notable Supreme Court decision concerning criminal law rendered by Washington: Over the dissent of Justice Story and one other justice unnamed, but with the authority of *The Federalist Papers* in his favor, Washington held that the states and the federal government had

concurrent jurisdiction to punish federal crimes under federal law, unless Congress expressly provided that federal jurisdiction would be exclusive. *Houston v. Moore*, 5 Wheaton 1 (1820). See also the discussion in David P. Currie, *The Constitution in the Supreme Court: The First Hundred Years, 1789–1888* (Chicago: University of Chicago Press, 1985), 108–10.

44. *P. Butler, Esquire, v. Hopper*, 1 Wash. C.C. 499 (1806); *Brig Tryphenia v. Harrison*, 1 Wash. C.C. 522 (1806); *United States v. Kennedy*, 4 Wash. C.C. 91 (1821).

45. *Niles' Weekly Register*, September 1, 1821; September 29, 1821. See also Gerald T. Dunne, "Bushrod Washington and the Mount Vernon Slaves," *Supreme Court Historical Society Yearbook* 1980: 25–29.

46. See the letter of Joseph Story to James Kent, of August 31, 1844, quoted in Warren, *The Supreme Court in United States History*, 2: 121–22.

47. *Corfield v. Coryell*, 6 Fed. Cas. 546 (No. 3,230) (C.C.E.D.Pa. 1823, 1825), at 551.

# Editor's Note

To preserve the multidisciplinary flavor of this collection, the contributors' respective citation and indexing styles have been retained so as to reflect the style that exists in their respective disciplines.

# Contributors

*William R. Casto* is at the School of Law, Texas Tech University, Lubbock.

*Daniel A. Degnan,* S.J., is at the School of Law, Seton Hall University, Newark, New Jersey.

*Scott Douglas Gerber* is at Florida Coastal School of Law, Jacksonsville.

*Mark D. Hall* is in the Department of Government, East Central University, Ada, Oklahoma.

*James Haw* is in the Department of History, Indiana University/Purdue University at Fort Wayne.

*Wythe Holt* is at the School of Law, University of Alabama, Tuscaloosa.

*Stephen B. Presser* is at the School of Law, Northwestern University, Chicago.

*James R. Stoner*, Jr., is in the Department of Political Science, Louisiana State University, Baton Rouge.

*Sandra Frances VanBurkleo* is in the Department of History, Wayne State University, Detroit.

*Willis P. Whichard* is at the Supreme Court of North Carolina, Raleigh.

# Index

# About the Editor

Scott Douglas Gerber is Associate Professor at Florida Coastal School of Law in Jacksonville. He received both a Ph.D. and a J.D. from the University of Virginia, and a B.A. from the College of William and Mary. He is a former law clerk to a federal judge. He is the author of *First Principles: The Jurisprudence of Clarence Thomas* (in press) and *To Secure These Rights: The Declaration of Independence and Constitutional Interpretation* (1995), both from New York University Press.